The Word as Scalpel

THE WORD AS SCALPEL

A History of
Medical Sociology

Samuel W. Bloom

OXFORD
UNIVERSITY PRESS

2002

OXFORD
UNIVERSITY PRESS

Oxford   New York
Auckland   Bangkok   Buenos Aires   Cape Town   Chennai
Dar es Salaam   Delhi   Hong Kong   Istanbul   Karachi   Kolkata
Kuala Lumpur   Madrid   Melbourne   Mexico City   Mumbai   Nairobi
São Paulo   Shanghai   Singapore   Taipei   Tokyo   Toronto

and an associated company in Berlin

Copyright © 2002 by Oxford University Press, Inc.

Published by Oxford University Press, Inc.
198 Madison Avenue, New York, New York 10016

www.oup.com

Oxford is a registered trademark of Oxford University Press

Library of Congress Cataloging-in-Publication Data
Bloom, Samuel William, 1921–
The word as scalpel : a history of
medical sociology / Samuel W. Bloom.
p.   cm.
Includes bibliographical references and index.
ISBN 0–19–507232–4; ISBN 0–19–514929–7 (pbk.)
1. Social medicine—United States—History.
2. Sociology—United States—History.   I. Title.
RA418.3.U6 B56 2002
306.4'61'0973—dc21   2001037042

1 3 5 7 9 8 6 4 2

Printed in the United States of America
on acid-free paper

Acknowledgments

Among the many who helped me with this book, Kurt Deuschle stands out. He first suggested the idea for a proposal to the Commonwealth Fund Book Program on the Frontiers of Science. At the time, Kurt was the distinguished and much loved chairman of the Mount Sinai School of Medicine Department of Community Medicine. My first large debt, therefore, is owed to him and to the Commonwealth Fund, especially to former staff members Lester Evans, John Eberhart, and Reginald H. Fitz. Special thanks are also due to Susan Garfield and the Rockefeller International Conference Center at Bellagio, Italy, where I developed the first detailed outline of what this book eventually became. Soon afterward, my appointment as a Visiting Fellow at the Russell Sage Foundation relieved me of academic duties for six months of total immersion in writing. From these sources, the short book first proposed evolved into the present much more ambitious history.

Most of the work was done in the old-fashioned off-line way, at typewriter and then word processor, heavily dependent on documents, interviews, and libraries. Reference librarians at the Levy Library of Mount Sinai School of Medicine, the New York Academy of Medicine, and the New York Society Library were particularly helpful. The kindness and efficiency of archivists regularly solved critical problems, especially those at the Meiklejohn Institute in California, the New York Public Library, the National Archives of the United States, and the University of Wisconsin Center for Film and Theatre Research. Organizations like the National Institutes of Health and the American Sociological Association were always accessible and responsive. But more than any other, I owe thanks to the staff of the Amagansett Free Library. There seemed to be no request too difficult for this remarkable public library of a small New York village.

When it comes to individual contributions, it is much harder to assess influence and to adequately express my gratitude. For example, my students in the Ph.D. Program in Sociology at the City University of New York were my primary readers and critics of chapters in draft. I could not possibly list them individually, but collectively, they are at the top of my list of the most helpful. There are also friends and colleagues who served the writing process in what I can only describe as an intellectual context rather than in specific helping roles. Sol Levine, for example, was someone who never waited to be asked. He initiated contact, asked about my work, and then critically responded to anything I sent him. My debt to him cannot be estimated, and my sorrow for his recent death is deep. Robin Badgley and Bob Straus have played similar roles. Both were partners in various professional activities. Badgley always behaved with quiet humor and unsparing dedication; it was a joyful experience to work with him. Straus has been both friend and co-worker for almost fifty years, so it was fitting that he was selected by the publisher to read the manuscript. His critique included many helpful suggestions. Robert K. Merton, Patricia Kendall, Renee Fox, George G. Reader, and Mary E. W. Goss were there at my entry to the field when it was not yet known as medical sociology. Merton's influence never ended, and all of them have remained both friends and professional models.

Those individuals who were interviewed are credited throughout the text, and all of their contributions are important. Some, however, deserve special mention, including Eugene Brody, Donald Light, Albert Wessen, David Mechanic, James McCorkle, and Fred Hafferty. Among historians, I am indebted specially to Milton Roemer, Milton Terris, Rosemary Stevens, and David Rosner. Robert H. Felix, Raymond V. Bowers, Herbert Klerman, Kenneth Lutterman, and Herbert Pardes generously shared their experiences at the National Institute of Mental Health.

Chloe E. Bird, Peter Conrad, and Allen M. Fremont, editors of the fifth edition of *The Handbook of Medical Sociology*, commissioned my article, "The Institutionalization of Medical Sociology in the U.S.: 1920–1980," a task which served in unexpected ways to help complete the final draft of this book.

Edward W. Barry, the former president of Oxford University Press, encouraged and supported me through many years and two earlier books. He is a rare example of the type of publisher every writer wants. I am also indebted to Valerie Aubrey, my first editor at Oxford, and to Dedi Felman, Jennifer Rappaport, and Robin Miura, my current Oxford editors.

Caroline Helmuth was my secretary during the early drafts, but that hardly describes the part she played. She was also research assistant, friend, editor, and genial ally. When Caroline went to California and I was forced to work mostly on my own, Josephine Greene saved me from disaster regularly, serving as my word processing consultant. When I needed to return to early sources, Mary Lou Russell at the Commonwealth Fund was gracious with her time and knowledge.

Although my debt is great to everyone mentioned so far, there is another level of gratitude that is reserved for my daughter Jessica, my son Jonathan, and my grandchildren Alexander and Sonia who are the anchors and joy of my existence; but it is Anne, my wife, who, more than any other, has given not only what I needed to write this book but also the greater portion of what is valuable in my life.

Contents

The Word as Scalpel

Introduction

"Medicine has many faces. Whatever your interests and talents are, there is a place for you to express them in this profession." These words have always stayed with me, even though they were spoken almost fifty years ago on a September day in a large auditorium at the University of Pennsylvania School of Medicine. The speaker was the dean, Dr. John Mck. Mitchell, addressing the freshman class on its first official day. I was there as an observer, part of a team of research sociologists from Columbia University, just embarking on a study of medical education. Little did I realize that Dr. Mitchell's words would apply to me as well as to the neophyte medical recruits. Within a few years, I was to become a faculty member of a medical school, embarked on a career that was just being identified with a name, "medical sociology."

At the time, I thought Dr. Mitchell was reminding his students that the boundaries of medical subjects included much diversity, but still within the limits of biological science. Even public health and psychiatry, though different from the mainstream, were still traditional "medical" specialties. I was wrong, of course; Dr. Mitchell, a pediatrician himself, was saying what the famous medical historian Henry Sigerist had said in a different way a few years earlier: "There is one lesson that can be derived from history. It is this: that the physician's position in society is never determined by the physician himself but by the society he is serving."[1]

We were, Dr. Mitchell and I, captives of the spirit of the years immediately following the Second World War. Part of the fallout of that terrible event, with its ghastly statistics of human destruction, was that it brought into question our understanding of human behavior. Never had human reasoning, in the form of science, advanced so far, but, at the same time, never had the capacity for human destruction reached such depths. In medicine, the profession assigned to be the arbiter of both health and illness, the reaction was to seek redemption through the application of the scientific method to human behavior. "Without an adequate understanding of the human habitat, and of the characteristics of human organism and environment," Norman Cameron wrote in 1952, "the medical student cannot be competently prepared for the role he has chosen—that of the physician in modern American society."[2]

Because of farsighted medical educators like Cameron, courses in behavioral science emerged, usually in the curricula of either psychiatry or preventive medicine, and sociology was virtually always an important ingredient. Medical schools became interested enough to add social scientists to their faculties, for the first time, in more than token numbers and with more than token responsibilities.[3]

Out of these origins, medical sociology emerged as a new subdiscipline to play roles in both research and education. As an early recruit to teach behavioral science to medical students, I began to chronicle its history.[4] Soon, however, my attention was diverted to the past. I discovered that sociological inquiry about health and medicine can be traced back at least to the beginning of the nineteenth century. Most intriguing is the excellent quality of these early studies. Their methodology was advanced, comparable with modern work. Why, then, the question arises, did they fail to become part of a body of knowledge, growing with continuity in the manner of contemporary science? Instead, these early investigations were typically episodic and were conducted by individual scholars. Each was associated with major, disruptive social events like war or political and technological revolution but afterward disappeared from public consciousness, only to be repeated later as though nothing like them had existed before. Not only continuity was lacking but clear scholarly identification. What was new to the modern period, therefore, was not an innovative type of intellectual work but rather the establishment of an institutionalized intellectual activity called "medical sociology." But could such a field be understood without reviewing its past? I found myself drawn both to the prehistory of modern medical sociology and to its social development.

As I explored further, it also became evident that this was not a story of interdisciplinary discovery and cooperation. Both medicine and sociology sought to deal with similar problems, and in the process medicine attempted to create its own social science of medicine. Why did this effort fail? The question pointed to the general histories of both professions. Each profession, for example, responded in its own way to the forces inherent to the growth of higher education in the United States. In the process, they were driven by the often competing purposes of advocacy and objectivity. Drawn together by common interests, their partnership was uneasy.

In the end, I expanded the purpose of the book. The focus would still be on the modern period, but only after a review of medical sociology's earlier intellectual origins. And on the whole, I decided to emphasize the institutional history. Academic subjects characteristically offer two dimensions for historical study, the development of knowledge and professional or institutional formation. For example, Merton, in his analysis of the sociology of science, differentiates the specialty's *cognitive identity*, "in the form of its intellectual orientations, conceptual schemes, paradigms, problematics, and tools of inquiry," and its *social identity*, "in the form of its major institutional arrangements."[5] The former is the most common in the literature of medical sociology, but the focus here will be on the latter, following the steps of institutionalization.[6]

For such a task, my own occupational history was an advantage. I was an early participant in the rapid institutionalization of medical sociology. The pattern of my career followed a mirror-course of the major developments in the field. During the period when research offered virtually the only role open to sociologists in medical institutions, I apprenticed at perhaps the best research organization in sociology, the Columbia University Bureau of Applied Social Research (BASR), working in its first foray into a medically related project.[7] In 1956, when sociologists were just beginning to be accepted on medical school faculties, I joined the Baylor University School of Medicine and have been a medical educator ever since. Periodically throughout this time, I served on special commissions that studied and made policy recommendations concerning the role of the behavioral sciences in medical education. At the same time, I was drawn into activities of professional organizations, particularly in the early years of the Committee on Medical Sociology founded by August Hollingshead and Robert Straus. As the Committee evolved into the Section on Medical Sociology of the American Sociological Association, I served as the principal administrative officer.

In the meantime, a literature grew that showed medical sociology to be concerned about its own development.[8] However, just as my own publications on these themes have been limited in scope, the review papers of the field tend to be specialized, each dealing with a subtopic such as the contribution of sociology to mental health, public health, medical education, or health services. Even in its textbooks and commissioned reports, the history of the field does not yet emerge in full detail.[9] Once the writing began, the book expanded from the more limited task originally conceived, a direction that was encouraged by colleagues with whom I checked and reviewed the material to be included.

These informal "conversations" soon evolved into organized, lengthy interviews, and a dimension of oral history began to take shape as part of the work's methodology. This, of course, changed a relatively straightforward library task into something more complex and expensive. The generosity of the Commonwealth Fund has made this possible, allowing me to conduct in-depth interviews with many of those, both from medical education and from sociology, who have made this history.

My natural tendency in the beginning also was to screen my own personal involvement behind the "objective" facts. But soon such a constraint came to seem artificial and somehow less honest than a frankly acknowledged personal view.[10] There is an obvious advantage to being part of the story one is telling, and I decided to use it fully.

The Plan of the Book

The overall problem-focus of the book is on the modern period in the history of medical sociology, beginning with its clear identification as a subfield fifty years ago. However, the roots of medical sociology are much deeper historically, and they share common soil with three conceptions: *medicine as social science; public health;* and *social medicine.* These were activities developed internally within medicine during the nineteenth century, whereas medical sociology grew as a separate field, drawing mainly from currents within its own parent field of sociology and, to a lesser extent, from social psychology. Together, I have treated these as the antecedents, or prehistory, of medical sociology. They are presented as "Part I, The Origins of Medical Sociology," consisting of five chapters. In chapter 1, the search for knowledge about how social factors influence illness is reviewed in a very condensed form, going back two thousand years, but with more detail beginning with the eighteenth century. This degree of historical background is necessary to engage the question: Why did a systematic social science of medicine fail to emerge from the long effort by public health and social medicine to create a theoretical framework and continuous development of knowledge about the relation between social factors and illness?

In the second chapter, the organizing premise is that the emergence of medical sociology can only be understood within the context of the special characteristics of the American university. The effort is made to describe how a more organized social science was produced in American universities than anywhere else in the world. A special comparison is made with the English and German universities, which, though in many ways the models for American institutions, produced a very different sociology. Particular attention is paid to the role of the private foundations in the growth of both the university and social science.

The third chapter discusses medical sociology as an intrinsic and important part of the history of sociology itself, when, during the period 1920–40, the parent discipline becomes fully legitimate as an "autonomous intellectual activity." Two major events, the Committee on the Costs of Medical Care and the President's Research Committee on Social Trends, are described in detail to show that the sociology of medicine, as an approach, was already developed to a high level at that time and was much more than an academic activity, playing an important role in issues of public health policy.

Chapter 4, still dealing with the period between the two World Wars, turns to the origins of what would be two major methodologies of the specialty. The first is the sociology that grew at the University of Chicago from 1893 to 1935, with special attention to the social ecology of mental disorder and urban life developed by R. E. L. Faris and Warren H. Dunham. The second is concentrated in the work of Harry Stack Sullivan. Sullivan, a psychiatrist who was an early American follower of Freud, introduced a shift from the Freudian emphasis on instincts and early childhood experience to the etiological significance of interpersonal relations. Two papers by Sullivan, published in 1931, are generally cited as the beginning of a movement toward a therapeutic orientation as opposed to the custodial care practices that then dominated hospital care for the mentally ill.[11] The conception of the hospital as a "therapeutic community" grew from these origins to become one of the most active substantive areas for sociological study immediately following World War II. This chapter describes the study of interpersonal relations in therapeutic situations and analyzes the importance of its adaptation of ethnographic field methods of research.

Chapter 5 shifts the focus from the substructure of medical sociology in both social medicine and general sociology to the intellectual origins most specific to the field. Two contrasting scholars and their influences on medical sociology are described in biographical and intellectual detail: Lawrence J. Henderson and Bernhard Stern. Each laid foundations for subsequent major paradigms that for a time were to dominate sociology as a general science and the special study of medical sociology. Henderson, who was a biochemist as well as a physician, adapted in midcareer the functional theory he had pioneered in physiology to early structural-functional interpretations of social relations, and this theory, for the next three decades, was the guiding theory of much of American sociology. In medical sociology, his analysis of the doctor-patient relationship as a social system had a seminal effect. Stern, on the other hand, was a Marxist whose social history of medicine emphasized a sociopolitical perspective that was only to come into its own in the 1960s as an important approach in medical sociology.

A summary of part I deals with the major questions this extensive prehistory raises for the modern phases of medical sociology. It is argued that the *cognitive identity* of the specialty was established prior to the modern period's emphasis on its *social identity*. Henderson, Stern, the Chicago sociologists, and Harry Stack Sullivan served primarily the development and consolidation of the cognitive identity of medical sociology. Their heirs continued to build the knowledge of the field, but the framework in which they worked was one of rapid institutionalization.

Part II turns to the first steps in the emergence of modern medical sociology, from 1940. A series of questions are addressed about the process of becoming a visible special field of general sociology. How was this initiated? What were the major determining factors, the underlying patterns of development in its parent discipline, the barriers, the major accomplishments? World War II is shown to be an event that established the role of sociology in national affairs in a way comparable to the emergence of psychology under the impetus of the First World War. Through the biographies of early medical sociologists and some of their medical sponsors the influences of contacts and experiences of this war are traced. Although the Defense Department was the most significant source of social science support during the war, medical sociology is shown to have received financial sponsorship in the postwar years mainly from private foundations, especially the Russell Sage Foundation, the Commonwealth Fund, and the Milbank Fund.

Chapters 8 through 10 describe the role of external support, both federal and private, and of professional associations in the institutionalization of the field. The story is one of the rise of federal support, for both research and training, and then its decline. This is also the period when institutional legitimacy is secured with the establishment of the Section on Medical Sociology of the American Sociological Association (ASA) and with the creation of several journals, including the official ASA sponsorship of the *Journal of Health and Social Behavior*. Within medicine, this legitimacy is represented most dramatically by the creation of a new subject matter committee for Part I of the National Board of Medical Examiners (NBME), the Committee on Behavioral Science, signaling the full acceptance of sociology in the education of future physicians concerning the psychosocial aspects of health and illness.

Part III assesses the current status of medical sociology. Since 1980, the field has been attacked in both its intellectual and institutional identity. Acceptance has not meant security. Institutionally, there has been a precipitous contraction of federal support for the social sciences, all the more devastating because it comes as an added thrust to what was already a downward curve of federal resources for academic work in general. Compounding the problem is evidence that medical sociology is losing its favored position in the behavioral science movement. In the market of scarce academic resources, the competition of "behavioral medicine" and "health economics" has intensified. In addition, psychiatry is acting to withdraw from collaboration with medical sociology, preferring instead to keep to itself the responsibility for teaching medical students about the social aspects of behavior as well as the psychological. In spite of these challenges, medical sociology in the United States enjoys a status unequaled by its peers anywhere in the world.

My main motive in approaching medical sociology's history from these vantage points is to find meaning in what, for me, given the everyday pressure to inquire and to teach, ends up so often as "interesting" but disconnected arrays of ideas. Medicine is, after all, a basic social institution that, because of its importance, must reflect the society's changing values about patterns of human relationship. For sociology, therefore, the study of medicine is an opportunity to find and test general—not specialized—conceptions of human behavior. Always, in this history of sociology's efforts to understand health and illness as social problems and to describe and interpret medicine, I have tried to be alert to the more general social meanings and have not hesitated to comment on what I find.

Finally, the title testifies to the influence of Lawrence J. Henderson's warning: "A doctor can damage a patient as much with a misplaced word as with a slip of the scalpel."[12] There is for me a compelling simplicity and precision to these words, just as strong now as when I first read them almost forty-five years ago. Their initial attraction is not difficult to explain. Sociologists were still a rarity in the halls and classrooms of medical schools, and I was groping in this unfamiliar terrain. Here was a famous physician from the past, whose name was part of the lore of the basic science of medicine[13] and who became in midcareer a sociological scholar and teacher of sociologists. His statement about "the misplaced word" struck me on first reading with the force of Old Testament prophecy. If words, the main substance of human relations, are so potent for harm, how equally powerful can they be to help if used with disciplined knowledge and understanding? And where more certainly does this simple truth apply than in the making of a physician? Within this frame, it is essential to study and understand the sociology of medicine.

PART I

MEDICAL SOCIOLOGY BEFORE 1940

1

The Origins

Medicine as Social Science,
Public Health, and Social Medicine

Medical sociology is an old conception but relatively young as a field of endeavor.[1] From early in the nineteenth century, one can trace research activities that are remarkably close, at least in style, to their modern counterparts in medical sociology. Until about seventy-five years ago, however, such studies were episodic, linked to major events like the struggle for political and social rights of the European middle class in the 1840s, the similar struggle of the English working class later in the nineteenth century, and the radical technological and social changes caused by the Civil War in the United States. These events typically heightened public feelings of social responsibility and, in the process, stimulated early variants of social science. Edwin Chadwick's *Report on the Sanitary Conditions of the Laboring Population of Great Britain* in 1842 is a good example.[2] Just as typically, however, at least with inquiry about health, the motive force of such movements was not sustained. It was not until almost 1930 that an unbroken development began in the sociology of medicine, and only after World War II were individuals identified as "medical sociologists."

Medical sociology, in its nineteenth-century origins, derived from three overlapping concepts: medicine as social science; social medicine; and the sociology of medicine. All three are concerned with explaining the linkage between social conditions and medical problems, the idea that human disease is always mediated and modified by social activities and the cultural environment.[3] "Medicine is a social science," wrote Rudolph Virchow in 1848.[4] Even earlier, French and German investigators used similar terms as they became concerned with the social problems of industrialization. The French social hygienists of the 1830s are one example, and, in Germany, another well-known physician, Salomon Neumann, studying the influence of poverty and occupation on the state of health, shared Virchow's view.[5]

However, "social science" as Neumann and Virchow perceived it was quite different from what it is today. For them it was a partisan, utilitarian activity, identified with advocacy and reform. Although Virchow is now remembered as the father of modern pathology, his "medical reform" was far removed from the academic natural science model that social science later adopted in its struggle for professional legitimacy.[6] Instead, the "right to health" and the obligation of the state to provide for it were inherent parts of these early conceptions. It was, after all, the mid–nineteenth century, a time of revolution and the consolidation of the values of the Enlightenment. Like the rights to education and religious and political freedom, the right to health was inserted into the basic discourse of the Western European nations. It was a belief that these pioneers of modern medicine fought for ardently, utilizing as they went early variants of epidemiology, bio-statistics, and survey research.

Virchow, for example, studied and reported on the epidemic of typhus fever in 1847 in Upper Silesia. He identified the causes of this outbreak to be a complex of social and economic factors, and he concluded that little should be expected from medicinal therapy when political action is required to deal with epidemics.[7] Neumann, similarly, conducted in 1851 a study of the medical statistics of the Prussian state. What is so striking, however, is that although such research iden-tified the social and economic conditions of particular groups of people as risk factors for disease, it rarely included the type of theoretical analysis that is the basis of continuous, cumulative research, nor did it attract discussion by a com-munity of scholars with similar interests. As a consequence, it was not until the early twentieth century that a distinguishable field of academic study emerged to seriously explore the social aspects of medicine.[8]

From within medicine, it was the field of public health that was most receptive to social science. Public health, or social medicine as it was called in Europe, is population based medicine, the special field concerned with prevention and the politics of health and devoted to using scientific medicine as an antidote to the social ills brought about by the Industrial Revolution. In the United States, "so-cial" has been a charged word, associated with socialism and radicalism, so that "public health" and, more recently, "community medicine" are preferred. Espe-cially in Europe, this field saw the poor as medicine's natural jurisdiction and was oriented to health related social reform.

Until the mid–nineteenth century, medicine equated social science with activ-ism, as often political as it was professional. Sigerist, for example, was the physician-historian who, between the 1920s and 1940s, identified himself more closely with sociology than any other medical scholar. Yet, although he conceived an ambitious project in the "sociology of medicine," for him the sociological en-terprise was believed to stand "at the intersection of social analysis and social reform":

> Not yet entirely differentiated from economics, political science, anthro-pology, and social work, "sociology" . . . was broadly understood by intel-lectuals and policy makers, even by many sociologists, as a countervailing point of view and a moral disposition rather than as a specialized academic discipline.[9]

The differentiation of roles within medicine also gave social science relevance. For Virchow, especially, medicine as social science is a direct expression of that aspect of the history of medicine in which the physician, as physician, takes the role of public benefactor.

In modern Western medicine today, all the various possible roles of the physician are assigned to separate places within the profession. Recruits to the profession have a choice to focus their activities in a particular role, whether as healer, physician-scientist, or public benefactor. At the same time, the society chooses one or more aspects of a profession to press for emphasis by adding or subtracting the allocation of public resources, but all receive some substantial measure of support. It was not always so.

The Physician as Public Benefactor: Early Origins

Ancient Greece tried on each professional mantle known today but never in the full combination we now take for granted. Individualized medicine, our 2,400-year-old link to Hippocrates, seems to have arisen only in the fifth century B.C., just prior to the appearance of Hippocrates himself. Before that time, the physician appeared as "a dispenser of predetermined modes of practice"[10] and not as individual healer. Independence of thought, speculation about a patient's condition, rational explanations to the patient about the facts and possibilities of his/her condition, and the freedom to make the best possible choice of therapeutic action—these basics of professional behavior so taken for granted today were hard to come by. Nevertheless, they are included in Hippocratic writings, and soon after, the physician-scientist appeared.

At first these different aspects of physicianhood were the specialties of sects, but each in itself always evoked ambivalent response in society. In effect, one finds in history rehearsals for each of the various styles and dilemmas of modern medicine. The role of physician-scientist, for example, varied with the structure of society and was both promoted and feared. "Suspicion of the scientist," Temkin tells us,

> depended partly on the prevailing mode of research and partly on popular imagination molded by the sensibilities and morals of the times. In antiquity, when medical research was sporadic, the fear that the unscrupulous physician misused his knowledge of poisons was probably greater than the fear that the scientist might use man's body for research.[11]

As public benefactor, an early model was Hippocrates himself, who was honored by his own society "for having sent his people to various places in Greece to teach the inhabitants how to save themselves from the plague which had invaded the country from the lands of the barbarians."[12] Not until the nineteenth century, however, did the role of the physician as public benefactor find its full expression. Only then did a genuine public health movement occur. For Western European societies, the intervening millennia, from antiquity, were dominated by a search for both knowledge and healing skills that focused on human biology. In the prevailing dualism of the body and the soul, of matter and the spirit, the body was the domain of the physician and the remainder of human experience the province of the philosopher or the priest.

The Renaissance and After

The pattern of social change described here is not so much conceptual as institutional. Since antiquity there was awareness and, during the Renaissance and immediately after, a heightened consciousness about the effects of social conditions on the health of populations. What was lacking was the systematic investigation of these relationships and the institutionalized expression of such ideas in public policy.

Although some of the early-nineteenth-century rhetoric spoke of medicine as social science, the first step toward the institutionalization of public responsibility in the role of the physician was in the medical specialty of public health. Although concepts of social medicine were inherent in studies of the last half of the nineteenth century, the institutionalization of social medicine in Europe and public health in the United States only crystalized at the turn of the century. The field was emerging as it is currently defined: "the effort organized by society to protect, promote, and restore the people's health. The programs, services, and institutions involved emphasize the prevention of disease and the health needs of the population as a whole."[13] From such a perspective, health problems, instead of being considered "as they occur in a series of individuals," are seen in the context of the community as a whole. Emphasis is on the "organized nature of the efforts involved" and on prevention.[14] The more specific elements of the public health concept include:

- The need to study the relation between the health of a given population and the living conditions determined by its social position
- The noxious factors that act in a particular way or with special intensity on those in a given social position
- The elements that deleteriously affect health and impede improvement of general well-being[15]

Such ideas did not emerge into clear and substantial operational form by the force of their inner logic or by their persuasiveness as ideas. They only emerged as part of policy with the aim of placing social and economic life in the service of the power politics of the state.

Of course, some form of community life has existed as far back in time as we are able to describe, and always with the need to deal with health problems in some organized way. The supply of acceptable food and water, the prevention and control of epidemic and endemic diseases, and the provision of some type of health care are as old as civilization in its most primitive forms. Public health as a concept emerged from the need to deal with the health problems of group living.

Similarly, although the biological character of disease and physical disability have always been recognized, community action concerning health has been filtered through cultural belief systems; and attributions of cause have in turn been influenced by social and economic circumstances, including the available knowledge and technology. Thus, for thousands of years, epidemics were seen as the acts of spirits or gods, retributions for wickedness or other transgressions, not as natural events; avoiding them therefore required some form of appeasement of these forces. Even though the Greeks developed the idea that disease results from natural causes, the use of effective community action to prevent and control disease followed a very uneven course until modern times. To deal with the menace of illness and disability, agencies have been created and laws established and procedures to implement such laws have been instituted. In these ways, public health has been closely linked with government activity since early times.

As long as the influence of the Periclean Greeks survived, public health practice was rational. The Romans, for example, were engineers and administrators who built sewer systems and baths and created systems of water supply and other health facilities. They also organized medical care, so that "by the second century A.D., there was a public medical service, and hospitals had been created."[16] Although these institutions were the models for later Christian practices, the disintegration of the Greco-Roman world led to a decline of urban culture and with it to a decay of public health organization and practice. This does not mean that medieval Europe jettisoned entirely the earlier organization of public health. The protection against epidemics, for example, even though filtered through the religious and superstitious ideas that prevailed at the time, "led to a mode of public health action that is still with us, namely, the isolation of persons with communicable diseases."[17] This is the institution we now know as quarantine.

During the thousand years prior to the modern era, the administration of public health was decentralized to the local community. The first major step toward linking health to the state was in the eighteenth century, when, within the political paradigm of mercantilism, European governments assumed responsibility for the protection of individual and group health. Absolute monarchy was the continuing political foundation but was no longer based on a system of personal loyalties to the monarch. Especially as exemplified by German Cameralism, Rosen argues, this was a crucial stage in the development of the modern state.[18]

As the state took over public administration, managing material and human resources, health became a matter of public policy. The state had a vested interest in the health of the populace. To best serve the state—at this point represented by monarchy—the physician was enjoined to act in the best interests of his patients in effect as medical police; the state, in turn, acted to assure the welfare of the land and the people.[19]

Rosen describes "an almost fanatical emphasis" at this time (the eighteenth and nineteenth centuries) on the increase of population and consequently on the reduction of disease mortality.[20] The benefit to the individual patient was real, but it was secondary to the central *motif* to serve the state. If one asks, "What does it matter?"—the answer is found in the different histories of France and England compared with Germany, where the medical police concept survived longest and developed most deeply.

England and France, in the first half of the nineteenth century, moved away from absolutism and mercantilism. The French Revolution and the rapid industrialization of England produced the first phase of a genuine social medicine, including the use of the survey as a tool for documenting the class differences and their consequences in disease that resulted from the new social order. In Germany, meanwhile, the heritage of the medical police was the traditionalization of the ideal of orderly efficiency. As a result, "by the middle of the nineteenth century in Germany, the concept [medical police] had largely become a sterile formula. Once Germany encountered the health problems connected with the new industrial order, a new approach was necessary."[21]

The ideology of the medical reform movement, meanwhile, fared no better than the organizational vitality of the medical police. Voices like Virchow and Neumann were tuned out of the public consciousness with the defeat of the Revolution of 1848. Their broad conception of health reform as social science was transformed into a more limited program of sanitary reform, and the importance of social factors in health was downgraded while the biomedical emphasis gained overwhelming dominance from the scientific revolution caused by the bacteriological discoveries of Robert Koch. Social medicine, in Germany, was aborted until it emerged again in the early twentieth century.

In England, meanwhile, the economic liberalism of classical economists like Adam Smith forestalled for a time public consciousness of the consequences for health of the Industrial Revolution. Within this philosophy, "the 'naturalness' of an economic system was said to flow from the objective necessity of labor, industry, value, and profit; just as the 'naturalness' of Newtonian physics flowed from the perfect harmony of matter and its 'universal' laws of attraction and repulsion."[22] Not until the second half of the nineteenth century did this theory about the absolute necessity of submission to the "laws of society" yield to the facts of industrialization. Inexorably,

> the industrial revolution . . . changed the living conditions of millions of people: ill health, poor housing, dangerous and injurious occupations, and excessive morbidity and mortality could not be overlooked and investigations of the causes and possible remedies of these social problems were undertaken, often by medical men.[23]

One of the most frequently cited of these early English studies is the Chadwick report. Prepared in 1842 by Edwin Chadwick, a lawyer and administrator, this report to the Poor Law Commission was not the first of England's pioneering social surveys. In 1832, James Philip Kay, M.D., published *The Moral and Physical Conditions of the Working Classes Employed in the Cotton Manufacture in Manchester*, in which he documented how poverty and illness were infinitely interlocked.[24] Peter Gaskell in 1833 presented a survey, "The Manufacturing Population of England," with similar conclusions. Both Gaskell and Kay, however, interpreted the meaning of their data in ways that reinforced the existing social order. Poverty was seen as part of the "natural order." The poor were more vulnerable to disease, it was reasoned, because of their "moral condition." Therefore, it was necessary to change the morals (not the socioeconomic conditions) of the poor in order to improve their health. Today, we would see this as "blaming the victim." Early economic liberalism did not recognize the paradox of survey documentation that revealed high morbidity and mortality among the poor and then using these data to justify the practice of child labor.[25] The Chadwick report, however, broke with the traditions of economic liberalism, recognizing the relations between social problems and medical conditions. Proposals to change social organization and to initiate government action concerning public health and medical care were soon to follow. Such proposals, however, did not result in a rationally argued policy, drawn from the evidence-based theoretical formulations that were inherent in the Chadwick Report. Instead, only partial solutions were instituted, especially focused on the specifics of the most evident problems, such as sanitation in the rapidly growing cities.

One example was Chadwick's recommendation that a "district medical officer" should be appointed in each locality. The Public Health Act of 1848 provided for such appointments, and by 1855 the law was extended to include London as well as the other regions of England. The medical officer became a model public health role for physicians of the future.

Another consequence was the establishment of public health as a course of study. In St. Thomas's Hospital, a course of lectures on public health was started as the first of its kind in England.

There were advances, therefore, but mainly in public health practices, not in the systematic organization of knowledge about the relations between medical problems and social and economic conditions. The readiness was for the inclusion of new medical measures for the prevention of disease and the promotion of health. Much slower was the recognition that social measures were necessary as well.[26] Pressures arising from the emerging political strength of the English working classes produced some partial reforms but were not strong enough yet to break the dominance of economic liberalism as the guiding philosophy of Britain.

The United States

In the United States, during the eighteenth and nineteenth centuries, attitudes and practices concerning health and illness were similar to those in England. The prestige of the medical profession was quite low generally.[27] Except for an elite few who traveled to the medical centers in Edinburgh or Germany, physicians learned as apprentices, even after the proliferation of private proprietary schools of the nineteenth century. With little faith in the efficacy of medicine itself, America was dominated even more than its mother country by the "moral" concept of illness. Although the individualism that was promoted by the frontier rejected older ideas of immutable fate, it saw individual intelligence as bounded by the "rules of nature": that is, man is motivated to learn the rules of nature and thereby to be able to order his behavior toward a perfect society. "It was reasoned that sickness, disease, and poverty resulted from immorality; conversely, health, wealth, and happiness were proof of one's adherence to the moral laws."[28] The concrete results of this philosophy, in hindsight, were striking:

> It was this assumption which enabled a prominent New Yorker during the 1832 cholera outbreak to thank God that the disease remained almost "exclusively confined to the lower classes of intemperate, dissolute, or filthy people huddled together like swine in their polluted habitation." At the same time, a minister proclaimed that the epidemic was promoting "the cause of righteousness by sweeping away the obdurate and the incorrigible . . ." A Special Medical Council appointed by the Board of Health during the outbreak lent its authority to this belief by asserting that the disease was confined "to the imprudent, the intemperate, and to those who injure themselves by taking improper medicines."[29]

Not until the shattering impact of the Civil War was there serious challenge to the concept that disease was a punishment from God, to be alleviated only when the lower classes learned "to observe the moral laws—personal cleanliness, temperance, hard work, thrift, and an orderly life."

The deadliness of the American Civil War is well known. Although the records are not adequate to allow an exact accounting, it is certain that more United States soldiers died than in any other war, probably over six hundred thousand. What is less well known is the impact of sickness and disease on the military casualties. Dr. Joseph Jones,

> an indefatigable Confederate medical inspector who kept voluminous records, estimated that . . . the ratio of battle deaths to those from disease was roughly one to three: i.e., 50,000 deaths from battle injuries to 150,000 from sickness and disease. The ratio for the Union forces, which were better fed, clothed, and housed, was approximately one to two: 110,000 deaths from battle and 225,000 from disease. In other words, "grim as the battle statistics are, the troops faced an even greater threat from sickness."[30]

The United States was poorly prepared for the health problems caused by the massive movements of populations and the destruction of the war. In spite of warning signs, virtually no organized public health system existed. "Only two or three cities had any kind of decent water system . . . [and] no city had a sewerage system worthy of the name." As Duffy reports:

> The reek of overflowing privies in the impoverished sections must have been beyond imagination. Adding to the foul atmosphere were dairies, stables, manure piles, and heaps of garbage scattered through the towns. Butchers and slaughterers frequently let blood flow in the gutters and simply piled offal and hides on vacant ground next to their places of business. Tanners and fat-and-bone boilers gathered offal and hides in open wagons, thus adding further to the already pungent city aromas. Rivers, creeks, streams and brooks flowing through the cities had all become open sewers by mid–century. Shallow wells, which still supplied most city-dwellers with water, were polluted beyond redemption. The wonder is not that mortality rates were soaring but that so many of the poor survived.[31]

In spite of these conditions, and the additional warning provided by major outbreaks of yellow fever and Asiatic cholera during the 1850s, no national public health organization had yet been formed. Moreover, the prosperity of America during this period did not help. On the contrary, commercial interests generally opposed the establishment of codes and regulations for sanitation and improved social conditions. On similar grounds, the Army Medical Department was small and poorly financed. In March 1861 the Congress voted only $115,000 for the Army Medical Department. It remained for a civilian organization of reformers, the United States Sanitary Commission, to pressure Congress into a reorganization of military medical, and eventually, of public health practices in the United States.

Another little-known aspect of this important chapter in American medicine is the role of women. The United States Sanitary Commission came into official existence on June 13, 1861. Three prominent New Yorkers are credited with its founding and its effectiveness: Dr. Elisha Harris, who was a significant public health figure; the Reverend Henry W. Bellows, a well-known Unitarian minister; and Frederick Law Olmsted, famous later as the designer of New York's Central Park. But, Duffy tells us, "the real impulse came from the thousands of women who were anxious to emulate the work of Florence Nightingale and her cohorts in the Crimean War."[32] Custom was against any form of participation by women in the war. Any combat role was, of course, out of the question, and that was where attention was focused. As the devastation of battle wounds, injuries, and sickness became overwhelming, however, women forced their way into important medical roles as nurses. It was not easy:

> Shortly after the outbreak of fighting, Dorothea Dix, whose activities on behalf of the insane had made her a national figure, offered her services and was appointed Superintendent of Female Nurses. Subsequently Congress authorized the employment of female nurses in general hospitals. A public controversy immediately broke out whether or not delicate females should be exposed to the horrors, brutality, and moral dangers of war. . . . Army surgeons were opposed to the introduction of women into [army] . . . hospital wards as a matter of principle.[33]

Nevertheless, the women persisted. The Union Army officially enlisted over three thousand women as nurses, and many more served as volunteers. They were recognized to be far more effective than the male nurses. Their record of accomplishment notwithstanding, there was little carryover after the war. Although the prejudice against women in medicine was modified, the prejudices of the prewar society were reasserted and did not yield appreciably until much later in history.

The same can be said for the public health movement generally and even more so for social science in medicine. The United States Sanitary Commission, just like the Chadwick report, was part of a major historical episode. The public awareness that these dramas forced into being did not survive the crisis event itself. There was no institutionalization of lasting reforms, and—most important for the story being told here—there was no theoretical insight about the relation between social factors and medical problems. Not for another half-century would substantial progress be made toward the goals of social medicine.

The Twentieth Century: The Beginning of Both Social Medicine and Medical Sociology

At the midpoint of the nineteenth century, Western societies appeared to be ready for a different and more systematic conception of how social factors relate to medical problems. The grip of economic liberalism's "natural laws of society" had been loosened by gradual recognition that industrialization was a manmade force against which "moral reform" was puny. Major disasters like the Civil War in the United States and the typhus epidemic that Virchow investigated in Silesia led people in the Western world to reconsider the causes and to reassign responsibility for problems of health and illness. However, there were other interferences with the emergence of the field that is now called "social medicine."

This was a period when the terms "public health," "social hygiene," and "social medicine" were often used interchangeably. The idea of "medicine as social science" was dropped. In spite of the farsighted efforts of men like Virchow, however, the perspective of organized medicine narrowed rather than broadened, and there was not yet an independent social science to take over the task for itself. In retrospect, it appears that the rapid growth of medical bacteriology during this period turned attention away from the promising beginnings of systematic conception and control of the social environment as major means of reducing disease and promoting health.

The latter half of the nineteenth century saw public health as a special field join forces with those who believed the new bacteriology would solve all of medicine's problems. The social perspective in medicine was frozen, set aside more than rejected, to reappear in the early twentieth century. Emil Behring, one of Virchow's chief academic critics, epitomized this historical trend. In 1893, writing about the etiology of infectious disease, Behring referred to Virchow's study of the 1847 typhus fever epidemic as characteristic of the attribution of "social misery" as the major cause of disease. Remarking that "while these views . . . had their merits, now, following the procedure of Robert Koch, the study of infectious disease could be pursued unswervingly *without being sidetracked* [my emphasis] by social considerations and reflections on social policy."[34] Virchow himself, after the defeat of his medical reform policies in the aftermath of the European revolutions of 1848, achieved an outstanding career as a basic scientist, the pioneer of modern pathology. At the same time, he continued to see "medicine in its organic relation to the rest of society, and [he] recognized health and disease as enmeshed within the web of social activity."[35] Virchow's reputation survives, while Behring, who condescendingly dismissed Virchow's social medicine in favor of a narrower biological view, is virtually forgotten today. There is a double irony to this story: at the time, it was Behring's view that prevailed, and today, Virchow's identity is mainly for the kind of biological focus that Behring stood for, while Virchow's advocacy of social science is known to only a few.

Soon after the turn of the century, the social medicine perspective was revived. Alfred Grotjahn, who was a young medical student when Behring proclaimed bacteriology to be the ultimate medical truth, published in 1904 a statement of theory that he called "social hygiene." Medical problems, he believed, should be systematically investigated "in the light of social science," so as "to arrive finally at a theory of social pathology and social hygiene, which with its own methods . . . would be used to investigate and to determine how life and health, particularly of the poorer classes, are dependent on social conditions and the environment."[36]

Grotjahn, more than any other medical scholar up to that time, was able to create a complete set of principles for a systematic study of human disease from a social viewpoint. Nor was his a lonely vision. Similar ideas were given expression during the first decade of the twentieth century, suggesting that there were new conditions in the social climate that favored such development. It was probably not coincidental that sociology, independent of medicine, was going through a major growth phase at this time or that the social work profession emerged. All three, medicine, social science, and social work found a common ground for action—in the prevention of tuberculosis and the securing of decent working conditions in factories, better housing, and the like.[37] Harvard University is a case example of the interprofessional cooperation and competition among them. At Harvard, medical social work was introduced as a distinct specialty in 1905 and was combined with sociology within the Department of Social Ethics that was created in 1920. Richard Clarke Cabot, the first Harvard professor of social ethics, is generally considered the founder of medical social work. Cabot, Kane tells us, although he was a physician, emphasized the discrepancy between medical recommendations and their feasibility, especially because of what he saw as the distance between the world of the medical practitioners and the realities of their impoverished patients. Medical social work was expected to bridge that gap, Cabot believed, and he was an eloquent spokesman for teamwork between physician and social worker.[38] One of his first acts as chair of social ethics was to create a two-year graduate program for social work, signifying his preference for the "normative" science of social work, meaning a discipline that "continually tests social action with reference to norms," trying to determine "whether each given policy is good, just, or consistent with moral ideals."[39] Sociology, in comparison, was seen as "a pure or descriptive science."[40]

Although Cabot was instrumental in leading the trend toward the professionalizing of social work, he lost in the struggle for academic legitimacy at Harvard. By 1930, the issues surrounding Cabot's tenure as the head of a joint sociology and social ethics department were resolved by the creation of an independent sociology department. A department of sociology was first instituted at Harvard University in 1931, and it replaced the Department of Social Ethics.

The last decades of the nineteenth century were also the time when the term "medical sociology" first appeared. In the United States, in 1879, John Shaw Billings linked the study of hygiene with sociology.[41] Because of Billings's prestige as one of the original faculty of physicians at the Johns Hopkins University School of Medicine, this was a notable event. Billings was also the organizer of the Surgeon General's Library, later to be the National Library of Medicine, and the compiler of the *Index Medicus*.[42] In 1894, Charlie McIntire defined medical sociology as

> the science of the social phenomena of the physicians themselves as a class apart and separate; and the science which investigates the laws regulating the relations between the medical profession and human society as a whole; treating of the structure of both, how the present conditions came about, what progress civilization has effected and indeed everything related to the subject.[43]

In 1902, Elizabeth Blackwell[44] also wrote about "medical sociology," and in 1909, James Warbasse published a book called *Medical Sociology*.[45] In the same year, Warbasse started the Section on Sociology of the American Public Health Association (APHA). The members of this group, however, included few sociologists: they were mainly social workers and physicians. Their deliberations reflected the sociology of the time: the study of and attempt to ameliorate the exploitation of child and female labor and the social problems associated with mass immigration—race relations, slums, housing.

The Section on Sociology of the APHA was disbanded in 1921. The time was not yet ripe for medical sociology. The atmosphere of the time was, as in the early part of the nineteenth century, moved mainly by the spirit of medical reform. The intervening century had created vastly different conditions, however, and medical reform now had new strengths as well as new problems.

As the Western world moved into the period between the two world wars, two distinct patterns emerged to express the heritage from twenty-five hundred years of searching to explain the relations between social factors and medical problems: one was within medicine, the other separate from it. There were the medical fields of public health and social medicine, which, unsuccessfully up to this point, had sought to integrate social science with medicine to create a systematic theory and methodology. Medicine itself was now radically changed in its basic knowledge, its technology, and its therapeutics, and so was the social organization of medical education and medical care.

Medical sociology was in existence but barely, a foundling of social work in the United States and of social hygiene in Europe and England. It was to have a rich period of intellectual development that began in the 1920s, but to understand medical sociology, it is important to look further at its nineteenth-century antecedents, shifting focus from the efforts to incorporate social science within medicine to the birth of American sociology and its development from the last decade of the nineteenth century till the first world war.

Summary

The early history of medical sociology, from antiquity to the beginning of the twentieth century, is richer, more complex, and more relevant to modern theory and methodology than has been generally perceived. Its highlights can be summarized in the following propositions:

- Social factors in health and illness have been recognized by physicians for most of civilized history, going back at least to Hippocrates.
- The actual menace of illness caused action related to the social conditions of disease; that is, such events as epidemics caused the introduction of organizational structures for public health, especially in urban societies, including effective sanitation and sewer systems. Ancient Rome is a good example.
- Social medicine emerged in the nineteenth century as a movement to investigate medical problems in the light of social science, but its earlier variants—such as the efforts of Frank, Virchow, and Neumann in Germany, Guerin in France, and Chadwick in England—did not get beyond providing added thrust to the public health movement; that is, elaborating the infrastructure of sanitation and various organized efforts to "clean up" the worst pockets of industrial exploitation of the poorer classes.
- What was most consistently lacking until the appearance of medical sociology was the effort to develop a systematic theoretical basis for the administrative program of public health.
- The nineteenth century movement that developed under the banner "Medicine is a social science" did not achieve its goals. It was strong enough to force a dialogue with the biomedicine that emerged from bacteriological science, but the new germ theory so dominated medicine that the development of a genuine social medicine was aborted.
- With Grotjahn, in the early decades of the twentieth century, social medicine revived. It continued, however, to be dominated by a biomedical orientation. It was pragmatic and applied.

2

American Sociology before 1920

From Social Advocacy to
Academic Legitimacy

The emergence of medical sociology can only be understood within the context of the American university. Even though the English and German universities were, in many ways, the models for American institutions, a more organized social science was produced in American universities than anywhere else in the world, and medical sociology developed as an intrinsic part of its parent discipline. The character of this historic development did not become clear until after the American Civil War.

At that time, in the last quarter of the nineteenth century, both social science and medicine in the United States took great leaps forward. Before that, they were intellectually dependent on European scholars. To be professionally current, many Americans studied at the universities of Germany, France, and England. Separation from these scholarly roots and independent national growth was only possible with the radical reorientation of American universities away from the scholasticism of their Christian theological sources and their transformation into secular, empirical science–based institutions. This happened when the first generation of college teachers with Ph.D. degrees were beginning to make their careers within the nation's universities.[1] Both intellectual development and the institutional arrangements were fundamentally changed. The research university was born, and all of the major types of intellectual activity were included in this transformation, including both sociology and medicine.[2]

This was also the period when the modern medical school first emerged in the United States. Medical education became closely aligned with the university, grafting the basic biological sciences of the graduate school to the bedside teaching model of the English hospital schools. Medicine, during the prior century, had been dominated by clinical private practice. Even medical education was largely private and for profit, in schools where local clinicians lectured for a fee, followed or paralleled by individually supervised apprenticeship toward qualification. There were some university medical schools as early as the 1770s, but they were few and were poorly supported. Not until the late nineteenth century did medical education begin grafting the basic biological sciences of the university graduate school to clinical instruction in teaching hospitals.[3]

In a similar way, the use of social science by medicine began to change. Instead of the ad hoc efforts of physicians themselves to create a social science of medicine, there was a new differentiation of tasks. Out of the university's graduate school a specialized subfield began to emerge, a sociology of medicine that competed with public health and social medicine in the effort to understand the relation of social factors and problems of health and illness.

Today, medical sociology is an intellectual activity both inside and outside of medicine. In the university college of arts and science, it has achieved an institutional structure autonomous from medicine. In medical schools, a parallel role exists. Like the preclinical "basic sciences," medical sociology has a dual identity, basically within its parent discipline and secondarily as a participant in medical institutions.[4]

Because sociology was, at the turn of the century, still in its early stages of development as a social science, it was to be another fifty years before the conditions were right both within medical education and in sociology itself for the subspecialty of medical sociology to begin its modern course. Nevertheless, this was a period of intense preparation, for both medicine and sociology. There were, however, important differences in their histories. Medicine had already completed a substantial part of its intellectual journey from "an empiric art into a rational science"[5] and, as shown by the circumstances surrounding the Flexner Report, was in the process of institutionalizing the new rationality into medical education and clinical practice. Sociology, on the other hand, was in the very early stages of emergence as a social science. Medicine, despite its already established practice of welcoming newly emerging intellectual disciplines into research and educational partnership, was not yet ready to extend such an invitation to sociology. As I have shown, this was not because of any lack of interest in the relation between social factors and medical problems. Rather, it was because the dynamism of biomedical discoveries, especially the bacteriological sources of germ theory, was at its most overwhelming and because sociology as an academic profession was in its infancy, too weak to challenge the still strong conviction that medicine itself could develop and institutionalize its own social science.

Against this background, medical sociology's history, both before and after institutionalization, reflects the pressures of medicine as its host profession and general sociology as its parent discipline. This growth can be summarized in the following three propositions.[6]

1. Medical sociology is closely connected with and follows the patterns of development in its parent discipline. Unlike some specialized intellectual activities that take sharply divergent directions away from their origins,[7] medical sociology's theory and research follow closely those of mainstream sociology, and its institutional structure similarly has been strongly integrated with that of general sociology.

2. Throughout the discipline's history, there has been a dual thrust toward progressive reform on the one hand and the development of knowledge on the other. The tension between advocacy and objectivity, between applied and basic science has always been present as a dialectical challenge.

3. There has been, for more than a century, a substantial overlap between the work of subgroups within medicine and that of social scientists who, from roles external to medicine itself, conducted research about problems of medicine. The two have had tempestuous relations, at times courting and collaborating, at others competing or excluding. Two medical specialties were particularly involved inside medicine: community medicine, including public health and preventive medicine, and psychiatry, which has tried to fit "behavioral science" within its knowledge base. This "insider-outsider"[8] ambiguity has been central to the struggle for legitimacy by medical sociology in both the medical world and the academic world of sociology.

From such determinants, the major roles of medical sociologists have emerged:

- Basic scientist of behavior
- University teacher in sociology departments and teaching collaborator with physician colleagues in medical school
- Policy analyst and consultant

This range of activities and roles emerged gradually. Today medical sociology is one of sociology's most active subspecialties. Only by looking in depth at its preinstitutional history, however, can medical sociology as we see it today be fully understood.

American Sociology: The Beginnings

The beginning of modern American sociology is usually dated to the creation of the American Social Science Association (ASSA) in 1865.[9] The general multidisciplinary character of this organization and its expansive social reformist objective is evident in its own statement of purposes:

> To aid the development of Social Science, and to guide the public mind to the best practical means of promoting the Amendment of Laws, the Advancement of Education, the Prevention and Repression of Crime, the Reformation of Criminals, and the Progress of Public Morality, the adoption of sanitary regulations, and the diffusion of sound principles on the Questions of Economy, of Trade, and Finance. It will give attention to Pauperism and the topics related thereto. . . . [It will aim to obtain] by discussion of the real elements of Truth; by which doubts are removed, conflicting opinions harmonized, and a common ground afforded for treating wisely the great social problems of the day.[10]

Both the time of its founding and the broad reformist mandate of the ASSA reflect the social impact of the Civil War. In the most detailed study of the ASSA conducted to date, Mary Furner wrote, "The industrial America that grew up after the Civil War made people conscious of society in new ways. The factories, the corporations, the railroads, the burgeoning cities—those powerful totems of a modern age had seemed so promising one by one. Considered together, they had a more ominous look."[11] To answer the social questions posed by industrialization became the need and opportunity that spawned the modern social science professions.

In the beginning, the recruits to social science were concerned citizens from various walks of life, amateurs for the most part, energized more by humanitarianism than by the drive to contribute to basic understanding of society. And so they remained for the most part in the ASSA for the next two decades. Gradually, however, some ASSA leaders and the new universities "shifted their attention from the unfortunate victims of social change to processes affecting society as a whole and then embarked upon empirical studies to discover how society worked [and] took the first tentative steps toward professionalization as social scientists."[12]

Inevitably, the ASSA was too broad in its scope to satisfy the needs of the varied interests of its early membership. It began to spawn new, more specialized organizations. Initially, these were still, in emphasis, groups interested mainly in the application of a social perspective on public policy. In 1874, for example, the National Conference of Charities and the American Public Health Association (APHA) were created. The former was to become, in 1918, the National Conference of Social Work, while the latter became the major professional association of public health specialists in medicine.

Gradually, though not without much internal and public struggle, there was a shift away from the advocacy of the reformers, and academics emerged as the leaders of the ASSA. Unlike the antebellum colleges, "which placed primary emphasis on transmitting a cultural tradition and developing the civic morality of students, the emerging universities developed an ethos of their own which stressed the creation of new knowledge above everything else."[13] For both non-academic and academic social scientists, tension between reform and knowledge persisted, but the impulse toward professionalization was inexorable. Like the reform-oriented professions of social work and public health, the university-trained disciplines began to break away from ASSA. Beginning in 1884 when ASSA was not yet twenty years old, the academic professional associations appeared in the following order:

The American Historical Association, organized in 1884

The American Economic Association, in 1885

The American Anthropological Association, in 1902

The American Political Science Association, in 1904

The American Sociological Society, in 1905

These groups became the main source and expression of social science in the United States.

Medical education, at this point in time, was regarded by most educators as seriously deficient,[14] but it was certainly alive and active. Fully four hundred medical schools were founded in the United States between 1800 and 1900, but most were private or "proprietary" (organizations for profit). They also came and went, so that, by 1905, the year when the American Sociological Society was founded, there were 155 operating medical schools. This is still a large number, substantially more than there are today. Also, the doctor-to-population ratio was one to 700–800, more favorable in terms of the available supply of physicians than today. The American Medical Association (AMA), founded in 1847, grew from eighty-four hundred members in 1900 to seventy thousand in 1910. It was estimated in 1901 that approximately six thousand people were graduating yearly from the medical schools.[15]

Graduate education in sociology, on the other hand, had barely begun. In 1893, the first graduate department in sociology was created at Chicago University. Following close behind were Columbia, Brown University, Yale, and the new state universities of the Midwest, Wisconsin, Nebraska, and Michigan. The American Sociological Society was inaugurated in 1905 with 115 members, and by 1910, only 141 more had been added.

It is important to keep in mind that secondary and higher education, at the turn of the century, was nothing like it is today. Less than 10 percent of high school–age children, in the year 1900, actually attended a secondary school, and the students in colleges and universities were only 4.01 percent of Americans of college age.[16] The secondary schools themselves were largely private and almost entirely academic, geared to the classical and sectarian approaches typical of higher education at the time. Donald Light, in a recent discussion of the development of professional schools in America, writes that through most of the nineteenth century there was

"no academic profession as we understand it today. . . . The traditional colleges concentrated on mental discipline and piety. In the 1870s, President McCosh of Princeton affirmed: "Religion should burn in the heart, and shine . . . from the faces of the teachers . . ." One was to avoid education "which puts a keen edge on the intellect while it blunts the moral sensibilities . . ." This meant that through recitation of the classics and pages of disciplinary rules, colleges attempted to control the mental and moral lives of their students. They believed that restraint produces self-restraint, hard work produces diligence, and precise memorization and recitation produced a disciplined mind in any field of endeavor. Such goals provided no support for an academic profession. Faculties spent their time being disciplinarians and hearing memorized recitations of ancient languages or mathematics. There was no academic career, salaries were low, and as President Eliot [of Harvard] remarked in 1869, few men of talent were attracted to the academic calling.[17]

From such a background came virtually all of higher education's recruits, a situation that did not change significantly until the twentieth century.

When, in 1908, Abraham Flexner conducted his survey of all 155 medical schools in the United States and Canada, he found that the residue of the scholasticism of nineteenth-century higher education was still pervasive. Flexner was himself a product of the Johns Hopkins University soon after it was founded in 1885. Like the University of Chicago and Stanford, Johns Hopkins was a model of the research university that emerged to replace the old religious scholasticism, and its orientation to graduate study and the scientific method throughout the curriculum was a radical departure for its time. Flexner, as he made judgments about the state of medical education, saw the university through the prism of the Johns Hopkins model. Therefore, he believed that the problem with medical education in the United States was that it was dominantly proprietary. If it had been part of the university from the beginning, none of the important problems that his survey described need have existed.

Critics of Flexner focused on this point. Duffy particularly criticized what he saw as Flexner's ignorance of the actual state of higher education in America during the nineteenth century:

> In his classic study of American medical education in 1910, Abraham Flexner blamed the University of Maryland for the introduction of proprietary schools—a system, he wrote, which divorced American medical schools from universities and led to a progressive lowering of educational standards. It is clear, however, to anyone who studies conditions in nineteenth-century America that *the universities to which medical schools might have been grafted simply did not exist* [my emphasis]. When the Maryland legislature established the College of Medicine of Maryland, there was no university within the state. The same was true in 1845 when the Louisiana legislature transformed the Medical College of Louisiana into the medical department of the University of Louisiana. The University existed only in name. Moreover, even in the case of schools such as Harvard and the University of Pennsylvania, the medical school professors collected their own fees and remained virtually autonomous for much of the school's history.[18]

A close reading of Flexner suggests that he based his judgment on the early colonial history of medical education in the United States. At that time, shortly before the American Revolutionary War, the earliest medical schools were indeed part of the university. The first was by John Morgan in 1765 at the College of Philadelphia, later to be the University of Pennsylvania, and the second at King's College in 1768, which became Columbia University. There followed the medical departments at Harvard in 1783, Dartmouth in 1798, and Yale in 1810. The case of Maryland, in his judgment, interrupted this development, establishing what Flexner called "a harmful precedent."[19] His opinion on this matter, as on most, was direct and unqualified:

> The sound start of these early schools [Pennsylvania, Columbia, Dartmouth] was not long maintained. Their scholarly ideals were soon compromised and then forgotten. True enough, from time to time, seats of learning continued to create medical departments . . . but with the foundation early in the nineteenth century at Baltimore of a proprietary school (Maryland) . . . a harmful precedent was established. Before that, a college of medicine had been a branch growing out of the living university trunk. This organic connection guaranteed certain standards and ideals, modest enough at that time, but destined to a development which medical education could, as experience proved, ill afford to forego.[20]

Flexner was not totally impervious to the historical realities of the nineteenth century. "Even had the university relations been preserved," he wrote,

> "the precise requirements of the Philadelphia college would not indeed have been permanently tenable. . . . The rapid expansion of the country, with the inevitable decay of the apprentice system in consequence, must necessarily have lowered the terms of entrance upon study (of medicine).

But for a time only, the requirements of medical education would then have slowly risen with the general increase in our educational resources. Medical education would have been part of the entire movement instead of an exception to it. The number of schools would have been well within the number of actual universities, in whose development as respects endowments, laboratories, and libraries they would have partaken; and *the country would have been spared the demoralizing experience in medical education from which it is but now painfully awakening* [my emphasis].[21]

What Flexner seemed to ignore was the changing nature of the university during the preceding century and especially the pervasive Christian traditionalism that placed such severe constraints on the university's ability to open itself to the rational orientation of science. His analysis also neglected the interaction between socioeconomic and political factors and education.

Whatever one decides about the different interpretations of Flexner and Duffy, the conditions in which both sociology and medical education began a new era were the same: it was a period of intense, widespread expansion of educational institutions and of the intellectual standards of colleges and universities. The industrial growth of the post–Civil War years with its explosive increase of technology made very clear the need for a more educated population. Basically, the pioneers of American sociology were part of a social science movement that was seeking both intellectual integration and social reform. It was, as the Bernards have documented so extensively, part of a movement that was utopian in aspiration, humanitarian in idealism, and directed toward establishing realistic principles of social welfare and reform.[22] From the outset, however, there were differences between the primary work roles of sociology and its sister social sciences. Sociologists, from the beginning, were more part of the university.

This close association, in the United States, between sociology and the university may be explained by the fact that, in its birth order, it was the last of the social sciences to professionalize. Consequently, as the major chroniclers of the field point out, "the span of sociology's biography is almost identical with the rise and development of graduate studies and the 'university' proper in America."[23] One result of this association appears when one compares the presidents of the professional societies from their beginnings up to 1930. All in sociology were university professors. The American Historical Association included judges, ministers, and representatives of the army, navy, and public service. The presidents of the American Economics Association and the American Political Science Association also included many who were not from academic institutions.[24] The least academic among all the social sciences was the national Conference of Social Work, which, in its first seventy-five years, included very few leaders who were from the universities.

The first historical phase of American sociology, however, in spite of its close ties with academic institutions, exhibited little of the ivory tower elitism of its European counterparts. Quite the opposite. As Lazarsfeld and Reitz tell us, "[W]hen sociology first came to the United States, it was akin to a crusade for social improvement." Moreover, there was one highly visible result of the alliance between social reform and early sociology: the social survey movement. In the beginning, wages and housing conditions and social relations in the family were surveyed. The study of more varied social attitudes came later.[25]

The founding of the American Sociological Society occurred in the middle of this development. The membership was small, beginning with 115 and growing to 1,021 by 1920.[26] For the purposes of this discussion, it is notable that Lester F. Ward, the first president, had a medical degree. This should not be interpreted as more than an intriguing footnote to this history of medical sociology, though it does indicate something about the nature of medical qualification at the end of the nineteenth century. Ward gained his qualification at a time when the M.D. degree could be obtained in as little as six months of part-time attendance at lectures. It was precisely to this shallowness of professional standards that Flexner directed his withering criticism of 1910. Ward was medically qualified in name only; but the fact that he took the trouble to study both medicine and law while at the same time fashioning a career as a sociologist should be judged against the most prestigeful model, the universal scholar, that prevailed at the time.[27]

In the post–Civil War era, the social backgrounds of most leading sociologists were rural and religious. "Of the nineteen presidents of the American Sociological Society who had been born prior to 1880, who had completed their graduate studies before 1910, and who had achieved some prominence before 1920, not one had experienced a typically urban childhood."[28] They were, like many American scholars of that time, either ministers or the sons of ministers and were deeply committed to personal involvement in social reform. Although they did not use sociology to endorse the ideology and practices of conventional, institutionalized religion, they were "almost without exception fundamentally concerned with ethical issues."[29] The quality of their reformism appears to have deep roots in this combination of rural and religious backgrounds:

> These men grew to maturity at a time when the religious and ethical traditions of Protestantism still dominated the nation. Often their reformism was a secular version of the Christian concern with salvation and redemption and was a direct outgrowth of religious antecedents in their personal lives. Lester F. Ward's maternal grandfather and Franklin H. Giddings' and William I. Thomas' fathers had been ministers; William G. Sumner, Albion W. Small, George E. Vincent, Edward C. Hayes, James P. Lichtenberger, Ulysses G. Weatherly, and John L. Gillin had themselves had earlier ministerial careers. This recurrent combination of rural background with inculcation of religious ideals was an important part of the experiential framework within which so many early sociologists interpreted and evaluated the conditions and problems of urban, industrial life.[30]

Ward and his most prominent contemporaries, Sumner, Giddings, and Small, present a mix of American and European approaches to scholarship. Like their European models, they were intellectually rooted in philosophy and unafraid to attempt comprehensive theories of society. They also accumulated wide-ranging experience outside of the university and were prodigious "heroic" workers, writing, editing, and joining in a variety of lay and professional organized activities. They were, like their contemporary medical colleagues, "emerging" into a new identity.

Sociology is presented to students today with attribution mainly to European intellectual origins; it is defined as a special science for "the study of social aggregates and groups in their institutional organization, of institutions and their organization, and of the causes and consequences of changes in institutions and social organization."[31] The early models for American sociology were mainly French and British. From France, August Comte (1798–1857), in his writings from 1830 to 1854, is described as the source both of the name "sociology" and its conception of society according to analogies drawn from natural science. From England, Herbert Spencer's theories of social evolution were paired with Comte's views of society as a social organism. Comte's biological analogies fit well with Spencer's evolutionary perspective. Their "laws of society" appealed to Americans, especially the purposive rationality of Comte, the individualism of Spencer, and the naturalistic interpretations of both. Although Spencer's translation of the evolutionary doctrine of survival of the fittest into a defense of laissez-faire individualism appealed more to industrial leaders than to the reform-minded American sociologists, his work nevertheless was the main point of departure for the early pioneers, including especially Sumner and Ward but also Giddings, Thomas, and Snaniecki.[32]

By 1910, the influence of Comte faded and was replaced by that of Durkheim, who was able to take the strong heritage of the French hygienists of the early nineteenth century and wed its empirical research methods to theory that was comparative and closely linked with anthropology. Germany meanwhile assumed the dominant position in the development of theories of social behavior, social structure, and social change. Americans like Albion Small, the founder of sociology at the new University of Chicago, received their graduate training in German universities, bringing back the teachings of Max Weber and his polemical exchanges with Karl Marx and the social psychology of Georg Simmel. From England at the same time came an influence strikingly different from that of Spencer: the development of quantitative methods of social research, particularly the surveys used for community study by Booth and Rowntree[33] and Sidney and Beatrice Webb[34] and the statistical analysis of Pearson and others.[35] Unlike American sociology, however, all of these developments were either outside of the university or in tenuous, proscribed status as partner to a related discipline, such as anthropology in France, political administration in England, and economics in Germany. It remained for the United States to provide formal instruction in academic departments throughout the system of higher education. Even today, no other country has given similar academic recognition to sociology, and the United States was the first to offer formal instruction leading to a doctorate.

The way sociology began as a derivative intellectual child of European thought but thrived in American academic institutions can only be explained by the special circumstances of social science at the time. Furner describes these first Americans to call themselves sociologists as "refugees from other disciplines." Both economics and political science quickly found a focus for harnessing their early post–Civil War activism to academic research, the former oriented toward "developing the skills to regulate the economy and the latter preoccupied with shaping techniques of administration for various government functions."[36] But that left social scientists who either were critical of what they saw as the co-optation of social science, especially economics, by the entrepeneurial marketplace or were in other ways left hanging in their search for solutions to broader social questions. "In quiet desperation," writes Furner, "a few serious social reconstructionists turned to a new alternative, sociology."[37] Even Albion Small, as late as 1908, admitted: "The chief obstacle which specialists of my sort encounter is the inveterate opinion that sociology is merely a convenient label for left-overs within the range of human knowledge that cannot be classified under any other head."[38] All the more remarkable, therefore, is the strength of sociology's academic growth once it got started.

The first recorded instance of a course called sociology in the United States was in 1876 at Yale University, offered by William Graham Sumner. By 1892 such courses were offered in eighteen colleges and universities. In the following year, the University of Chicago became the first to establish a department (joint with anthropology) that allowed students to get a doctorate in sociology. In 1894, the first graduate department devoted entirely to sociology was established at Columbia University. By 1910, most colleges and universities in the United States offered courses in sociology, but separate departments developed more slowly. Following World War I, this lag in the growth of strong institutional structure was corrected, as departments were formed in all of the major American universities. During the following two decades, a solid groundwork was laid for the important role sociological research was to play in the extraordinary effort to understand and influence social behavior in the armed forces and among civilian populations during the Second World War.

The intellectual history of American sociology during its early formative years is not so easily summarized. During this first phase—1880 to 1920—sociologists knew what they were not, that is "social workers or philanthropists," but they were less sure of what they were. In 1894, Albion Small actually had one of his graduate students conduct a survey of forty social scientists about their perceptions of the nature and limits of sociology.[39] There was much disagreement, but on one thing they were virtually unanimous: sociology should form a department of its own.

What can be said, then, to explain the strong thrust to establish a sociology separate and distinct from the other social sciences? When one compiles a list of early breakaways from economics, for example, there were more leaders than followers: Ely, Commons, Giddings, Ross. This was hardly a group of intellectual marginals in a survival crisis. Some were, in their time, distinctively radical. Ely, Commons, and Ross were all ardent activists who attracted enough controversy to be dismissed from their university positions. Others were conservative in their politics but dissatisfied with the concrete limits of academic social science. Sumner, for example, was a minister and moral philosopher who found in Spencer what he thought would be a scientific answer to the moral questions of the time.

Within this babble of voices, all calling themselves sociologists, the one clear American paradigm was pragmatism. Charles Horton Cooley at Michigan and then George Herbert Mead at Chicago gave a conceptual frame to social analysis that was distinctly grounded in the American experience. More than any other, the University of Chicago Department of Sociology, the first and leading center of graduate study, became an expression of this perspective. Pragmatism was also a philosophic paradigm that was hospitable to both advocacy and objectivity, thus providing a common frame within which two such different driving forces could operate together.

Sociology, therefore, grew in America out of dissatisfaction with the specialism of economics and political science. It followed the Comtean vision of unifying the social sciences, but there was little consensus on how. None of its boiling intellectual disagreement seems to have effected the growth of its institutional structure as a separate professional group.

By 1940, virtually all American universities had departments of sociology. During the next twenty years, there was a spurt of growth, but few new graduate programs were introduced. In 1960, there were seventy departments that were offering doctorates. There followed immediately thereafter the most intense growth of graduate education; by 1981, 118 institutions were granting doctorates in sociology, with another 109 granting M.A. or M.S. degrees. This number of higher-degree programs in sociology "is probably greater than that in all other countries combined."[40]

As a separate social science, sociology was able to achieve in the United States a strong position while in the Western European societies where sociology was born its institutional position was much weaker. The reasons, most agree, are connected to the social and political conditions that are unique to each society, but some general interpretations are possible.

National political ideology must be calculated as a significant factor. Certain countries have characteristically looked on sociology as a dangerous field, while others have allowed it relatively free conditions for expression and professional growth. The "totalitarian" governments, for example, have never been hospitable to sociology. Sociological inquiry as we know it was virtually forbidden by all the dictatorships: in Germany during the period of national socialism, in Communist Russia since 1924,[41] in Japan during much of its history, and in the eastern European countries since the late 1930s until their liberation from Soviet domination. Yet even among the Western democracies, all of whom have exhibited more favorable attitudes toward sociology than countries such as Russia, Spain, or Argentina, there are great differences that require other explanation. The existence of mass public higher education appears to be critical, but differences in the structure of the system of higher education also play an important role.

In the universities of England, for example, appointments to the faculties were closely controlled by the faculties themselves, not by separate administrative officers. The result was the creation of academic elites who resisted the type of innovation that the introduction of sociology as a new discipline represented. Both Hofstadter[42] and Shils[43] have commented at length about this consequence in the history of the British universities. They point out that, despite the spectacular success of Herbert Spencer in popularizing sociology in England in the latter part of the nineteenth century and the widely admired research achievements of Booth and Mayhew, as well as others, sociology as a separate discipline, and academic sociology in particular, developed very slowly in British universities. Shils explained this as a consequence of "the refusal of the British academic elite to raise questions about contemporary life in England." This "elite," Shils said, "based in Oxford and Cambridge, is self-sustaining and exclusive; since its existence is founded on privilege and class prejudice, it actively discourages a sociology which would make for critical investigation of the society that nurtures it."[44] Reiss has pointed out that British social anthropologists had no such inhibitions about studying the "primitive" inhabitants of British colonial territories, and anthropology was given precedence as a social science for academic chairs in universities.[45]

Similarly, in France, anthropology dominated sociology in academic appointment. Although these two subjects were often linked in the United States as well as in Europe, only in the United States did sociology grow more quickly and extensively than anthropology. In Germany, sociology grew from individual scholars, many of whom achieved academic positions more as economists or philosophers than as sociologists. Marx, of course, never achieved legitimate academic status because of his political radicalism. Simmel, though a lifelong teacher and brilliant scholar, was refused academic recognition until late in his life when he was finally granted a chair at the University of Strasbourg: the generally accepted reason is the discrimination practiced against Jews in German universities. Weber's chair was in political economy. Among the great early German sociologists, only Tonnies had what could be called in the Germany of that time a "normal" academic career as a sociologist.

In the United States, the preservation of sociology's early pragmatic orientation was one important reason for its strength. Although, as Reiss points out, "the alliances formed between sociologists and social reformers were sometimes uneasy, there remained an overriding concern in American sociology with developing an empirical science based on research into social problems."[46] Thus the exclusiveness of any tendency toward academic elitism was tempered with a perspective that directed both consciousness and the work of the discipline outward toward the realistic problems of the community.

American sociology also benefited from two organizational characteristics of the expansive growth of the university as part of the mass education movement. Because there were many students, there was less competition with older established disciplines. This resulted in less pressure to restrict professorships and created a favorable climate for autonomous academic departments, in contrast to the small centralized faculties of Europe. Within the resulting system, administration was separated from direct faculty control, a factor that, probably unexpectedly, allowed for easier introduction of new subjects and methods of education.

Another unique feature of American universities that, on its face, might not be expected to favor the kind of intellectual innovation represented by the introduction of sociology, was the importance of private foundations as a source of the financing of both professional development and research. Curiously, in those countries where universities have depended mainly on the government for finances, even when democratic political traditions were strong, the establishment of monopolistic intellectual elitism seemed to be reinforced. The role of private support, at least in the early stages of American higher education, served to open up the system and to encourage innovative educational styles and new disciplines like sociology, despite the conservative social interests that are regarded as intrinsic in philanthropic organizations that are created from large industrial fortunes.

The influence of private foundations is a complex question to which I will return repeatedly. In England, for example, the private foundations have also played an important role, but the character of the English university is very different from that of the United States. One is encouraged to speculate, therefore, that it is within a combination of factors that the role of the foundations must be interpreted.

What is clear enough is the fact that the great private family fortunes created by American industrial growth in the last half of the nineteenth century became very important indeed in the story told here. For medicine, in the first decades of the twentieth century, it was the Carnegie and the Rockefeller foundations that were most influential; for sociology, it was the Russell Sage Foundation and the Milbank Memorial Fund. In medical education, it has been argued that the effect of the private foundations was to create an elite, using three hundred million dollars between 1910 and 1930 to mold American medicine into a professional group that subordinated itself to the class interests of the industrialist donors.[47] However one interprets their effects, the foundations were, as Rosemary Stevens writes, "the most vital outside force in effecting changes in medical education after 1910, and for a long time they took the place of government support."[48] For sociology, the influence of the private foundations has not been as fully documented, but it is certain that the difference is more a matter of the degree of their importance than a question of whether they played a significant role.[49]

The Russell Sage Foundation was founded in 1907, just five years after the General Education Board, the first of the Rockefeller foundations, and two years after the Carnegie Foundation for the Advancement of Teaching, which, in 1908, sponsored the Flexner study of medical education in the United States and Canada. Founded by Margaret Olivia Slocum Sage, the wife of the congressman and financier for whom the foundation is named, the Russell Sage Foundation was started with ten million dollars, "the largest single gift to philanthropy in the history of the world" up to that time.[50] The goals of its charter were action oriented, stated broadly as "the improvement of social and living conditions in the United States." Very early, however, it developed a special interest in sociology, particularly in its research methodology, establishing in 1912 a Department of Surveys and Information.

For at least one historian of sociology (Oberschall), the Russell Sage Foundation played a direct and critically significant role in the development of empirical sociology. "The sociology survey movement flowered in the decade after the 1910s," writes Oberschall,

"especially after the Russell Sage Foundation was established in 1907. . . . The foundation supported Kellogg's Pittsburgh Survey with $15,000, the investigations by students in schools of social work, and the investigations of women and child labor conducted under the direction of Florence Kelly at the Consumers' League. Russell Sage had close links with the C.O.S. (Charities Organization Society) of New York, the New York School of Philanthropy, and Paul Kellogg's *Charities and Commons* (later the *Survey* magazine). The origin of the social survey idea was in the COS's effort to arouse public opinion for social reform. Its tenement house committee in 1899 arranged a public exhibit of models of tenements . . . that presented to the public "in accurate and scientific form the results of bad housing conditions upon the health and industrial welfare of the community. The Pittsburgh Survey originated in 1907. . . . After Russell Sage financing was secured, it was vastly expanded in scope and pushed beyond the goal of a quick journalistic survey. . . . After Pittsburgh, a series of surveys on a smaller scale followed.[51]

From its start, the Russell Sage Foundation established a pattern of activity that involved close linkages with both the professional organization of the social sciences and, at the same time, with related agencies of philanthropy and government. In its interest in social surveys, for example, it joined hands immediately with the Social Science Research Council when the latter was formed in 1923. The American Sociological Society was one of the seven national scientific societies that joined to establish the Social Science Research Council. The others were societies of anthropology, economics, history, political science, psychology, and statistics. Russell Sage was to be involved with all of these disciplines, but it established a special concern with sociology as the companion science of the profession of social work, which, together with the direct funding of social reforms, became the overriding focus of the Foundation's first thirty-five years. After World War II, the orientation of the Foundation shifted away from social reform and the problems of the social work profession to support of the development of sociology as a scientific discipline. Medical sociology was a primary focus of this revised policy direction.[52]

Margaret Sage was also active in more direct financial support of medicine, but this was not, at the time, connected with medical education. It was another heiress, Elizabeth Milbank Anderson, the daughter of the New York financier Jeremiah Milbank, who, in 1905, created what was to become the major private source of funds for public health and social medicine. The Milbank Memorial Fund, founded as the Memorial Fund Association in 1905, was increased to ten million dollars in 1921 at the death of Elizabeth Milbank Anderson and, under its revised name, continues to the present as a major force in social medicine and, during the last fifty-five years, in medical sociology and health economics.

By the end of World War I, sociology was, both intellectually and institutionally, ready for the full thrust of its modern development. Although American sociology was distinctive, it was by no means independent of European scholars and institutions. For at least another decade, until Hitler and the preoccupation with totalitarian threats took hold, American sociologists continued to travel to study in Europe. Even before 1930, the influence was reinforced as European scholars were imported to American universities. Petirim Sorokin at Harvard is a good example. From 1930 on, many more came.

Lazarsfeld and Reitz called this the second historical phase of American sociology, characterized by the search "for an autonomous sociology":

> By the end of World War I, a sizable number of sociologists were operating. Some had come out of the social-survey movement, others had required systematic training abroad or in the early graduate departments of the United States. Not surprisingly, these new sociologists wanted to win prestige and academic recognition for their work. This effort was characteristic of what we call the second phase.[53]

The groundwork for medical sociology was dominated by the same forces that shaped its parent discipline. Like general sociology, medical sociology found its place mainly in the university. Medical sociology also struggled with the dualism of applied and scientific orientations, on a parallel course with sociology itself. The growth of sociology as an academic discipline in the period immediately following World War I appeared to require certain underlying conditions:

> These conditions—free inquiry both within and without the university, mass public education, a loosely organized, decentralized university system, and large resources for the financial support of research—therefore appear essential to the rise and rapid development of sociology. . . . Sociology is among the sciences that may become dangerous to the state and to society; the growth of such sciences as academic disciplines is therefore intimately bound up with the state of society.[54]

The society, Reiss is saying, must be willing and able to tolerate the most searching and unrestricted inquiry about itself. Otherwise, there can be no flourishing of scientific sociology.

What, if anything, does this tell us about the necessary preconditions for medical sociology? First, of course, the parent discipline must be established. That would seem to be a given for the emergence of any subfield within sociology. Does it also follow that the environment within which a subdiscipline must conduct its inquiries, in this case the profession of medicine, must also be willing and able to tolerate the most searching and unrestricted inquiry about itself before a field like medical sociology can develop? The answer to this last question was not yet clear in 1920 when the sociology of medicine as a specialized subfield was just beginning.

Although during this time there were active efforts to start such a field within medicine as part of public health and social medicine, no similar effort occurred so early as part of the growing academic profession of sociology. Surveys conducted as late as 1950 show that no sociologists yet were identifying themselves as specialists in medical sociology.[55] Studies related to psychiatry were mentioned as a secondary field of interest in Odum's 1950 survey, but these appear to date mainly to the period after 1920. None of the major textbooks included health, illness, or medical care among the important problems of society. Only in the work of individual scholars does one find examples of what medical sociology would later become. McCartney, in a study of the earliest American professional journals, found that, during the decade 1895–1904, articles that can be categorized as the sociology of medicine (including *mental health and gerontology*) ranked ninth in the percent of articles published. McCartney surveyed the full range of topical fields in sociology, including nineteen categories. The actual number of articles in the sociology of medicine was small, 3.1 percent, compared with "social theory, history and change," which contained 31.6 percent and ranked first. The sociology of medicine was to continue as a low-ranking but continuously visible publication area until the decade following 1955 when, with 7.5 percent, it became the fourth-ranking area of sociological publication.[56]

At the end of what Lazarsfeld called the first phase of American sociology, there was as yet no identifiable sociology of medicine as a field of institutionalized intellectual activity. During the next two decades, however, from 1920 to 1945, very important developments for the history of medical sociology occurred. The mainstream of sociology's development was toward "an autonomous sociology."[57] As a relatively new field, sociology was engaged in winning prestige and academic recognition for its work. Medical sociology would not be ready for a parallel move toward autonomy as a subspecialty until twenty-five years later; but it existed to the extent that there were important sociologists who undertook research about medical problems and who received assignments within public commissions to study the most critical health-related problems of the time. This would be the period, the decades between the two great wars, when the foundations of medical sociology were firmly set.

3

Between the World Wars

The period between the two world wars was, for sociology generally, a time of growth and of institutionalization. As for medical sociology, this was when much of its intellectual foundation was built. Bernhard Stern,[1] Michael Davis, and Henry Sigerist carried forward the traditions of social medicine, both scholarly and activist. Within academic sociology, on the other hand, a quite different approach was initiated. Lawrence J. Henderson, in a Harvard seminar on Pareto in 1931, used medicine as the illustrative case for the development of social theory.[2] Functionalism, on the model Henderson himself pioneered in physiology, was his prime concern, applied to the phenomena of social behavior. The doctor-patient relationship, Henderson said, should be conceived as a social system, and his colleague Talcott Parsons and his student Robert Merton developed the theory further as structural-functionalism, including among their substantive illustrations the social roles, organizations, and processes of socialization in modern medicine.[3]

These decades also saw the development of social psychiatry and the social ecology of disease. A physician, Harry Stack Sullivan, pioneered the former, but in close association with social scientists. Robert E. L. Faris and H. Warren Dunham built on the primary sources of empirical sociology at Chicago to apply the most advanced survey methods of sociology to the social epidemiology of mental disease.

All of these activities were rich, both in their published results and in influence on future work, but they represented a classic pattern of individualized academic scholarship. These were efforts of individual scholars, working without membership in a defined and organized "field." Included were a mix of physicians and sociologists. Henderson, Sullivan, Sigerist, and Ackerknecht were physicians; Stern, Parsons, Faris, and Dunham were sociologists. They related to and affected one another but not on a continuing, institutionalized basis. At the same time, however, two remarkable historical events occurred that produced a very different style of inquiry about medical problems, bringing social scientists and physicians together in a cooperative attempt to work directly from scientific study to policy decisions. The Committee on the Costs of Medical Care (CCMC) and the President's Research Committee on Social Trends (the "Ogburn Commission"), were both started in a time of economic prosperity by farsighted groups. The Great

Depression overtook them at midpoint, and their potential effects upon public policy, for the most part, were aborted. Yet, as I will show, these two large-scale public commissions, much like the development of knowledge in the sociology of medicine by individual scholars between the wars, were previews of the patterns of relationship that were to be stabilized after the Second World War.

The failure of such episodes to achieve their goals, despite substantial resources and achievements, underscores the importance of the organization of an intellectual activity. The development of knowledge, in itself, does not provide the sufficient requirements for continuous existence. Therefore, the institutionalization of a new scientific role and discipline is presented as the dividing line of this history. The history of social research about medical problems is at least one hundred and fifty years old, yet we speak of medical sociology as only fifty years old. What finally demarcates an institutionalized field?

Institutionalization: Sociology, Social Research, and Medical Sociology

Oberschall, in the most thorough historical analysis of empirical sociology I have been able to find, documents the fact that sociology and social research followed independent histories until they were combined in one discipline.[4] Looked at in this way, it becomes clear that social research about any particular substantive area, such as health and illness, could not establish a separate identity until there were the necessary conditions of intellectual and scientific interest, social demand, sponsorship, and resources. Moreover, no type of social research appears to be sustained, each step building on the other, except as part of a basic discipline that is well along in the process of established institutionalization. One of Oberschall's major illustrations of this principle is from public health:

> The most interesting and prolific period of social research in France occurred between 1815 and 1848, when public hygienists and medical reformers became concerned with the condition of the working and lower classes in the urban and increasingly industrial environment. It is to the public hygienists that we owe such a classic as Parent-Duchatelet's treatise on prostitution, which stands as the most thorough and empirically documented work on that topic.[5]

Yet, immediately thereafter, during the reign of Napoleon III, the research precedents of the public hygienists disappeared. Similarly, in both Germany and England, as we discussed above, health-related research emerged, flourished for a time, and then disappeared: "Time and again a promising research tradition melts away, techniques of research discovered and fruitfully applied at a particular time are soon forgotten and fall into disuse only to be rediscovered quite independently by later investigators, and even within the same research groups the high quality of earlier research deteriorates over time."[6] Only with institutionalization, says Oberschall, does this episodic and noncumulative history of any intellectual activity change. Whether it is social research or the broad, universal theories favored by the early academic sociologists, each needed the conditions favorable for institutionalization before a sustained and continuous intellectual development could occur.

For sociology in the United States, the full process of institutional development began after the Civil War and entered its final stage during the period between the world wars. In other countries the process was to occur later. Condensing a model constructed by Ben-David, the institutionalization of an intellectual activity (or "new scientific role and discipline") proceeds in four steps:

> First, there is some differentiation in subject matter, method, and technique from earlier disciplines.

> Second, this hitherto peripheral subject matter comes to be regarded as a meaningful part of culture.

> Third, these beginnings lead to increasingly patterned recruitment of talented people into the new scientific activity, which thus gains in numbers, in its resource base, and in stature.

> The fourth and final step consists of the successful consolidation of a distinct scientific community with its own subculture, a broad operational base, a communications network, publications, and scientific associations.[7]

At this point, Oberschall continues, "The members of the new discipline have developed a separate identity and the new science becomes a self-perpetuating domain of culture and to a large extent independent of its environment. It is now assured of a resource base and it generates its own problems and concerns from within the discipline."[8]

The first step in this process is the clearest and most easily demonstrated. Even at this stage, however, when the focus is on intellectual distinctness, development is not explained (as historians of ideas so commonly argue) by the force of ideas in themselves, by intellectual discovery and the supercession of the more powerful ideas over the less. Such explanation of the history of ideas is not adequate. To be sure, conception and theory, their origins, their fusions, modification, and inherent worth or excellence are important, but comparative analysis shows they are not sufficient. One need only compare sociology in England, France, and the United States to see that the same intellectual conditions are not, in themselves, enough to spur the equivalent processes of institutional development.

> There existed toward the end of the nineteenth century widespread intellectual dissatisfaction [in the United States] with the approaches of the several existing disciplines—economics, psychology, law, the philosophy of history—in the sense that their concepts, methods, and concerns did not adequately deal with an entire order of social phenomena. But this intellectual malaise and the widespread concern with the social problems of an urban-industrialized society were also present in Europe and by themselves did not provide the opportunity for the establishment of sociology in universities, although it allowed sociology to be pursued as a semi-respectable intellectual enterprise.[9]

In England, for example, in spite of the advanced tradition of survey research and social statistics and the popularity of such theory as that of Herbert Spencer, sociology's position in the British university system was precarious until after World War II. Between the two world wars, there was a department that awarded an undergraduate sociology degree only at the University of London, "but even there sociology appeared to be a specialty within economics and economic history and attracted only a small number of undergraduates."[10]

By comparison, sociology in the United States rapidly was differentiated from the other social sciences. In 1908, a survey by the American Sociological Society showed there were fifty full-time professors of sociology in existence. Economics was the major discipline from which sociology differentiated itself in the United States, with the process beginning in the 1880s. Overlap between membership in the American Economic Association (AEA) and the American Sociological Society continued to be considerable until the 1920s, but the differentiation of sociology as an academic discipline was by then secure. In England, it was not to be for another thirty or more years.

The second step is more problematic. It requires both conditions of intellectual demand and supply and, as Oberschall and Ben-David show, they cannot be conceptualized along classic supply-demand models. On the demand side,

> the emerging discipline must acquire a sponsor group which backs it with its resources . . . [and] on the supply side, there should exist a group of people whose professional advancement and career chances are enhanced by engaging in a new activity, who assure recruitment into the new discipline, who fight to defend and expand the initial institutional footholds gained, and who themselves become a powerful lobby in favor of institutionalizing the new role in addition to the original sponsor group.[11]

It is generally agreed that, in sociology, the original ideas and theories that have withstood the test of time originated in Europe, not in the United States. Yet well before American sociology became the source of important new knowledge and research methods, sociology as an autonomous academic discipline was "a smashing success," even while European universities blocked it.[12] Nor were there unique, favorable social conditions in the United States; rapid industrialization and urbanization, growth of slums, labor struggles, and other social problems were shared by both continents, except for the massive immigration into the United States. The unique and probably most critical factor that differentiated the development of sociology in the United States from Europe was the rapid expansion of higher education in the United States, "with unprecedented resources at its command, and its growth as an extremely competitive system, favorable to innovation."[13]

During this period, in the later decades of the nineteenth century and the first of the twentieth, the major actors in both the history of medical education and of sociology play parallel roles. For example, as the initiator of the "first competitive spurt" in the sponsorship of sociology as an autonomous discipline, Oberschall attributes the most importance to Johns Hopkins University, which for graduate education became as powerful a model as it was to Flexner in his proposals for the reorganization of medical education. When Johns Hopkins opened in 1876, "Columbia University was a day school with no afternoon classes [and] no dormitories, and the library opened only two or three hours a week."[14] The same was true of the other leading universities of the time. Daniel Coit Gilman, the first president of Johns Hopkins, decided to act boldly with what was then an unprecedented three and a half million dollars in endowments. He used the entire endowment income for salaries, establishing professors with salaries of five thousand dollars, double the average at the time for Yale and Harvard. In the social sciences he borrowed from Germany the seminar method, a lighter teaching load to encourage research, and he created publications for both dissertations and scholarly journals. This model was to be imitated soon by most of the leading universities of the time, but initially their leaders tried to discourage Gilman. As Flexner reports, President Eliot of Harvard advised Gilman that his proposed university model would not work. Eliot told the Hopkins trustees, just before the plan was instituted, "A university is not built in the air. It is a growth, and I should doubt very much whether any institution, old or young could cut loose from the community in which it is placed. . . . We could not deliberately undertake that (at Harvard) even if we were starting anew."[15] Despite the prestige of Eliot and of Harvard, the advice was ignored. Fortunately for sociology and other intellectual activities in the United States, Gilman persisted, and his donor, Johns Hopkins, had provided him with full responsibilities and freedom to follow his own professional judgment. Even President Eliot was later to be grateful, as shown by the graceful way in which he ate his earlier words on the twenty-fifth anniversary of Gilman's presidency of Johns Hopkins:

> President Gilman, your first achievement here has been . . . the creation of a school of graduate studies, which not only has been in itself a strong and potent school, but which has lifted every other university in the country in its departments of arts and sciences. I want to testify that the graduate school at Harvard University started feebly in 1870 and 1871, [and] did not thrive until the example of Johns Hopkins forced our faculty to put their strength into the development of our instruction for graduates.[16]

At the same time in history the private foundations of America's largest industrial and financial family fortunes were founded. Their influence has been interpreted as a force for elitism and conservatism in American higher education. Especially in medical education, recent historical analysis has argued that the Rockefeller foundations "used their immense wealth ($300,000,000 given to medical education and research between 1910 and 1930) to force specific reforms in medical education [that] . . . would make medicine serve the needs of capitalist society rather than the interests of the medical profession."[17] Another similar argument is that the foundations were instrumental in changing, under the banner of progressive reform, medical education and the medical profession to conform to business models of efficiency and scientific management.[18] More detailed attention will be given to these ideas later. Most important in the immediate context is the specific criticism that both the foundations and the Flexner report acted to limit the number of positions and to cut back the number of medical schools.

For the arts and sciences in general, and sociology in particular, I would argue that the influence of the foundations was the opposite: it acted to expand the training of social scientists and to foster competitive innovation. The founding of the University of Chicago, where the first graduate training program for the doctorate in sociology was started in 1893, is probably the best illustrative case. Here again the resources came from the Rockefeller family. As Oberschall recreates the story, William R. Harper as Chicago's first president played a role for his university that was to be as important to the history of graduate studies as was Gilman's at Johns Hopkins earlier. Indeed,

> "just when the competition generated by the Hopkins and Columbia undertakings [Columbia followed the Hopkins model beginning in 1880] . . . was beginning to dampen, the second and more extensive round of competition and innovation was started with the founding of the University of Chicago. . . . If there ever was an academic innovator and entrepreneur, it surely must have been William R. Harper. . . . When fellow Baptist John D. Rockefeller offered him $1 million to start a college, Harper replied he needed $15 million to create a truly great university. He eventually got $30 million and delivered on his promise in a remarkably short time. The immense resources of the new university and Harper's aggressive tactics immediately threw other universities on the defensive."[19]

The effects of this bequest and Harper's method of using it was to create a new demand for young social scientists with doctorates and in no way to limit the development of social science. Quite the contrary.

The foundations were a vital force in the second and third steps of sociology's institutionalization, in terms of the supply-demand model in which the emerging disciplines must acquire a sponsor group that backs it with resources.[20] For sociology in the United States, the necessary sponsorship came from the universities that were recently organized, highly competitive, and generously financed and from private foundations like the Russell Sage Foundation.

For someone like Margaret Olivia Sage, an early suffragette, deeply religious in terms that linked her sympathies to the poor, the support of social work became a logical way of using the large fortune that, without children of her own, she inherited from her husband with the full responsibility for deciding, herself at the age of seventy-eight, how over sixty-five million dollars should be allocated. At the time, the connections between social work and sociology were very strong. On the supply side of the institutionalization paradigm, American sociologists were more often than not Protestant ministers (Albion Small of Chicago, Summer of Yale, Gillin of Wisconsin) journalists (Park of Chicago), and "social scientists with the scientific inclination and academic aspirations to throw in their lot with sociology when they found economics as a discipline closed to them."[21] They fitted the model that Margaret Sage was advised to follow by men like Daniel Coit Gilman, who urged her not to attempt to use the foundation itself to finance solutions to problems of "social betterment" but to use only the income of a large endowment to provide the means for "the permanent improvement of social conditions." Gilman, as one would expect from the prime mover of the Johns Hopkins, recommended as the means to that end "research, study, teaching, publication, initiation of concerted effort, establishment of necessary agencies and institutions, aiding such effort already existing and such agencies and institutions already established."[22] Economics in the United States at the turn of the twentieth century, even though it shared some attributes with sociology, had become opposed to social reform.

Samuelson describes the economics of the period as optimistic, theological in character, protectionist, nationalist, and pro-business. . . . Max Lerner calls this period "the triumph of laissez-faire diffused through economics departments . . ." According to the orthodox view, *private charity and government intervention to correct social evils would in fact lead to collective harm* for the entire society, not to its improvement or cure. Reform in all its aspects stood condemned as a socially harmful activity inspired by sentimentalism and irrationality.[23]

In similar ways, the other, older social sciences did not fit the needs of reform-minded philanthropists like Margaret Sage, but the new discipline of sociology did. With the push of men like Gilman, therefore, the research and education objectives of the Russell Sage Foundation met in sociology the potential for rational, disciplined investigation of the problems that were at the focus of their mission and "a course of instruction . . . thought to be vocationally useful to social workers, . . . philanthropists, [and] social reformers."[24] From reform-minded private philanthropy, therefore, the demand side of sociology's institutionalization found powerful support.

When the demand for a new discipline and a supply of potential recruits come together, as they did for American sociology in the 1920s, the fourth and final phase of its institutionalization was achieved. The University of Chicago continued to be the leading department in the rapidly expanding field. The *American Journal of Sociology (AJS)*, published at the University of Chicago since July 1895, was joined by *Sociological Monographs* in 1915 (changed to *Journal of Applied Sociology* and then finally to its present name, *Sociology and Social Research*, in 1927), by *Social Forces* in 1922, and by the *American Sociological Review* in 1936, the latter replacing the *AJS* as the official journal of the American Sociological Society.[25] With these developments during this period between the two world wars all the basic characteristics of a scientific discipline were in place.[26]

It was at this time that medical sociology entered the first stage: differentiation as a scientific activity. Only when sociology grew to the point of dividing its labor was such differentiation possible, and, at first, other subspecialties took precedence. The earliest were from sociology's main sources in the European heritage of social philosophy and theory and were followed by those that expressed the American emphasis on social reform. Because of its early incorporation into the teaching curriculum of the university, American sociology was a textbook subject before it had a chance to develop a strong base in empirical research. In this phase, sociology relied most heavily on the intellectual heritage of European social thought. Very soon, however, influenced by its connections to reform-minded philanthropy, social problems and social pathology became categories of specialization. The other major areas were "the community, rural, urban, and industrial sociology; the family, marriage and institutions; race, ethnic minorities, folk; population, demography, ecology, regionalism."[27] Problems of health and illness, the study of how social factors influence medicine and its organizations, and theories of social behavior that have special implications for medicine as a social institution began to be differentiated in interdisciplinary study of psychiatry and mental hospitals and within such categories as population and ecology and social psychology. The same principles of institutionalization were to apply for the subdiscipline of medical sociology as for the parent discipline.

Medical Sociology: Phase 1—Intellectual Differentiation

There were many "firsts" for American sociology between the great European wars: the first laboratories of social research in 1925 at the University of North Carolina and the University of Washington, the creation of the Social Science Research Council in 1923, the first large-sample public opinion polls, the first American studies of American life typified by the Lynds' classic work, *Middletown*,[28] the first presidential commission devoted primarily to social research,[29] and the first distinctively American theories to dominate sociological scholarship internationally. What was to be known later as medical sociology grew largely within these important developments of sociology's mainstream, distinguished only by the use of medicine or medical problems as the empirical subject for otherwise generic sociological approaches and concerns.

There were, however, also separate, more specialized developments in close synchrony with previous types of research in social medicine. For example, Edgar Sydenstricker, Michael Davis, and William F. Ogburn conducted studies directly concerned with social problems. Within their research, the relationship between social factors and illness was basic and, for Sydenstricker and Davis would be a lifelong preoccupation. Moreover, their research, unlike that of predecessors, did not "melt away—only to be rediscovered quite independently by later investigators."[30] Instead, their work attracted a continuity of inquiry, becoming the foundation of slow but regular accumulation of knowledge that was later to be identified as medical sociology.

The question is what made for continuity at this particular point in history? To answer this question, I will first describe in some detail each of the major cases, beginning with Sydenstricker.

Continuities with Social Medicine

Sydenstricker, like a great many social scientists of the time, began as an economist. He is identified variously as a statistician, an economist, and a public health professional. His major work, however, *Health and Environment*, published in 1933, was an advanced theoretical discussion of how health is in dynamic equilibrium with the environment. Rosen credits Sydenstricker with "masterly analysis" that was an exception to the trend toward "almost exclusive concentration on the economic aspects of medical care. . . . He broke down the idea of the environment into its component aspects, and then showed the relation of each of these to health problems. Sydenstricker laid the basis for a theory of social medicine."[31] Much like the first American sociologists of the late nineteenth century, many of whom also began their careers as economists, Sydenstricker found the perspectives of economics too confining, too probusiness.

Sydenstricker first achieved professional notice as a statistician in the Public Health Service. In 1914, he joined the team directed by Dr. Joseph Goldberger to conduct a study that would be the definitive explanation of pellagra as a diet-dependent disease. The study was based on a design to survey seven villages in South Carolina. It was to prove that pellagra was dependent on diet, that diet was determined by economics, and that the economics of the South was determined by its one-crop system.[32]

Goldberger was not the first to recognize the social and economic implications of pellagra. Rudolph Virchow made a similar assertion about pellagra in the mid–

nineteenth century, close to the time when he conducted his pioneering epidemiological study of typhus fever in upper Silesia. Goldberger, however, "was the first to gather enough facts so that the ancient connection of the disease with poverty would be more than a surmise."[33] This achievement was only possible because of Syndenstricker, who provided the scientific tools. Once the problems of scientific proof were solved, however, unexpected new problems emerged. Troublesome cultural values interfered. For the medical profession, attitudes were fixed in germ theory enough to resist quantitative evidence to the contrary. For the main body of physician-scientists, the data of statistics and epidemiology were alien: they accepted only the proof of the laboratory. The lay public was equally resistant; especially in the South, where the disease was so widespread, ordinary people found the solution contrary to regional culture, and the political leadership did not like the publicity and acted to suppress the study. Still, Goldberger and his associates persisted, and eventually, after two decades, won their case to the point that the disease began to be treated routinely according to their findings. Their vindication was to be in the virtual elimination of the disease in the United States.

Sydenstricker, in 1916, while still in the Public Health Service, joined the surgeon general in recommending legislation for national health insurance.[34] In 1926, shortly after he joined the Milbank Memorial Fund as scientific director, he became a member of the CCMC. Again, he identified himself with the problem of discrimination in access to medical care by dissenting from the final report of the CCMC which, he felt, did not go far enough in its recommendations for the reorganization of the delivery of medical care.

Sydenstricker, unlike predecessors such as the French social hygienists a century earlier, was able to sustain his role beyond an isolated research episode. He also retained and defined his own professional identification with social science, even as he became an acknowledged theorist of social medicine. In retrospect, this was possible for two reasons: first, his research fitted into the health insurance movement, a policy perspective that, though supported by a minority in the United States, was strong in other Western countries; and second, he was identifiable by the scientific tools that he used so effectively with a visible field of endeavor. Both the health insurance movement and his profession survived, though not without difficulty, to become part of a continuous historical effort. Sydenstricker's role was to help differentiate the subject matter, method, and techniques of the sociology of medicine from earlier disciplines, the first step in institutionalization.

Michael M. Davis played a similar role. One of the earliest graduates of the Columbia University Department of Sociology, he wrote his thesis[35] under Franklin Giddings, the third president of the American Sociological Society. Following his mentor's deep interest in urbanization, he studied problems of health to illustrate how sociological principles contributed to explaining the effects of social status, particularly with reference to the massive waves of immigrants that were then coming to the United States. His book, *Immigrant Health and the Community,* published in 1921, is one of the first monographs of modern medical sociology.[36]

Davis, like Sydenstricker, was quickly drawn into a leadership role in social policy. His interest in immigrants made him aware of deficiencies of access to health care that were related to poverty. Just prior to the First World War, a community health center movement was started. Beginning with a demonstration center for maternal and child health in Milwaukee in 1911, the concept of neighborhood health centers for the poor grew rapidly. By 1920, there were seventy-two such centers in forty-nine communities. By 1930, the number had grown to 1,511. Davis studied this movement and was active in its implementation, and when the CCMC was created in 1927, he was on its executive committee. By this time, he was, like Sydenstricker, a functionary of a philanthropic foundation: director for medical services of the Julius Rosenwald Fund of Chicago. Also in the CCMC was William F. Ogburn, who, like Davis, was an early sociology Ph.D. from Columbia University. Ogburn, professor of sociology at the University of Chicago, was elected the nineteenth president of the American Sociological Association in 1929. That same year, President Hoover made him the director of the President's Research Committee on Social Trends. This national endeavor, more than any other prior event, signaled the arrival of sociology at full legitimacy as an intellectual activity in the United States. These two major interdisciplinary studies, the CMCC and the Hoover Research Committee on Social Trends, are important markers in the historical development of medical sociology as a special field. They are part of the differentiation of the sociology of health at the same time that they mark the legitimation of sociology itself as a policy science. For these reasons each one is given detailed attention here.

The Committee on the Costs of Medical Care

On May 17, 1927, a Tuesday, Lou Gehrig's homer and a "timely single" by Babe Ruth made front-page headlines in the *New York Times,* but no mention appeared of another event that was of historic importance for the future of health care in the United States. In Washington, D.C., a group of some sixty physicians, health officers, social scientists, and representatives of the public created the CCMC. For the next five years, the CCMC, consisting of fifteen members, met twice a year and produced twenty-eight reports on fact-finding studies. They were supported by a consortium of eight private foundations, including the Milbank Memorial Fund, the Russell Sage Foundation, the Carnegie Corporation, and the Rockefeller Foundation. Their aggregate support of CCMC was $750,000, an enormous amount of money for research at that time.

The CCMC was an expression of two basic perspectives: medical economics and public-preventive medicine. Harry H. Moore, described as "a public health economist,"[37] was the director of the study, and I. S. Falk, who was trained originally in bacteriology, was associate director. Sociologists appear to have acted in relatively minor roles. However, Moore's major book, *American Medicine and the Peoples' Health,* published in 1927, was "structured on the theory of social lag,"[38] the theory of social change enunciated by William Ogburn in 1922. Ogburn himself was a member of CCMC, and Michael M. Davis was one of the eight-member executive committee. Their contributions, together with those of Sydenstricker, were hardly minor.

In the final analysis, however, more important than sociology's direct contribution to CCMC was the effect that CCMC's reported findings and recommendations were to have on the future activities of the sociology of medicine, especially its future health services research, and related public policy. Most influential was the testimony that CCMC gave on the issue of health insurance and the organization of health care delivery. The committee's majority concluded strongly, but with some equivocation, in favor of national health insurance. On health care they reached a more radical (for the time) judgment that group practice and group payment plans should be allowed to compete equally with individual fee-for-service health care. Also emphasized were the needs for comprehensive services equally distributed to all sectors of the population and improved education for all health professionals. What CCMC did was to create an agenda and to buttress it with supportive data such that when "the pressures of the 1920s were brought to a head in the social turbulence of the early 1930s," the health professions, especially medicine, and the federal government were unable to avoid intense debate about the issues of public policy that CCMC so clearly articulated.[39] Among those issues were problems of the social organization of medical institutions, of the relations between psychosocial and sociocultural factors and their impact on health and illness, and of the sociology of professional education. These were to be, two decades later, the focal questions for a new type of partnership between medicine and sociology. Especially in the educational institutions of the health professions, sociologists were to be invited to study the problems and to provide some orderly body of data on which the instruction of future doctors and the resolution of health care dilemmas could be based. In this respect, CCMC can be interpreted as a major source of the emergence two decades later of the subspecialty of medical sociology. For the moment, however, the critical financial situation of the depression obscured the problems of developing an appropriate structure for modern medicine. Concern for the costs of health services overwhelmed all others.[40]

The timing of CCMC is one of its most striking features. Though it ended during the depression, the year of its founding, 1927, was at the height of the nation's most heady prosperity, a time of national growth and general feeling of optimism. Why, under such conditions, would such a broad-based group of organizations and individuals come together and the CCMC emerge as a self-created and private organization? The answer, according to I. S. Falk, the associate director in charge of research for the CCMC, was the unexpected consequences of the changes in medical education that occurred in the United States so rapidly after the Flexner report of 1910.[41]

Falk, looking back on the event forty-five years later, reasoned as follows. The need for government participation in providing health care started with the Industrial Revolution. Prior to that, responsibility for providing care for the sick and injured rested on the family, the neighbors, the church, "often on the master for his servants, [and] on the employer for his employees. With the beginning of the Industrial Revolution in Europe, first the journeyman's guilds and then the labor unions and the emerging socialist political parties assumed roles to provide for their members."[42] The inadequacy of these separate and private systems, however, led in Europe to increasing government intervention, including compulsory group payment of costs. "On a national scale, this happened first in Germany in 1883 as a political move by Prince Bismarck to check the growth of Socialist parties, and many other countries followed suit."[43]

The United States at first followed a pattern closely similar to that of Europe. From colonial years there were provisions by the government against epidemic diseases and for the poor and the destitute but at the level of local government. The national government, when it became involved, introduced a method of support different from that of Europe, what has become known as *categorical support*. It began very early, with the Marine Hospital Service Act in 1798, to provide for the temporary relief and maintenance of sick or disabled seamen, financed by a charge of twenty cents per month on all seamen, mainly to pay for care in marine hospitals and managed by the Treasury Department.[44] "It was in effect," writes Falk, "a compulsory, contributory national health insurance program for a *particular category of persons*" (my emphasis).[45] This pattern of categorical federal support for health services has remained dominant to this day but with increasing controversy. It contrasts with the universal coverage of European health systems, which do not selectively separate categories by age, occupation, or socioeconomic class, as the United States has done.

The Marine Hospital Service evolved into the Public Health Service (PHS) by 1912. At that time, the successful achievements of workmen's compensation laws seemed to forecast as the next step the protection by the government against non-work-connected risks, services, and costs on a pattern similar to that of the British National Health Insurance Act of 1911. Indeed, such a movement had wide support, including that of the AMA. A campaign for such insurance was waged between 1912 and 1920. The PHS surgeon general, Rupert Blue, supported it, and from the PHS a strong brief for it was published by Surgeon General Benjamin S. Warren and public health statistician Edgar Sydenstricker.[46]

Subsequent events, according to Falk, were influenced primarily by science and technology. He attributes to "the scientific revolution" the establishment of a new base in knowledge for medicine and medical care. Most important was the modernization of medical education and training set in motion by the Flexner report. The incorporation of "the exploding mass of new knowledge and medical art and technology . . . into medical education," Falk believes, made specialization inevitable, which in turn "resulted quickly in fractionation in medical care, increasing complexity of personal health services, rising costs, and the outmoding of the general practitioner and family doctor."[47]

Against this background, in the early 1920s, leaders in medicine, public health, and social science began to "sense an urgency to assess trends . . . and to consider what could be done . . . [with] the medical care system. This," says Falk, "was the genesis of the Committee on the Costs of Medical Care."[48]

There are large gaps, however, in Falk's explanation of CCMC's origins. Why, for example, did the AMA withdraw the support it gave to national health insurance in 1912? In general, what interrupted the apparently smooth transition early in the century toward the models of payment and delivery of medical care represented by England and Germany? After all, the research university was adapted from those countries with important but relatively minor adjustments to the special conditions of the United States. Why not the health care system?[49]

One answer is that the war happened. Certainly, World War I marks the sharp turn of American health care away from collective action in the public interest. During the war compulsory health insurance came under attack from all its previous supporters: not only within the medical profession but from commercial insurance companies, employers' associations, organized labor, and other groups. "Compulsory health insurance was attacked," Stevens tells us, "as being class legislation, socialistic, tyrannical, and in the surge of nationalism as the United States entered the war, as 'un-American' and 'German.' "[50] The irony was that this attitude of the profession against collective public action to provide medical care to the population as a whole coincided with reports that would be expected to produce just the opposite effect. For example, about 25 percent of draftees were rejected for military duty and over 46 percent were revealed to have some physical or mental defect.[51]

At the same time, as it rejected collective action that might ease and equalize the access of the public to medical care, American medicine was deeply preoccupied with its own professional organization. Standardization was effectively initiated through the AMA Council on Medical Education, created in 1904. The Association of American Medical Colleges (AAMC), started in 1876 as a means of reforming medical education from within, was reorganized in 1890 and joined the National Confederation of State Medical Examining and Licensing Boards, created in 1891, in setting higher standards for training physicians. Their purposes were reinforced and consolidated in 1915, when the National Board of Medical Examiners, a voluntary national examining body, was created with a subsidy from the Carnegie Foundation for the Advancement of Teaching. It took time to disentangle the overlapping roles of these organizations and to establish the identity of the American medical profession. Only when the competing forces they embodied and the problems of undergraduate medical education set in motion by the Flexner report were resolved did the concepts of "need" and "demand" for medical care begin to be explored analytically in relation to the supply of service available and the kind of personnel required.[52]

Until 1920, the AMA appeared to favor legislation for compulsory social insurance. Thereafter AMA policy changed: such legislation was seen as "a threat to private practice," which, for American physicians, was "the very basis of American professionalism." As Stevens summarizes,

> [h]ealth insurance would require participating physicians to accept fee schedules, regulations, possible work reviews. It would set up an organization outside the doctor-patient relationship, over which the individual physician would have no control. It might limit the patient's choice of physician. One physician described the proposed California legislation in 1916 as an "assault upon the rights of every man practising medicine in the State of California." Thus, *the interests of professionalism diverged from the pressures for social action.*[53] (my emphasis)

This was the context in which the CCMC was created. In April 1926 fifteen people who were prominent in medicine, public health, and the social sciences came together "to launch a definitive evaluation of the organization and the availability to the public of scientific medicine."[54] It was at this meeting, with no links of any official nature to any existing professional or governmental organization, that the 1927 conference was planned and the CCMC came into being.

The Intellectual and Political Outcomes of the CCMC

"The Committee," Falk reminds us, "had no authority to compel any action, and its appeal was to reason, responsibility, and the public interest. Thus, from its beginning in 1927 to its end in 1932, CCMC was an undertaking *to achieve social progress through voluntarism*" (my emphasis).[55] Such a preference for the private and the voluntary over governmental means to achieve social progress is a unique heritage of the United States. "Americans have always tended to view government as inherently illegitimate," writes the political scientist Andrew Hacker.[56] "We give it power only grudgingly and then object to its exercise." Yet when we assign to voluntary groups the responsibility for social progress, how are they expected to work? Can the types of change that the CCMC charted occur without any participation from the government? Before that question can be answered, of course, one must look at what the CCMC actually did, and what it proposed.

The CCMC conducted a variety of studies, from which the staff prepared twenty-six reports, a final staff volume,[57] and a summary report with recommendations adopted by the Committee on October 31, 1932.[58] The result was the most complete factually based portrait of the health system that had ever been made available to the American public. Included were studies of the resources for health and medical care; actual availability and receipt of care by families in many communities; costs, expenditures, and their impacts; and standards for the measurements of adequacies and applications for evaluations. A national survey of over eighty-six hundred white families found that nearly half of those in the lowest income category (under twelve hundred dollars) received no medical, dental, or eye care in a period of twelve consecutive months, while those in the highest income category, ten thousand dollars and over, contained only 13.8 percent who received no care. This was in spite of the fact that there was substantially the same incidence of illness per family or per individual in the various income groups.[59] It was also determined that medical costs were unequally distributed. Regardless of income, less than 4 percent of families incurred 80 percent of the costs. This made clear the potential catastrophic effects of illness on individual families unless effective protection could be supplied both of access to medical care and against the financial costs.[60]

The CCMC was unanimous in its conclusion that medicine is a necessary social service. In the interpretation of what such service meant and how it was to be supplied there was, however, a split among factions of the Committee. These factions clustered according to the interests of the public and those of the medical profession. Even within the factions, however, there was equivocation about recommendations that were believed could—and subsequently did—cause the medical profession to feel threatened about its basic laissez-faire approach to the organization of medical practice.

For example, the majority of the CCMC recommended that medical personnel should be organized in group practices, including physicians and other health professionals, preferably focused in hospitals. Prepayment for such services was also recommended as a method of dealing effectively with costs. Opinion was divided, however, on whether such financing should be private or tax supported and whether it should be voluntary or compulsory. Thus, as Stevens notes, "the proposals for financing were vague, [but] the philosophy was clear."[61] The recommendations, in effect, opened the way equally to "a system of compulsory government-sponsored health insurance [or] . . . a spontaneous development of local private schemes with no compulsory element nor any public subsidy."[62] The former would have guaranteed an integrated scheme whereby the providers as well as the consumers of health services would be brought into cooperative relationships, the goal of CCMC's deliberations. The latter private scheme, however, prevailed, producing a coordinated system of payment schemes without a coordinated system of medical service. The result is the system we have today: "a mixture of government prepayment (Medicare), tax (Medicaid), commercial and nonprofit insurance, and other prepayment schemes. Until the recent development of managed care, it was a system that was designed to protect consumers from excessive costs and to guarantee providers high financial rewards and autonomy, including the right to expand the technological aspects of the system, regardless of cost."[63] For the society, on the other hand, this system has proven to be uncontrollable in its costs and created the conditions that, it can be argued, allowed the system radical transformation into today's market-driven health care industry.

The CCMC recommendations were based on a model that combined the successful private, hospital-based group practice structure of the Mayo Clinic with prepayment. It was a change from the concept of a completely free and voluntary transaction between an individual patient and a doctor to one in which each person would purchase an insurance policy or contract for specified services to be given by a health service organization. It was, for all that, evolutionary rather than revolutionary. In Stevens's analysis, "[i]ts importance lay in the fact that the model was designed not only for reasons of economy but also to tackle a major problem of scientific medicine, the control and efficient use of specialists [, and] . . . emphasized the particular relevance of multispecialist group practice as an organizational solution to the egalitarian structure of medicine in the United States."[64]

For organized medicine, however, the CCMC majority recommendations, in spite of the care that was taken to avoid radical confrontation with existing practices, were not politically acceptable. A minority report detailed the dissent of seven CCMC members who represented private practice, one from the medical school representatives, and the secretary of the AMA. They stated that they were in conflict with the general tone or trend of the report. On the strengthening of PHS and basic educational improvements, they agreed with the majority. But "the majority report makes it appear," they said, "that the medical profession has been static and unprogressive." Such an implication, they believed, was "unjustified by the history of medical progress."[65]

The minority report by the physician members specifically opposed what they called "government competition in the practice of medicine." They were also concerned that CCMC "ignored the central position of the general practitioner." Flatly opposed to both voluntary and compulsory health insurance, they nonetheless strongly endorsed the "duty of the state to give complete and adequate care to the indigent."[66]

In fact, the majority had *not* recommended compulsory health insurance, but this became obscured in subsequent debate. Part of the blame, according to Stevens, can be ascribed to the ready identification of the report with the Roosevelt administration. Of course, CCMC was conceived and appointed during the Coolidge administration, and its major work was conducted while Hoover was the nation's president. Although its tone may seem legitimately to be more in the spirit of Roosevelt, Stevens is more specific in her explanation. "The Roosevelt administration," she wrote, "was personified in Edgar Sydenstricker, a member of the Committee who was appointed to the technical board of President Roosevelt's Committee on Economic Security, where he did indeed advocate compulsory health insurance."[67] The irony, Stevens adds, is that Sydenstricker also refused to sign either the minority or majority Committee report on the ground that neither dealt with the fundamental economic questions.

Whatever the reasons, the AMA reacted strongly and negatively to the CCMC summary recommendations. Whether they misread or misinterpreted the truth of the report, they labeled the very modest recommendations of CCMC socialist dogma: "There is the question of Americanism versus Sovietism for the American people."[68]

In the immediate short run, the opposition by the AMA prevailed. The recommendations of the CCMC were left unimplemented by either the private or the public sector. Early statements by the Roosevelt administration that were favorable toward a health insurance system were dropped after the AMA House of Delegates, at a special session in February 1935, strongly repeated its opposition to all forms of compulsory insurance. "Following the AMA's action, the administration, anxious not to jeopardize other aspects of Social Security, did nothing. Thus the Social Security Act of 1935 was passed without health insurance provisions," in spite of the recommendations of Sydenstricker's Committee on Economic Security.[69]

Taking a longer view, both Falk and Roemer find in the CCMC a more positive achievement. Falk, for example, speaking about the CCMC twenty-five years later, called its final report "a document which changed the course and the pace of evolution for the health services of the United States."[70] Even though the opposition of interest groups like the AMA rendered ineffective the immediate implementation of the CCMC recommendations, through the extensive documentation of its report a baseline of data was established on which the struggle for health legislation over the next forty years was able to draw. Certainly, CCMC was a fountainhead of modern medical economics. As Margaret Klem records, CCMC contains reports on the costs of adequate care that have never been duplicated since.[71]

One of the clearest consequences of CCMC was the precedent it set for the importance of continuing collection of data as the basis for logical health care planning, especially as represented by the family-cost-of-illness survey.[72] In particular, CCMC provided the model for the National Health Survey of 1935–36. Using the manpower and facilities of the Federal Emergency Relief Administration and the Works Progress Administration, the PHS made a series of studies during the thirties, giving national figures on the extent of various disabling conditions and on the relationship between changes in income and standard of living and the costs of sickness and medical care among families of wage-earners.

In summary, the intellectual heritage of the CCMC was rich, but the public policy results were much less impressive. The quality of the scholarship and the courage of individual members of the staff like Falk, Klem, Sydenstricker, and Walton Hamilton set a standard of quantitative health services research that in medical sociology was followed in subsequent decades by such scholars as Odin Anderson, Jack Elinson, Leo Reeder, Howard Freeman, Sol Levine, and David Mechanic. The spirit of this important early work was not lost.

At the same time, it is important to note the lessons of public policy that, at least for some time, appear to have been lost. In the work of CCMC, there is a clear split between the members from the public health professions and the practicing physicians, including both those from the private practice group and others. The tendency of the members of the Committee who performed the data-based work and who were from public health was to rely in their arguments for legislation on data and analysis, within the framework of the norms of science reporting. The physicians, on the other hand, depended much more on ideological rhetoric based on the prevailing political realities. Through the AMA, particularly, they mounted a powerful force in support of what they thought as their self-interest. The result was that "[i]n the final CCMC days (1929–32), we had been spending as a nation $3.7 billion for all health services, about $29 per capita per year—about 3.6 percent of the gross national product (GNP) of about $100 billion. By 1950, the expenditures were up to $12.0 billion—about 4.6 percent of the GNP of $263 billion. Nor was there end in sight for the escalation."[73] This is an accurate description of the heritage of the public policy decisions that followed the reports of CCMC. The CCMC itself, it must be said, furnished the data and sounded the alarms that could have been used to prevent this costly and disorganized result in the health care system of the country.

The Ogburn Committee: 1929–33

The large-scale utilization of social science for public policy in the United States is usually associated with liberal Democratic administrations, beginning with Franklin Roosevelt's New Deal.[74] Actually it was Herbert Hoover who first assigned to social science a high level of prestige and public responsibility. Known to history primarily as the man who presided over the Great Depression in 1929, Hoover entered the presidency with a very different image. He personified, in his role as Coolidge's secretary of the interior, the ideal leader of American progressive liberalism. Even his successor, Franklin Roosevelt, shared this view, as shown in a letter written to a friend in 1920: "I had some nice talks with Herbert Hoover before he went West for Christmas. He is certainly a wonder, and I wish we could make him President of the United States." Hoover conceived a national program for social reform, and immediately upon his election he sought to instill among his associates the same type of what he called "rational scientific nationalism" that defined his approach to cooperation between science and industry, but with the focus redirected to social reform.

Radical in its scope, Hoover's national program to abolish poverty was expected by the progressives of the time to establish what was actually called "the Great Society." Its strategy was to apply scientific research to social problems.

Even before he won the election of 1928, Hoover decided that a survey of the nation's social resources was needed, "a counterpart in human terms to the famous survey of natural resources undertaken before the war to establish scientifically the appropriate national priorities concerning waterways and their uses, mineral sources, forests and recreational areas, and other interests of the conservationists."[75] Immediately upon his election, Hoover acted to correct "a shocking lack of data on which to base policies for coping with social problems."[76] His assistant, French Strother, when assigned to this problem, found his way to Howard W. Odum, professor of sociology at North Carolina.

Odum, in turn, enlisted the cooperation of the recently formed Social Science Research Council (SSRC), which devoted its annual summer meeting entirely to planning a response to the president's request. The meeting fitted perfectly with Hoover's style. In Karl's description,

[t]he Council's summer meetings had been, for several years, a center of communication and intellectual stimulation and communication in the social sciences. . . . [These] meetings served many purposes, including the setting of policy for the coming year's distribution of grants, the bringing together of representatives of the foundations which provided the funds and the academics who profited, and the mixing of local, state, and federal officials who might provide useful ideas and benefit the discussions. Held in a fraternity house in the isolation of the Dartmouth campus, the occasion provided recreation and a Chautauqua-like atmosphere—not unfamiliar to many participants—for reflection and inspiration.[77]

Working with the SSRC was not a new experience for Hoover. Since 1923, when he chaired the President's Conference on Unemployment, he had expanded his industrial management interests to look at the human side of scientific management. Eyre Hunt, a close associate since the war, was his chief assistant in establishing working relationships with social sciences for governmental use. Together Hoover and Hunt had made warm contacts with SSRC, the National Research Council, and the National Bureau of Economic Research.

In a similar way, they had made contact with those private foundations that were the main early supporters of social science. Among these were the Russell Sage Foundation, which by the 1920s had attached an interest in the study of the effects of migration to its already well-developed concerns with urban social conditions.

By the time he became president, therefore, Hoover had established relationships with the working institutions of social research and with their sources of funds. All were represented at the Hanover, New Hampshire, meeting of the SSRC in 1929. First, there was a unique interdisciplinary blend of the best-known social scientists of the time. Included were Charles Merriam, professor of political science at the University of Chicago and the founder and head of the SSRC; Wesley Mitchell, professor of economics at Columbia University and the founder of the National Bureau of Economic Research; and William F. Ogburn, who was in the process of moving from Columbia to the chair of sociology at Chicago. Second, there were the representatives of the foundations. Of these Shelby Harrison, of the Russell Sage Foundation, played a key role in this event.

There were many more, amounting to thirty-eight actual participants at Hanover in August 1929. The list reads like an exclusive club of the best-known social scientists of the time: they were from all the disciplines and a broad spectrum of ideologies, ranging from Alvin Johnson, Robert Lynd, and W. I. Thomas to Beardsley Ruml.[78] Ogburn was the person who was most immediately interested in a scientific social survey, and he became the meeting's choice to direct the effort to implement Hoover's mandate. In several ways, Ogburn seemed the perfect person for the job. He had a reputation both for active participation in social reform movements, and by 1929 he was perhaps the most prominent spokesman for the scientific emphasis in social research.[79] He had already combined these two interests in the study of social trends, collecting long-range empirical data on election returns, scientific developments, legislative acts, and so on. The quantitative interrelations between these diverse social indicators were the main theme of his work. What better person, therefore, was there to be in charge of what was to be called the President's Research Committee on Social Trends?

On September 6, 1929, Ogburn conferred in Washington with Strother. A small dinner party was planned for September 26, to include Merriam, Mitchell, Ogburn, Odum, Shelby Harrison, Ray Lyman Wilbur (the new secretary of the interior), Strother, and the president. The Committee, as eventually constituted, made Mitchell its chairman and Merriam its vice-chairman. Shelby Harrison acted as secretary-treasurer, Ogburn as director of research, Odum as assistant director, and Edward Eyre Hunt as executive secretary.

As it turned out, the initial apparent general agreement of purpose by the members of the group concealed differences in point of view that were fundamental. For example, the meaning of "survey" was interpreted in two different ways. For Shelby Harrison, for example, it meant a philanthropic reform survey, best illustrated by the Pittsburgh Survey of 1907. Hoover, on the other hand, was using the model of "engineering" surveys, which looked to the mechanical and industrial efficiency of the city as the source of its social problems rather than to issues of child welfare and education, which were the main focus of the social survey. The Harrison concept emphasized the definition and measurement of the behavioral factors in American society and the Hoover concept emphasized the statistical correlations of disease, degrees of poverty, and the number and condition of tenement buildings. Both were optimistic and with absolute faith in the ability to apply science to the solution of public problems, and in that sense, "Hoover and his social scientists were of the same generation, riding in the same boat." There remained a question whether "Hoover's sense of the industrial engineering survey, Harrison's commitment to the social survey of the professional social worker, and the social science of Mitchell, Merriam, and Ogburn, provided them all with the same set of oars."[80]

There would be more points of conflict between the politicians who were the decision-makers and the social scientists who were asked to provide the data and analysis that was necessary for "rational scientific public policy." The social scientists themselves were divided about the ability to preserve scientific objectivity while working directly in the service of the president. In the end, they were persuaded that Hoover's "scientific rationality" would be nonpartisan if it was provided with a sufficiency of factual information. Interestingly, they were also persuaded by Hoover's decision to have the work of the Committee financed through private rather than governmental resources.

Comfort with the admittedly "political," if not "partisan," source of their assignment was, for the Committee, just one part of the rationalization. Their reasoning about the funding was another. The budget was, for the time, huge. The initial estimated budget request for $560,000 ended up in a total cost of $750,000. Hoover himself suggested $200,000 for research, $100,000 for conferences and $100,000 for "follow-up." The latter is again a curious item when considered within the framework of the obsession of all parties to "scientific objectivity." As Karl wrote,

[i]ncluded [in the "follow-up"] was the whole publicity campaign for the program: publication of the research, magazine and newspaper campaigns, and radio broadcasts. That such a campaign, scheduled presumably for early 1932, was not to be considered "political" was part of the interesting set of illusions about politics which surrounded the committee's formative stages.[81]

As the private donor, the Rockefeller Foundation was chosen. Here again, however, an interesting sidelight of the issue of "objectivity" presents itself. The source of funding for the committee was to be the "Spelman Fund." Who exactly was the Spelman Fund?

The Spelman Fund was actually the Laura Spelman Rockefeller Memorial Fund, with a changed name. The name change in 1920s was part of an effort among philanthropists to separate themselves from connections with political reform. In their published statement of purpose, the Spelman Fund said: "The Spelman Fund has no political objectives; it is interested only in helping to provide experience and wisdom in executing public programs which have already been adopted and which are no longer matters of political controversy."[82] Undoubtedly this was to some extent the reaction of the Rockefellers to public attacks, including some from Congress. Despite the Committee's links to Hoover, however—or perhaps because of them—the request for funds to the Rockefeller Foundation was successful, with formal support given through one of the family's foundations that, by coincidence or design, did not include the Rockefeller name.

Thus was the work of the President's Research Committee on Social Trends launched by a president who believed in "a definition of democracy that in some strange way omitted politics"[83] and financed by a powerful family's philanthropy that considered itself "above" politics. No one, it seems, thought about the external factors that structure the situation in which intellectual activity occurs and about how such factors might influence both the activity and its outcomes. The Ogburn Committee submitted its plan to Hoover on October 21, 1929, less than a month after its first meeting and "three days before the first crashing jolts the stock market gave the society which the Committee had been asked to examine." The Committee's work, born in the confident belief of progressive liberalism that the "dispassionate objectivity" of science would solve social problems just as it was thought to be solving the technological problems of industrialization, would actually take place against the background of a deepening recession.

In spite of the depression, the Committee worked during the next three years and produced a massive two-volume report. Its scope was awesome.[84] The interconnections with government are clear enough in the lengthy acknowledgments to government bureaus for their statistical and research aid; but the involvement of philanthropically supported research institutions is also important. Warren S. Thompson and P. K. Whelpton of the Scripps Foundation for Research in Population Problems provided the basic essay, "The Population of the Nation," that opened the volume. The Brookings Institution, the Russell Sage Foundation, the Milbank Memorial Fund, and the various universities associated with those and other philanthropic agencies gave staff time and clerical assistance to the Committee. "The report," Karl said, "serves an interesting function as an inventory of the network of Americans and American institutions committed to social science."[85]

The ambiguity of the "objective" stance of the Committee and of the "rational scientific nationalism" of its sponsor evolved into open conflict sporadically throughout the three years, both between the White House and the Committee and within the Committee itself. Various constituencies saw the Committee as an instrument of their interests, including Congress and the business community, and they pressed for access to and free use of the data as it was collected. In 1932 Harper's magazine wrote of "The Great Fact-Finding Farce." The president himself increasingly pressed for access to the data through his representative, Hunt, whose requests in early 1932 made it clear that the White House wanted to use the Committee materials in the election campaign. Merriam and Odum objected strongly. "We are certainly dealing with dynamite," Odum remarked to Ogburn on March 5, 1932.[86]

Part of the dynamite were the data on health as collected and analyzed for the Committee by Edgar Sydenstricker and Harry H. Moore. Both, as I have shown, were also prominent in the work of the CCMC. Moore was the CCMC's director of research. Sydenstricker, already known for the high standards of his quantitative research, now struck out courageously in opposition to both the majority and minority report of the CCMC. Moore and Sydenstricker agreed on the basic principles of the CCMC majority, as presented in their five main recommendations:

1. For better organization of personal health services, especially through comprehensive group practice
2. For strengthening of the public health services
3. For group payment of the costs, whether through nonprofit insurance, taxation, or combinations
4. For more effective coordination of the services
5. For improvement of professional education, with increasing emphasis on the teaching of health and the prevention of disease

As Falk was to recall later, these recommendations in the aggregate "constituted a first formulation of a national health program in a pattern reflecting the circumstances, the needs, and the perspectives of the times, with implementation to rest mainly on voluntary actions."[87] On the dynamic of voluntary action, however, Sydenstricker dissented from both the majority and the minority positions. Moore joined the majority in a reformist approach that fit well within the framework of the utopian scientific progressivism of Hoover. Sydenstricker argued that volunteerism was not enough and, in prophetic terms, said that runaway costs would result.

In the Ogburn Committee report, however, Moore takes the more radical position, whereas Sydenstricker confines himself to a detailed elaboration of statistics about the state of "vitality" in the American people. Moore, in his chapter, "Health and Medical Practice," after detailing what he considered remarkable advances made by medical science during the previous century, wrote:

A considerable proportion of the people of this country are still suffering from a multitude of preventable defects, disabling diseases and minor ailments. An unnecessary toll of millions of dollars is imposed on the nation annually, thousands of human beings are needlessly destroyed and there is widespread suffering, inefficiency and disability. Though knowledge is at hand to prevent much of this suffering and premature death, it is not being fully utilized. Human life in this country is wasted quite as recklessly and continuously, quite as surely in times of peace as in war. "The health field has a woefully ineffective distribution service, as compared with its marvelously effective production service in the laboratories of the world," declared William H. Welch, late in 1925. "We know how to do a lot of things which we don't do, or do on a wretchedly small scale." One important reason why existing knowledge and equipment are not fully utilized is that medicine, in the midst of a highly organized economic world, remains fundamentally individualistic. Private medical practice, health department, private agency, hospital and clinic—each is going its own particular way. Medicine today is essentially an unorganized professional service.[88]

In his discussion of trends, Moore outlined with remarkable foresight the patterns of conflict that were inherent, given the history and the nature of social institutions in the United States, between increasing expansion of a role for government in the provision of health care and continued reliance on a private system dominated by the profession of medicine. Looking at his carefully worded and documented statement seventy years later, his position seems eminently reasonable and even conservative. Nevertheless, given the conditions of the time, it was "dynamite."

For other reasons, however, the 1,500-page book that was published by the Ogburn Committee in January 1933 caused very little reaction, certainly no "explosion." To begin with, the report was released only after Hoover had lost the 1932 election to Roosevelt. In the struggle between Hoover and the Committee concerning how to preserve the objectivity of the Committee's work, to protect it from the charge of partisanship, the Committee prevailed. Hoover, on the other hand, never received the social science data that he wanted to present for his own approach to the problems of unemployment and old age, issues that were central to the election. The Committee itself seemed secure in their satisfaction with the work they had done, saying in their introduction: "The clarification of given values . . . in terms of today's human life . . . is a major task of social thinking." Others, however, thought differently. As Karl put it: "Firm in their faith, they entered oblivion."[89]

Summary

The Ogburn Committee was a high point in the legitimization of sociology as an institutionalized intellectual activity. In spite of the fact that *Recent Social Trends in the United States,* as Lazarsfeld remarks, is now and was in its time "a book that stands unread on the library shelves," it also was "the cradle of the modern social indicators movement as well as an outstanding example of another issue which commands increasing attention today: the relation between historiography and sociological data in the broadest sense—from cultural documents to demographic calculations."[90] Most important, despite the deep divisions between the social scientists and their sponsors that emerged, the Committee's work did not fall between the cracks of intellectual history. There was a sustaining continuity between the social research it conducted and the work of sociologists and other social scientists that followed. If both the CCMC and the President's Research Committee on Social Trends were failures as far as their direct intended effect on public policy, they succeeded in establishing a national role for social science as part of the processes of public policy. Within the next ten years, by the time World War II broke out in 1939, "social research activities had become so ubiquitous that the government turned to the social researchers almost as a matter of course."[91] Once the United States entered the war, all government agencies started social research activities on a substantial scale. All of the research armamentarium was in place and in operation: content analysis, sampling surveys, detailed interviews, laboratory experiments, group dynamics, and so on. There was no question that sociology was a major partner with the other sciences in the United States.

Medical sociology was part of this development but not yet identified as a subfield in its own right. The major participants were part of public health and social medicine more than of medical sociology as it would develop after the war. Sydenstricker, Davis, Falk, and Moore were the outstanding individuals who can be traced as direct contributors to the Social Security Act of 1935, including federal grants-in-aid to the states for maternal and child health and for crippled children's health services (Title V), and the first permanent authorization to the PHS for grants to the states for public health work and authorization of funds for PHS "investigation of disease and problems of sanitation."[92] Although their work continued after enactment of the Social Security Act, these men's efforts to deal with problems of medical care services, costs, and burdens failed. Even though they contributed to the Wagner National Health Act proposed in 1939 and thereby forced their research data and analysis into the consciousness of Congress, the Act itself was not passed, and their work was pushed off the national agenda by other priorities associated with the war.

What they did was, nevertheless, vital preparation for the history of medical sociology that was to follow after the war. At the same time, a parallel intellectual development occurred in the universities. Particularly at Harvard, Yale, and Chicago, scholarship of a different, more theoretical cast was building the foundation of medical sociology. To that aspect of the period between the world wars I now turn.

4

The University of Chicago

In 1920, American sociology was still dominated by the University of Chicago. Not only was it the first university department of sociology in the world, it quickly became the single main source of both the intellectual and institutional development of the field, including research on the sociology of medicine.

Albion Small (1854–1926), the founding chairman, was from the same mold as the other leading American sociologists of that time: he was a Protestant clergyman, deeply concerned about the human consequences of the rapid industrialization and urbanization of post–Civil War America, with a "passion for reform" combined with pragmatic optimism that a systematic science of society would solve these problems. However, Small's leadership included no "party line." He is remembered to have urged his students "to proceed as quickly as possible to make everything he taught them out of date." Of even greater importance "was the intelligent perception by Small, accepted enthusiastically by his colleagues and successors, of the inhibiting consequences of doctrines, schools of thought, and authoritative leaders."[1]

Chicago attracted a variety of adventurous minds, strong-willed and different but, in the open environment created by Small, able to work side by side. Sociology itself was, in the beginning, a haven for "well-trained students, unhappy with the fast hardening boundaries of the slightly older disciplines, [who] . . . settled upon sociology as a frontier field where professional ideology did not yet preclude experimentation."[2] But while the other pioneer sociology departments each came to be dominated by the doctrine of a founder—Columbia by Giddings, Yale by Sumner, Brown by Ward, Wisconsin by Ross—Chicago was for two full generations a department with a team of equally able men, with the metropolis of Chicago as their laboratory. Albion Small must be given much of the credit for this achievement.

Nor did this talent for institutional leadership end at the boundaries of the University. Small also assumed as part of his mission the establishment of sociology in America as a legitimate social science. In 1895, he started the *AJS*, and in 1906 he was a founder and subsequently the fourth president of the American Sociological Society. The *AJS* was made the official journal of the Society, giving to Chicago for the next thirty years extraordinary centrality in the institutionalization of American sociology.

Against this background, it would seem appropriate, almost inevitable, that Chicago would become the source where some of sociology's major tools of inquiry would first be tested on problems of the sociology of medicine. Perhaps the most important, in terms of its subsequent influence on research methodology, on the development of knowledge, and on public policy, was the research by Robert E. L. Faris and H. Warren Dunham on mental disorder in urban areas. This study was to become a classic in the field of social epidemiology. As such, it is often treated as part of the history of social medicine rather than of sociology. Even when it is acknowledged as the product of sociologists, there is a tendency to see this type of research as a special case, outside of the mainstream of academic sociology. As Milton Terris, an important physician in modern social medicine, has remarked,

> [t]here are a couple of sociologists who went over into chronic disease epidemiology, like Saxon Graham. But I can tell you that my personal view of the sociologists was a very dim one. So much above the battle, pontificating all over the place with their theories, and not into the real things that are going on. I think this is a fairly common opinion about sociologists among people in the social medicine field. It was inevitable that there be this kind of attitude since their orientations were so very different.[3]

Terris is speaking, of course, about academic sociology. The Chicago School hardly fits his description. Far from being "above the battle," it was always close to and active in the social problems it studied—poverty, race, delinquency. As early as 1894, for example, the sociology department set up its own settlement house and maintained thereafter close and complementary ties with social work. Yet none of this active involvement interfered with Chicago's role simultaneously to provide the foundations of academic sociology. Indeed, the history of this department illustrates the fact that the differences between social medicine and the academic sources of medical sociology are not so wide as popular belief would have it.

The special character of the Chicago studies of mental disorder in urban areas becomes clear only by understanding in some depth what it was like at Chicago in 1930, when Robert E. L. Faris and H. Warren Dunham, then young graduate students, were guided by Ernest W. Burgess to test some of his theories with the most advanced survey methods of the time.

Urban Sociology at Chicago: The Theoretical Foundations

"America in the early 1920s," writes Martindale, "sensed itself as having come of age and having arrived at the status of a world power.

> Both the muckraking of the first decade of the twentieth century and the xenophobia of the war years were over; the 1920s were characterized by a sense of sophisticated objectivity and scientism. The trek of sociologists to Europe for orientation was over. American sociology was experienced as equivalent, if not superior, to European sociology. There was a surge of student enrollments and the shift into social science classes for orientation to the twentieth-century world was underway. Finally, a reorientation had

quietly been brought about by the war years and there was an unconscious acceptance of the idea that America was no longer a nation of small towns and farmers, but of metropolitan aggregations, and members of the [University of Chicago] department acutely experienced the city of Chicago as a great experimental laboratory.[4]

This was when the succession of power between the first and second generations of sociologists at Chicago occurred. Albion Small retired in 1923, and Ellsworth Faris, who had returned in 1919, was appointed in his place. Park, Burgess, and Faris took over from Small, W. I. Thomas, and Charles R. Henderson. The basic orientation was laid down in Park and Burgess's *Introduction to the Science of Sociology*.[5] "It thrust the social process into central focus and urged a program of systematic, objective empirical research."[6] It was the time when the Chicago sociologists began "the painstaking task of gathering the facts of urban life . . . just the course of development [needed] to lift sociology from its former speculative, philosophical character."[7] At the same time, the ideological perspectives of the founders were maintained, including that combination of Protestantism and pragmatism peculiar to the American Midwest.

The religious heritage of American higher education was particularly strong at Chicago, and, in sociology, the marriage between Protestant theology and progressive liberalism that was growing in the Midwest was epitomized not only in the founding generation but also in the 1920s. Chicago's first president, William Rainey Harper, was a Baptist minister and biblical Hebrew scholar. He used the large bequest of John D. Rockefeller to create a university that released energies of missionary zeal, applied to the modern metropolis instead of to the more traditional "heathens" of backward and "colored" countries. For sociology, this was of special significance, "because the philosophy underlying the young institution gave the adventurous social scientist an unusual degree of freedom, both from administrative restraint and from a sense of embattled inferiority engendered in older institutions by the entrenched humanistic scholars' contempt for the upstart discipline of sociology with its bastard name and barbarian terminology."[8] The major goal of President Harper, according to Matthews, was to break down the barrier between the university and the life outside its walls. "Harper was determined to build a graduate school which would combine original scholarship with community service."[9] Small was the ideal social scientist to help in this mission.

Small, like Harper, was a Baptist minister. His early recruit to sociology, Charles R. Henderson, was also a Baptist minister. They helped to link closely together the three departments of divinity, political economy, and sociology and make them "not only the most popular, but . . . also the outstanding centers of creative work, since they had been given a remarkable degree of freedom to criticize the social conditions of industrial America."[10] Small wrote to Lester F. Ward in 1895, for example, to express his belief that competent "Christian sociologists" would make important contributions to the field specifically because of their religious beliefs.[11] But Small was meticulous about the boundaries of religion. He criticized the existing camp of Christian sociologists for "their lack of scientific rigor and claimed that they had much to gain by being attentive to works by secular scholars."[12] Small was an early social engineer who shared with Ward the belief in the intelligent application of scientific knowledge to social affairs but rejected Ward's belief in the scientific management of society as part of "systematic socialism." Small also was careful to differentiate "systematic sociology." He was thus an ideal person to represent at Harper's Chicago the corporate-liberal theories that were so strong in nineteenth-century America. He typified the type of men being recruited to the new discipline. Matthews describes this type as follows:

> Sociology lends support to Donald Fleming's hypothesis that the academic boom of the late nineteenth century represents in part a secularizing of moral concern and of the moral career, a displacement of personnel from clergy to academy. The young man of good family with a conscience too sensitive for business more often chose lectern to pulpit as a place from which to pass ethical judgment upon his fellows.[13]

Small was the prototype, and a quick look at the major figures at Chicago, those who created its special climate, shows how much they shared in background even while all of them followed Small's precept "to proceed as quickly as possible to make everything they had been taught out of date" and in the process made their own unique contributions.

Of the first generation, next to Small, W. I. Thomas was the strongest intellectual force. Like Small, he was the son of a Congregational minister, but—except for Park—comparisons between him and his faculty colleagues end there. Considered by many to be the most creative sociologist of his time, Thomas was born in 1863 and raised in a small Tennessee town. After spending his childhood largely in the woods, he took an A.B. degree at the University of Tennessee in 1884. For four more years he remained at that university, teaching English and modern languages, and then spent a year studying philosophy in Germany, followed by a teaching position in English at Oberlin in 1889. During this time, he began to become interested in sociology, teaching a course at Oberlin, and in 1895 he became a fellow in Albion Small's new department. His doctorate in 1896 was one of the earliest granted in sociology in the United States. Very quickly, Thomas established himself at Chicago and as a leading theorist in the field. He also

> gained firsthand knowledge of an alien milieu by tramping around Chicago. This practice made him invaluable to his colleague, Henderson, since he could report on his visits to a variety of saloons. (Henderson, Thomas claimed, had never visited a saloon or tasted beer.) By 1910, the prodigiously energetic Thomas had become a full professor and the center of the department's intellectual life."[14]

Thomas was the social psychologist who built the most lasting body of conception and knowledge on the foundations of Dewey, Cooley, and G. H. Mead. He was also the most significant influence on Robert Park, and at least indirectly, on the later conceptions of Burgess and his students. However, his penchant for "firsthand knowledge" together with ideas that were unorthodox politically for his time became his undoing. In 1918, Thomas's formal academic career terminated after he was arrested in a Chicago hotel room with a young woman on charges of disorderly conduct, false registration, and violation of the Mann Act. Matthews summarizes this event:

Public interest was fanned by the fact that the woman's soldier husband had just sailed for France, and that Thomas was a prominent defender of female emancipation. He had already evoked protests to the university from concerned citizens; an indignant Iowan, for example, had found a talk by Thomas on American women so shocking that he complained to President Harry P. Judson, denouncing it as "a vicious attack upon the social system of America," defending "institutions not recognized by the moral code," and offering "a psychological defense of the moral evil."[15]

Thomas denied his guilt as charged in the hotel incident, but he acknowledged that he was "guilty of the whole general charge in the sense that I hold views and am capable of practices not approved by our social tradition."[16] Dismissed by President Judson and the university board of trustees, Thomas was defended most vigorously by Robert Park but without success.

It was Park (1864–1944) who stepped into the breach created by Thomas's loss. He, too, although his family background was commercial rather than clerical, fit easily into Chicago's cast of old American stock from the Midwest. Born in 1864, Park studied first at the University of Minnesota and the University of Michigan. The former was, in 1882, a "tiny college of the sort which struggled for life throughout the Midwest just before the period of massive development of higher education."[17] Ann Arbor, on the other hand, was already in 1883 the outstanding state university in America. At Michigan, Park was more a campus politician and typical fraternity member than a scholar, but he studied with John Dewey and became editor of the campus newspaper. His first career was as a newspaper reporter, beginning at the *Minneapolis Journal* and working on several Midwest dailies before he got a job with the *New York Journal* in 1892. He loved New York, but he went on to be city editor of the *Detroit Tribune* and, finally, drama critic and reporter of the Scripps's *Chicago Journal.*

Park was working as a press agent for Booker T. Washington of Tuskegee Institute in 1912 when, at a conference, he met W. I. Thomas. They became friends immediately, and Thomas invited Park to Chicago to give some lectures on the Negro in America. At age forty-eight, this was the turning point of Park's life. His age notwithstanding, Park went on to become one of the nation's outstanding sociologists. His background in the "real world" was hardly wasted, serving instead as the ideal balance to Burgess, who became his chief collaborator. On the surface, these two could not have been more different: Park an extrovert who loved to wander through the streets and savor the life of each of the cities he lived in; Burgess another minister's son (Congregational) who like most of his colleagues was a Chicago Ph.D., was described as "slight, pale, harried, [and] a prodigious worker," never married, living with his father and sister in an apartment near campus. Yet they were close friends and coworkers, each complementing the other. Interestingly, though Park had the charisma to attract students, Burgess was the one more interested in identifying and solving social problems. Burgess was able to get funds for research and to keep research and teaching running smoothly. Thus, though the city was Park's special interest, it was Burgess who recruited Robert E. L. Faris, the son of Ellsworth, who was then chairman of sociology, and H. Warren Dunham to do research on mental disorder in the city.

Mental Disorder and Urban Life

Both Faris and Dunham came to Chicago as undergraduates, Faris in 1924 and Dunham in 1926. They met, as Dunham tells the story, while "painting seats at the stadium in Stagg Field, to make money. Faris was one of the first fellows I met."[18] Burgess brought them together again as graduate students to do the study of mental illness in urban life, Faris receiving his doctorate in 1931 and Dunham in 1941. Their book based on this research was published in 1939; it was a landmark study, both for urban sociology and for social epidemiology.

Robert E. L. Faris, in his memoir about life at the University of Chicago in the 1920s, says very clearly that the research was not intended to establish social ecology as a "distinct and separate subject, partitioned off from general sociology."[19] Quite the contrary; it was, like the two dozen books about a variety of forms of urban behavior written by the Chicago graduate students of these two decades, intended to be just one route into the subject. The focus on social disorganization had roots in the theories of Simmel and Durkheim. Park, while studying in Germany, was influenced by Simmel's ideas about social distance, the characteristics of the stranger, and other phenomena of individuation and isolation. He and Burgess regularly sent students into the city to conduct firsthand observation. One of the most important of the resulting dissertations was *Suicide,* published in 1928 by Ruth S. Cavan. One of Cavan's basic findings was "that the incidence of suicide in Chicago was greatest in the highly disorganized central hobo and rooming-house areas of the city and lowest in the most stable residential areas. The highest of all occurred in the Loop, with the next highest rates in areas contiguous to it."[20] Faris, in his M.A. thesis, traced the connections of the Cavan studies to Durkheim and Halbwachs.[21] What the Chicago sociologists sought were data to verify, extend, or disprove these theories.[22] Building on the Cavan study of suicide, Burgess guided Faris and Dunham toward a more general documentation of the effects on individuals of social disorganization and the association between social variables and "insanity," operationally defined as rates of hospitalization for mental disorder.

When they began, Dunham writes, "the study of mental disease and abnormality had come to be the exclusive concern of the medical men both in Europe and America."[23] Although ecological, statistical, and case studies had been applied to a variety of social problems since the 1890s, no significant attempt was made to study insanity by these methods. The medical approach, in turn, had been dominated by the germ theory for at least half a century, so that hypotheses of somatogenic etiology prevailed in the study of mental disorder as well as physical disease.

There were only a few prior attempts on the record. In 1901, J. S. Sutherland studied the geographical distribution of mental disorder in Scotland.[24] At about the same time, W. A. White presented an article on the geographical distribution of insanity in the United States. Dunham, describing the background of White's research, notes that no actual maps were presented; but on the basis of statistics White concluded that the older and longer settled sections of the country had a much higher incidence of insanity than the newer and more recently settled sections. White also computed separate rates according to race and found that among Negroes (as they were called at that time) in the southern states there was a much lower rate of insanity than among the Negroes in the North. Both these early studies compiled statistics for all cases of mental illness, an indication of the difficulties with diagnostic categories that plague this type of research to this day.[25]

White and Sutherland were only the beginning part of the literature on the epidemiology of mental disorder that had accumulated by 1930. Dunham singles them out because they were the closest in method to the subsequent Chicago studies. Quite separate from the sociological hypotheses that linked insanity to social disorganization, there were a series of explanations for mental illness that derived from the data of censuses of hospitalized patients that began to be collected in the United States in 1850. The story they told was watched with growing alarm because the proportion of hospitalized mental patients seemed to be increasing sharply. Faris and Dunham began their work, therefore, not so much at the beginning as at the midpoint of a developing series of epidemiological studies focused on two linked hypotheses:

1. There has been a substantial increase in mental illness in the United States over the previous century.
2. The increase in mental illness is associated directly with industrialization and urbanization.

Summarized, this was the "urban hypothesis." It reflected the fact that as the United States grew into one of the most urbanized countries in the world, it preserved the romantic myth that the rural and small-town experience that was giving way to the city was more pure. The city is the Temple of Mammon in this picture—a vortex of temptation. With its dirt, noise, and confusion, the city "corrupts" the reason as well as the body. The urban is mistrusted as the unnatural, and the unnatural is one step removed from the mad.

Nourishing such beliefs were the data about increasing rates of mental illness. The result was to highlight the difficulties of urban adjustment and to idealize the rural. In more specific sociological terms, it was reasoned that

> rural life partakes more of the characteristics of the familistic *Gemeinschaft* than urban life of the contractual *Gesellschaft*. This overall comparison yields the following special hypotheses; the greater precision and stability of social roles in rural society, less marked status-striving, more intimate and personal forms of authority, the greater security of primary group ties, the specification of norms, for all life's situations, the relative homogeneity of the rural population which reduces the risk of value conflict, and the greater integration of religious groups, occupational groups, etc . . . helps a person in unifying his roles.[26]

Adding to the "urbanism hypothesis of mental illness" were evidences of increasing rates of crime and delinquency. In the interpretation of some, these were similar types of social deviance, different but on a common basic continuum with mental disorder. As others have pointed out, this raises a fundamental question about how mental illness is defined in relation to social norms and social pathology.

As the urban hypothesis came under more intense research scrutiny, however, its validity was challenged. As early as 1920, a study of rejection figures for mental illness during World War I showed that the rates for urban rejectees was lower if mental deficiency was included (see table 4-1).

Table 4-1 Rejections of Army Recruits for Mental Illness in World War I
(Rates per 1,000)

	U.S.	Urban	Rural	4 large cities
Total	18.12	12.64	21.15	13.25
Total without mental deficiency	3.67	3.87	3.56	4.97

Adapted from Leacock 1957 (see note 26).

Again, a definitional problem is raised. One could exclude mental deficiencies for purposes of analyzing the relations of social factors to mental illness. This, however, raises perhaps more difficult questions concerning the physical as compared with the functional components of mental disease.

Even the higher rates that were found in four large cities (Boston, Chicago, New York, and Philadelphia) have been explained by evidence that psychotics in cities are more likely to be hospitalized than in rural areas.[27] Moreover, in several studies of foreign countries with large rural populations, no rural-urban trends were found; and Mangus, in Ohio, found that the highest rate of admissions to mental hospitals came from predominantly rural counties of that state.[28]

The Faris and Dunham research was part of the slow climb in search of the truth about the urban hypothesis. In the pattern of all detection narratives, there were false leads and unexpected suspicions and, inevitably, a new set of hypothetical formulations with which to start the cycle of research all over again. It became more and more clear that the urban hypothesis had been an expression, at least in part, of a "rural bias" that runs strong in the values of Western cultures. One of its basic assumptions has been that rural and urban environments represent coherent, mutually exclusive types of human experience that in themselves constitute specific causal factors influencing the personality of their participants. The "bias" in this hypothesis prejudges the adjustment and integration challenges that adhere to these two differing life experiences, arguing that "complex, heterogeneous, value-conflicting urban cultures produce intrapersonal organizations which are correspondingly heterogeneous and unintegrated," whereas simpler folk (or rural) cultures "produce simpler unified personality integration."[29]

As more epidemiological data were accumulated, so did the doubts about the validity of the urban hypothesis increase. There were no consistently higher urban rates of mental disorder found, either for general categories such as "psychoses" or for specific types of disease. Greater differences were found between one city and another than between urban and rural settings. As it became clear that some rural areas had very high rates of mental disorder,[30] a revision of the hypothesis was suggested in which "urbanization" was separated conceptually from "social integration." Whereas previously the degree of social integration was believed to be a direct function of urbanization, the relation between these two variables became itself a focus of study rather than an assumption.

As revised, the question for investigation became not what degree of urbanization was associated with the incidence of mental disorder but instead what type of rural area was involved or what type of section of the city. The special distribution or "ecology" of mental disorder replaced urbanization as the major concern of epidemiological inquiry about mental illness. The Faris and Dunham study became the most influential research in the development of the "ecology" hypothesis. In their mapping of the residential distribution of all patients admitted to public and private mental hospitals from the city of Chicago, they found that high rates of mental disorder were concentrated in and around the central business district of the city. Following the Burgess conceptions of "natural areas" that were believed to be applicable to all American cities, Faris and Dunham charted the relations between rates of mental disorder and the types of residential areas in the city. Their general conclusion was that hospitalized mental illness was distributed indirectly according to socioeconomic status. Those areas of Chicago with low socioeconomic status tended to have more mental disorder than urban residential areas for higher socioeconomic status.

The most important contribution of the Faris and Dunham research, however, derived not from their conclusions about psychosis in general but from their breakdown of the data into specific categories of psychosis. The most frequent disease entities, schizophrenia and manic depression, were chosen in the belief that they were the most reliable diagnoses in the statistics reported by psychiatric institutions. Each of these forms of illness, it was found, followed a different pattern of relationship with socioeconomic status. Especially for manic depression psychosis, the general curve of hospitalized mental illness did not apply.

It should be noted that, even at the most general level, the findings of Faris and Dunham raised important questions about the social etiology of mental illness. In the concentric pattern that the Burgess model plotted of increasing social status as one moves outward from the center of the city, Faris and Dunham found that mental disorder appeared to decline in every direction toward the periphery of Chicago. On this basis, one could reason that the earlier conceptions of the chain of determinants leading to mental disorder would need to be formulated so that social disintegration, instead of being a response to urbanization, becomes a cause in itself of mental disorder. In other words, where earlier interpretation asserted that urbanization produced, in and of itself, an effect on personality that was disintegrative, Faris and Dunham showed that, for some members of the urban society, the opposite could just as validly be asserted. It was not urbanization per se but how one adapted and the success of status achievement that, at least for schizophrenia, was the more critical determinant. The relevance of Durkheim's conception of anomie is unmistakable here.

Put another way, the findings of the high rural rates in some areas but not in others and equally high urban rates in some sections of the city but not in others appear to eliminate the significance of the rural-urban variable in itself and to point to the existence of some common factor or factors, independent of the rural-urban dimension, which is shared by high-rate areas, wherever they may be.

For some students of the problem, this left untouched the assumption that certain environmental conditions were, as general determining variables, conducive to all forms of mental illness. Socioeconomic status simply replaced the rural-urban variable as the villain. This assumption was challenged by Faris and Dunham in their studies of disease-specific rates.

Calculating the rate per one hundred thousand of first admissions with a diagnosis of schizophrenia into Chicago hospitals during the period from 1921 to 1931, Faris and Dunham found that "an ecological map . . . indicates very definitely that schizophrenia shows a great variation in frequency in the different [local] communities [of Chicago]."[31] Further, they recorded that "the pattern formed by the rates is a regular and typical one and follows in the gradients of its rates Burgess's scheme of the circular growth of the city." More specifically,

the distribution of rates ranged from 111 in community 1 at the extreme northeast end of the city to 1,195 in community 32, the Loop, or central business district. The average rate is 289 and the median rate is 322, and these figures indicate that the bulk of the community rates are clustered at the low end of a skewed frequency distribution. In other words, there are a few communities close to the center of the city which have extremely high rates, while the great bulk of the communities have much lower rates. The highest rates for schizophrenia are in the hobohemia, the rooming house, and the foreign-born communities close to the center of the city. There are no glaring exceptions to this regular pattern."[32]

A strikingly different picture emerges from the mapping of manic depressive psychosis. The typical pattern is absent to the point where a random distribution may be described.

In their interpretation of these data, Faris and Dunham considered a variety of possible explanations. Two emerged as the most challenging to subsequent researchers: (1) the so-called drift hypothesis, which was constructed with particular reference to the ecology of schizophrenia, and (2) the conclusion, from the differential distribution of the two illnesses, that schizophrenia is more significantly influenced by social factors than manic depression.

The "drift hypothesis," most simply stated, is that "the concentration of cases (of schizophrenia) at the center of the city is caused by the fact that the emotionally and mentally unstable fail in their economic life and thus drift to the depressed areas from which they are committed to hospitals." This "drifting" theory was suggested by Faris and Dunham only as an explanation of that portion of their data that showed a high concentration of schizophrenic illness in the most severely disorganized central portions of the city. It was, however, embraced by others as a more complete explanation that, in Dunham's critical appraisal, "is analogous to an earlier biological explanation for city slums: namely, that it is not the slums that make slum people but slum people who make the slums." In fact, Dunham went so far as to say that he suspected

that when we have a sounder knowledge of both sociological processes and schizophrenic etiology, we shall see the "drift" hypothesis for what it really is, namely, an attempt to annihilate the significance of the ecological findings in much the same fashion that certain persons during the thirties tried to dismiss the Depression by explaining the loss of a job on the basis of a person's neurotic makeup or emotional instability."[33]

Faris and Dunham themselves prefer an explanation of their data that combines predisposing personality or psychogenic tendencies with a differential impact from the social environment. Thus schizophrenic illness would be explained at least in part as a response by a particular personality type or types to the special social conditions of the urban slum. The manic depressive also represents predisposing personality organization, but because the behavior associated with this illness fits in many respects into the success requirements of our society, it is found as often in the higher as in the lower-status groups of the society.

The Faris and Dunham study signaled the two directions that epidemiological studies increasingly were to emphasize in later years: namely, (1) the intensive study of nationality and cultural variables as they relate to mental disorder and (2) a more thorough appraisal of socioeconomic status in its relation to mental illness. The former direction was indicated in their data concerning both racial and cultural minorities and the latter by the consistent findings of schizophrenia in association with the lower socioeconomic status groups and, to a lesser extent, the association of manic depressive illness with high socioeconomic status.

The social ecology research concluded that, in the urban strata of lower socioeconomic status and in communities of cultural miorities, one's chances of growing up and developing a personality that can adjust in some fashion to our cultural life are less than in those communities at the periphery of the city. Faris and Dunham generalized that such communities deny many persons "adequate breathing space" in growing up, "as is so well depicted in Wright's portrayal of the life of Bigger Thomas in *Native Son*." They added:

> This analysis can be made without any smug reference to "disorganized areas." It is not that these communities are disorganized, as Whyte and others have shown, but rather that life is hard, the struggle is sharper, and consequently more personalities have difficulty in coping with it and finding acceptable social economic niches than in other communities of the city.[34]

With reference to the urban hypothesis, the increased interest in the ecology of mental disorder was consistent with the accumulation of evidence that the rural-urban variable was too general and undifferentiated to offer promise in the search for greater understanding of the problem. Furthermore, it became increasingly clear that, in a society such as one sees in the contemporary United States, the designation of rural-urban distinction has little but historical relevance. It has been observed that "rural-urban social differences are gradually being erased because the country as a whole is becoming more concentrated in large urban agglomerations and the remaining rural areas have increasingly taken on urban characteristics."[35] Further, "each of the supposedly urban characteristics—density, impersonality, mobility, etc.—[has] a significance in the daily life of the individual which has been exaggerated for cities and minimized for rural situations."[36]

With the blurring of the distinction between urban and rural life, it would seem inevitable, therefore, that the focus of inquiry into the social origins of mental disorder would shift. If the challenges presented by social environment are indeed significant in the problem of mental disorder, these early studies clarify the need to define the specific kinds of demands that a given position in society involves before the adjustment of individual and family life to such social placement can be fully evaluated.

Indeed, these were the directions social epidemiology was to take following World War II, and Faris and Dunham played perhaps the major role in establishing the groundwork on which the critically important epidemiological research on mental disorder of the postwar era was to be built.

The Chicago studies of the social ecology of mental disorder were made possible by the maturing methodology of the social survey movement. Although the community survey had roots deep in the history of nineteenth-century Europe, in the United States a genuine social survey movement did not appear until 1909 when the Pittsburgh survey was started by Paul Kellogg. This is usually cited as the first systematic study of an American community. As Pauline Young has documented, the Pittsburgh survey was rapidly followed by others in the United States, and they have continued in an unbroken pattern to the present. Just as in Europe, the social survey movement began by focusing on wages and housing conditions among the poor, but "the range of topics became more and more subtle."

> Soon, social relations in the family were added, subsequently supplemented by descriptive material on attitudes. In 1912, the Russell Sage Foundation created a Department of Surveys and Information. By 1928, the director of this department, Shelby Harrison, was able to review more than two thousand social surveys—some national in scope, others local.[37]

By the end of World War I, there were in the United States a sizeable number of working sociologists, and a developed quantitative methodology was embedded in the sociological perspective of that time. When, therefore, the pursuit of the urban hypothesis raised questions about the distribution of mental disorder according to social variables like size and type of community, socioeconomic status, race, and ethnicity, the quantitative survey methodology necessary to answer such questions was available. Chicago sociology provided the skilled manpower for both the theoretical conception and the methodological capability to pursue such questions.

However, a different type of question about mental illness had been raised by the experience of World War I, for which a clear research strategy and methodology was less immediately evident. Involved were questions about the efficacy of the treatment methods for the mentally ill and the possible contribution of interpersonal theory. This became the source of a second major antecedent of medical sociology.

Interpersonal Relations in Therapeutic Situations

In the early 1920s, the therapeutic methods changed for seriously ill psychiatric patients at Saint Elizabeth's Hospital in Washington, D.C., and at the Sheppard and Enoch Pratt Hospital near Baltimore. Particularly from the work of the psychiatrist Harry Stack Sullivan (1892–1949), a social psychology of interpersonal relations emerged. Two articles by Sullivan, published in 1931, are generally cited as the beginning of a movement toward a therapeutic orientation—as opposed to custodial—to hospital care for the chronically ill, especially the mentally ill.[38] The conception of the hospital as a "therapeutic community" grew from these origins to become one of the most active areas for sociological study immediately following, and very much influenced by, World War II. Also from these origins, observational techniques developed by social anthropologists were adapted to the study of hospitals conceived as small communities.

During the half century preceding Sullivan, "hospital care" came to be synonymous with "doctor's care." In effect, the hospital functioned as an expanded waiting and examining room, a special accommodation for the physician. Therapy was conceived of as the time spent with the doctor or under the specific order of the doctor. All else was secondary. Even the nurse was an instrument, more or less, primarily designed to carry out the doctor's orders. For the patient, the hospital was a place for two distinctly different experiences: there was the doctor's "therapy" and, lumped together, all the rest. For the hospital staff, the dichotomy was similar. There was the specifically therapeutic part of their job, and the rest was "custodial."

The attitudes associated with the therapy-custody dichotomy may have been appropriate for the acute and dramatic types of illness that dominated the general hospital until recent decades. However, when medical science gained control over many of the most dangerous elements of acute infections, such attitudes became outdated. The recognition of the radical shift in the patterns of illness from acute to chronic problems is generally dated to the period following World War II. However, the implications of large-scale chronic illness for medical care were anticipated twenty-five years earlier in the experience with mental disability associated with the First World War. Even though American involvement in that war was brief, there were 97,578 admissions to neuropsychiatric services in army hospitals. Nor were they all casualties of battles. This fact, plus the high rejection rate for mental illness among recruits, forced into social consciousness questions about how many persons in the society were mentally incapacitated, who they were, and why. A new awareness of the ineffectiveness of known treatment methods was also created. At the time, the mental casualties of war were not treated but merely separated from others; their care was not therapeutic in any sense, only custodial. If they did not recover spontaneously, they were given pensions for life. The general attitude toward these men was one of pity and guilt. They were the awesome residue of war, whispered about as victims of "shell shock," killed in spirit as surely as those who were dead physically on the battlefield.

It was this type of patient that first stimulated Harry Stack Sullivan's interest in psychiatry. Receiving his M.D. from the Chicago College of Medicine and Surgery in 1917, Sullivan went to work immediately as a civilian with the United States army during the remaining days of World War I. In 1922 he became a liaison officer for the Veterans Administration at Saint Elizabeth's Hospital in Washington. At that time, Saint Elizabeth's Hospital was a major center of psychiatric activity. William Alanson White had introduced many new treatments there—in particular, the application of Freud's psychoanalytic principles to the diagnosis and treatment of hospital patients. White's influence on Sullivan was profound and was freely recognized by Sullivan throughout his life.[39]

In 1923, Sullivan moved to the Sheppard and Enoch Pratt Hospital near Baltimore as assistant physician. In 1925 he became director of clinical research. Attending staff conferences at the neighboring Johns Hopkins University's Phipps Clinic, he came to know the chairman of psychiatry, Adolph Meyer, and his group, particularly Clara Thompson. They influenced and were in turn influenced by Sullivan. Together they adapted the basic psychoanalytic framework of Freud to include a strong interpersonal dimension that was to be known as the neo-Freudian school or, more simply, as interpersonal psychiatry.

At Sheppard Pratt, Sullivan conducted detailed studies of schizophrenic patients. From his records on several hundred patients, his first achievement was to bring schizophrenia back into a "human" perspective. This was important, because much of schizophrenic behavior was treated as though it were *not* human. Sullivan, however, demonstrated "that even the most disturbed patients did not develop any type of symbol activity that is entirely outside the realm of the human, no matter how bizarre it may appear to be."[40] Therefore, he argued, it is never impossible to understand the patient in some sense if sufficient contact with him/her is possible.

A second principle of his theory was that illness is a problem-solving effort. He saw early schizophrenia as an attempt to reintegrate masses of life experience. In contrast to the usual view at that time—that nearly all such patients were damaged, if they recovered at all—Sullivan found patients who were more competent after a schizophrenic episode than before.

His conceptions of the importance of patient contact and of a deep understanding of the factors that contribute to illness episodes led Sullivan in 1929 to organize a special ward for young male schizophrenic patients where he could test the application of these principles by creating a special therapeutic environment. This experimental work seemed to follow naturally from the style of life that Sullivan had developed in association with Sheppard Pratt.

> Sullivan lived on the grounds and he made his home available to all his coworkers for discussion of clinical problems. These discussions made him progressively more aware that the interactions of the patient with other persons is a primary determinant of the outcome of his effort to reintegrate masses of life experience. [For his experimental ward] . . . he selected his staff with great care, with a preference for candidates who had experienced psychological disturbances similar to those of the patients. . . . Sullivan not only had frequently lengthy informal interviews with the patients but also talked freely and informally with the staff, often in the evenings at his home. This type of indirect intervention was based upon a number of newly developed views—a recognition of the potential benefits to be gained when persons with similar background share their experience and of the therapeutic import of human interactions other than the patient's interview with the psychiatrist. Although the experience of the ward was never analyzed systematically, the outcomes for the patients were extraordinarily favorable.[41]

These experiences led Sullivan to the conclusion that interpersonal relations were more important both to the onset of illness and to therapy than had been previously conceived. Therefore he turned to social scientists for help. In particular he came to know and often to work with Lawrence K. Frank, W. I. Thomas, Ruth Benedict, Harold D. Laswell, and Edward Sapir. As Gordon Allport has commented, "Sullivan, perhaps more than any other person, labored to bring about the fusion of psychiatry and social science."[42] "Personality and its disorders," he wrote, "manifest themselves only in interpersonal relations, and it is by the psychiatrist's participant observation of his patient in such relationships that he does his clinical and scientific work. Psychiatry then is a social science (regardless of what its practitioners may think), and recognition of this prevents many common misconceptions."[43]

From these ideas, it is easy to see how Sullivan influenced both the therapeutic community approach to hospital care and the use of field methods to study the hospital experience. The direction Sullivan took was also influenced by the writings of patients in the years preceding his work. These constitute a remarkable series of personal documents, autobiographical writings by individuals who described their experiences as psychotic patients. Probably the best known of these is that of Clifford Beers (1907).[44] Such documents continue regularly to appear, including those by Seabrook (1935),[45] Kerkhoff (1952),[46] Ward (1955),[47] and Frame (1961).[48] In these personal documents the hospital is vividly portrayed as a small society. They form a rich background of illustration for the ethnographic approach. "One of the greatest secret societies in the world," said Beers, "is the psychiatric hospital," and he proceeded to record a patient's view of the culture of this society, its structure and content. Sullivan's observations are closely parallel, forming the basis of his interpretation that psychosis itself is "disordered interpersonal relations nucleating . . . in a particular person." Differentiating "social recovery" from "personal recovery," Sullivan weighed heavily the importance of social environment in the therapeutic process.

By turning the spotlight away from intrapsychic aspects of mental disorder and toward the interpersonal, Sullivan inspired a generation of ethnographic studies of the mental hospital as a small society. Two of these, by Rowland (1938, 1939)[49] and by Devereux (1944),[50] were conducted prior to World War II; they provided lengthy descriptions of patient culture in hospitals, based on participant observation.

After he moved to New York in 1930, Sullivan's direct collaboration with social scientists intensified, especially with Sapir, the linguist and cultural anthropologist. Sapir organized a seminar in culture and personality at Yale in 1932 and 1933 in which Sullivan made the central contributions. Many prominent social scientists who later studied culture and personality trace their interest in large part to this seminar. When Sullivan founded the Washington School of Psychiatry in 1936 and the journal *Psychiatry* in 1938, Harold Laswell was very active in the school and social scientists were frequent contributors to the journal.

Sullivan's importance to psychiatry, and especially the modifications of psychoanalytic therapy that followed from his theories, have tended to obscure his direct contributions to social science. Even though Sullivan himself focused on problems connected with psychotherapy, his conceptions of personality and of human development tended to merge with the social psychology of his time and to add significantly to it. This was recognized by no less a person than W. I. Thomas, who, in 1927, in his presidential address to the American Sociological Society, described Sullivan's work at Sheppard Pratt in the following terms:

> Dr. Harry Stack Sullivan and his associates, working at the Sheppard and Enoch Pratt Hospital, Baltimore, are experimenting with a small group of persons now or recently actively disordered, from the situational standpoint, and among other results this study reveals the fact that these persons tend to make successful adjustments in groupwise association between themselves.[51]

Sullivan did not reject the significance of biological determinants on personality and behavior; rather, he left room in his theory to include biology as it became known, selecting for himself what he believed it was possible to study with the tools at hand. What he did reject was the Freudian concept that the basic structure of personality is laid down during the first five years of a persons's life.

Accepting the Freudian emphasis on maturation as the result of previous experience, he believed that personality structure takes fifteen or twenty or even more
than twenty years for its essential development, depending partly on sociocultural
conditions and partly on the unique aspects of each individual's career.

> Favorable or unfavorable influence may significantly modify development
> at any of the "eras," or stages of development. . . . The quality and kind of
> interpersonal relations that one experiences in the home, school, play-
> ground, summer camp, and neighborhood are crucially important. But in
> human life there is nothing static. Everything changes . . . hence, significant
> personality change, for better or for worse, can occur at any time in life,
> depending to a great extent on the nature and course of one's social life—
> on one's interpersonal relations.[52]

These ideas subsequently were to have a profound influence on the social
psychology of socialization, particularly the emphasis on adult stages of the life
cycle, which, in very recent times, has become a subject of inquiry where sociological conception has contributed significantly, compared with the previously
dominant developmental psychology and psychodynamic theory.[53] Perhaps more
important in 1930 was Sullivan's ability to document from his patient data the
importance of the sociocultural context and the structure of the situation in which
an individual functions. These ideas were compatible with the principles of
American social psychology that derived from Charles Horton Cooley and were
developed by George Herbert Mead. W. I. Thomas was himself a major contributor
to this theory. Thus we see the influence of Sullivan on the Chicago school and
on the qualitative methods of participant observation that would be so important
to the future of symbolic interaction.

Sullivan's biographers separate his life into three distinct periods. The first
was during the 1920s, represented mainly by his work in hospitals, when he
shifted and modified his conception of mental illness from a Freudian psychoanalytic base to the beginning of his interpersonal theory. The focus of his experience during this period was with patients, and his intellectual life was con-
centratedly involved with mentors like William Alanson White at Saint
Elizabeth's, and Adolf Meyer at Johns Hopkins, and such psychiatric colleagues
as Clara Thompson. The second period began with a move to New York City in
1929, where he opened a private practice on Park Avenue. During the next ten
years, Sullivan broadened his intellectual scope in every way; his theories expanded beyond the borders of psychosis "toward a psychiatry of peoples";[54] and
his personal contacts expanded to include the growing colony of European refugees in New York at that time—Franz Alexander, Karen Horney, Erich Fromm,
Frieda Fromm-Reichman—and also a variety of social scientists. His return to
Washington in the late thirties marks the third phase, when he engaged in the
institutional development of the Washington School of Psychiatry and the *Journal
of Psychiatry*. Perry sees the move to Washington as

> a direct outcome of this collaboration with social scientists in and around
> New York. . . . In Washington, Sullivan and his social science colleagues of
> the twenties and thirties—particularly Sapir and Lasswell—hoped to found
> an institution that would significantly collaborate on a formal or an informal

basis with the government in an ameliorative plan for a broad program of preventive psychiatry, politically informed and dynamic.[55]

Undoubtedly Sullivan was responding to the "same climate that produced the dedicated men and women throughout the nation who followed Franklin D. Roosevelt and his New Deal into Washington, in the hope that the government could offer some meaningful help to one third of the nation."[56] He also was responding directly and personally to a remarkable person, Lawrence K. Frank, who together with Beardsley Ruml played an important role earlier in this narrative as intermediaries between President Hoover and the world of social science.

Ruml, who received his doctorate in psychology from the University of Chicago in 1917, was the director of the Spelman Fund, and Frank worked for him. It was Frank, however, who was the stronger intellectual influence, and it was Frank who, according to Perry, was the earliest and most important midwife for Sullivan's emergent sociological perspective, just as he was to continue to be for psychiatry and social science perspectives more generally for three more decades. Perry believed that Sullivan's introduction to American social science was facilitated by a trip to New York in the middle twenties when he first met Lawrence K. Frank through a mutual friend. If Sullivan, more than anyone else, brought about the fusion of psychiatry and social science, Frank for many decades represented the dedicated middleman in the process of fusion, chairing scores of conferences on mental health throughout the world and gaining the respect and trust of both disciplines. At the time of his meeting with Sullivan, Frank, like Ruml, was employed by the Laura Spelman Rockefeller Memorial Fund. This was the period when the various great foundations were moving from philanthropic enterprises into the support of social science research. From the beginning of the friendship between Frank and Sullivan, they recognized a common interest: the urgent necessity for bringing the dynamic findings of psychiatry into a meaningful relationship with social science, for the benefit of both disciplines. Increasingly they felt that remedial attempts in the society were necessary and anticipated the ultimate inability of the casework approach, then developing in various outpatient clinics, to meet the overall problem at all class levels.[57]

With the exception of Frank, all of the social scientists who worked with Sullivan were either on the faculty of the University of Chicago or former students. The "mosaic of Chicago social science," as Perry calls it, fit neatly into Sullivan's clinical and life experience. The social psychology of George H. Mead, especially, provided the American idiom that was needed for Sullivan's clinically derived shift in emphasis from the Freudian *id* to the *self*, a concept close to the European-Freudian *ego* but adapted to social interactional theory. Although Mead and Sullivan did not meet personally—Mead died in 1931—Sullivan knew his writings and, more important, learned his social psychology through close personal associations with W. I. Thomas and Harold Lasswell. Thomas, of course, was Mead's colleague at Chicago and perhaps his major theoretical disciple in the early stages of American social psychology. Lasswell was a student at Chicago in the early twenties and learned Mead's theory largely through his close relationship with Robert E. Park. Mead and Park both began their intellectual development with Cooley at the University of Michigan and then studied at Harvard with William James, completing their intellectual apprenticeship in Germany. The influence of German romantic philosophy was strong in American pragmatism, and Mead became the major theorist alongside Dewey of the peculiarly American translation of nineteenth-century German thought into the rational, problem-solving optimistic spirit of the New World. Both Mead and Park were thoroughly conversant with Freud, Marx, Darwin, and Hegel, but they found the Freudian idea of emotional catharsis through understanding more appealing than the concept of the unconscious. In Perry's interpretation,

> The importance of Mead to sociologists and social scientists at Chicago was precisely in the fusion that had taken place in his own thinking. The sociologist did not have to be trapped into explaining whether his sociology was Freudian or anti-Freudian, Marxian or non-Marxian. The useful insights from European and American thinkers of the nineteenth century had been sorted out and placed into a meaningful whole, a consistent and intellectually vigorous social psychology. This was Mead's gift to Chicago social science. Once Sullivan had incorporated some of this thinking into his own theory, he too was able to avoid some of the needless competition between various cults and simply try to place his own observations within a central body of American knowledge and philosophy.[58]

The influence of Park on Sullivan was more direct than that of Mead. They met for the first time at the First Colloquium on Personality Investigation, held in 1928 at New York City under the auspices of the American Psychiatric Association's Committee on Relations with the Social Sciences. This was the first of two large formal meetings between social scientists and psychiatrists that emerged from the early conversations among Sullivan, Frank, and Lasswell. It should be noted that both the first and second colloquium—the Second Colloquium on Personality Investigation was held in New York City under the same auspices in 1929—were financed by a grant from the Laura Spelman Rockefeller Memorial Fund. At the 1928 meeting, Sullivan was able to formalize the collaborative thinking that had come out of his earlier meetings with W. I. Thomas and Edward Sapir, who was also a professor at the University of Chicago at that time. Also present at these colloquia were Ernest W. Burgess, Charles E. Merriam, and others from the University of Chicago.

It was at about this time that Sullivan read *Introduction to the Science of Sociology*, by Park and Burgess. He himself acknowledged that he was deeply influenced by what he called "a richly documented sociological text."[59] The use of participant observation and more generally methods adapted from social anthropology to study Sullivan's concepts can be traced particularly to the influence on Sullivan of Park and Sapir. Park came to such methods from his training in journalism. He stimulated many of his students to use them in the wide-ranging investigations of the city of Chicago. Sapir was a cultural anthropologist who, during his years at Chicago, found that cultural anthropology was adaptable to the study of contemporary American subcultural groups. There was a natural affinity between him and W. I. Thomas. "Sapir saw that cultural anthropology need no longer confine itself to the study of the languages, customs and so on, of primitive cultures; it could, like sociology, study various cultural groups in transition."[60]

This combination, the theory of Sullivan and methods derived from Sapir and Park, found expression in a study by Howard Rowland of two mental hospitals in New York State.[61] Using a method of direct observation and participation in the activities and events of a mental hospital, Rowland's objective was "a systematic description of the more commonplace aspects of hospital life in order to permit some degree of generalization as a guide to further study."[62] He was immensely successful in achieving this purpose. As sociologists turned increasingly to the descriptive study of the hospital, Rowland's study was a guide and model.

In brief summary, Rowland's picture of the typical patient experience includes the following steps:

1. First, the mental patient "loses caste" in the world outside the hospital. "He loses civil rights, social class position, economic power, and neighborhood and community esteem. Socially and politically, the individual is disenfranchised. He is lifted out of a complex society and is placed in a new social order which is vastly different."[63]
2. He enters a new society but is always conscious of the old "real" society. He is on the *inside* looking *out*.
3. He learns that in this new society, the social field is split into staff and inmate worlds, living together in the closest proximity but separated sharply by a high sociological wall.

The patient, Rowland continued, can be seen as uprooted from his family and community, subordinate to the authority of a professional staff that is distinctly separate from him and therefore inaccessible in significant ways, and forced to be dependent on his peers—the patient world—for the fulfillment of a variety of emotional and social needs.[64]

This was the first of what was to become ten years later a large-scale effort by social scientists to study the hospital as a social environment. It was a major step from Sullivan's reports and his experimental ward for schizophrenic patients at Sheppard Pratt to the beginning of psychiatry's systematic concern with the hospital as a "therapeutic community." Sullivan and his followers turned a spotlight away from the intrapsychic to the social context of mental illness. In this step, social scientists played a major role, especially the Chicago school.

Thus the stage was set for the shift in attitudes within both psychiatry and social science that was to lead to a fresh look, soon after the then impending Second World War, at "the other twenty-three hours" in the mental hospital. The period since World War II has witnessed a remarkable effort to understand the contributions to therapy that recognize the hospital as a *total* social experience. The groundwork for this effort was set by Sullivan and the Chicago sociologists. For medical sociology, soon to embark on its major period of growth as an institutionalized subfield, this was to be one of the richest veins in the development of knowledge through sociological research.

Summary

The social identity of medical sociology, I have argued, did not take visible shape until after World War II. The cognitive or intellectual identity was antecedent, enjoying a remarkable growth during the preceding quarter-century interval between the great wars. Theoretical paradigms like functionalism and Marxism were only part of this development. There was also a testing and expansion of the tools of inquiry of sociology as a social science, and medicine provided one of the major areas for the applications of such inquiry. Two research methods stand out, the one quantitative and other qualitative. In the sociology of medicine, the former is represented by the surveys of the social ecologists at the University of Chicago and the latter by field research on the interpersonal relations of health care deriving from the experimental schizophrenia ward of Harry Stack Sullivan at the Sheppard and Enoch Pratt Hospital in Baltimore. Both, notably and in my opinion not coincidentally, were substantively focused on the problems of mental disorder and therefore have been treated by some scholars as a separate field in itself, social psychiatry. Thus in a narrower sense historical analysis is forced into the same kind of comparisons and questions I raised earlier concerning the relations between medical sociology and social medicine. No matter. Such questions can only sharpen the search here for an understanding of the patterns of institutionalization in the full range of their historical continuities and discontinuities.

However, the picture of this formative period in medical sociology is not complete without a description of the influences of the theoretical developments that were taking place. The effort to make sense of the effects of war and of the economic depression produced some of the most influential theories of the next half century. The forces for stability—for the functional dynamics of social change—produced structural-functional theory, and the forces for conflict and revolution produced Marxist theory. Medical sociology was no less affected by these forces than general sociology, and representing them were two major figures, Lawrence J. Henderson and Bernhard Stern. Using a biographical method, the next chapter discusses their contributions.

5

Regional and
Intellectual Influences

After dominating American sociology for the first third of the century, the University of Chicago yielded to the East Coast Ivy League Universities of Harvard and Columbia as the center of influence.[1] Included was a change of focus from the field-centered study of Chicago as an urban laboratory to European-based theory. The strength of the Midwestern research preference for positivism and data-based methods was by no means lost, but the paradigms of structural-functionalism and Marxist dialectical materialism now found distinctive American interpretations, heightened by the deep economic depression of the thirties and the events that anticipated the oncoming European war. At the same time and in similar ways, medical sociology groped for a distinctive voice. However, it was still too early for a collective, institutionalized identity. Medical sociology was represented by several outstanding individual scholars who, through theoretical and historical writing, placed their stamp on the work of the next generation. Their contributions were close in pattern to the parent field but found in the study of medical problems a rich empirical base. The history of medical sociology in this important formative stage, because it is so much the product of a small group of outstanding individuals, can be told through their biographies. Leading this intellectual development were Lawrence J. Henderson and Bernhard J. Stern, each in a different way.

Henderson was a well-known physician-scientist who, attracted to sociology in midcareer during the 1920s, conceived a model of social systems theory that was one of the early sources of functionalism, the dominant sociological theory during the next thirty years. Stern, trained at Columbia by Ogburn in sociology and by Boas in anthropology, was a social historian of medicine who was a Marxist. Whereas Henderson built his theoretical model from the dyad, seen as the most fundamental type of human relationship, Stern studied society in sociopolitical terms, always working as a concerned intellectual in close touch with the social problems of his time. Henderson was committed to creating a social science with a rigor comparable to that of natural science, and he saw no proper place in such a science for sociopolitics. Indeed, in contrast to the activist, policy-oriented Stern, Henderson epitomized the value-neutrality that many sociologists idealized as the model of all types of science.

As different as these two men were as scholars, the contrast in their personal lives was, if anything, greater. Henderson was from an old New England family, and he took very seriously his role as the Abbott and James Lawrence Professor of Chemistry at Harvard University. He was a "gentleman" in both dress and manner. He believed, for example, that no self-respecting man wore shirts buttoned down the front, continuing himself to wear a foldover shirt well beyond its time of fashionable requirement. When he despaired at the way such shirts were laundered in Massachusetts, he sent them to a laundress in France every two weeks.[2] Stern, on the other hand, was from a middle-class Jewish family in Chicago. Never fully achieving academic legitimacy, Stern started and ended a twenty-five-year connection at Columbia University as a lecturer. Although his colleagues admired him, attacks on his right to teach during the McCarthy period colored much of the last decade of his life. Such ideological controversy distracted from Stern's influence as a scholar, even though, in life, he was clearly more active *as* a scholar than as an ideologue.

As would be expected, their academic and social worlds were far apart. Henderson was by choice as well as birth a Brahmin; his friends were in the upper stratum of Boston and Cambridge society, academics, professionals, and businessmen. A devotee of French culture who spent many summers in France, he was a close friend of Harvard presidents Eliot and Lowell. Stern's close associates were very different, a mix of New York's radical intelligentsia and such likeminded scholars as the medical historian Henry Sigerist and the pioneer medical sociologist Michael M. Davis. Even in the expression of his politics, Stern functioned primarily as an intellectual; his role as a founder and editor of the Marxist journal *Science and Society* is an example. To this day, the journal continues with a well-established reputation for high scholarly standards but also as a voice dedicated to left-wing politics.

Each man, in a distinctive way, represented opposite ends of the objectivity-advocacy dualism of modern sociology. Henderson's theory appealed to those who believed that legitimacy was to be found in knowledge. By the methods of science, this view asserted, society could be understood and made better, but only if science was "value free." Stern, though no less committed to rigorous scholarship, linked his work directly to social change. "Unlike the current fashion in medical sociology," the editors of his selected papers wrote, "his research illuminated the real and pressing problems to be faced [in society]."[3] His commitment to social democracy suffused his work and, although it was generally agreed that he was not dogmatic in his opinions, he was a nonconformist politically who believed that scholars should address independent social criticism to the broadest possible public.

Each man, in addition, was a teacher who left a heritage through influential students. Among those who testified to the great influence of Henderson on their work were the authors of the famous Hawthorne experiment, Elton Mayo, Fritz J. Roethlisberger, and T. North Whitehead. Others included the sociologists Talcott Parsons, Robert K. Merton, and Kingsley Davis; the economist Joseph Schumpeter; Crane Brinton, the historian of science; and the literary scholar Bernard DeVoto—all members of his famous seminar on the sociology of Pareto, which was started in the fall of 1932 and continued for seven or eight years.[4] Similar testimony to his influence came from such diverse individuals as Chester I. Barnard, the businessman and social scientist, Clyde Kluckhohn, the anthropologist, Eliot D. Chapple, the anthropologist, and many others. Stern, in the opinion of some, exerted a similarly strong but less direct influence on students.[5] Milton Terris believed that Stern especially influenced the field of social medicine. "His students in the medical field," writes Terris, "were essentially the same as Sigerist's—Herbert Abrams, Leslie Falk, Milton Roemer, Richard Weinerman, Jonas Muller, S. J. Axelrod, to name but a few."[6] Terris added in a subsequent interview that "it was difficult for Stern in his precarious situation at Columbia . . . to develop a group of graduate students; unlike Sigerist, unfortunately, he was not director of an institute. . . . [However] he was indeed the father of medical sociology, a pioneer in this field who founded an important tradition."[7]

Together the works of Henderson and Stern anticipated the central theoretical paradigms of the next half century of both general and medical sociology: the functionalism of social system theory, conflict theory, and neo-Marxism. In addition, as sociology emerged, after World War II, to contend for equal status with the rest of science, especially in the support structure of government and private foundations, the competing conceptual frameworks attracted public controversy. Sociology was seen as "radical" and suffered from contradictory reputations, both as "unscientific" and as "socialistic." Functionalism, although considered a conservative perspective by critics within sociology, was just as likely to be labeled the opposite by outside critics. Henderson and Stern epitomize the divergent approaches of this intellectual debate in terms reflective of both general sociology and medical sociology.

Each, therefore, is described here in some detail with attention to the full context of his contributions to knowledge.

Lawrence J. Henderson (1878–1942)

For many years, Henderson's sociology was not widely known, even though his conception of interpersonal behavior as a social system is a fundamental step in the history of functionalism in sociology.[8] Talcott Parsons, who is generally credited with being the major exponent of both sociological functionalism and its expression in social systems theory, acknowledges repeatedly his debt to Henderson, though not as a primary influence.[9]

Functionalism, by 1930, was already widely known in biology, and Henderson himself was credited with giving it, through the Henderson-Hesselbach theorem,[10] mathematical expression in research on the physiology of the blood. Anthropology established what was probably the earliest social functionalist school, based on Radcliffe-Brown and Malinowski,[11] and the latter are acknowledged sources for Parsons. On the other hand, Parsons was a regular at the Pareto seminar, beginning in 1932, where Henderson developed the ideas that, in 1935, were published under the title "The Patient and Physician as a Social System" and two years later in the book *Pareto's General Sociology: A Physiologist's Interpretation* (1937).[12] Both the sociologist George Homans[13] and the psychologist Henry Murray[14] dedicate their widely known books to him. It is, therefore, one of those curious footnotes in the history of ideas that for almost three decades Henderson was more a cult figure to a small sociological and academic elite, mainly his former students from Harvard, than he was acknowledged generally for his seminal contribution to basic sociological theory.

As Barber wrote in his biography of Henderson in 1970, "[i]t is probable that nine out of ten sociologists, on first learning of this book or otherwise hearing about L. J. Henderson, would respond with the question, 'Who *is* L. J. Henderson?' "[15] That this is less true today owes much to medical sociology. The interpersonal relations of medicine, and most particularly the doctor-patient relationship, became a focus of medical sociology's concern very early in its modern post–World War II history. In the process, Henderson was rediscovered and his more basic contributions to general sociological theory were reexamined, culminating in 1970 with Barber's book devoted entirely to Henderson and with Alvin Gouldner's inclusion of Henderson in his detailed critique of functionalism as part of what he called "the coming crisis of Western sociology."[16] Fittingly, Barber was a former student of Henderson, and his account, both the biography and the exposition of theory, was affectionate and respectful. Gouldner could not be more opposite. He saw Henderson as the center of Harvard's Pareto cult of the 1930s, providing to an elite group of scholars "their rationale for optimism and conservatism in the midst of the great crisis."[17]

Biography

Lawrence Joseph Henderson was born in Lynn, Massachusetts, near Boston in 1878 and died at the age of 65 in 1942.[18] Only the most spare details of his early life are known. He was the son of a ship chandler, a dealer in supplies and equipment for ships. His father's headquarters were in the old port of Salem, Massachusetts, near Lynn, with business interests in the French islands of Saint Pierre, and Miquelon, off the coast of Canada. Although unlike his father, Henderson spent his life in an academic career, his respect for his origins in the world of commerce never flagged. Robert Merton, Henderson's student in the 1930s, reports that

> One of Henderson's favorite phrases (was) "a man of affairs," meaning that someone knew his way around and had an intuitive grasp of reality, for which Henderson had an incredible respect.
>
> Henderson was always drawing the parallel between a real physician with his intuitive sense, making diagnoses and so on, and a really thoughtful businessman, who also dealt in such a way, with reality, social reality, and understood it.[19]

Throughout his life, Henderson was a Bostonian, living in Cambridge close to his beloved Harvard, where he studied both as an undergraduate and medical student and soon afterward joined the faculty. After graduating from Harvard College in 1898 and from Harvard Medical School in 1902, he immediately went to the University of Strasbourg for further study and research in chemistry. Biochemistry was a newly emerging field and became Henderson's special area of interest. Upon his return from Strasbourg, Henderson was first a lecturer, then an instructor, and successively an assistant, associate, and full professor of biological chemistry in both Harvard College and the Harvard Medical School. He never practiced medicine,

> but he had a great knowledge of and influence on the scientific medicine that was rapidly developing in his lifetime. Although Henderson was a scientist rather than a medical practitioner, he always admired a certain kind of medical man—the decisive therapeutist who bases his judgments on a

combination of science, experience, and intuition and who is reflective about his own behavior. He felt that there were many such men among his colleagues and friends in the Harvard-Boston medical community . . . and [he] invited such men to help instruct his students in his sociology course at Harvard.[20]

Throughout his career, Henderson displayed in combination the attributes of researcher, including abstract conception and methodology, and philosopher. Functional theory, derived from the classic generalized description of physico-chemical systems by Willard Gibbs, was the point of departure for his own central achievement as biological scientist. In the tradition of the laboratory, Henderson built on the works of predecessors by demonstrating the validity of his central ideas in mathematical terms and by experiment. His friend Dr. Arlie Bock wrote at his death in 1942:

> His formulation in 1908 of the acid-base equilibrium has far-reaching sig-nificance. The second great contribution made by Dr. Henderson was in furtherance of Claude Bernard's insistence upon the necessity for synthesis of physiological systems. By simple mathematical methods, Henderson was able to demonstrate for the first time the quantitative relationship in eight variables in the blood. His thinking concerning the equilibrium in the body had long been influenced by Willard Gibbs' study, *On the Equilibrium of Substance*, and is best exemplified in his book, *Blood—A Study in General Physiology*, published in 1928.[21]

As early as 1917, Henderson turned his attention to more general questions about human behavior. His book *The Order of Nature* (1917) established him internationally as a philosopher, but a closer look reveals that he was continuing the pattern of his earlier scientific work.[22] The concepts of equilibrium, of regu-lation, and of homeostatic mechanisms were continually at the center of his con-cern. This is evident in his biochemical and physiological research until the late 1920s. At that point, having established his scientific reputation on a level equal with men like Pavlov, J. B. S. Haldane, and Walter B. Cannon, Henderson turned his central attention to the phenomena of social behavior.[23] Here again, theories of functional systems remained his central intellectual focus, but now he "became interested in social equilibria, stimulated greatly by the kind of thinking, familiar to him as a scientist, brought to the subject by the Italian engineer-sociologist, Pareto."[24]

Henderson's Sociology

Pareto's efforts to work out a mathematical formulation for a system of economic equilibrium in society held a natural appeal for Henderson. Henderson had made his reputation by applying the method of simultaneous equations to Gibbs's phys-icochemical system theory while Pareto used indifference curves to formulate equations of economic equilibriums. Moreover, Pareto, like Henderson, came into the social sciences late in life, after an education mainly in mathematics and physical science. Pareto began his scholarly career after about twenty years' ex-perience as a practicing engineer.

Homans and Barber credit William Morton Wheeler with introducing Henderson to the writings of Pareto. Wheeler is another scholar who is generally unknown to most sociologists, despite the fact that he was one of the first faculty members in the Department of Sociology when it was created at Harvard in 1931. Wheeler was professor of entomology at Harvard, cross-listed to the Department of Sociology on the basis of his interest in the social life of insects.

Henderson, reports Barber, "was immediately and enormously impressed by Pareto. It was just what he had been looking for, and for the rest of his life he devoted more and more of his time and activities to Pareto and to social science. Yet, curiously enough, it was not mainly Pareto's ideas that Henderson passed on to some of the young social scientists of the 1930s, who are themselves very influential today. His influence consisted more in teaching his own methodological ideas about such essential matters as systems, equilibrium, mutual dependence, and the functions of conceptual schemes."[25] This influence and its considerable impact on sociology has not gone completely unnoticed. Russett offers the opinion that "Henderson may have given greater impetus to the diffusion of equilibrium concepts among American social scientists than any other single individual. To a whole generation of Harvard students he passed on his conception of scientific method, of social science methodology, and specifically, of the place of equilibrium analysis in social science."[26]

Often neglected in the estimates of Henderson and his effect on the world of science is one activity in which his physiology and social science were combined, the Fatigue Laboratory.

In 1927, Harvard University set up the Fatigue Laboratory to study physical and mental stress in workers. The laboratory was in the Harvard Business School and sponsored both physiological and social research. Henderson was the first director of the Fatigue Laboratory. As a physiologist he took an interest in and influenced the physiological work of Dr. David Dill; as a social scientist he took an interest in and influenced the social research of Elton Mayo, Fritz J. Roethlisberger and T. North Whitehead, especially their now famous work at the Hawthorne Plant of the Western Electric Company. In its turn, this "industrial relations" research had a considerable influence on American sociology in the period after World War II.[27]

Through his work in the Fatigue Laboratory, Henderson came in contact with Chester I. Barnard. Homans reports that it was Henderson who encouraged Barnard to write *The Functions of the Executive* (1938).[28] Henderson's influence on the corporate world was further verified when in 1939, he was appointed chairman of the Committee on Work in Industry of the National Research Council, and under his leadership the Committee surveyed and evaluated much research in this field, both physiological and sociological.[29]

Henderson's Fatigue Laboratory was the model for Yale University's Applied Physiology Department, created during the 1930s. This department, its history following the war, and its effect on sociologists like Robert Straus is a good example of how Henderson's influence was diffused and why it is so little known.[30] Straus went on to become in 1958 the founding chairman of the first department of behavioral science in a medical school. Thus, in a very direct way, Henderson's approach to medical sociology was transmitted.

Better known than Henderson's relationship with the Harvard School of Business Administration is his influence on the Society of Fellows at Harvard.[31] However, a recitation of what Henderson did, of what he wrote, and of the institutions he directly worked to create is not enough to convey the nature of his influence. Despite its small volume, the available biographical testimony establishes that Henderson was, in his person and type, a force in the lives of all who came in contact with him. Especially in the description of his Pareto seminar, this is most vivid. For example, Robert K. Merton, one of Henderson's most distinguished students, recalls the experience:

> The composition of the Henderson seminars was extraordinary. It was not just another graduate seminar. It was a very personal construction. In it were such people as Bernard De Voto, an editor of "The Easy Chair" at *Harper's* and a very well-known American historian, a good friend of Henderson's and someone for whom Henderson had an inordinate respect. Well . . . there was Benny DeVoto sitting there, in this luxurious room in one of the houses. It was not a classroom, it was a lounge. A great sofa in front of the fireplace, and just a collection of chairs that had been put together for members of the group.
>
> How did the seminar proceed? Back then, Pareto had not been translated into English, of course, so you had your choice: you either had the Italian edition or the French edition. . . . Henderson would assign a chapter or two, which was an immense amount of material. We went through the whole of Pareto in one year, discussing it in detail. Then we would sit there with copies of the book in our respective laps and he [Henderson] would expatiate, and there would be a give-and-take conversation. There was no question that Pink Whiskers—which was the affectionate behind-his-back term for Henderson—Pink Whiskers dominated. And he had some very strong opinions as to what was significant in Pareto. . . . All you have to do is read Henderson's brilliant little book on Pareto . . . to see the use of Pareto's conceptual scheme which he applied to physician-patient relations. . . . I am sure that was the first time that I and the rest of us were exposed to the idea of looking at the relationship between physicians and patients from a sociological standpoint.[32]

Repeatedly, his students speak about his "passion." His red beard was like a flag to his character. Homans and Bailey wrote: "His method of discussion is feebly imitated by the pile-driver. His passion was hottest when his logic was coldest."[33] Barber agrees and adds: "Nowhere, as my own experience as a student of Henderson showed, was this more evident than in his teaching. Yet it made him a great teacher. Whether he agreed or disagreed, a student could never forget Henderson's words because of the passion so clearly expressed in them."[34] There was another side to Henderson that, obviously, was just as important: "If he [Henderson] felt a man had something in him, no one could be more patient than he in helping it come to light. He had the gift of taking a scholar's raw data, no matter how far they might be from his own field of biochemistry, and bringing out the pattern that lay in them."[35] In somewhat the same way, Barber adds, "Henderson helped bring out patterns not fully manifested in Pareto's work, particularly in the concept of a social system."[36]

It would be easy to limit discussion of Pareto's appeal for Henderson to the intellectual. Without doubt, he was powerfully drawn to Pareto's ideas because of the two men's common origin in science and because Pareto gave expression to a functionalist interpretation of society that expanded Henderson's physico-chemical perspective. However, Pareto's other appeal was that the two men shared a deeply conservative politics. As Homans and Bailey—in full sympathy with Henderson's views—tell us: "His beard was red, but his politics were vig-orously conservative."[37]

Functionalism as a Political and Regional Force

Gouldner has argued that the appeal of Pareto's politics for Henderson was not coincidental. Moreover, Gouldner also believed, the extraordinary triumph of functional theory during this period of sociology's history is linked to political implications, and Henderson's Pareto seminar is illustrative.

> In particular, the crisis of the 1930s led some American academicians to look to European academic sociology as a defense against the Marxism that was recently penetrating American campuses, for Europe had far longer experience with it. European social theory was thrown into the breach against the crisis-generated interest in Marxism. It was with such ideolog-ically shaped expectations that a group of Harvard scholars which centers on L. J. Henderson . . . began to meet in the fall of 1932.

With heavy sarcasm, Gouldner added:

> The political implications of the circle's interest in Pareto were expressed by George Homans, who candidly acknowledged—Mr. Homans never says anything except with forceful candor—that "as a Republican Bostonian who had not rejected his comparatively wealthy family, I felt during the thirties that I was under personal attack, above all from the Marxists. I was ready to believe Pareto because he provided me with a defense."

What was for Homans a defense, however, was the opposite for Gouldner, who quotes Crane Brinton's assertion that Pareto himself was then called "the Marx of the bourgeoisie"—when he was not, less grandly, simply termed a Fascist.[38]

Henderson himself is, for Gouldner, a central influence within what he calls "the Parsonian synthesis." Its emergence, Gouldner argued, was neither part of a developmental theoretical sequence as both Henderson and Parsons conceived it nor a brilliant breakthrough departure from previous theoretical paradigms. Rather, in Gouldner's interpretation, it was a defensive response to a "deep crisis" in middle-class societies, marked by a series of major sociopolitical convulsions:

> (1) World War I, which undermined the middle classes' confidence in the inevitability of progress, destroyed old nation-states and created new ones throughout Europe, increased American influence in Europe, under-mined mass confidence in the old elite, and set the stage for—
> (2) The Soviet Revolution, which for a period intensified the revolution-ary potential in western and central Europe, acutely heightened anxieties

among the Euro-American middle class, began to polarize international tensions around the United States and the Soviet Union, and, converging with growing nationalism in underdeveloped areas and particularly in Asia, undermined the colonial empires of the victorious Western powers;

(3) The international economic crisis of the 1930s, which . . . created mass unemployment among the working class, acute deprivation to small farmers, sharp status anxieties and economic threats to the middle class, and finally accelerated the growth of the welfare state in the United States.[39]

Gouldner saw Henderson and his younger Harvard colleagues and students as the direct heirs of a sociological tradition "that stressed the importance of developing shared belief systems, common interests and wants, and stable social groupings."[40] The lineage reached to the founders of modern sociology, Saint-Simon (1760–1825) and Comte (1798–1917). The philosophical climate of the early nineteenth century was dominated by positivism and utilitarianism, and, Gouldner argues,

[t]he newly emerging sociology did not reject the utilitarian premises of the new middle-class culture, but rather sought to broaden and extend them. It became concerned with *collective* utility in contrast to individual utility, with the needs of *society* for stability and progress and with what was useful for this. In particular, it stressed the importance of other, "social" utilities, as opposed to an exclusive focus on the production of economic utilities. Sociology was born, then, as the counterbalance to the political economy of the middle class in the first quarter of the nineteenth century.[41]

Gouldner consistently interprets each new development in sociological thought as a response more to its underlying politicoeconomic conditions rather than to the historical chain of ideas. Therefore, much as Gouldner saw the sociological position of Comte as a restorative philosophy following the early nineteenth century's "emotionally exhausting quarter century of revolution and war," so also he saw the functionalism of Henderson/Parsons as a "positive" reaction to the cataclysms of war and depression in the twentieth century.

In addition, Gouldner finds a natural affinity between the early French social positivists and the "detachment" of academic science. "Positivism," Gouldner said, "was congenial to those among whom science had prestige, especially educated sectors of the middle class, and who sought a prudent way of producing social change—progress within order, skirting political conflict so as not to risk the mobilization of uncontrollable allies, the radical Jacobin potential, and simultaneously to minimize the reactionary, restorationist backlash."[42] According to Gouldner, this was an important part of the reason why the sociology of the French founders and their classical European successors of the late nineteenth century, such as Durkheim, Weber, and Simmel, was institutionalized in the academic sociology of the universities.

Like Oberschall, Ben-David, and others,[43] Gouldner is impressed with how sociology just prior to World War I was "increasingly institutionalized within the supporting university contexts of the different countries [of Western Europe]."[44] Sociology is seen as an instrument of each historical period's struggle, used by the dominant emerging class to supersede its prior master class. Sociology, by 1910, "was no longer the avocation of stigmatized reformers but the vocation of prestigious academicians."[45] Gouldner adds, however, that the university had become state sponsored, "an agency for the integration of society on a national and secular basis."[46] Thus, even as intellectual freedom and autonomy became an institutionalized right for the new breed of full-time career academicians, they were constrained, says Gouldner, by a "larger loyalty" to the essential institutions of the social order of the nation. As evidence, Gouldner notes that the classical sociologists enthusiastically supported their nations at war in 1914 and "rarely manifested autonomy from the claims of the nation-state."[47] The university, he concludes, had been coopted by the state. Basically this is Gouldner's explanation for the separation between an academic sociology inside the university, dominated by functional theories that supported the national status quo, and a sociology outside the university that was dominated by Marxism. This was a time when sociology, in its institutionalized centers, acted to prevent itself from being "confused" with socialism. The same type of effort to avoid a similar confusion becomes important in the anticommunist backwash of World War II and plays a special role in the early phase of the establishment of medical sociology.

Whether or not Gouldner's interpretation is correct, there is no questioning the fact that the center of academic sociology in the United States shifted at just the time, the early 1930s, when Harvard created a department of sociology. It shifted from the Midwest, where its cultural headquarters was the University of Chicago, to the eastern seaboard. Henderson himself, with his impeccable academic credentials, his devotion to Harvard, and his leadership position among its Brahmin elite, personified the type of individual that Gouldner believed emerged because of the sociopolitical crisis of war and depression in Europe and the United States; emerged, that is, to fit the circumstances, not to determine them. The "Pareto Circle," as Henderson's seminar was known, articulated the type of academic sociological perspective, international in scope and focused on the preservation of social order, that, Gouldner believed, the conditions of the time required. Spawned from this seminar were the leaders of the Parsonian synthesis that would carry forward the structural-functionalist orientation in its domination of American sociology during the next three decades. Gouldner's explanation epitomizes the critique of structural-functionalism that rose to challenge the dominance of the Parsonians in the 1960s; his view is that of the critical conflict theorists who argue "that scientific change, though mediated by intragroup conflict, is caused primarily by processes extrinsic to the scientific group, specifically societal level changes in economy, class and ideology."[48] The structural functionalists, on the other hand, saw themselves as agents of an intellectual development, in the continuous differentiation and accumulation of objective knowledge, theoretically formulated and empirically grounded.

About the meaning of the regional shift of sociology's professional centrality, from Chicago to Harvard and Columbia in the East, there is considerable difference of opinion. Faris, for example, argues that the rebellion against Chicago was "the work of an activist faction, politicized and socially involved, who challenged Chicago's stand on scientific detachment and value neutrality."[49] This is the opposite picture from that presented by Gouldner, who saw the positions in the reverse. Martindale[50] and Kuklick[51] interpret the events of the thirties in terms that appear to be closer to those of Gouldner. Lengermann[52] finds all three views too neat a fit to ideology, whereas the facts that she presents are more complicated and contradictory.

At issue is a question that is critical for the remainder of this discussion of medical sociology: What are the nature and sources of scientific change? The overwhelming weight that Gouldner attaches to politicoeconomic determinants fails to account for the intrinsic quality of the scientific method as a value orientation that drives toward critical and independent thinking, regardless of political consequences. It *is* possible to argue that both the roots and the limitations of Henderson's social system theory are more intellectual than political, an idea that Gouldner does not seriously consider.

Henderson was passionate about what he saw as a fallacy in linear cause-and-effect reasoning in both the natural sciences and the social sciences. In his own words:

> Because every factor interacts in a social system, because every thing, every property, every relation, is therefore in a state of mutual dependence with everything else, ordinary cause and-effect analysis of events is rarely possible. In fact, it is nearly always grossly misleading: so much so that it must be regarded as one of the two great sources of error in sociological work.[53]

Exception has been taken to Henderson's theoretical reasoning on the basis, quite different from the ideological critique of Gouldner, that Henderson argued from models that were primarily mechanical or physiological. On the other hand, his descriptions of the doctor-patient relationship, the central illustration he used to bridge his functional analysis of physicochemical systems with social systems, were eloquent and deeply sensitive to the human complexities involved:

> A patient sitting in your office facing you is rarely in a favorable state of mind to appreciate the precise significance of a logical statement; and it is in general not merely difficult but quite impossible for him to perceive the precise meaning of a train of thought. It is also out of the question that the physician should convey what he desires to convey to the patient if he follows the practice of blurting out just what comes into his mind. The patient is moved by fears and by many other sentiments, and these, together with reason, are being modified by the doctor's words and phrases, by his manner and expression.[54]

He used a concrete clinical problem that, prophetically, gained increasing relevance between 1935 and the present:

> Consider this statement, "This is a carcinoma." . . . We may regard this statement as a stimulus applied to the patient. This stimulus will produce a response, and the response, together with the mechanism that is involved in its production, is an extremely complex one. . . . For instance, there are likely to be circulatory and respiratory changes accompanying many complex changes in the central and peripheral nervous system. With the cognition, there is a correlated fear. There will probably be concern for the economic interests . . . of wife and children. All those intricate processes constitute a response to the stimulus made up of the four words, "This is a carcinoma."[55]

His analysis, however, lacked the clarity of his work in the biological sciences. His social science did not go very far beyond a challenging but limited formulation of the problem of interpersonal relations in the terms of functionalistic theory. As Barber notes, "[he] knew little of the experimental and survey research techniques that were just emerging in the social sciences."[56] His contribution was a framework, the point of departure for Parsons, Merton, and his other students and junior colleagues during the next generation of sociology.

For medical sociology, his most direct contribution was probably through Parsons, especially in chapter 10 of *The Social System*.[57] Medical practice, in this chapter, is used as a concrete illustration of Parsons's conception of the social system. It is regarded by many as one of the clearest representations of his ideas in all of his work. Henderson is credited in the very first footnote in the chapter: "For general comparison with this chapter," Parsons writes, "the reader may be referred to L. J. Henderson, 'Physician and Patient as a Social System.' "[58] The influence that spread from this source was to powerfully affect medical sociology during subsequent decades.

Henderson would have been pleased with the way medical sociology as a subfield became established both in its parent discipline and in medicine more generally. Just as he thought sociology could learn from medicine, especially the technique of concrete case illustration, he also believed that medicine's understanding of its social aspects was backward, even somewhat worse than it had been in earlier historical periods. Scientific medicine, to which he was a major contributor, was recognized by him as an achievement that included some important costs. "There is a need," he wrote, "to fix and clarify the ideas of physicians concerning the half-forgotten sociological aspects of medical practice and to give appropriate instruction to medical students."[59] To achieve this end, his own tendency was to focus on the two-person physician-patient social system, but not because he was unaware of the importance of larger social systems in which physician-patient encounters were involved.[60] However, his consideration of the larger societal social system was no more than background to his intensive small group focus. The kind of frame of reference used by Gouldner and others was essentially foreign to Henderson. The world was, during the time when Henderson worked mainly as a sociologist, in turmoil. Sociology itself was undergoing rapid institutionalization, including deep conflicts about the official journal of the American Sociological Society, the proliferation of regional professional societies, a growing service relationship to national public policy, and the growth of methods of quantification. Henderson, at least in his writings, remained oblivious to these turbulent events.

Bernhard Stern could not be a more opposite case. Curiously, Gouldner in all of his main critique of American sociology during the thirties never mentions Stern even once, though Stern was an eloquent and accomplished scholar of just the type that Gouldner found missing in American sociology at that time.

Bernhard J. Stern (1894–1956)

Bernhard J. Stern's importance to medical sociology, like Henderson's, was embodied in both scholarship and in deep influential effect on students.[61] He was also, in his beliefs, a symbol of controversies that were to plague medical sociology for decades after the Second World War.

Stern's intellectual legacy is broad in scope. He wrote nine books and coauthored three books, ranging in scope from the sociology of science to anthropology.[62] In addition, he edited four books and served as an editor of the *Encyclopaedia of Social Sciences*, to the first edition (1932) of which he contributed seventeen articles, including such topics as slavery and the position of women in society. Yet there is no biographical entry for Stern in the second edition of the *Encyclopaedia of Social Sciences* (1968), nor does his name appear in the index.

Among those who believe that Stern has been unfairly neglected or even rejected by the leaders of sociology during and since his lifetime, the explanation usually points to another side of his life. He was a left-wing political thinker, editor of a Marxist journal, and a publicly active supporter of progressive causes. From 1938 to 1953, Stern was a target of congressional investigating committees. How much professional hardship these activities caused is debatable. His most ardent supporters are scathing in their opinion of his colleagues and of his employer, Columbia University. Stern himself, however, and his widow did not share these feelings, and there is strong evidence that the Columbia University Faculty supported him, especially against the public charges of the McCarthy congressional investigations.[63]

Against the evidence that Stern was a pioneer of medical sociology, it is hard to ignore that he is most often omitted or, at best, neglected in the textbooks and published historical accounts of medical sociology. Here, however, the task is to set the record straight. Who exactly was Bernhard Stern, and what did he contribute to medical sociology?

Biography

Stern was born in Chicago on June 19, 1894, the third of seven children of Herman B. and Hattie Frank Stern, who had immigrated from Germany.[64] The Stern family lived in the Polish section of Chicago where they owned a department store. Looking back on his youth, Stern described a situation typical of many immigrants in that period of American history. Both parents worked long hours at the store, and the children, five girls and two boys, worked with them whenever possible. All the children went to public schools where they were harassed as Jews and also beaten on the street by the neighborhood children.

Similar to other immigrant families, the Sterns were strongly linked to their ethnic origins but also enthusiastically patriotic about their newly acquired nationality. Judaism and Jewish identity were pervasive themes in the Stern household, as was a commitment to the principles of the United States Constitution. In Stern's adult years, these two themes, a passion for the democratic freedom and social justice associated with the founding fathers of the United States and the historical-philosophical perspective of Jewish tradition, both of which were inculcated in childhood, continued to be critically important.

Stern studied for his bachelor's and master's degrees at the University of Cincinnati from 1913 to 1917 and simultaneously enrolled at the Hebrew Union College, graduating as a rabbi in the Reformed Synagogue movement. Although he earned his living as a rabbi for only a few years, there seems little doubt that the intensive preparation in history and philosophy that was part of his rabbinical training had a strong influence on his scholarship. Moreover, some of the friendships that he made at the Hebrew Union College continued throughout his life.

These positive effects of his Jewish heritage and identity, however, were coupled with negative experiences with anti-Semitism. For example, his desire to be a physician crystalized during this period, but he was unable to gain access to a medical school. He believed he was stopped by the policy of *numerus clausus* for Jewish applicants that was common at the time. In 1923, however, he was accepted at the University of Graz Medical School in Austria, which he considered one of the best schools in Europe.

Stern's poor health, however, finally ended his aspirations of becoming a physician. While honeymooning in Italy in 1923, he became critically ill. He and his wife abandoned their plan to go to Graz and went to Berlin, where a surgeon operated on Stern for ulcers. This was not a sudden or new experience, for Stern's health had been frail since childhood. Eventually, after months of fighting his illness, he decided to go to the University of Berlin. During the next year, Stern studied in Berlin and at the London School of Economics, dogged by his illness. In 1924, he returned to New York and entered Columbia University, doing a year of intensive work in anthropology with Franz Boaz and with the sociologist William F. Ogburn, who supervised his dissertation.

According to Charlotte Stern, Ogburn was a warm and strong supporter who did everything possible to help Stern. Ogburn was interested in the role of invention in social change, which Stern investigated in terms of social resistance to medical innovation. His thesis was written in 1925–26 and published in 1927.[65] The objective was to find and demonstrate the principle of "social inertia," a concept derived from Ogburn, referring to the forces of custom and authority, vested interest, ignorance, and tradition and the fear of new ideas. Although the dissertation was conceived as a test of Ogburn's sociological theories of social change, it was reviewed in medical journals and quickly gained Stern a reputation as a medical historian.[66]

Much like the great medical historian Henry Sigerist, Stern turned away from the previous dominant emphasis on great doctors and their discoveries toward the analysis of medicine within "a matrix . . . at once cultural, social, and economic."[67] The comparison with Sigerist is not mere coincidence. They were friends and are often compared in the significance of their influence on the writing about the history of medicine. There are, however, important differences. Sigerist was a physician-philologist, trained as a medical historian under Karl Sudhoff at the University of Leipzig's Institute of the History of Medicine; Stern was primarily a sociologist by training, developing the historical method in the service of his analysis of the role of medicine in society. Sigerist's focus tended always to be on medicine and became more so as his career proceeded. Stern focused more on the social factors and, therefore, seems most legitimately to come by the title "The Father of Medical Sociology."[68]

Stern's dissertation established a standard and substantive focus that infused much of his subsequent scholarship. In his examination of social resistance to medical innovation, the illustrations he used covered a very broad range, from the opposition to dissection to the opposition to prevention of puerperal infection. His analysis of the seventeenth century, for example, that critical historical point in the assertion of modern scientific thinking for western Europe, achieves a perspective that presages the sociology of science that Robert Merton was to amplify in his own dissertation ten years later.[69] Merton himself wrote about the achievement of Stern on the subject:

Vestiges of any tendency to regard the development of science and technology as *wholly* self-contained and advancing irrespective of the social structure are being dissipated by the actual course of historical events. An increasingly visible control and, often, restraint of scientific research and invention has been repeatedly documented, notably in a series of studies by Stern who has also traced the bases of resistance to change in medicine.[70]

Stern, in this first of his major writings, asserted the priority of the social structure in the development of knowledge, precisely the same conclusion that Merton emphasized: "And the limitations of any unqualified assumption that science or technology represents the basis to which the social structure must adjust become evident in the light of studies showing how science and technology have been put into service of social or economic demands."[71]

Merton's comments highlight what was perhaps the most effective achievement of Stern's first book when it was published, that is, to challenge the assumptions that prevailed among medical historians that scientific discovery and innovation determined the pace and course of the history of medical practice. Stern was able to refute this idea with special effectiveness in his study of the power of tradition and authority to obstruct the acceptance of Harvey's demonstration of the pulmonary circulation of the blood. In the seventeenth century, despite the century's historical significance as the turning point for the final triumph of rational science over medieval scholasticism, Harvey, like Galileo shortly before him, was subjected not only to intense public opposition, led particularly by the Church but also by his fellow scientists. Even Descartes rejected Harvey's theory of propulsion of the heart; Bacon never mentions him; and Thomas Sydenham includes no reference to him in his writings. More than a century after his death, authoritative textbooks of medicine continued the opposition to Harvey. Even more dramatic, and more costly to the effectiveness of medicine, was the opposition for centuries to the idea of asepsis. Stern documents how, for six centuries, from the thirteenth to the nineteenth, the methods of asepsis (clearing of foreign bodies in wounds, suturing of the edges of wounds, the soaking in wine of pads and pledgets used to foment the suture wound) were known and demonstrated. Yet, even against Holmes and Semmelweis in the mid–nineteenth century, the opposition to practices of simple asepsis and antisepsis was furious.[72]

These ideas, relatively commonplace today, were novel and exciting when Stern began to write them in 1927. He was by no means alone. Sigerist was already embarked on the same course. Sarton was in the middle of his life's work to revise the narrow scope of the existing history of science. Henderson at Harvard was teaching quite similar ideas as part of his constantly expanding sociological perspective. Stern, nevertheless, must be regarded as an important innovator.[73] But it was for young physicians entering the field of social medicine that Stern may very well have had the greatest impact. Milton Terris, for example, tells in an interview how he felt when, as an undergraduate at Columbia University in 1932, he took a course with Stern:

My God, he was a terrific teacher. Remarkable, very Socratic, very patient. He had a tremendous influence on a person like myself, brought up in medicine. An eye opener. His Ph.D. thesis is a very important book . . . showing that medical discoveries are not just a question of medical genius. . . . The time was ripe for it. And his *Society and Medical Progress* had a very important influence on a whole generation of medical care people who were coming forward at the time.[74]

The years following his dissertation were extremely productive for Stern. In addition to his writing on medical sociology, his anthrological interests found expression in books about the Lummi Indians of northwest Washington State (1934), race (1942), and the family (1938) and a general textbook in anthropology written with Melville Jacobs (1947).[75] His biographical research on Lester F. Ward and Lewis Henry Morgan also was initiated and would continue throughout his life. In 1936 he was founder and on the editorial board of the Marxist social science journal *Science and Society*; he contined to serve this journal for the next twenty years. Despite his reputation as a man in delicate health, he appears also to have been very active working for a variety of types of institutions. In 1932, he was appointed to the faculty of the New School for Social Research as a lecturer in anthropology, where he worked parallel with his Columbia University appointment until 1943 and again from 1948 until his death. In 1930, immediately upon his return to New York from Washington State, he was appointed assistant editor of the *Encyclopedia of Social Sciences,* contributing to fifteen volumes of that most important source book during the next four years. He worked at various times for most of the institutions that supported the early steps toward bringing social science and medicine into partnership; for the Commonwealth Fund he wrote three books;[76] for the New York Academy of Medicine he participated in the work of the Committee on Medicine and the Changing Order; for Michael Davis and the Julius Rosenwald Foundation he participated in the Committee on Research in Medical Economics in 1938–39 and for Carnegie, in their study of the Negroes in America, in 1939. He also worked for a variety of government and private organizations: for the State Insurance Fund of Puerto Rico he wrote a report on a proposed industrial hospital and rehabilitation center; for the New York Heart Association he prepared a report on the socioeconomic environment and cardiovascular disease; for the U.S. Senate he testified on the Wagner-Murray-Dingell Bill.

Stern's academic career, however, never reflected his performance as a scholar. The pattern was established in 1925–26 in his first appointment as a tutor at the College of the City of New York, where he went as a substitute for a professor of sociology who was ill. As in all of his later appointments, he was liked by his students and regarded as an excellent teacher.[77] By the end of the year, his thesis was completed and accepted, and a tenure line position became available at City College. With the strong endorsement of the Sociology Department faculty, Stern expected to be appointed, but he was not. From the evidence, it appears that Stern's independence and convictions about the right of free speech were the reasons underlying this administrative decision. What follows is a key episode, as recounted by his widow:

> Robert W. Dunn was an economist from Yale who had been to the Soviet Union. When he came back, he traveled throughout the country lecturing. ... The students at City College wanted to hear him lecture, but they had to get permission from a faculty member. They went to Bernhard because they knew he was so staunch about freedom of speech. They asked him to

sponsor the meeting, which of course he did. . . . The result was that he became persona non grata with the college officials.[78]

Stern's political activities at this time (1926–27) were no more than what would now be called "liberal." He was not yet identified with any political movement. The event, therefore, shocked him. It cost him his job because the president of the college accused him of bias, while acknowledging that he was an excellent teacher. This was to be the pattern of his career. In the following year, at the University of Washington, the experience was repeated. According to the Meiklejohn archives, "[l]ocal religious groups were critical of a speech he gave before the Auto Mechanics Local in which he claimed that environment was a greater force than heredity. What convinced them that Stern was beyond redemption was an analogy he drew between Easter sunrise services and the pagan rites of Indian idol worshippers."[79] Even though he won awards for his teaching, his lectures about local Indian tribes raised intense local controversy, enough again to prevent his advancement to tenure. These setbacks notwithstanding, the trajectory of his intellectual career achievements was very swift and full.

During these first, richly productive ten years of Stern's professional career, his sociology of medicine was dominated by the same general type of problem he addressed in his Ph.D. thesis. The second book, published the same year as his thesis, for example, was on vaccination: *Should We Be Vaccinated? A Study of the Controversy in Its Historical and Scientific Aspects*, published by Harper in 1927. This book was an amplification of part of his thesis, showing how the medical profession itself impeded medical progress toward what would later be a standard practice of preventative medicine. It told a fascinating story of how the financial interests of specialized segments of the profession caused them to exploit the ignorance of the public, using campaigns to promote fear and revulsion among the masses. Stern told the detailed story, with all its interplay of professional envy and jealousy, of the role played by various religious and medical sects, and of the questions raised about authority and spheres of control among the official bodies that became involved. The same types of themes were developed in a long essay he wrote for the National Resources Committee in 1937: "Resistance to the Adoption of Technical Innovation."

Looking at the body of his work between 1927 and the late thirties, it would appear that Stern was giving full play to his interests in all their breadth. He was writing actively in anthropology, reading and publishing the articles of Ward and Morgan, and establishing the premises of his Marxist critique of society in his new journal. Toward the end of the 1930s, his work shifted, and he began to focus more on the sociology of medicine. The historical case studies concerning technological and scientific innovation are replaced by a deep and broad analysis of medicine and society. Five books in medical sociology were published within a five-year span, from 1941 to 1946; two of them are considered the outstanding products of his whole career and remain topical and relevant to the problems presented by medicine today.

Society and Medical Progress, published in 1941, was requested by Michael M. Davis and funded by the Committee on Research in Medical Economics.[80] In the preface, Stern testifies generously to the influence of Sigerist, and the confluence of their points of view is unmistakable. This is a work of social history, covering the whole span of medicine from ancient Eygpt to the present. It is also an up-to-date analysis of the status of contemporary medicine, at the time establishing the context of urbanization and its effects and the relationships between income and health, ending with an analysis of the most important ways that medicine interacts with science and society. A detailed historical demography and a discussion of epidemiology remind the reader of the critically important recent work of Thomas McKeown.[81] Like McKeown, Stern sets the record straight about those advances in health that have been the result of improved living standards and public health measures as compared with those advances that more directly derive from advances in medical care itself.

Beginning with the two traditions of medicine, the scientific and the magicoreligious, Stern charts the long rivalry and slow progress to medical science. Starting with Egypt and including Babylon, the ancient Greeks, and the Romans, Stern documents how progress in medicine is always related to changes in the total society. In the Western world, the advances and retreats of practical-secular medicine are charted through the declines of the Middle Ages to modern times. The scientific foundations that are represented in each historical period are fully discussed. In the process, Stern discounts the "great men theory of history," showing how discoveries are often made by several people at the same time and the importance of the cultural context in the advances of science. Each historical period is shown to include its own type of advances, including the Middle Ages, as well as its own inhibiting factors. There is no gradual and continual progress along evolutionary lines, Stern argues. The advances occur in "sudden spurts."

The role of institutions receives extensive treatment. The development of medical schools are described from the earliest examples in the West, in Salerno, Italy, in the twelfth and thirteenth centuries. The universities, the scientific academics of the seventeenth century, and the changes in American medical education from the seventeenth through the twentieth century are described. The development of the modern hospital is also treated in depth, including the effects on costs, the consequences for the poor, and the effects on the distribution of physicians. A long section on urbanization and its effects disputes the theories of social Darwinism.

His chapter on medical advances and social progress could easily be exchanged for current statements of medical problems today. The effects of changing morbidity and mortality rates on the types of disease, the changing age composition of the population and the problem of the aged, the change in the psychology of the world caused by the reduction of some of the major problems of illness that characterized the past, and the effects on other sciences are all discussed in detail.

The book ends with a number of conclusions. First, Stern asserts the need to study medicine as an integral part of society. "The traditional approach to the study of medicine as a unique discipline has, as a rule, violated reality by ignoring the essential and all-important relations of medicine and socioeconomic conditions, with prevailing social attitudes, and with other scientific disciplines."[82] Second, he says physicians should understand the social and psychological factors that affect patients and medical practice as experts, not as novices. In this sense, he anticipates the behavioral science movement of the next two decades in medical education.

Equally, he criticizes social scientists for a failure to study medicine adequately. This was the book that Milton Terris says "had a very important influence on a whole generation of medical care people who were coming forward at the time."[83] Its full impact, however, should be considered together with that of a second major book, *American Medical Practice in the Perspective of a Century*, that Stern published in 1945. This book was commissioned by the Committee on Medicine and the Changing Order established by the New York Academy of Medicine in 1942. The objectives of the Committee were to address the following issues:

1. The quality of care, especially methods of maintaining and improving quality
2. Accessibility to preventative and curative care
3. Problems of cost, especially the distribution of services at the lowest possible per capita cost

The members of the Committee included a wide array of both medical and lay members.

Read against the situation of the 1990s, Stern's *American Medical Practice* seems remarkably contemporary in its ideas. His major areas of concentration—the trend toward specialization in medicine, the supply and distribution of physicians and medical resources, and the utilization of and access to medical care—are among the most important problems of medicine today. Stern's method involved the use of a wide array of data—statistics of demography, the epidemiology of disease, and the economics of the distribution of health professionals—from which he developed the argument that medicine can only be understood in the context of socioeconomic changes in the society in general. Stern's conclusions about the discrimination in medical services available to the poor, especially the black population, continue to be accurate today, and his advocacy of the "right to health" is expressed with a remarkable clarity.

As fresh and revelant as these fifty-five-year-old pages strike the contemporary reader, one also cannot fail to note how modest and unremarkable their political judgments now seem. This book was the centerpiece of Stern's teaching as a visiting professor of sociology at Yale in 1944. For several years, he was an inspiration to young graduate students like Robert Straus, who testified that Stern "inspired excitement for the opportunities which the study of medical systems provided for testing and extending sociological theory and the ways in which the social scientist could reinterpret the history, clarify the processes, and even predict the future of medicine."[84] Stern's 1945 book on American medical practice became "the Bible of medical sociology at Yale.[85]

The irony for Stern was that despite his reasoned scholarship and the lack of dogmatism in his writing, he was during the last decade of his life publicly judged mainly as a radical. His open sympathy for a Marxist interpretation of history caused him increasing trouble as the United States postwar obsession with communism found expression in "McCarthyism." His experience, of course, was not unique. It was part of the experience of all U.S. colleges and universities, for whom 1945–55 have been called "the difficult years" and for educators "a time of considerable if not extreme stress."[86]

Sigerist also suffered during this period, although his political position was no more than that of social democracy. From Sigerist's autobiographical writings,[87] which unfortunately are not matched by comparable diaries from Stern, one learns what it was like to have the kinds of opinions they had in the 1930s.

Without similar autobiographical materials, we can only make inferential comparisons with Stern. We know their views were similar. On the other hand, Sigerist came to the United States as an international authority on the history of medicine, to a chair established by the beloved William Welch at Johns Hopkins when that school was at the zenith of its prestige as the model of American medical education. Therefore, his position was the opposite of that of Stern, who worked mainly for others and never with the protection of a secure academic position.

As the American reaction against left-wing values intensified after the war, Sigerist and Stern took different paths. Sigerist returned to Europe; Stern remained in New York to face what must have been the most difficult trial of his life—a demand from the Senate McCarron Committee and later from the McCarthy Committee to Columbia University that he should be fired as a "danger to the security of his country." Sigerist, it must be noted, denied what many of his friends believed, that he left the United States because the attacks on him became intolerable. Characteristically, he expressed some guilt about leaving under fire, expressing his anger at the opposition and the wish to stand and fight.

Nevertheless, Sigerist was honored by the American academic community as he was leaving. He was swamped with invitations; there were nine banquets and testimonials in May 1947, the month before he left, then fifty-six years old, to work full-time on what he regarded as his most important life's work; and only poor health cut short the eight-volume history he had planned.

For Stern, there was quite another fate—the attack from the McCarthy Committee in 1953. Unfortunately, popular belief is actually very different from the true facts.[88] Stern *was* charged with being a security risk, and the officials of Columbia University conducted a hearing on the charges. No action was taken, but there was also no public statement. Among Stern's friends, one finds today a residue of bitterness about this episode. Many feel that Stern was either attacked or left "to swing in the wind" by his colleagues. Neither is true. Stern was granted a special hearing by a committee of faculty. Although Stern himself was the main witness at the hearing itself, he was joined by the executive officer of the Sociology Department, who had prepared a lengthy analysis of his professional work and career. At the end of that meeting, a report was made to the president of the university, and the final outcome was that the university authorities wrote to Stern, congratulating him on his scholarly achievements and the integrity of his teaching as well as his scholarship. His appointment was renewed. In addition, the final judgment of the investigating committee was an eloquent testimonial to Stern and to the rights of academic freedom:

> Dr. Stern is not a member of or otherwise under the subjection of any group to which he has surrendered his intellectual freedom. Dr. Stern's unresponsiveness during questioning by Congressional committees is explicable on grounds that do not touch his integrity, though his wisdom in these circumstances may be debatable. . . . He accepts fully and without reservation his obligation to the community of scholars of which he is a part. That is, we believe that he is honest in his work, that his goal is that of impartiality and objectivity, both in his research and his teaching, and that the conclusions he draws are those dictated by his work and his own rational judgment thereon. Our estimate of Dr. Stern as an honest scholar and teacher rests in part upon our own impressions after three hours of very earnest

discussion with him. It rests even more firmly, however, upon the appraisal of his immediate colleagues in the Department of Sociology as reported to us by its Executive Officer. . . . In his estimation the entire discussion serves to confirm the Department's previously expressed opinion that Dr. Stern is an honorable as well as effective teacher and an objective contributor to the literature of his field. In his judgment we concur. We join in advising favorable action upon the recommendation of the Department of Sociology that Dr. Stern's appointment be renewed.[89]

This endorsement, sadly, was soon to become the basis of remarks by Robert K. Merton to the memorial meeting at Columbia University of November 26, 1956, four days after Bernhard Stern died at the age of sixty-two and barely three years after the challenge to his loyalty at Columbia.

In both cases that have been reviewed here, L. J. Henderson and Bernhard Stern, the ideological passions of the time tested the values of the academy. Objectivity was challenged by advocacy from forces both within and outside the university. Henderson was attacked as a reactionary, Stern as a radical. Nor is this their special experience. Many others were similarly victimized. The basic point is that for Stern, as was true for others, myths were propagated and persisted regardless of the available facts to the contrary—myths that fit the heroic stereotypes of the radical dissident. The myths were unnecessary; the courage and honesty of Stern is secured by his work.

In the field of Stern's major contributions, the social history of medicine, what was his fate? Again, it is difficult to avoid comparison, especially with his friend Sigerist, whose method and perspective were so similar and who died within six months of Stern (March 17, 1957) also at an untimely age, sixty-five. Two types of answers can be offered to this question. First, concerning the perspective that both represented, both had failed to convince the field at the time of their death. As Reverby and Rosner write,

> [t]he history of medicine remained primarily intellectual history. In addition both the prevailing political conservatism and the lack of institutional support served to isolate those who were writing left social history. With the rise of McCarthyism in the post–World War II years, the left political import of the social history approach was stifled.[90]

There were fine scholars who carried on their work, but at least for another decade or more they worked in isolation and neglect from the growing field of medical sociology and, to a lesser but still notable extent, by social medicine.[91]

Other social historians[92] began their work in the period between the world wars. In spite of the excellence of their work, however, the social history of medicine remained for a long time a neglected approach in medical sociology. Nevertheless, after World War II, they and other individual scholars[93] continued their work, and at Yale University and Johns Hopkins longstanding traditions in the history of medicine were sustained. Freidson's very important study of the professions draws heavily on historical materials and methods.[94] Stevens, a student of Abel-Smith, has completed important studies of the impact of specialization and state medicine on medical practice in England, of American medicine, of Medicaid,[95] and of hospitals.[96] George Rosen continued research that dates to the early 1940s on public health in the United States and Europe.[97] Historical scholarship has contributed also to two very current social problems as they relate to health care, the poverty of minority groups[98] and the social and ethical implications of advanced technology.[99] Along the same lines of direct address to current health-policy issues, Reverby and Rosner (1979) have collected a remarkable group of essays in social history.

For Stern, however, the ironies persist. One might have thought that the emergence in current American sociology of a strong representation of the Marxist interpretation of society would include a revival of interest in Stern, but this is not the case. In basic works by Vicente Navarro[100] and in Waitzkin,[101] two of the major Marxist writers in medical sociology and social medicine, Stern gets not a single mention. Among the other Marxist interpretations of medicine in the United States, the same gap is found.[102]

Summary Discussion: Medical Sociology before 1940

In its earliest origins, what we now call medical sociology is part of public health and social medicine. The intellectual history of the eighteenth and nineteenth centuries tells us that the effort to understand the relations between social factors and medicine was always a continuing presence within medicine. The tension between explanations that focused on the biological on the one hand or on the psychosocial on the other was also always there. The tendency for interest in social factors to become greater during periods of social and political conflict and change caused such tension only to become deeper. As a result, public health/social medicine has a long history of identification with radical political movements. For physicians, to identify more closely with what is called "the social science of medicine" was often confused by more conservative members of the profession with "socialism" a political movement that was developing at the same time.

The sciences basic to biomedical knowledge advanced so swiftly in the latter half of the nineteenth century that medicine as a profession was transformed. The social sciences also developed at this time, though at a slower pace. The effects of this dual development were highly significant for social medicine. As Rosen writes,

> [t]he concept of social medicine could become more precise only with the advance of medicine and the development of social science. One cannot emphasize sufficiently that *social medicine rests equally upon the social and the medical sciences* [my emphasis]. Anthropology, social psychology, sociology and economics are as important for this field as the various branches of medicine.[103]

In other words, the development of both social medicine and medical sociology as continuous institutionalized intellectual activities required the convergence of their growth patterns. In the period between the world wars, this convergence began to occur. The context was "a crisis in medical care" that was, in its outlines, not unlike the crisis in the United States health care system of today—a crisis of cost, of the distribution of professional manpower, and of equality of access by social class and minority group status.

It would seem paradoxical that this crisis developed within a situation in which the United States possessed an abundance of physicians. At the beginning of the twentieth century, there were more physicians in the United States in proportion to the population than "had ever existed anywhere before at any time."[104] In contrast to Europe, where a distinct two-class system of medical care was rigidly established—the wealthy had private doctors and the masses had "poor" doctors—everyone in the United States could have a personal physician, and most did.

Beginning in the 1920s, the scientific revolution was used to change this situation. Medical schools in the United States became scientific and laboratory oriented; they became selective and much more costly, educating far fewer doctors; and their graduates became increasingly specialized. One of the results of this combination of technological expansion and manpower contraction was the increased cost of medical services, exacerbated by increased demands. Within this cycle, access to medical services was curtailed for the working classes and the poor. The paradox, in other words, was that out of a situation of abundance, both in knowledge and in skilled manpower, there grew a crisis of shortages—of manpower, of services, and of finances.

The paradox deepens when the trends of health indicators for the general population are taken into account. During the first half of the twentieth century, the average life expectancy of U.S. citizens was dramatically increased: it almost doubled. Epidemic and infectious disease were reduced: in 1900, when the population of the United States was 75 million, over thirty thousand people died of infectious disease, but in 1953, with a population at 160 million, only nine thousand did. Recent analysis shows that these advances were essentially signs of the triumph of social medicine and public health. It was in the improvement of conditions in life, both through effective public and preventive health and in better standards of living, that the general health of the public improved.[105] Ironically, however, the "crisis," as it was perceived, only grew more intense. The most accepted explanation attributed the problem to the changes in the prevailing pattern of disease prevalence and incidence, coupled with changes in basic social institutions, especially the family, caused by the Industrial Revolution. Silver, for example, explains the increased medical demand as follows:

A staggering amount of responsibility shifts to the doctor. . . . Shifting from acute to chronic disease as major cause of death and disability results in increased demand for medical service quantitatively and qualitatively. The doctor has to see people who are less seriously ill, be prepared to do less in physical care, recognize more of socioeconomic aspects and look after psychological and emotional aspects, prevent disease at interval stages, and restore the patient to relative social usefulness. The role is more complex, more demanding, and advisory as well as therapeutic.[106]

Put in another way, as the science and technology of medicine became effective for the control of the major diseases of the nineteenth century, especially tuberculosis and the communicable diseases of childhood, a new pattern of health care, dominated by cardiovascular-renal diseases, malignant neoplasms, accidents, and psychosomatic diseases, was introduced. To manage the advanced technologies as well as the changes in health care, problems of social organization both of the medical profession and in methods of health care delivery became more visible and critical.

For closer association to occur between sociology and medicine at the time would seem to be only logical because sociology, by definition in actual practice, was focused on the study of social structure, social behavior, and their consequences. Out of the earlier close liaison between sociology and social reform and consequently with social work, the young discipline had focused its attention on poverty, racial prejudice and discrimination, and urbanization's effects on the sense of identity among its mobile new populations.

At this point in their history, however, a different order of association begins between social medicine and sociology. The episodic, discontinuous course of social research disappears, only to be replaced by tensions of status and legitimacy.

In their earlier historical experience, social science and social medicine were unable to join hands in common purpose *consistently* in the study of social factors in health and illness. There was a logic to such partnership that periodically brought the two together, but their love affairs were never sustained in a lasting marriage.[107] The problems, to extend the metaphor more precisely, might be compared to those that so commonly beset lovers who come from disparate types of families and whose unions are called "intermarriages." Social medicine was, after all, heir to a higher class of the professions than was nouveau, upwardly mobile sociology. Moreover, social medicine could always "call on" sociology when it wanted. Why marry? In truth, as I have shown, the field of public health and preventive medicine, parents of social medicine, periodically pulled back from their liaison with social science, preferring an emphatically biomedical orientation.

When, however, social science, and more particularly, sociology, became established as a discipline, the possibility of a closer association—the "marriage"—with social medicine became more attractive. Then indeed they began to work together consistently. The time was in the early decades of the twentieth century. However, the medical world they faced together was more technologically developed, more biomedical in its prestige-orientation than ever. Social medicine and sociology were together "against the world," as it were. At the same time, sociology (the "wife"?), feeling the thrill of its own independent growth, became dubious about being the subordinate partner. The tables turned. A newly legitimate sociology was willing to "use" medicine as a subject to test its own growing science, but, at the same time, its independent status *as* a science was more prestigeful a goal than the secondary "applied" status of research handmaiden to medicine. Reinforcing this tendency was the research university, which, by 1920, had become the established home for most sociological work, where the focus was on the academic goal of developing knowledge and therefore on theory and basic research. Within this situation, health and illness became only one among several social problems that the new discipline chose to test its more generic theoretical conceptions. In the process, sociology claimed a separate identity, separate from two of its major professional alliances of the past: social work and social medicine.

For medical sociology, the period between the two world wars produced two types of social inquiry dealing with medically related problems. The first continued an association with public health that was rich in precedents from the past, with the work of Michael Davis, Edgar Sydenstricker, and Bernhard Stern as the best examples. These were sociologists who were involved in the world of medicine, working side by side with medical counterparts, committed not only to their academic inquiry but to playing an active role in making medicine as an institution work more effectively for the society. Unlike those sociologists who preceded them, however, they directly played important roles in establishing the groundwork of the new intellectual activity that would be called "medical sociology." The second type of sociologist was identified primarily with general sociology: medicine was merely a reality-source for gaining theoretical understanding of social behavior and of society. Major examples of the latter type were Talcott Parsons, Robert E. L. Faris, Warren Dunham, W. I. Thomas, and Edward Sapir. Both types shared a pioneering role in establishing the theoretical foundations of medical sociology.

The intellectual origins of medical sociology were complete, in every important respect, by 1940. Put another way, the substructure of the discipline's "cognitive identity" was established, even though there were no signs yet that any visible awareness existed among sociologists about a distinct subfield concerned with the sociology of medicine. To be sure, there were those, especially in social medicine, who conceived of medicine as a social science; but essentially for those sociologists who studied the problems of health and illness—and they were many and prominent members of the field—the major concern was to advance the knowledge of sociology and to test the rigor of its research methods. The general pattern of development for medical sociology's intellectual origins, therefore, follows that of its parent field.

More specifically, the antecedents of medical sociology contain the following distinct characteristics:

1. The discipline was, like sociology itself, dominated by the Chicago school, or what has been called the "mosaic of Chicago science." This was evident not only in the discipline's early theoretical conceptions of social epidemiology and of the interpersonal basis of mental disorder; it was also reflected in the development of both quantitative and qualitative methodologies of research.

2. At the same time, studies of social behavior in medical relationships were at the heart of the emergence of social system theory in the 1920s. As the domination of Chicago sociology yielded to Harvard and Columbia at the end of the period between the wars, the structural-functionalism of Parsons and Merton became the guiding paradigm of both sociology and the newly emergent subfield of medical sociology.

3. The social crises of economic depression and approaching war in the 1930s were stimuli to strong voices of political radicalism within sociology. Bernhard Stern, for example, was an outspoken Marxist whose pioneering socioeconomic histories of medicine were outstanding. However, despite the strength of Stern's appeal to the field of social medicine, his theoretical contributions were buried in the conservative political reaction of the post–World War II period.

4. The medical crisis in the 1920s, so modern in its general contours, produced two remarkable interdisciplinary efforts that established for sociology an active role as expert consultant to the federal government: first, the Committee on the Costs of Medical Care, and second, the President's Research Committee on Social Trends.

5. Parallel with and closely related to the importance of the research university in the growth of American sociology is the role of the private
family foundation. Several foundations marked the sociology of health
and illness as a field for their special interest. Foremost among these
were the Russell Sage Foundation and the Milbank Memorial Fund. The
Laura Spelman Rockefeller Memorial Foundation also played an important early role, especially in the fusion of psychiatry and social science
that was achieved around the work of Harry Stack Sullivan.

World War II served as an interruption but also as a stimulus. It became the
marking point for increased drive in the history of medical sociology. Indeed, it
is the point of origin for the first steps toward the formation of medical sociology's
social identity—its formal institutionalization as a field.

____ PART II ____

MEDICAL SOCIOLOGY,
1940–1980

6

First Steps toward
Social Identity

Effects of the War and
Its Aftermath on Medical Sociology

Introduction to Part II

The substantial intellectual and methodological foundations for a sociology of medicine that had accumulated by 1940 did not immediately spawn an identifiable special field. Even the name "medical sociology," in spite of its appearance at the end of the nineteenth century,[1] disappeared, and exactly when it surfaced again is obscure. Nevertheless, the subject matter began to be taught, in the thirties by Bernhard Stern at Columbia, in the early 1940s at the University of Chicago by Everett Hughes and by Leo Simmons at Yale.[2] Research on medical problems was part of the generally enhanced role of sociologists in the Second World War, and several of the field's outstanding pioneers trace their entry into medical sociology to wartime research.[3]

Development in the postwar years began slowly until formal organization as a subspecialty began in 1955 with an ad hoc group called the Committee on Medical Sociology of the ASA.[4] Despite the prominent role of sociology in the war—in the Research Branch of the army's Information and Education Division under Samuel A. Stouffer, in the War Relocation Authority and the Foreign Morale Analysis Division under Alexander Leighton, in the Wartime Communications Research Project under Harold D. Lasswell, and in the Foreign Broadcast Monitoring Service run by Hadley Cantril—the first steps were very modest, even uncertain. When the war ended, almost all the social science research programs of the government were disbanded.[5] The researchers themselves returned to the universities, and included among them were those who would be the future pioneers of medical sociology.

Yet by 1965 medical sociology had become one of sociology's most active subspecialties, and it continues to be so today. The Medical Sociology Section of the ASA averages close to eleven hundred members, one of the largest numbers of any section. The *Journal of Health and Social Behavior,* originally published privately, is now an official journal of the ASA in its forty-second volume.[6] Special activities of the section have attracted financial support from the Milbank Memorial Fund, the Carnegie Foundation, and the Robert Wood Johnson Foundation. At the same time, in the universities, federal support was directed to health-related sociological research. Beginning with the National Institute of Mental Health (NIMH), eventually a wide range of agencies joined the effort, including the National Center for Health Services Research (NCHSR), the National Institute for Child Health and Development (NICHD), the National Institute on Aging (NIA), the National Institute on Drug Abuse (NIDA), and others. Once support for the research activities was established, large sums of money were committed to recruit and train medical sociologists by means of doctoral and postdoctoral training programs.[7]

It is also clear from a spate of recent textbooks that the teaching of medical sociology is established as part of the standard undergraduate college curriculum,[8] and, in medical education, the Behavioral Science Committee of the National Board of Medical Examiners has consolidated the legitimacy of medical sociology as one of the basic subjects of medicine. By all the criteria that Shils and Ben-David describe for the institutionalization of an intellectual activity, therefore, medical sociology qualifies.[9]

What were the forces that produced medical sociology as a specialized field at this particular time in history? Why was it successfully able to develop a continuous institutional history when earlier spurts of activity and promising beginnings were aborted after episodes of national crisis passed?

More important than the slow pace of development during the decade immediately following the war was the continuity that was sustained with the intellectual patterns of prewar research on the sociology of medicine. In addition to the major prewar domains of inquiry (social history of medicine, social psychiatry, social ecology of mental illness, and the doctor-patient relationship as a social system), medical education conceived as socialization for the profession became a major new problem for inquiry.[10] At the same time, new roles for the sociologist appeared in medical settings, as teacher and research collaborator with physicians and as consulting advisor in medical organizations. The latter were the sociologists *in* medicine, identified by Straus as distinct from the sociology *of* medicine.[11]

Until 1960, the support for these activities came mainly from private foundations, and the most active site was the university. Among the groups within medicine who were sociology's most welcoming hosts, psychiatry was foremost and public health–preventative medicine a close second. At that point a discernible favorable shift occurred in both financial and organizational sponsorship, resulting in accelerated development of both research and teaching. The preparation for this shift during the first two decades of medical sociology's institutionalization, 1940 to 1960, will be the focus of this part of the story.

In 1942, Franklin Ebaugh, a prominent psychiatrist and medical educator, published (with his collaborator, Charles Rymer) a nationwide survey of psychiatric teaching in medical education.[12] Psychiatry during the 1930s had just begun to establish a place for itself in American medical schools, and Ebaugh provided a valuable assessment of its current role, with guidelines for the future. The Ebaugh-Rymer report was only the first of what would soon be a continuing series of surveys and reports about medical education in the United States. After thirty years of using the Flexner report as its blueprint, medical education began again to review its purposes and methods. It was still too early, however, for public or professional awareness of medical sociology. No mention was made by Ebaugh and Rymer of any role for social or behavioral science in either psychiatry or elsewhere in medical education.

In public health and preventive medicine, the situation of sociology in 1940 was similar, despite the fact that their prior liaison had been so close: social science was utilized episodically, as needed for research purposes only. In part, this must have been influenced by the experience of public health in its own role within the medical profession. At a time when specialization was medicine's watchword, the field of public health—or, more broadly, "social medicine"—was slow to gain acceptance as a medical specialty. While thirteen specialty boards were constituted during the decade preceding the war, it was not until 1948 that the American Public Health Association and the AMA Section on Preventive and Industrial Medicine were brought together to form the American Board of Preventive Medicine and Public Health.[13]

Within ten years, however, the situation changed dramatically. When the AAMC began its annual series of teaching institutes in 1951, the social sciences were not only included but given a prominent place.[14] One notes, however, that medicine preferred to invoke the social sciences by other names; in the case of the first AAMC Teaching Institute, Norman Cameron used the term "human ecology":

> We are today witnessing an expansion of undergraduate medical teaching into areas which, two or three decades ago, would have been regarded as the provinces of social workers and visiting nurses, but not of physicians. Progress has been made in the scientific study of *human ecology* (the interaction of human organism with human environment), and of *personality* (the characteristics of human organisms resulting from this interaction) which compares favorably with the progress of physiology during the nineteenth and early twentieth centuries. There has gradually emerged, out of the empirical, experimental and field studies in anthropology, psychology and sociology, a large and systematized body of immediately useful knowledge which is steadily growing. . . . The role of the physician in contemporary American society is coming to require more and more that he become thoroughly familiar with the systematized knowledge concerning human ecology and personality, and that he gain at least an elementary understanding of the scientific methods used in gathering and validating data in this area of human biology.[15]

Human ecology did not catch on as a name, but "behavioral science" did. The content, however, was the same, based on the fields of sociology, anthropology, and psychology as they applied to issues of health and illness.

The second AAMC Teaching Institute, "Preventive Medicine in Medical Schools," at Colorado Springs, restated the message of Cameron, with an emphasis on "comprehensive care." The proceedings concluded that

> a physician must consider the variety of factors which bear on health, not just those of organic disease or impairment, [and] must understand each patient as an individual, taking into account his ambitions, his feelings, why

he behaves as he does. Similarly, it is necessary that the physician know how to evaluate the effects of a patient's way of living, his habits, his family, his job or other factors in his life as they bear on health.[16]

By these and other quasi-official endorsements, the inclusion of social science was mandated for medical education at midcentury. It was a propitious time. The war had catapulted all academic institutions into rapid expansion. The depression-inspired decision by the medical profession in the midthirties to cut back on health manpower training was reversed, setting off an immediate acceleration of training the skilled manpower needed for the military and, in effect, a thirty-five-year process of unprecedented growth for medical schools and education for all the health professions. The war also meant that the social sciences were swept into the general wind pattern of intensified government-science collaboration whereby research and development of all types became a watchword of modern war.

The emergence of medical sociology, however, was not without obstacles. The close liaison with public health and preventive medicine, for example, that had been so promising between the wars was undermined by the postwar reaction against a "social medicine" that was confused with "socialized medicine."

Thus the new respect for the "basic sciences of behavior" was focused in academic medicine, and psychiatry became its conduit into the teaching centers. The role of sociology in medical care was more problematic.

The Wartime Experience

The war was an interruption as well as a stimulant to both sociology and medicine. What appeared to be well-established patterns of development in the organization of health care delivery, especially those recommended by the CCMC and the Ogburn Committee, were critically interrupted, and some incipient changes lost their momentum entirely. For the research that was so rapidly creating medical sociology's "cognitive identity," the opposite was the case: social research expanded, as the war raised new kinds of questions. For higher education generally and medical education in particular, the effects of the war were more radical, shaking the premises at their roots.

For medical sociology, the war strengthened those aspects of its growth that were academic, both in the university more broadly and in the medical school specifically, and at the same time weakened its ties with social medicine, especially in the active public effort to reform the delivery of medical care. During the next two decades, the major thrust in the institutionalization of American medical sociology was in research and teaching roles. Paradoxically, this was the time when "action research" had achieved an accepted place in policy decision-making, and social research on health would seem to fit more into the action pattern than the academic. How can this be explained?

In their history of the development of applied sociology, Paul Lazarsfeld and Jeffrey Reitz write that when World War II broke out in 1939, social research activities, by then, had become "so ubiquitous that the government turned to social researchers almost as a matter of course. In one federal office, the Department of Agriculture, sociologists had played a major role for quite a while, particularly with respect to the land-grant colleges, whose specific task it was to improve the life and work of farmers. But once the United States entered the war, new moves followed, at first slowly and then with almost explosive rapidity. In 1939, Roosevelt began cautious support of the Allies through Lend-Lease and similar policies. The country was in no way united behind this effort, and apparently the president watched public opinion polls rather carefully. Hadley Cantril had left Princeton University to head a special opinion research agency, originally financed by Nelson Rockefeller. . . . Cantril tells of several instances of how he provided the Executive Office with information on public opinion here and abroad. At the same time, the United States Army was greatly enlarged and took the unprecedented step of creating a Division of Research and Information."[17]

Lazarsfeld and Reitz go on to describe how, after Pearl Harbor, all government agencies became involved in large-scale social research activities. "The Office of War Information concerned itself with civilian morale; the Armed Services worried about training soldiers; the overseas operations of the Office of Strategic Services tried to anticipate enemy moves." These were only some of the many agencies that called on the social sciences for help.[18] Although the full range of wartime social research has not been systematically documented, the record clearly shows that all the available techniques developed in social research were used: content analysis, sampling surveys, detailed interviews, laboratory experiments, group dynamics, and so forth. Lazarsfeld's conclusion about these activities is notable: "When the war was over it was clearly impossible to revert to the separation of sociology as an academic pursuit from the problems of governmental and private organizations. The convergence had become a fact."[19]

How then can one explain the academic direction in which medical sociology would move immediately after World War II? In part, this followed from the fact that medical education was one of the major early clients for the application of social research in the postwar period. Medical educators, concerned about the potential dehumanizing effects of scientific specialization, sought a method of better understanding the medical school as a social environment, whereas previously they had focused entirely on the individual medical student and his/her character and qualifications. There was, fortunately, a matching interest among sociologists who were studying the role of the professions in society. The principal scholars were two outstanding sociologists, Robert K. Merton and Everett Hughes, each of whom was primarily interested not in medicine as such but rather in adult socialization and the role of the professions in society. "Socialization for the profession" was to become one of the most important areas of inquiry in medical sociology.[20] Although such research was "applied sociology" in the sense that it was solicited with direct reference to important policy questions for medical educators, it also at the same time brought sociologists into the university medical school. This contact contributed to the creation of new roles for social scientists as teachers of medical students and strengthened the academic identity of the young subspecialty of medical sociology.

More direct applications to the practice of medicine, however, found a less favorable climate in postwar United States. For sociologists who were most directly involved in social medicine, studying and analyzing problems of medical care, the postwar decade became a dark period of trial and rejection. Scholars like Sigerist and Stern experienced their most difficult days. Although Sigerist, when he returned to Switzerland in 1947, denied that he was leaving because of the attacks that he suffered at the time,[21] there is no question that Sigerist and the field of social medicine generally were perceived, quite accurately in large part, as part of the political left and as such were stifled by the rise of McCarthyism in the postwar years.

The boom of academic sociology, and with it medical sociology, therefore, was balanced by the bust of sociology's role in medical care.

Sociology and Medical Care: The Background of Postwar Policy

As I have shown, the CCMC resulted in the first full-scale conception of a national health program for the United States. This was a high point of close liaison between social science and social medicine. However, the violent opposition by organized medicine to the CCMC's recommendations undercut sociology's role in social medicine.[22] Although the CCMC proposals were moderate and reflected the circumstances, needs, and perspectives of the times, the opposing view of the Committee's physician members prevailed. The latter advised the continuation of solo practice, fee-for-service payment, and continued leadership and guidance by the medical profession instead of group practice and prepayment; they were totally opposed to community, governmental, or other intrusions into the field of medical care, a view that was formally endorsed by the AMA. There was no effective counterbalance to the AMA at the time, and it appeared that the Committee's proposals would die.

The conditions of the national economy, however, saved the CCMC's work from the "innocuous desuetude" to which the *Journal of the American Medical Association* consigned it.[23] The severity of the depression revived the argument of need that was in the CCMC's report, but it also cast doubt on its recommendation of voluntary action.

The first emergency measures proposed by President Roosevelt included programs for the federal financing of medical care costs. They addressed the need to protect the society against the kind of insecurity that was highlighted by the depression, including the risks of wage loss and costs of health care arising out of illness. Roosevelt appointed the Committee on Economic Security to deal with these problems, and Edgar Sydenstricker and I. S. Falk were on the Committee's staff. In Falk's own words: "[We] recommended separation of income protection [through temporary and permanent disability insurances] from group payment of medical care costs, and proposed a broad national health program embracing both personal and community-wide health services, all of which was generally acceptable to the Committee."[24] Again, however, there was a mobilization of protest from those who defined these proposals as against their interests, the medical profession and the insurance industry particularly. They mounted a formidable campaign of protest to both the White House and Congress. Fearing that controversy about government-sponsored health insurance might delay or even block passage of the entire economic security program, some members of the Committee on Economic Security argued successfully for compromise. Therefore their preliminary report recommending a broad health program was given to Congress as a program designed only "for study." Without organized group support for these proposals, they were filed away.

I. S. Falk was the major government staff person who worked to keep alive the concept of a national health program. In 1936 an interdepartmental committee to coordinate health and welfare programs developed a new formulation of a national health program, and this was used as an agenda for the National Health

Conference in 1938. On January 23, 1939, a report and recommendations on a national health program by its technical committee were transmitted to Congress by the president in a "health security" message. The essential elements of these reports were incorporated in a bill by Senator Wagner of New York, the National Health Act of 1939. Extensive hearings were conducted about the Wagner Bill in the Senate, but, because of the intense conflict among opposing groups and what Falk reports as "persisting coolness in the White House," not to mention the increasing preoccupation with the impending war, the only result was a committee report and a promise of further pursuit.[25]

The campaign to accomplish federal legislation based on the recommendations of the CCMC continued. During World War II and in the immediate postwar years, the congressional discussions were focused mainly on the bills of senators Wagner of New York and Murray of Montana and Representative Dingell of Michigan, the so-called Wagner-Murray-Dingell bills. It is interesting to look at the evolutionary changes that successive proposals went through. The bill started with a national health program based mainly on federal assumption of responsibilities through grants-in-aid to the states, with wide latitude in implementation. However, there were two kinds of reactions, both in opposition to the bills: (1) The same groups that were in opposition from the beginning, such as the AMA, continued to oppose them even though they became more and more mild in their recommendations of change; and (2) the groups that were strongest in support in the first place withdrew as they saw the principles of change steadily eroded. Falk reports that it was clear from the results that the federal-state government programs of the Social Security Act, especially for public assistance and for unemployment compensation, caused fiscal and administrative confusion, "while the completely national old age and survivors social insurance was progressing smoothly."[26] The Wagner-Murray-Dingell bills successively increased their recognition of these results by incorporating proposals for national health insurance in the pattern of national social insurance instead of the earlier design of federal grants-in-aid to the states for multiple and variable state-by-state programs. The design of the programs developed in the Social Security Board was essentially the product of Falk and his staff. The bills themselves stimulated intensive national debates and consequently intensified organized opposition.

Roosevelt signified his support for the Social Security Board recommendations during World War II by including a recommendation of hospital insurance in his 1942 budget message. He did not vigorously press for these proposals, however, responding to the counterpressures from the AMA and others. President Truman, on the other hand, immediately upon his succession to the presidency in 1945, expressed his own strong support of the Wagner-Murray-Dingell bills in a health message on November 19, 1945, to Congress. This was followed with two other messages in 1947 and 1949, but he was not able to overcome the opposition, and the stalemate continued through his term in the White House to 1952.

It is worth noting that in those times of insignificant inflation nationally and moderate increases of prices and costs generally, medical care costs increased at rates far in excess of other costs. This is precisely the pattern that is causing so much concern today. Consistently, over the period from 1950 to the 1990s the rate of increase in medical care costs was substantially higher than that of the national inflation rate. Thus, the outlines of the problem that we face today were clear at least fifty years ago. The medical care system has steadily become more and more complex for providers and more and more frustrating to both urban and rural consumers. Demands for medical care and for quality assurances, Falk writes, were intensified while maldistributions of resources for care were becoming more pervasive and more inhibiting to receipt of care. The gap between the potential of medicine and its performance was widening.[27]

This was the situation in medical care during and immediately after the years of World War II. The pressure of fiscal and distribution problems intensified. There was a continuing rapid increase in medical knowledge and in the complexity and costs of its technology. At the same time, there was an increasing dominance of the medical care system by the providers themselves. Finally, and contributing particularly to the latter development, medical care financing was patterned mainly through a growing private insurance industry that provided open-ended financing of the providers linked to government responsibility for substantial portions of the cost.

For the leaders of the field of social medicine, especially scholars such as Sigerist and Stern, the years of the war and the immediate postwar period were particularly frustrating. All the evidence concerning the pattern of development of the nation's health care professions and services was in support of the projections made from their research of the twenties and thirties. Yet their recommendations were denied a hearing, not on the basis of the evidence but rather because they were labeled political radicals. Not only Sigerist and Stern but also men like Falk, Davis, and Sydenstricker and others who were not politically identifiable in the same way were also denied a full hearing of their ideas. The irrationality of McCarthyism swept most of the recommendations coming from social medicine into the same box and labeled it "socialism." What had been a promising growth in cooperation between social scientists and public health and preventive medicine physicians suffered particularly from this postwar reaction.

Psychiatry and Social Science

Between psychiatry and social science, however, relations were better. One reason was that the collaboration was much more recent. There were also no past associations with politically sensitive policy questions. Perhaps most important, the work they shared focused on basic research and teaching in academic settings. The circumstances that brought them together were strongly influenced by World War II.

As mentioned earlier, the experience with mental disorder during World War I dramatized both the extent of the problem and the difficulties of effective treatment. The experience in the Second World War was to be completely different. When admissions to neuropsychiatric services in World War II soared to one million, ten times the figures of World War I, they were treated with hope and with much success. Many of these men were able to return to duty and not a few to combat duty. By 1945, seven out of ten who were admitted for psychiatric disorder to military hospitals went home rather than to a Veterans Hospital.[28]

Moreover, much of the treatment of these men was given by physicians who had no prewar experience in psychiatry. Under the pressure of war, the crowded neuropsychiatric services were staffed by doctors who either learned at the elbow of a psychiatrist or in brief, highly condensed training courses. In this way, a forced educational process occurred within the medical profession. Doctors learned, in a way that was not yet available in most centers of medical learning, about the effective advances psychiatry had already accomplished, and, probably more important, many learned to view mental illness in a new frame of reference. The psychotic ceased to be the hopeless, "different" patient, and the neurotic was not just a malingerer, or "crock." Instead, emotional disorder came to be recognized as a threat to every individual just as physical illness was considered a danger to which all are susceptible. In addition, concepts of prevention were increasingly applied to mental illness.

Another lesson of the war was that it was understood that "cure" in the sense of removal of symptoms was not required for effective functioning in life situations. This was a way of thinking, of course, that had long been accepted for physical illness; for example, a person might have a serious chronic illness like arthritis or diabetes but continue to work and live "normally" within given limits. The war showed that many personalities thought to be unstable functioned surprisingly well in combat and under other stresses. Some neurotics gave good account of themselves in battle but were unable to stand those aspects of army life that so-called normals found less stressful—the regimentation, the discipline, the autocratic organization. In other words, mental sickness was not an absolute, either-or phenomenon. Both psychosis and neurosis came to be seen as the product of a complex set of factors. Among these, the individual's personality was critical but not sufficient in itself. Also significant were elements in his social experience, both in his life history and in his current definition of the social situation.

Each of these steps by the medical profession toward better understanding of its own psychiatric branch brought it closer to the social sciences. If a neurotic can function well under some life conditions and poorly under others, obviously his neurotic condition involves not merely a personality but a personality "in interaction with the patterned situation in which the individual behaves."[29] If most "normal" individuals may be assumed to have a "breaking point," then it becomes critical that we understand why, for example, the experience of combat was so much more stressful under certain social conditions and not under others. The spotlight of medical attention changed from a narrow focus on the individual; its circle widened to include the individual in interaction with his social environment, a proposition that had been well developed by the psychiatrist Harry Stack Sullivan and his social science collaborators.

While interest in the social psychology of the American soldier was emerging in the medical branches, it was already well established in other parts of the military. One of the unique and highly productive intellectual enterprises stimulated by World War II was the work of a group of social psychologists and sociologists working in the Research Branch of the Information and Education Division of the War Department.[30] The formation of this unit was actually accomplished against an explicit prohibition of Henry Stimson, the secretary of war. When the army's Intelligence Division planned a survey of the morale of combat soldiers in the army in 1941, Stimson ruled: "Our Army must be a cohesive unit, with a definite purpose shared by all. . . . Anonymous opinion or criticism, good or bad, is destructive in its effect on a military organization where accepted responsibility on the part of every individual is fundamental."[31] Fortunately, Stimson's directive, although never rescinded, was ignored, and the Research Branch was formed under the direction of Samuel Stouffer and allowed to conduct its many surveys. From these studies, the details of interaction between personality and social environment were charted in ways that were to prove useful to questions of mental health. For example, the researchers found a hitherto unsuspected loyalty and dependence by combat soldiers on the small group, the squad or platoon that was the primary focus of their participation in the war. Later, evidence collected by the Germans indicated that their soldiers, as different as their ideology was, behaved in much the same way. Their loyalties were less to the Nazi regime, it would seem, than to each other.[32] Feelings of sharing and belonging to such groups proved to take precedence for many over even their desire for personal survival. Thus soldiers who were evacuated with injuries often showed impatience to get back to their outfits, even though this meant return to an otherwise dreaded combat situation. Moreover, replacements in such groups found that they had to watch out for themselves while the "old-timers" watched out for each other with fanatical devotion and self-sacrifice. When removed from their original group, men not infrequently showed feelings of intense loss, rebelliousness, or worse, in spite of the fact that their replacement situation was much less physically dangerous than previously. "In general," a retrospective study concluded, "most soldiers required support from their immediate group in order to function effectively. And when their close ties were suddenly severed, many broke down."[33]

The kind of research that would soon be the special province of medical sociology was embedded within the work of such units as Stouffer's I and E Branch. Only later would it be recognized as special. Jack Elinson, for example, who became one of medical sociology's acknowledged major figures, speaks of his entry into medical sociology as an event "without choice or forethought" while he was a member of Stouffer's research group. He was assigned the task of surveying the morale of patients in three army hospitals. In a memoir, Elinson tells about the experience:

> It was the custom to keep military patients in hospitals until such time as it was determined that they were either too disabled for further military duty and were to be discharged, or that they would be returned to full military duty. . . . Unexpectedly, my survey showed that, as abhorrent as military service was, patients who would *not* be discharged were next highest in morale. The lowest in morale was the group for whom it had not yet been determined what their fate would be. . . . The uncertainty apparently contributed more to low morale than either severe medical disability or the certain knowledge that indefinite further military services was their lot even though most were unwilling soldiers—men who had been drafted for military duty in the most unpopular service—in the army.[34]

Even more surprising, Elinson found that men in the amputee wards were the most cheerful by far. The critical morale factor was certainty-uncertainty. Since the amputees knew where they were in relation to future service, they were, despite their mutilation, higher in morale.[35]

Elinson's study so shocked the policy-makers in Washington that he was called to testify before a military hearing of generals and colonels. Only twenty-four years old at the time, he records how it felt to be so held accountable personally for a piece of social research. Apparently, he passed the test because he was ordered immediately afterward to go overseas to study a variety of questions about solders' attitudes under battlefield conditions. A Washington columnist thought

differently, reporting that Elinson had been sent overseas as punishment for uncovering low morale conditions in army hospitals.[36]

Another wartime activity that was to influence subsequent research in medical
sociology was under the War Relocation Authority (WRA) with Alexander Leighton, a psychiatrist, as director. In the first Japanese relocation center in Poston,
Arizona, on Indian land in the Colorado River Valley, a social science research
unit was organized in March 1942. In this group, anthropologists like John Prov-
inse and sociologists such as Dorothy S. Thomas and Leonard Broom studied the
effects of varying social conditions on mental health. Leighton himself continued
to do similar research in the postwar period, pioneering the type of large community studies that, in the 1950s, preoccupied social psychiatry.[37]

Leo Srole, who was to be the senior investigator of the Midtown Manhattan
Project,[38] tells of a different kind of wartime experience that influenced his later
involvement in medical sociology:

> Through historical accident I was myself exposed to in-service experiences
> in programs that had the general philosophy and some of the methods
> which later evolved into what we now call community psychiatry. Classi-
> fied as a military psychologist in the U.S. Air Force, in 1944–45 I was as-
> signed to the staff of a rehabilitation hospital for "combat neuropsychiatric
> casualties." In nuclear form, the hospital's regimen for these men had the
> makings of a milieu-oriented, day-care center of a kind that has become one
> of the service pillars of contemporary psychiatry. Then, in the year imme-
> diately following [1945], I served as UNRRA Rehabilitation Officer in a Ba-
> varian Displaced Persons (DP) Camp for 6,500 recently liberated Jewish sur-
> vivors of Nazi concentration camps. Given their numbers, psychological
> conditions and the barren military barracks nature of the ex-Wehrmacht
> installation, it was my role to guide, coax, push and help these traumatized
> survivors to create a new and rehabilitative community of their own, with
> most of the institutions and agencies requisite to a normal population oc-
> cupying a normal residential environment. As a result of these rather spe-
> cial in-service experiences, I think I can say that my scientific interests in
> the development of community psychiatry are more than "merely schol-
> arly."[39]

These illustrations of the wartime experiences of people who later became
identified as medical sociologists need to be seen only as segments of the larger
story of sociology during the war. Many cases can be cited to show how wartime
social research established the efficacy of sociological inquiry for important policy issues. Only two brief examples need to be added to fill out the picture. The
first occurred early in 1944, when Hadley Cantril was a research advisor to President Roosevelt:

> The President was concerned that further bombing in Rome might upset
> American Catholics. The research group decided to ask a previously se-
> lected sample group this question: "If our military leaders believe it will be
> necessary to bomb Rome, but take every precaution to avoid damage to its
> religious shrines, would you approve or disapprove this decision?" Al-
> though Catholics disapproved more often than Protestants, two-thirds of

them nonetheless did approve. Cantril reports that two days later, railroad yards and airports in Rome were heavily bombed.[40]

Another case in which a specific policy question was addressed by wartime social research concerned the planning of the return of American troops following the German defeat.

> The soldiers could not be brought back simultaneously. Who then should have to wait behind? The army made a survey to see what the troops them-selves would consider fair. Should the wounded men precede those who had children waiting at home? Which should count more heavily, total length of service or actual combat experience? From the answers to such questions, the analysts developed a sophisticated point system which gave each soldier a potential score from one to eight. The higher the score, the sooner the man could leave. At the time of demobilization, the point system was explained to each member of the armed forces stationed in Germany. There seemed to be general agreement that the procedure ultimately avoided a great deal of potential friction, and it has recently been applied by the Navy in assigning personnel to ships.[41]

To end with these illustrations of relations between social science and policy-makers during World War II would be misleading, however; the consequences were not, by any means, always so favorable. The scientific findings sometimes were not utilized in such direct and rational terms. For medical sociology, this would repeatedly be a troublesome problem; therefore, one of the most interesting illustrative cases is inserted here. *The lesson was that decision-making can and often does ignore very clearly demonstrated knowledge when it conflicts with strongly rooted predispositions.* We are indebted to Lazarsfeld and Reitz for a full and fascinating description of this case.[42]

Policy–Knowledge Conflict: An Illustrative Case

Between the Civil War and World War II, the U.S. army maintained a rigid policy of racial segregation. Negro units (as they were called then) were rarely assigned to combat duties, with the official explanation couched in terms of morale and military efficiency. The argument was that any attempt to integrate Negroes into white units would undermine morale among the white troops and might even lead to violence. In addition, official explanations were not above claiming that Negroes were inferior fighting men and better suited to service roles within the military. As Dalfiume documents, these ideas constituted well-established doc-trine in the military.[43]

When the Army Research Branch began to study this problem during World War II, the initial surveys seemed to reinforce some of the basis of army segre-gation doctrine. Surveys showed that the majority of black soldiers were opposed to segregation on principle, but as many as half of them accepted it as a "practical necessity." At the same time, 90 percent of the white soldiers approved of seg-regation. The social researchers, however, pointed to previous studies that dem-onstrated that attitudes do not always predict behavior, arguing thereby that gradual desegregation would "not necessarily" be met with violent resistance from whites. Army officials, nevertheless, chose to emphasize the 90 percent approval by white soldiers of segregation, reasoning that if segregation was abandoned, it would be a blow to morale. They also feared the possibility of conflicts while arguing that Negroes would accept segregation in the army because they were accustomed to it in civilian life. As Lazarsfeld and Reitz concluded: "The findings had little effect on anyone, because they could so easily be interpreted as consistent with the rationale for practically any policy position."[44]

Later in the war an opportunity arose to conduct further research on this question. A shortage of white infantry replacements after the Battle of the Bulge was made up with platoons of black soldiers who volunteered for the previously all-white companies in the European land war. Thus a living experiment was created, which the Research Branch studied, concerning the desegregation problem. Rather surprising findings emerged. "The experience of desegregation produced a favorable rather than unfavorable change in the attitudes of whites toward blacks in the Army."[45] "White men of the integrated units had experienced a profound change of opinions toward Negroes. Whereas only a third of the white soldiers had expressed a favorable opinion of having Negroes in their companies before this experiment, afterward 77 percent said they had become more favorable and none said they were less favorable.[46] A similar improvement was found in the attitudes of the officers and sergeants in integrated units. "Of the white officers, 84 percent of the white sergeants said that the Negro soldiers in their companies performed well in combat. Only 1 percent of the sergeants and none of the officers said they did not do well."[47]

The attitudes of men in integrated units contrasted sharply with the attitudes of men in divisions not participating in the experiment, 62 percent of whom opposed the inclusion of Negroes in their units.

One would expect that the results of this real-life experiment and the careful, data-based analysis by the social research unit could not be denied by army officials. Nevertheless, the official reaction tended to reflect the basic opposition to desegregation that had existed before. Army officials rejected the study as based on an experience that was "only an experiment that proved little."[48] The study itself was criticized by general officers as being biased. Further, one general officer argued that findings could not be transferred between emergency and nonemergency situations. "The report is based upon opinions formed while the informants were in combat, and is admittedly limited to impressions received during such periods."[49] In fact, the experience and the study had little immediate effect on army policy. When the war ended, the Negro platoons were detached from their white units.

However, some members of the War Department, albeit a minority, persisted in proposals for integration. They used the findings of the army's research branch to urge a change in army policy. They were successful in convincing secretary of war Paterson to establish a board of inquiry, the "Gillem Board," to review research on Negro manpower in the military. This board interpreted the findings to support the concept of desegregation. Though their recommendation did not include complete desegregation, they proposed steps in the form of continuing experiments. For example, they suggested integration in certain kinds of assignments and in recreational facilities and equal opportunities for advancement within the military hierarchy. Off-duty housing, however, was to remain segregated. Full integration was proposed only as a long-term goal to be achieved at some unspecified date in the future. In other words, the Gillem Board struck a kind of compromise. In the opinion of Lazarsfeld and Reitz:

> This case study indicates that even when the gap between knowledge and decision is reduced and initial objections to a recommendation are refuted in subsequent research, changing a policy-maker's initial predisposition may require political action. In this case, certain groups within the policy-maker's organization already were predisposed toward integration. But their political effectiveness may well have been enhanced by the availability of strategic information which forced top authorities to keep the door open for possible policy changes.[50]

The Lessons of War

As medical sociology progressed, similar problems were encountered in the efforts to translate knowledge into policy. Much like other areas of social science, medical sociology increasingly has been assigned research questions that are policy relevant. Yet the resistance to utilization has often proved to be independent of the quality of the work. How then can one explain the rapid growth and acceptance of the field?

One can only speculate that a chain reaction was set off by the new interest in social science that grew out of the circumstances of the war. Medicine, on the one hand, became more respectful of its own subspecialty, psychiatry. Psychiatry, in turn, was drawn toward increased collaboration with social science, especially sociology, anthropology, and social psychology. The social sciences themselves were in the process of developing methods of inquiry and knowledge that converged with the needs of psychiatry and the health sciences more generally. Underlying these developments was a public sense of frustration at the irony of war. Instead of "making the world safe for democracy," the aftermath of hot war was the Cold War, which too often appeared to be a preface to nuclear obliteration. One explanation for the new faith in the sciences of human behavior is the hope that humanity's triumph over the natural sciences would be matched by new knowledge about psychosocial problems.

Some of this hope was quickly tempered by the Korean War. In that conflict, North Korea utilized advances in basic psychological sciences to brainwash prisoners, and thus demonstrated how new knowledge about behavior could be used to destroy as well as to heal. There was no longer any escape. The knowledge of social science became as crucial as that of atomic science because, ironically, the struggle to heal is thus impelled by the forces of destruction.

Sociology in the Immediate Postwar Period

When the war ended, sociology as a discipline entered what Lazarsfeld calls its third phase. In its earliest American origins sociology was close to social work and even in its impressive first steps toward quantitative methods of research was guided by the urgent social problems of the time: poverty, urbanization, and the cultural and racial conflicts that accompanied massive immigration and rapid industrialization. This was followed by a preoccupation with winning prestige and academic recognition for the work, a struggle "for an autonomous sociology." In the third phase "it was clearly impossible to revert to the separation of sociology as an academic pursuit from the problems of government and private organizations. The convergence had become a fact, though a troublesome one."[51]

In 1948 the Social Science Research Council sponsored a small conference entitled "The Expert and Applied Social Science." At this conference, some participants introduced the question whether "applied social research" was indeed a worthy activity. Lazarsfeld, a participant in the conference, reports that this started a continuing debate about possible role conflict and tensions. One position was that applied research is radically different from basic scientific work and therefore detracts talent and resources from true progress in the discipline. For Lazarsfeld, this was a false comparison with the natural sciences. Nevertheless it was a strongly held view and continues to the present day. Another question raised asked whether applied research automatically serves the prevailing system. This was a position that would be articulated by C. Wright Mills and become a basic tenet of radical sociologists.[52]

Medical sociology emerged against this background. While the depression of the thirties had momentarily halted the rapid growth of American universities, sociology was not severely affected. The Roosevelt administration built on the pattern begun by Hoover and the Ogburn Committee: it used more social scientists than any previous administration.

In this period sociological teaching was also expanded in the university, despite the constraints on the general growth of higher education from the depression. As Martindale described it,

[l]arge numbers of young people crowded into the universities because of an inability to find employment and with the assistance of the NRA, many young people, out of serious concern for what was happening to society, were turning to the social sciences rather than the humanities for orientation. The foundations were expanding their programs of social science research. Refugee sociologists from European totalitarianism were arriving on American shores and adding a new leavening to American social thought.[53]

All these growth forces came together in the mobilization for the Second World War. The war focused all energies, for the moment, on the military, but the momentum of prewar developments carried over into the postwar years.

For sociologists, as for most Americans, the war was a heady experience. After decades of essentially parochial preoccupations, when, intellectually, the United States was dependent on European social thought as the theoretical foundation on which to build, American sociology emerged from the war with new confidence in itself. All the major observers of the period agree on this point, but they also sound cautionary notes about its meaning. Lazarsfeld, as I have shown, talks about the "troublesome" nature of the convergence between academic sociology and government-sponsored social research. Shils and Gouldner also qualify their descriptions of the wartime and postwar experience of the discipline.

Shils, for example, credits the success of social science at this time to its appeal for those who feel "they must manipulate their fellow men" and not to its achievements. By the end of the interwar period, Shils explained, sociological research seemed to offer a more acceptable sort of information than casual experience and random and occasional reflection. For circles which thought that they must manipulate their fellow men and which believed in science as the instrument of manipulation, social research appeared to be an appropriate handmaiden. The results of social research, uncertain as they were, began to exercise and to gratify that fascination which psychoanalysis met earlier in the century. Sociology had actually come to be about human beings and their society, in an age curious about and sensitive to the nuances of motive and conduct and eager to know what went on behind the face of reason and respectability. The Second World War drew all these impulses together and intensified them."[54]

Despite his disclaimers about the intrinsic scientific achievements of sociology, Shils interprets its history during the thirties as one of positive intellectual development that continued after the war. The dynamic, for Shils, is primarily ideational, a rational growth of knowledge. The definition of social problems, he argues, was founded in theory by the effort to assimilate European thought and in research by the relatively untried but rapidly developing methodologies of the interview, the sample survey, participant-observation, and the study of life-history documents. The major American theorists of the time, for Shils, were Parsons and Harold Lasswell and the methodologists were Paul Lazarsfeld and Lloyd Warner. They accomplished the necessary steps for the extraordinary wartime and postwar growth of sociology.[55]

Gouldner takes a different view. For him, the important determinants are politicoeconomic. The Great Depression of the thirties is the prewar challenge, and American sociology is perceived as a defense for middle-class fears about the possible radical consequences of the social conflicts and demoralization caused by the depression. Parsons's theoretical synthesis is seen as an attempt to solve the crisis by means of a new moral commitment rather than by changes in economic institutions. In these terms, Parsons was opposed to the New Deal and welfare state reforms. The war eliminated such differences and created "an all-embracing national unity" in which the state could and did call on sociologists for the use of their technical skills "on behalf of the collectivity." As Gouldner continues, "[m]any sociologists began to be employed by the federal bureaucracy. American sociologists acquired a firsthand and gratifying experience with the power, prestige, and resources of the state apparatus. From that time forward, their relationship with the state was a closer one."[56]

Neither Shils nor Gouldner, however, credit the importance of the network of institutions, such as the National Bureau of Economic Research, the Brookings Institution, and the Social Science Research Council (SSRC), that developed outside the universities and that, between the world wars, accumulated much firsthand experience in coordinating the work of social scientists with the activities of the government. One can argue, as Lyons does, that these organizations were among the most significant sources of the expanded role of social science in World War II.[57] All three were products of the 1920s, although the Institute of Government Research, the main parent group out of which Brookings was born in 1928, was founded in 1910 as part of the Taft Commission on Economy and Efficiency.

The case of psychology in World War I can be seen as a model of the pattern that has been followed by both medicine and the social sciences in their increased participation in government. As Lyons has said, "[i]n retrospect, World War I seems to have been a rehearsal for World War II in its effects on social science as well as on other aspects of the society."[58] The First World War gave psychology the chance to play an important role in government. By that time in Germany and the United States, experimental psychology had accumulated forty years of development, and research had been conducted in most of the types of human behavior associated with modern psychology, including the development of intelligence tests. Knowledge and technique, however, were not enough; it was also necessary that links should exist between acknowledged and respected agencies of science to whom the government returned when problems were identified.

For psychology, the key link was the National Research Council (NRC) of the National Academy of Sciences. Founded in 1916, the NRC included psychology and anthropology as its only social science members. Lyons describes what happened:

> Psychologists had thus accumulated knowledge and techniques directly applicable to the problems of manpower selection and training that confronted the military services. But there remained the task of bringing these to the attention of the military authorities and gaining their confidence in what psychologists had to offer and what they could do. . . . When the military turned to the Council [NRC] for assistance in 1917, it found a Psychology Committee organized and acting in cooperation with more than a dozen committees of the American Psychological Association, each specialized in an area of psychology applicable to military problems.[59]

These committees, because of their legitimacy both in the professional association of the academic psychologists (the American Psychological Association) and in the NRC, were able to influence the military services through the psychologists who were directly appointed to military units such as the Office of the Army Surgeon General and the Office of the Adjutant General.

> They thus had enough external authority and internal influence to make their weight felt. Their major contribution lay in the field of intelligence testing—organizing an extensive program for the controlled testing of military troops, and devising the classic Alpha and Beta tests, which set a precedent for the wide use of intelligence tests after the war.[60]

Unfortunately, although such activities demonstrated the relevance of organized knowledge from the behavioral sciences to emergency government in time of war, little of the wartime structure was retained in the permanent government once the First World War was over. Precisely to serve such a function, the SSRC, the National Bureau of Economic Research, and the Brookings Institution appeared. Through activities such as the CCMC and the Ogburn Commission, social scientists maintained their links to the government. Only in the Department of Agriculture did the government become directly involved in a systematic and sustained use of research in the social sciences. Otherwise, policy-related sociology and social science more generally were dependent on private resources for the maintenance of their work between the wars. More than any other group, the Laura Spelman Rockefeller Memorial Fund, under Beardley Ruml's guidance and, as already mentioned, with Lawrence Frank as a major intellectual force, was the source of support. During the seven years of its operation during the 1920s, the Spelman Fund gave forty million dollars, and the SSRC, the National Bureau of Economic Research, and the Brookings Institution were its chief beneficiaries.[61]

It is important to note that the prewar domination of private foundation support was not unique to the social sciences. In both the biomedical and physical sciences, the situation was similar. World War II served as the stimulus for change in government relations with all the sciences. This was not only for the allocation of resources but also in the quality of the role itself. Prior to this time, scientists saw themselves in a separate role from public policy positions. In any contribution that their knowledge might make to policy, therefore, the scientists saw themselves not as policy-makers but as instruments of policy and thereby in a subordinate status. There were some doubts, of course, that "the complete independence of science from political issues and governmental support were . . . the best means of advancing science."[62] However, not until World War II were these doubts turned into a radical change of science-government relations. As Price describes it,

> [i]n its [science's] military application, it was no longer merely an instrument for the improvement of weapons at the request of the military planners; it was a source of independent initiative in the invention of entirely new systems of weapons, to which war planners were forced to adapt their strategies and diplomats their systems of international relations. . . . Even more important, political leaders no longer assumed that basic research would be adequately supported as a by-product of the system of industrial enterprise or private education; in the United States, where private universities were most jealous of their independence from political control, the federal government was called on to support, on a unprecedented scale, the basic research carried on in universities. . . . At the same time, scientists and scientific societies began to think of their role in society, not as one of detachment from governmental affairs and not as one of subordination to industrial managers and bureaucrats, but as one of responsibility for the nature of policies and of the institutional system in which science would be fostered and protected.[63]

These changes continued because the conditions were favorable. The physical sciences gained importance, undoubtedly from the implications of the atomic weapon. Large-scale government support in the fields of national defense and space exploration were joined by organizational innovations that made the government itself the research entrepreneur and scientists part of government. A variety of forms were introduced:

> the establishment of government laboratories, administered by federal agencies or under contract to private companies; the extension of the contract method in order to finance research, development, and analysis by industrial or university groups; and the creation of non-profit, government-financed corporations like the RAND Corporation and the Institute of Defense Analyses (IDA). . . . Organizations like the RAND Corporation and IDA have also been created by government agencies to deal with problems of urban reconstruction and social progress, including the Urban Institute and the Institute for Poverty Research. These semi-autonomous institutions, as

well as the university and private research teams that operate under contract, have then served to promote the growth of expert staffs within the federal agencies that make use of their work.[64]

For the social sciences, the end of the war saw no break in the extraordinary range of research that had grown during the war. Some of these activities continued in the government, but the extent of such activities did not keep up with the pace set for the physical and the biomedical sciences. Most social scientists returned to their universities after the war. Another difference was in the type of support. For sociology, and even more for medical sociology, dependence for research support continued to be on the private foundations. But the amount of such support was increased dramatically, and the pattern followed that of the older sciences, moving toward what would become after 1960 mainly government-sponsored research and training programs.

The social sciences, fueled by the general productivity of the American economy, followed in other ways the patterns of the natural and physical sciences. Confident after their successful utilization of team research during the war and armed with more potent research technologies, the return to the universities did not mean a return to the prior fashion of independent inquiries by essentially single investigators. There were four major changes, two in the organization of research approaches and two dealing with the demand and supply of sociologists. All occurred within the university setting:

1. Research became more complex in technique, requiring large bodies of assistants, with finances and administration to support them. The Russian Research Center and the Laboratory of Social Relations at Harvard and the Institute of Industrial Relations at Berkeley are adaptations that were made by university structure to accommodate to these changes.
2. The technique of the sample survey became the core around which specialized institutions were created, affiliated to universities but independently financed from contracts for market research, government contracts, and contracts with private and civic bodies. The best-known examples are the Bureau of Applied Social Research at Columbia University, the National Opinion Research Center at Chicago, and the Survey Research Center at the University of Michigan.
3. Universities expanded rapidly after the Second World War, partly to accommodate to the returning veterans but also in response to the belief that grew in the society that higher education should be available to everyone. As a result, there were more students studying sociology and therefore more positions available for young sociologists to join faculties.
4. To fill the new manpower market, a different type of cohort became committed to the teaching and research opportunities in sociology. Unlike the early sociologists, drawn mainly from old, established, and often clerical Protestant American families, those who entered the field at this time were largely second-generation European-Americans. As Shils describes them, "[i]t was the coming-of-age during the later 1940s and 1950s of a new generation, European in its intellectual attachments through nativity, as in the case of Professor Reinhard Bendix, or through a sense of affinity, as in the case of the young Jews who received a form of worldly education in the radical political movements of the late 1930s.

The latter were offspring of the Eastern European Jewish immigrants who had come to America between the 1880s and the First World War, and they had quite a different outlook from the generation of social scientists which had preceded them . . . Professors Lipset, Selznick, Bell, Gouldner, and Janowitz came from such immigrant families."[65]

The capital of American sociology had now definitely moved from the University of Chicago to the eastern seaboard. Harvard, after a late start, and Columbia University dominated the field. At both institutions, outstanding scholars in both theory and quantitative research worked in close harmony, so that students could become fluent in both. At Harvard there were Talcott Parsons and Samuel Stouffer and at Columbia Robert Merton and Paul Lazarsfeld.

Just as these two universities were the leaders of general American sociology, so did they also become centers of medical sociology as it began to be widely identifiable as a special field of study and not just the province of individual scholars. In addition, Yale became another outstanding early proving ground for collaboration between sociologists and physicians in research and, as a result, for the training of young scholars who would become the leaders among the second age cohort of medical sociologists. Drawing from their published work and from interviews, this narrative now turns to the story of medical sociology from 1945 to 1960.

7

Postwar Medical Sociology

The Founders at
Major Universities, 1945–1960

Virtually none of those who became the first generation of medical sociologists were trained in any formal way to study problems of health, illness, or the medical profession. This should not suggest that they changed direction when they became medical sociologists. Quite the contrary; there are strong continuities between their early and later work. The career of August B. (Sandy) Hollingshead is typical of this pattern. His first major research was a study of "Elmtown," a midwestern town.[1] The central theme was the influence of social class on the lives of its adolescents. When in the early postwar years Hollingshead turned his attention toward studies of medical problems, the design and methodology remained consistent with his Elmtown research but the focus became the influences of social class on mental illness.[2] Leo Srole was also the author of a community study, conducted before the war.[3] In his case, the central variables included race, ethnicity, and social class. Following the war, he joined hands with a community-oriented psychiatrist and led an interdisciplinary team in a study of mental illness.[4] For Srole, like Hollingshead, the perspective and methodologies that had been fashioned on a small town were later applied to a city. The change was in the dependent variable but not in the overall character of the sociology.

Hollingshead and Srole are one type of the first cadre of medical sociologists. There was also a second, somewhat younger, and less experienced group. Typically they too did not train in any conscious way to be medical sociologists. There were no specialized training programs established until 1955 at Yale,[5] so that only in the doctoral dissertation could any specific training occur, and very few were devoted to medical problems. This group was either totally untrained at the time of the war or were just starting. They, like the older group, clustered mainly at Yale, Harvard, Columbia, and Chicago. Among the outstanding examples are Robert Straus and Jerome Myers at Yale, Mark Field and Renee Fox at Harvard, Patricial Kendall and Mary Goss at Columbia, and Eliot Freidson, Blanche Geer, Howard Becker, and Rue Bucher at Chicago. An exception to this pattern was Jack Elinson, who was trained more than anything "on the job" as a civil servant and then in the army Social Research Branch in Washington and got his Ph.D. at Georgetown soon after the war.

Although each of these universities developed its own style, there were strong links among them. There was much going back and forth, both among the leading teacher-researchers and among the younger group. Between Harvard and Columbia, for example, the ties were strong between Merton and his former teacher Parsons and similarly between Lazarsfeld and Stouffer, continuing their wartime research relationship. Merton went to Harvard as a graduate student in 1931, when the Sociology Department was only in its second year, and he remained devoted to it throughout his career. When Merton conceived and directed his groundbreaking research on the medical school as the socializing institution of the profession, the conceptual paradigm was structural-functionalism, with strong continuities reaching back to Henderson and Parsons. Following the same pattern was Renee Fox. Trained under Parsons at Harvard in the immediate postwar years, Fox is one of the few early medical sociologists who wrote a thesis on the sociology of medicine. Her study of a Boston metabolic ward was an empirical inquiry framed in Parsonian theory,[6] and when she went to Columbia to join Merton in his studies of medical education, she continued in the same research model, contributing several articles that have become as well known separately as the larger work of which they were part.[7]

There are equally strong connections between Chicago and the new centers of sociology in the East. Stouffer is the outstanding case. After a small-town, midwestern boyhood (Sac City, Iowa), he began graduate work at Harvard in English, withdrew to work on his family's newspaper, and only then, as a graduate student at Chicago, entered his career in sociology. He received his Ph.D. in 1930; Chicago was his major base for the next decade, with short side trips, first to London to do postdoctoral work with the statisticians Karl Pearson and R. A. Fisher and also to teach at the University of Wisconsin. The quantitative research style of Chicago sociology found perhaps its outstanding expression in Stouffer, both during the war in the I and E Research Branch and at Harvard, where he went immediately after the war. His Harvard laboratory of social relations reflected strong continuity with the team research approach to sample surveys.[8]

Other migrants to the East from Chicago were Leonard S. (Slats) Cottrell and William Caudill. Cottrell was a colleague of Stouffer at Chicago who came east first to Cornell and then to the Russell Sage Foundation, where together with Donald Young and Esther Lucile Brown he helped to create and implement a policy for the application of behavioral science to fields of social practice. A postdoctoral training program for sociologists and anthropologists to work in medical settings was part of the Russell Sage program, and with its help some of the outstanding careers in medical sociology were started. Caudill, as a young anthropologist, went from Chicago to Yale, where he conducted studies first of a psychiatric ward and then of a hospital, conceived as a small society. Hollingshead and Srole too came from prewar training in Chicago to careers in the East. Srole did his Ph.D. with W. Lloyd Warner, finishing just before entering the service; and Hollingshead, also working with Warner, had a postdoctoral fellowship at Chicago.

The telling of this important part of the history of medical sociology through the biographies of its founders does not imply a "great man" philosophy of history. The role of institutions, of socioeconomic and political forces, and of the development of knowledge are considered the major determining factors. Neverthless, the full context of the postwar history with all of its varied texture is enhanced by the biographies of individuals like Hollingshead, Srole, Straus, and others who played prominent early roles.

Place and individual, however, are hard to separate. The method of telling, therefore, will be to group the lives according to the major academic environments during the period 1945 to 1960. For sociology as a parent discipline, most would agree that Harvard and Columbia were the main centers of this period. Yale, however, plays a unique role that is particular to medical sociology. Especially in training but also in some aspects of research, Yale programs pioneered in this new field.

Yale: Its Postwar Role

Three activities emerged at Yale during the postwar decade that were to have strong influence on the institutionalization of medical sociology. In 1948, the preliminary steps were taken toward the New Haven study of social class and mental illness, a body of research that was to have wide influence on both scholarship and public policy concerning mental health.[9] In 1950, work toward the creation of the first training program in medical sociology was started. In 1955, a Committee on Medical Sociology was formed, the first national organization for sociologists interested in the problems of health and illness. All these activities were started by Hollingshead, who came to Yale from the Midwest in 1947. He was by no means a lone figure, however. Leo Simmons had been teaching the sociology of health for at least ten years before Hollingshead arrived. In the psychiatry department of the medical school, Eugen Kahn had appointed Simmons to his faculty in the midthirties, and Kahn's successor Frederick C. Redlich was strongly oriented toward collaboration with social science. In addition, there was the Laboratory of Applied Physiology with its links to the Harvard Fatigue Laboratory and to Lawrence J. Henderson.[10]

It is not surprising, therefore, that Yale attracted a remarkable group of young sociologists, anthropologists, and physicians who were drawn into close collaboration and productive scholarship on the social aspects of health and illness. Included were such well-known social scientists as Robert Straus, Jerome Myers, Edmund Volkart, William Caudill, Albert Wessen, and the physicians Eugene Brody and DeWitt C. Baldwin.

These activities were a radical departure from Yale's traditions. The teaching of sociology at Yale began very early. The first formal course in sociology in the United States was taught at Yale in 1876 by William Graham Sumner.[11] The second president of the ASA (1907–8), Sumner is considered one of the "big four" of early American sociology, along with Albion Small, Lester Ward, and Franklin Giddings. Unlike the others, however, Sumner never quite accepted sociology as a discipline. He saw himself instead as a creator of the "science of society" and concentrated all his energies on teaching based on his own work. Yale became, for generations, more the center of Sumner's version of social Darwinism than a source of research for new sociological knowledge. Instead of graduate students to carry on the work of the field, undergraduate teaching was emphasized. When Sumner died in 1910, his successor, Albert G. Keller, devoted himself to completing Sumner's multivolume *Science of Society*, a pattern that was to define sociology at Yale without much change until the Second World War.

The Sumner legacy fit with the conservative, Ivy League environment of Yale, with its complex prestige system and differentiated separate schools. The prewar faculty was characterized by class lines, with the faculty of many departments inbred with their own graduates who controlled promotions and tenure and discouraged both "outsiders" and those whose interests strayed from what they perceived to be the basic disciplines. Attempts by programs such as the Institute of Human Relations, the Child Study Center, and the Center of Alcohol Studies to integrate the thinking, the research, or the teaching of several disciplines were accorded second-class status. A. Whitney Griswold, an early postwar president of Yale, was particularly aggressive in his efforts to strip the university of programs that he did not believe belonged to the classical discipline–oriented mold. It was in this environment that the attempts to integrate behavioral science in the medical school with medical sociology initially failed, and although the environment has changed, they have never succeeded. Nevertheless, and in spite of these barriers, there were some bridges built between the university's subunits, and one of these was by Leo Simmons.

Simmons, on first impression, followed very much the model of Sumner and other early sociologists. Born in Kingston, North Carolina, in 1897, Simmons went to Bethany College in West Virginia, a small but very old (1840) denominational institution run by the Disciples of Christ. From there he went to Yale Divinity School and received a B.D. in 1925. Attracted by the sociology of Sumner, who was also originally a minister, Simmons earned his Ph.D. under Sumner's disciple, Albert G. Keller, in 1931.

Simmons the sociologist, however, was deeply committed to ethnographic methods. Perhaps his best-known work is *Sun Chief*,[12] an oral autobiography of a Hopi Indian that Simmons recorded and edited. Following Sumner and Keller, this part of Simmons's work rested on the assumptions of social evolution. The anthropological approach was used for the descriptive analysis of primitive societies as examples of stages of evolutionary social growth.

Simmons was an unassuming, dignified man who fit into the personal style of the Yale faculty community. Whatever the reasons, he appealed to Eugen Kahn when the latter was appointed as the first full-time professor of psychiatry at Yale in 1928, even though their professional values, on the surface, were very different. Kahn came to Yale directly from Germany, where he was one of the last *privat-docents* of Emil Kraepelin (1856–1926), a widely respected neuropsychiatrist, best known for his focus on a simplified classification, or nosology, of mental disease. In a period when Freud's theories were radically altering the traditional neurological emphasis of psychiatry and when people like Harry Stack Sullivan were steering a course toward interpersonal psychiatry, Kahn resisted these new trends. As Eugene Brody, who was a resident physician with Kahn from 1944 to 1946, describes him, "Kahn was pragmatic and skeptical. His service was one of mixed neurology and psychiatry, viewed mainly in terms of genetic and organic factors."[13] "Everything," Brody adds, "was psychopathic personality . . . and was due ultimately to organic drives."[14] The one leavening element in Kahn's orthodoxy was his interest in the effects of what he called "person-in-a-situation," and he turned to Leo Simmons to represent that interest.

The setting in which Simmons participated was a weekly departmental conference. The manner is described by Brody:

He [Simmons] was a very quiet, grey-haired man at that time. He always sat at Kahn's right . . . obviously a favored person. Kahn regularly spoke of person-in-a-situation, and that was his recognition that despite his tremendous emphasis on organic driven-ness and the hypothalamus, etc. that behavior was a function of the context. . . . It was an awkward way of saying it, but it was there. Leo [Simmons] was gentle, he spoke with us, but my memory of him is that he was "academic." Somehow he did not get into it in the gutsy way that people I got to know later did—like Bill Caudill who became a very strong personal influence.[15]

It appears that Simmons's style, the soft-spoken, old-fashioned dignity, and unthreatening anthropological emphasis on simple cultures helped to gain him access to the Medical School at Yale. There he had impact on young physicians like Brody and DeWitt (Bud) Baldwin, both later to chair medical school departments that combined medical and social sciences.

There was another side to Simmons, however, which led him to be the sponsor at Yale of Bernhard Stern. Stern's approach, of course, was in radical contrast to the conservative politics associated with Sumner and Keller, but this did not stop Simmons from arranging for Stern to be a visiting professor at Yale in 1944. Moreover, it was Stern's books, especially *American Medical Practice in the Perspectives of a Century*[16] that Simmons assigned in his medical sociology courses. The association between him and Stern at Yale was part of what made Simmons stand out in all the available memoirs of medical sociologists who studied at Yale during the years surrounding the Second World War.

Robert Straus, for example, writing of his first year of graduate study at Yale in 1944, gives Simmons primary credit for stimulating his interest in medical sociology: "Leo M. Simmons introduced me to the excitement and fruitfulness of life history material, took me with him to conferences in the Department of Psychiatry, encouraged me to take anthropology courses, and later directed my dissertation."[17] This is one of the very early dissertations in the modern field of medical sociology. Entitled "The Evolution of Public Medical Services in the United States," it was completed in 1947. Straus's testimony to Simmons's influence is coupled with praise for Stern:

Of great significance was the influence of a visiting professor from Columbia, Bernhard J. Stern. I consider Stern the unchallenged "father" of medical sociology. Many years before "medical sociology" was seriously identified at all, Stern inspired excitement for the opportunities which the study of medical systems provided for testing and extending sociological theory and the ways in which social scientists could reinterpret the history, clarify the processes, and even predict the future of medicine, If ever a sociologist deserved more and received less recognition from his profession, it was Bernhard Stern.[18]

When asked how he first became interested in medical sociology, Straus pointed to the two courses he took with Stern in 1944–45; and to the question about what published materials, if any, influenced his decision to become a medical sociologist he replied: "I think I would have to say in complete honesty that only Bernhard Stern's writings in formal medical sociology influenced me, and maybe a little bit of Michael Davis."[19] At that time, Simmons had not yet written any important work on medicine.

Simmons, however, was the conduit for Stern's continuing influence at Yale. Because Stern was only there for so short a time, and Hollingshead, when he arrived on the scene, was very negative in his attitude toward Stern, it was Simmons who made Stern's (1945) book the "Bible of medical sociology" at Yale.[20]

From a wide variety of testimony, therefore, a portrait emerges of Simmons in the role of mentor who supported and guided many students. His low-key, modest personality may be the reason he is so seldom credited with the several important "firsts" that he contributed to the newly emerging field. His courses in medical sociology, like those of Bernhard Stern at Columbia, were certainly among the first formal courses taught on the subject. They appealed, as did Stern's, to young physicians as well as to sociologists and are vividly remembered by both. This appeal, it should be noted, was to a different type of physician from those who responded to Stern. The latter were policy oriented and largely from the field of public health, a group that became the cadre of the social medicine movement in the United States. Simmons attracted physicians who were interested in social science theory, drawn to the concepts of interdisciplinary work with psychiatry.

Simmons was also the first social scientist, as far as I have been able to tell, who received a formal appointment to the faculty of an American medical school. Odin Anderson, at about the same time, was teaching in a full-time position in the Department of Public Health of McGill University in Canada, but in the United States Simmons broke this new ground. More important, the effects on the young physicians he taught appear to have been substantial and lasting. Gene Brody, for example, later became director of the Institute of Psychiatry and Human Behavior at the University of Maryland, where he assigned medical sociology to a significant place in the teaching of medical students that has continued from 1959 to the present. "Through Dr. Simmons' regular participation in departmental conferences," writes Brody, "we were reminded that with or without a background of constitutional factors, the behavior pattern of psychiatric illness was not a static entity existing in a vacuum. It evolved, and the way in which it unfolded and changed was very much a function of the social and cultural context in which the patient and his family lived."[21] For people like Brody, after their concentrated preparation in the biomedical sciences, Simmons was especially effective in conveying the significance of culture for understanding behavior, including illness. Brody speaks feelingly about this:

> It [Simmons' teaching, especially from *Sun Chief*] did tell the young psychiatric resident how individual thinking, feeling, and acting is shaped as part of "a socially inherited web of meaning"—to use Clifford Geertz's phrase. But it also underscored the universal humanity, the commonalities that, with care and patience, can be discovered in the experience of members of a variety of cultures.[22]

Simmons also wrote the first of a series of books in medical sociology that were commissioned and published by the Russell Sage Foundation. Written in collaboration with Harold G. Wolff, a well-known medical scientist at Cornell Medical School, the book was designed as a statement of basic knowledge in the field at that time. It was called *Social Science in Medicine* and appeared in 1954.[23] More than just a book was involved, however. The Simmons-Wolff collaboration was the pilot project in a major new policy direction taken by the Russell Sage Foundation soon after Donald Young became its director in 1949. Young joined with Esther Lucile Brown to develop a program for the application of the social sciences to the practicing professions. Brown, who preceded Young at the Foundation by almost twenty years, had single-handedly created its department for the study of professions. She was herself a graduate of Yale and the first anthropologist ever to work at the Foundation. When Young arrived, she had already completed her own series of books, including studies of nursing, social work, dentistry, and medicine.[24] Her department, however, had been more ancillary than central to the Foundation's main orientation. With the advent of Young, it became part of the main thrust of the 1950s. The program actually outgrew the Foundation's own resources so that in 1955, Russell Sage became itself the recipient of a large grant from the Ford Foundation to continue and expand the application of the social sciences to the professions.[25]

As Esther Lucile Brown recalls the events of that time, Leo Simmons was one of her first contacts when Donald Young asked her to implement a program to demonstrate how behavioral science can be applied to fields of social practice. She had already, during the course of her own prior work, made an "enormous number" of contacts in the health field. Among them were the leaders of Cornell Medical Center, where Harold Wolff was engaged in studies of psychosocial aspects of stress and was interested in having a social scientist join him for both research and teaching. When Esther Brown suggested Simmons, however, there was some hesitation on two counts, first because Wolff worried about hiring someone who was already so senior in his field, and second because he insisted on an anthropologist. The resolution of this problem is best told in Esther Lucile Brown's own words: "There was a question raised by Dr. Wolff about the fact that Leo was so senior that they didn't know whether they could absorb him. It would have been easier, he said—this was just a preliminary discussion—to have had a younger person."[26] The fact that Simmons came from Yale was also mentioned. Obviously, this represented a commitment that Wolff was unsure about, and to bring someone from a high-prestige university with a senior reputation in the field added weight to the decision. Explaining how she convinced him, Brown adds: "I said to Dr. Wolff, 'Are you clear in your mind that you want an anthropologist rather than a sociologist?' And he said, 'Oh, very clear. I have tried reading Talcott Parsons. I get nothing from that. This is not what I want!' So we provided somebody who was both an anthropologist and a sociologist."[27] It was this dual qualification that apparently won over Wolff to appoint Simmons.

Harold Wolff was an insider in the highest levels of prestige at the Cornell University Medical Center. In a school that prided itself mainly on its reputation in basic and clinical biomedical research, Wolff was part of the top echelons. His choice by Donald Young as a starting point for collaboration with social science in health was deliberate. Young reasoned that it would be easy to introduce sociology where it was already wanted, in psychiatry and public health. The difficult part was to get the hard core of the profession to work with and accept the entry of such new approaches. "We could have placed a social scientist with very little effort in practically every school of public health and every department of psychiatry," recalls Esther Lucile Brown when describing this episode. The Russell Sage support of Simmons's work with Wolff, therefore, was a planned strategy. Donald Young, in his years as director of the Social Science Research Council, learned firsthand about the pitfalls of interdisciplinary professional relations.

Moreover, he was naturally a hardheaded practical man and a dedicated sociologist. He would not be satisfied to take the easier way, helping to reinforce already broken paths. He judged from his experience how sociology could make its strongest impact on medicine and set about to help make it happen. Simmons was part of one of his early tests to find the best method toward that objective.

The strategy appears to have been successful. The collaboration between Simmons and Wolff continued beyond the initial program, and their book was published just five years after their association began. Furthermore, the Department of Medicine at Cornell expanded its collaboration with sociology by joining with the Columbia University Bureau of Applied Social Research in what became one of the most extensive studies of medical education of the time. The latter resulted in the appointment of Mary Goss to the Cornell Medical School faculty, one of the earliest of such appointments and one of the most lasting: she continues today as a full professor, working together with George Reader.[28]

What is generally not known is that Simmons was not the link to Reader and Goss. In fact, the long-term association between the Department of Medicine and the Columbia sociologists came about completely independently of Simmons. It seems that Simmons, in spite of his previous record of trouble-free relations with medical colleagues, unwittingly upset the Cornell faculty. One of the latter reports:

> Leo Simmons had gotten into all kinds of trouble because he stood up and made a speech at a national meeting [of the Association of American Medical Schools] and gave forth his insights in the social structure of the medical school. . . . [This caused] a lot of paranoia about having a social scientist who betrayed you in your midst at that point.[29]

Apparently Simmons, despite his characteristically gentle and unthreatening manner, was unable to resist just the gaffe that was most feared from a social scientist who was allowed entry into hitherto privileged medical situations. For him, this was no more than the fulfillment of the anthropologist's responsibility—to see and tell. But for his medical hosts, it was something else. Fortunately there was no lasting damage at Cornell, but this was only because of the very careful and dedicated work of George Reader and Mary Goss. How they managed under these circumstances to launch at Cornell one of the most ambitious and successful early medical sociology projects will be told later. It bears noting, however, that this experience was not unique; there were many cases where the new relations between social scientists and medical educators/scientists were difficult, where each rubbed the other's feelings raw. The important point is that the general pattern of this relationship survived and grew. The source determinants for working together were stronger than the discomforts of encountering each other's unfamiliar ways of doing things or even poor judgment.

Another interesting footnote to Simmons's Cornell experience is added by Edmund Volkart, who later at Stanford became the key figure in an even more ambitious Russell Sage project to help sociology penetrate medical education. It concerns the book that was written by Simmons and Wolff.

Volkart was a young instructor in the Yale Sociology Department at the time. His recall is that the year was 1952. He had just published a book based on his dissertation, a study of the sociology of W. I. Thomas.[30] In the meantime, Simmons and Wolff had submitted a book manuscript to the Russell Sage Foundation.

Donald Young and "Slats" (as virtually everyone addressed him) Cottrell wrote to Volkart asking him to review and edit the Simmons-Wolff manuscript. A fee of five hundred dollars was part of the offer. As Volkart himself tells the story of what happened:

> The point of my story is that I worked on the manuscript all that summer . . . revised it, excised it, and wrote a lot of things in it. I gave it to Leo at the end of the summer, and I didn't hear from him for about six weeks. Later, he said: "What have you done to my manuscript?" He was hurt. I mean, here's this young whippersnapper just joined the faculty, and here Leo was a senior man and I was messing up his manuscript. But I think I made it a better book.[31]

Apparently so did the Russell Sage Foundation because most of Volkart's revisions were kept in the published version.

Although Simmons continued to work for some time after this, his influence decreased. The mantle of leadership in medical sociology passed on to younger people, most prominently Hollingshead. For Volkart himself, this was the beginning of a decade or more of intense involvement in medical sociology.

Volkart's personal story is illustrative of several characteristic patterns of the development of medical sociology at Yale in these early postwar years. After the interruption of his graduate studies by the war, Volkart returned to Yale in 1945 and completed his dissertation two years later. His introduction to medical sociology was directly linked to his dissertation, even though there was no evident medical relevance in the work itself. There are two major reasons for this. First, the writing of the dissertation revealed a high level of professional ability. Second, for important persons outside of Yale, Volkart's work on W. I. Thomas was recognized to be relevant to social psychiatry, something Harry Stack Sullivan had discovered when he met W. I. Thomas twenty years earlier. Again, as in so many careers, the SSRC was the connecting institution. Alexander Leighton, then in the early stages of building his research on the social epidemiology of mental illness at Cornell, was the human link. As Volkart tells about it, this was "a piece of mosaic" that placed him in the field. The year was 1951. In the spring, his book on W. I. Thomas had been published. In the fall, Volkart was invited to give a paper on W. I. Thomas at the annual meeting of the SSRC.

> Alex Leighton was there, and the next day he came to me and said he would like to talk with me. I remember that we walked around for an hour or two. He was talking about his social psychiatry stuff, and Alex said: "We are trying to set up through the SSRC a Committee on Social Science and Psychiatry. Would you be interested in being a staff member? Some of your stuff on W. I. Thomas ought to tie in with this." I said, "Sure, it sounds good to me."[32]

On the basis of his work on that committee, Volkart became the staff person for the SSRC Committee on Social Science and Psychiatry, which produced *Explorations in Social Psychiatry*,[33] one of the important books of this period.

In 1954, Volkart moved to Stanford's Department of Sociology. It was for him a career step, a promotion, based mainly on his special competence in social psychology. When he got there, however, he found "three or four people teaching

social psychology." As a result, he decided to try something different and suggested a course on the social psychology of health and illness. "It was 1956–57,
and I started to build then a whole course . . . concepts of illness, interrelations
of social roles and stress. . . . I suppose I must have given it three or four times,
and each term, of course, gaining more knowledge of the literature."[34] At about
that time, Volkart recalls, David Mechanic came to Stanford as a student, and he
wrote a dissertation on illness behavior under Volkart's supervision. At first there
was some objection from colleagues in the department. But that did not last long.
About Mechanic's dissertation, Volkart recalls: "I remember we used to have
meetings in the night, Paul Wallin, Dick LaPierre, myself, Dave, and I don't know
if anyone else was involved, asking what is this dissertation all about?" The dissertation, of course, was completed, and soon articles appeared from it, quickly
establishing Mechanic as an important scholar in the field. Mechanic went on to
create one of the most successful training programs in medical sociology at the
University of Wisconsin and to write a series of books that make him a leader in
the field today. He continued to direct outstanding training and research programs
at Rutgers, where he is now.

During the period that Volkart was developing his course in the social psychology of health and illness, he wrote an article on bereavement that appeared
in the publication of the SSRC Committee on Social Science and Psychiatry.[35] He
also proposed a long-term study in the social epidemiology of illness, requesting
support from the Russell Sage Foundation. His interest in medical sociology had
deepened. At the same time (1958), he became chairman of the sociology department at Stanford. When the university decided to move the medical school
campus from San Francisco to Palo Alto, discussions began between him and the
planners of the medical school concerning some kind of tie-in with his course in
the social psychology of health and illness. Russell Sage turned down Volkart's
epidemiology proposal but suggested an alternative. Would Volkart be interested
in setting up a program in the medical school on social science and medicine,
they asked, and would Stanford be receptive to it? Volkart agreed, and Volkart,
Young, and Cottrell began to negotiate with the leaders of the medical school. In
1958, Russell Sage gave Stanford a grant of $250,000 to be spent over five years
on what was called the Stanford Program in Medicine and Social Science.

The Palo Alto campus of the medical school was opened in 1959. During the
previous year, Volkart commuted frequently to San Francisco, "helping them
work on curriculum, getting to know people in the medical school, and so on."
A strikingly revised curriculum was planned for the new campus, and after some
initial uncertainty among the medical people about the novel approach that he
represented, Volkart was welcomed. At the same time, he received a grant from
NIMH for a training program that provided predoctoral fellowships for sociology
students to specialize in medical sociology and for medical students to do work
in sociology. Within a few years, one of the largest programs in medical sociology
had crystalized at Stanford, despite the fact that as late as 1957, in Volkart's
words, "[n]obody knew quite how you deal with health and illness sociologi-
cally."

The fate of this program after 1960 is an important case example of basic
conflicts that created barriers for the growth of medical sociology even as interest
in the new field and its ability to command resources for development reached
their peak. To the uncomfortable surprise of those who were most deeply in-

volved, like Volkart, resistance was encountered more from sociology, in some cases, than from medical sources.

On the medical side, momentum developed rapidly. For Volkart, "it was a deeply satisfying experience . . . the kind of thing I was all revved up about, deeply involved in." More precisely, the program was deliberately interdisciplinary, though some parts of the medical faculty were more involved than others.

> Mostly we worked with the pediatrics department and psychiatry, public health, some internal medicine but not too much, because medicine wasn't too interested in this kind of thing. I was with two psychiatrists. The three of us gave the basic introductory course for all entering medical students . . . having to do with human development and social aspects . . . from the social psychological point of view. Every Saturday morning, I remember giving about ten of the presentations, including some aspect of society, family roles, illness, death, etc. Public health people would take part in seminars, and psychiatry took part in practically all case conferences with pediatrics, and in the teaching of residents in pediatrics and psychiatry.[36]

In the meantime, however, trouble developed between Volkart and his sociological colleagues. The Sociology Department had changed, and a faction was digging in its heels on a policy of building up its faculty in one particular theoretical approach. The conflict with medical sociology developed over a new appointment. As Volkart explains it,

> I had fallen out, so to speak, with some of my colleagues in the Sociology Department, because we were going in different directions. The thing I resented most about it was that under the grant we should have hired another person, an assistant professor in the field, and I could never get them to agree on anybody that was acceptable to them.

At this point in the interview, Volkart listed names of people he had proposed, most of whom later became very successful medical sociologists (David Mechanic was one example):

> They were setting up impossible criteria. We must have gone through ten names, and I could never find anyone who would please them. I was always batting my head against a blank wall, and the next thing there was a big blowup. . . . It was a combination of push and pull. I didn't think I was going to get too far with the Sociology Department; I didn't want to move entirely into the medical school, which I think would have been a possibility . . . Dave Hamburg was the chairman of psychiatry then. But I didn't want to do that, and I suppose in a way, I escaped the field by becoming a dean.[37]

In 1962, Volkart went to Oregon State as the dean of the School of Humanities. To replace him in the Russell Sage program, Benjamin Paul was brought in from Harvard. Paul was an anthropologist, so his appointment was able to sidestep the barriers that had so frustrated Volkart.

Volkart continued for almost a decade as an academic administrator, first at Oregon State and then as executive secretary of the ASA. He never returned to active involvement in medical sociology, choosing instead to specialize in theory when he returned to an academic appointment at the University of Hawaii. Even at the end of his career, however, he recalled this experience with satisfaction, despite the difficulties he had, and expressed pride in the field's accomplishments.

> I think a tremendous amount has been accomplished in those twenty-five years or so since it started. Medical sociology is now an established specialty. We have journals devoted to it. I don't know that any of us ever had the notion at the time that it was going to develop that way. We all kind of felt like we were out in left field, aberrant deviant sociologists and what not; but it's become a respected subfield of sociology, and I think its legitimacy in the eyes of the medical schools and medicine in general has been markedly improved in the last fifteen years. . . . It's come a long way from the time when there were four or five people that were engaged in it in one way or another. What about the future? The same, I think, at an expanding rate.

Volkart's professional biography is typical in several ways of those of the younger medical sociologists who emerged from the immediate postwar period at Yale. His professional identity began and remained strongly rooted in mainstream sociology. The study of medical problems and roles in medical institutions attracted his attention and commitments, but he could not, finally, take the step into full-time commitment to a medical faculty, even though an attractive opportunity presented itself. In spite of the frustrations caused by sociologist colleagues, he found a way to remain an academic sociologist by choosing a detour into administration.

This was only one pattern, however. Others were different, most notably Volkart's fellow Yale doctoral student Robert Straus, who, once drawn into the sociology of medicine, became a lifelong medical educator in the behavioral sciences. Like Volkart, Straus began his college studies before the war. Unlike Volkart, who was born in Maryland and received a B.A. from St. John's College (1939), Straus was a Yale undergraduate. A "townie," he was born in New Haven and spent his entire childhood there, entering Yale in 1940. Straus has published his own detailed autobiographical description of his career as a medical sociologist,[38] and references to him have already appeared in early parts of this discussion, so only a few selected facts will be added here.

Medical sociology did not enter Straus's field of vision until 1944, when an old sports injury cut short his army service and he returned to Yale as a first-year graduate student. Before that he had been attracted by Yale sociology because of people he regarded as outstanding teachers, such as Albert G. Keller—in his last class—James G. Leyburn, and Raymond Kennedy, and because Yale sociology encouraged a broad interdisciplinary scope. Immediately upon his return, however, he encountered Seldon Bacon, Leo Simmons, and Bernhard Stern. Maurice R. Davie was also one of the most important of Straus's teachers, but Davie was not involved in any way in the study of medicine. Nevertheless, Davie was co-supervisor of Straus's dissertation and is recalled by Straus as the person who supported and encouraged him to complete his degree in record time, three years from the beginning of study to the completed dissertation.

The dissertation seems clearly to reflect the influence of Stern. Straus describes it as a "social history of the entry of government into the field of health care." It focused on the case of merchant seamen who, Straus found, were

> a category of human beings going back into very ancient times for whom there were indications that nation-states and governments made special provisions in order to entice people to take on this very dangerous, hazardous activity in the benefit of the society. . . . In Britain, well before the establishment of colonies there were social provisions for seamen, and in most of the colonies there were the same provisions. Our first Congress established the United States Marine Hospital Fund, which was the predecessor of the United States Public Health Service.[39]

Following the same pattern of analysis as Stern, Straus used the historical method to ask the question: Why do governments get interested in providing health care? Viewing seamen as a beneficiary group, he then asked: Why seamen? This led to the history of other beneficiary groups who received federal health care in the United States and to an analysis that yielded a set of six conditions that Straus argued were present historically as consistent underlying determinants for the entry and expansion of federal government health care involvement.

Simmons, says Straus, was "quite disappointed in me because it was too historical, from his point of view." Nevertheless, Simmons used some of his available funds to arrange for the thesis to be published as a book.[40] There are several aspects of Straus's dissertation, and his reported experience with it, that seem to me to be notable. The general atmosphere of Yale in the late forties reflected its reputation of conservatism in sociological thought, continuous with its founders, Sumner and Keller, and reinforced by the snob values of the college. Yet Straus was able to write a dissertation that followed the sociopolitical model of Stern. Moreover, the work identifies the "categorical" method of federal financial support for health care that individuals like Sydenstricker had so bitterly opposed in the thirties and that Rosemary Stevens later analyzed brilliantly as the cause of escalating health care costs in the United States.[41] The basic conclusions of the work, in other words, are the same that the AMA called "socialistic" in 1933 when they editorialized against the recommendations of the CCMC, a charge they were to repeat whenever ideas like this surfaced. The official representatives of medicine continued in this stance up to and following the passage of the Medicaid-Medicare legislation in 1965. Straus himself, however, has never in any way been identified as a radical. Quite the contrary. He is best known as a quietly effective sociologist who has worked closely with the leaders of academic medicine for fifty years. At times, his smooth relations with the medical establishment have attracted criticism from sociologists that he is too conforming and identified with physicians. Yet his scholarly work has continued to be consistent with his early writing, and Straus never hesitated to stand up for Stern when he was attacked in the fifties. When Stern died, Straus strongly supported Milton Roemer, who arranged to publish a posthumous volume of Stern's writings.[42]

Straus and Volkart can be seen as illustrations of how Yale was structured at that time to both encourage and to tolerate a very broad and diverse sociology.

Certainly an institution that was built by and that saw its mission as serving the most privileged sectors of American society, Yale nevertheless did more than tolerate critically independent scholarship. For Straus and Volkart, it was an environment that stimulated unconventional inquiry, as well as being supportive and open intellectually.

Further comment is also suggested by the Straus and Volkart cases concerning my earlier statement that Yale's several subinstitutions—the college, the graduate school, and the centers and institutes—discouraged the integration of new subjects like medical sociology into the settings where they were most appropriate. Despite the very strong growth of medical sociology in the graduate school, therefore, the medical school never welcomed a teaching contribution from it. On the other hand, individuals moved quite freely across these internal boundary lines, enriching their own intellectual growth. Straus, particularly, is an illustration. With Simmons, he spent profitable time in conferences at the medical school. In addition, with Seldon Bacon's introduction, he joined Howard Haggard's unique Department of Applied Psychology.

Yale sociology also created a training approach that "took care of its own." It is often forgotten that the late forties and early fifties were a time of relatively scarce employment opportunities for new graduates. Yale used its multiplicity of suborganizations to help graduates like Straus and Myers to get launched in academic careers. Opportunities to work in medical settings or to do research on medically related problems were just opening up, while academic positions for young sociologists were still relatively scarce. Straus, for example, was offered three jobs when he graduated, two in teaching and one in research connected to medicine. He chose to work for his teacher, Seldon Bacon, in the Laboratory of Applied Pyschology as part of a research group that became later the Center of Alcohol Studies. "I went into it primarily as a research person doing some teaching in their summer program. . . . This was an appointment with a real supported research opportunity."[43] It was a follow-up to the first research he had done as a graduate student, also with Bacon, published in 1946.[44] The next six years are described in detail in Straus's memoir.[45] He calls it "a rare opportunity to learn from and share with men and women from varied disciplines, all looking at the same phenomena from different perspectives, and most looking for some common and meaningful conceptual framework." The work took him to the Bowery in New York for a study of 444 alcoholics and to studies of drinking in college and among Italians. Although none of this was connected to the medical school, it did contribute to his invitation to serve as staff director of the Governor's Commission on Health Resources in Connecticut in 1949–50. As it turned out, this part-time position with the Governor's Commission was fateful for Straus's future. The chairman of the Commission was William R. Willard, a physician who was then associate dean of the Yale Medical School. A few years later, Willard had gone to the State University of New York's Upstate College of Medicine in Syracuse to develop the school and medical center that had just been taken over by the State University of New York (SUNY) from Syracuse University. When he became dean of this medical school, he invited Straus to join him. There Straus was assigned the task of teaching behavioral science to medical students for a full freshman year, three hours a week. This was an astonishing assignment at the time.

The project at Syracuse began on a high note of enthusiasm and promise, but it encountered stubborn resistance almost immediately. Willard had recruited Edward Stainbrook at the same time as Straus to come from Yale to Syracuse as professor and chairman of the Department of Psychiatry. Like Willard and Straus, Stainbrook believed that behavioral sciences should be made an intrinsic part of the medical curriculum. With a Ph.D. in psychology as well as his M.D., Stainbrook had come to Yale in 1949 as an instructor, immediately after his residency at Columbia. He quickly gravitated to the social science and medicine group at Yale, working closely with Redlich and Caudill and meeting weekly with a group at the Institute of Human Relations that included Hollingshead, John Dollard, Neal Miller, Leo Simmons, and others. Clearly, Willard brought with him from Yale two faculty colleagues who could mobilize a formidable force for social science at Syracuse. It is instructive to look closely at what happened.

At first, it seemed as though there was already at Syracuse an equally strong group with the same educational ideology. Julius Richmond, the professor and chairman of pediatrics and later the undersecretary for health in the federal government, immediately joined Straus and Stainbrook's teaching program, together with Charles Willie from the Syracuse Sociology Department and George Stern from the Psychology Department. Straus was formally appointed to the Department of Preventive Medicine, but the interdisciplinary effort to create a teaching program for the medical students superseded anyone's departmental affiliation. The curriculum time was three hours a week, preempted from anatomy. Straus described what they did:

> Willard said, "Here it is. Do something with it." And that was the beginning of what, even today, I would call the teaching of "Health in Society." We groped. We got some other people, an internist, a social worker, a psychologist, and a sociologist [Chuck Willie] . . . and we took this time and did some lecturing and we met students in small groups. We were really very much exploring a way to select, make meaningful, and synthesize some concepts from the social and psychological sciences that would contribute to the creation of physicians who were both personally better integrated and had a better understanding of the processes of disease.[46]

Eventually, Straus became the head of a Section of Behavioral Sciences at the Upstate Medical Center of Syracuse. At the core of the Section were four faculty positions for sociologists, supplemented by people drawn from the departments. From psychiatry, Stainbrook and Murray Wexler, a psychologist, were integrated members of the teaching staff. Julius Richnmond and George Stern were also part of the inner circle of planners and teachers. However, the problems they encountered were formidable. Recalling the reception at Syracuse, Straus has written: "The school was steeped in tradition and inertia. The reception given a sociologist who had been hired on hard money and given someone else's curriculum time ranged from skepticism to overt hostility. There were a few friends, most of them like myself, brought in by the dean."[47]

Stainbrook evaluated the experience in a different way. He viewed the introduction of the behavioral sciences into the medical curriculum as essentially dealing with the incorporation of a new basic science. Up to that time, he observed, there was a pattern of expressing this need for new knowledge mainly in the clinical teaching. He wrote:

Medical facilities have been energetically attempting in recent years to define what knowledge of human action or behavior, derived from the psychoanalytic study of man, particularly, and more generally, from the behavioral sciences of psychology, sociology, and anthropology should be incorporated within the formal educational organization of the medical college. As a method of achieving this incorporation, collaborative teaching in the clinical years has been given a good deal of attention.[48]

More appropriate, Stainbrook argues, would be the creation of a basic science department of behavioral sciences. Without such formal structural change, he believed, there were difficulties in the social role of the teacher that would render the teaching ineffective. "We have ample evidence in the past year's experience with our introductory course," he wrote in 1956, "that as long as a behavioral scientist has a *de facto* appointment in a department of psychiatry, public health, or pediatrics, the set of expectancies others have of how he should be perceived and of how he will act are determined largely by the role behavior associated with the department of which he is a member."[49] To avoid the consequences of this tendency for students to perceive faculty in a "departmental role" rather than a "behavioral scientist role," the best method, according to Stainbrook, was to create a basic science department of behavioral science. "A basic requisite for the successful participation of the behavioral scientist in the medical school is . . . role specificity and role clarity as defined not only by him but also by others in relation to him."[50] These apparent differences should not suggest that Stainbrook and Straus were at odds. They both testify that their relations and collaboration were very effective and friendly. However, Syracuse was not ready for this type of change. Although good student response was reported, the resistance among the faculty was very strong. When, therefore, Willard was appointed the dean and president of a new medical school at Lexington, Kentucky, and he convinced Straus to join him, the new Section of Behavioral Sciences at Syracuse was not immediately eliminated, but it did not survive for long. Stainbrook and Wexler left at the same time, in 1956, leaving the program almost totally leaderless. Richmond, though a well-liked and respected teacher, was not able to keep it going. As Straus evaluates the outcome of the program,

> [w]e did not have an impact on the faculty. When a student complained to the Professor of Anatomy, the answer was: "Well, if it wasn't for this ridiculous behavioral science that has stolen our valuable time, you wouldn't have a problem." That was the climate of the time. It wasn't without its influence, but the effects were mainly on individuals.[51]

Although Syracuse was not ready for the type of behavioral science that Straus and Stainbrook created there, neither gave up the idea. Stainbrook seemed to be the most clear about the conviction that only with a department could the teaching of behavioral science be most effective in medical school. This is evident in his 1956 article[52] and his personal testimony. "Straus and I and Wexsler talked very much about it," he recalled, "and we tried to behave in those four years at Syracuse as if we were a department of behavior."[53] For Stainbrook, however, it took almost fifteen years before he could fulfill this belief. When he went to the University of Southern California (USC) in 1956, he headed the Department of

Psychiatry, attracted by the opportunity to fulfill a different kind of dream. "I really wanted to manage a Bellevue-like acute psychiatric center, and the County Hospital psychiatric unit was the Bellevue of the Coast."[54] In 1969, however, he created a new department at USC, the Department of Human Behavior, which he headed until his retirement in 1977. Straus, however, was to go immediately to the chairmanship of a new Department of Behavioral Science at the new medical school of Kentucky.

By 1959, Straus shared fully Stainbrook's earlier brief for the creation of a department of behavioral science. Only in such a department, Straus writes in 1959, can the behavioral scientist realize his full potential. The dangers are the same: role confusion according to the department of psychiatry, public health, or pediatrics, in which he/she is most likely to be appointed, or isolation and limitation of range of activity. In a separate department, the objectives that are most appropriate to the behavioral scientist can best be realized. Straus argued for a limited definition of the behavioral scientist to include the sociologist, anthropologist, and social psychologist. He also specified the objectives:

[f]irst, the delineation and synthesis of principles and content from the behavioral sciences which are specially pertinent to the understanding of human behavior in health and disease, and the biological and physical sciences in the development of a conceptual frame of reference useful for the practice of comprehensive medicine; second, the application of behavioral science concepts and research findings to a further understanding of the diagnosis, treatment and management of the individual patient, to the mobilization of health resources to meet the needs of society, and to the understanding of interpersonal relationships and social structure within medical institutions themselves.[55]

Recalling the experience of Volkart, the pattern of Straus's career, at first glance, looks very different. As Straus, like Volkart, was drawn steadily into full collaboration with medical colleagues, he did not suffer from the identity questions that plagued Volkart. Never fully certain that medical sociology was a legitimate expression of his sociological training, Volkart, despite considerable success both as a teacher and scholar in medical settings, turned away from the specialization when he encountered problems. Straus, on the other hand, encountered no less intense conflicts, but his adaptation was to dig his way deeper into a career as a sociologist–medical educator.

There is one problem, however, that Straus and Volkart shared. Both were invited to assume important administrative leadership roles, and they had difficulty choosing between working primarily as scholars and the opportunities to lead and create as educational administrators. Straus, from the beginning, responding to Willard's requests, functioned much of the time at Kentucky as a dean. Formally, he held two offices: coordinator of academic affairs and chairman of the Department of Behavioral Science. Like Volkart, however, Straus was to suffer conflict in the choice. In the beginning, the fit between his sociological training and the tasks of building a new medical school seemed to fit:

My own role during the first year and a half was not directly that of a sociologist, but I was bringing the perspective of one who was trained as a sociologist to the task of raising questions, interpreting answers, and thinking constantly about the relationship between program objectives, people behaving in groups and spatial arrangements.[56]

As time passed, however, the conflict between academic and administrative roles became too stressful, and Straus made a choice. In a recent interview I asked Straus about this. "How would you describe Willard's attitude toward you at that point?" I asked; "Was it in terms of what you represented professionally or was it more on the basis of the effectiveness that he saw in you personally?" Straus answered:

> I think a combination. Let me tell you this story about Bill [Willard]. Bill was in real conflict after we had been going here [Kentucky] for about three years, because by that time . . . I was developing the academic program and was really his academic subdean. . . . He gave me a choice, and I chose to develop the behavioral science department. I continued to do both actually for about three years. I think Bill was always in conflict because personally he wanted me to serve him in a staff capacity, but his respect for the importance of the behavioral sciences in medical education and for what this could accomplish and his convictions about it were such that he wanted this developed at the school, too. . . . There have been times when Bill . . . reflected with me on how things might have been different if I had made the other choice, or if he had been more persuasive in that respect.[57]

What Straus describes points up the often forgotten fact that during the time that medical sociologists were achieving a new professional position in medical education, there was another major effort to change the structure of medical education itself. Willard was focused on creating a new type of medical school, and in Straus he found someone who understood organization and interpersonal relations in a way that was valuable in the active, day-to-day administration of the institution. Inevitably these talents were associated with Straus's training as a sociologist, much as was the case with Volkart. Straus agrees that the sociological perspective was helpful to his role as educational planner and developer, but it was a specific cause of tension between his professional self-image and his administrative role. Moreover, the Department of Behavioral Science was used for what Straus calls "in-house study and evaluation of things going on in the hospital."[58] This type of policy-related function involving inquiry about the institution in which the sociologist works is in itself a source of role ambiguity.

The problem was compounded for both Straus and Willard by the fact that they saw a link between behavioral science teaching and the type of medical education program that was their goal. To neglect one was to jeopardize the other. The tension was not just a personal matter; it was inherent in the structure of the situation.

More important than any other problem, however, was something that affected all the innovations in medical education, including the new schools like Kentucky. This is what Straus calls the drift toward traditionalism:

> I think that all new [medical] schools have run into a problem of drift toward traditionalism as they moved from the planning and the early activation to the need to step up the pace of recruitment [of faculty] in order

to meet the pressures of students and patients. . . . The criteria for recruitment that initially reflect basic program objectives lose priority to criteria
that are connected with the bodies that can do the job. As this happened,
every medical school that I know of has experienced the need to modify
some of its objectives for change because there simply were not enough
people committed to change.[59]

In this statement, Straus discounts the significance of his own personal conflict.
The challenges and the barriers to both medical education and behavioral science,
he is saying, are larger than any particular person or situation.

In spite of these qualifications, however, Straus is proud of what has been
achieved in Kentucky. As a model for one type of development in medical sociology, a department of social behavioral science that stands separate and equal
with other academic departments of the medical school, Kentucky was not only
the first but it remains one of the strongest.

Straus, together with Volkart, Myers, and Wessen, was in the first cohort of
medical sociologists trained at Yale. They learned the new specialty together with
their teachers, groping toward conceptual synthesis, functioning as much or more
in planning and program development as in the development of knowledge. In a
formal sense, they were not trained to be specialists in medical sociology. They
became specialists by virtue of the work they did, the positions they were chosen
to fill, and the writing and research they accomplished. Yale provided the professional socialization, with Simmons and Hollingshead serving as models. From
medical educators like Kahn, Redlich, Milton Senn, and others, they learned early
that behavioral science knowledge was important to medicine and collaboration
between medical and social science professions was both exciting and possible.

The Development of Formal Research and Training Programs

Yale's key role in the history of medical sociology is best represented by the
formal programs it pioneered. Hollingshead was the key figure. He himself dates
the beginning of his own awareness of the need for collaboration between sociology and medicine to personal relationships he formed with physicians while
serving at Randolph Field at the Air Forces Training Command Headquarters
during the war, but the activation of this interest did not begin until 1948 when
he met Fritz Redlich. He had just completed the manuscript of his first major
research, a study of adolescents in a midwestern town,[60] and was exploring the
idea of continuing community research in one of the local Connecticut cities. He
consulted Mark May, a psychologist and director of the Institute of Human Relations. It was May who brought Redlich and Hollingshead together.

The Institute of Human Relations (IHR) was a prototype of the kind of special
organization that served Yale so creatively as alternative settings to academic
departments that had become too rigid for new ideas. Sociology was typical. It
was so strongly rooted in the Sumner-Keller tradition at Yale that the new developments in sociology, especially in social research, had difficulty gaining entry. Not until Maurice Davie became chairman just before the Second World War
was this to change. In the meantime, younger faculty members went to the IHR
to learn and to practice a different kind of sociology. It was at the IHR, for example, that Simmons had his first appointment. Created with private foundation

funds, the IHR was designed to be an interdisciplinary organization, a setting where the best brains of the time would be attracted to teach and do research. It was strongly influenced by psychoanalytic theory, which was the source of much intellectual excitement at the time, and among its members were Abram Kardiner, Ralph Linton, Mark May, and others, drawn from the various behavioral sciences. It was, for young minds, a haven from the limits imposed by the more traditional perspectives enforced on the departments by "great" leaders. The IHR was an important part of Yale for about two decades, and then in the early fifties it quietly went out of business, probably because its function as an alternative intellectual pathway was no longer so critical.

Maurice Davie, already active in quantitative social research (called disparagingly by his mentor Keller "garbage sociology"), was further shaken out of his own loyalties to the Sumner-Keller tradition by his wartime experience in a major study of victims of the European war.[61] The experience deepened his conviction that the Yale Department of Sociology must modernize, and toward that goal, he brought in a series of visiting professors immediately after the war. Included were Harry Alpert, Howard Odum, John Bossard, and Fred Strodtbeck. Hollingshead was the first major appointment reflecting the success of this policy.

Social class was, at the beginning, probably the central point of interest that brought the various people together who eventually were to launch Yale's extraordinary effort in the sociology of medicine. Davie, for example, was very interested in issues of stratification, so that his choice of Hollingshead must have been influenced by their shared research focus. Redlich, also, became convinced of the importance of social class well before he met Hollingshead.

Redlich first came to Yale in 1942 as a young refugee scholar. Leaving his home in Vienna in 1938, "for policial and racial reasons," he went first to a state hospital in the Midwest and then in 1940 to a neurology residency at Harvard. When he came to Yale, he gravitated to the IHR, where John Dollard became "the person who influenced me most."[62] In fact, his first effort at collaboration with social science was with Dollard, who at that time was on the staff of the IHR.

Dollard, the author of the well-known *Class and Caste in a Southern Town*, [63] seemed a perfect partner. He had worked with the Kardiner team, he was himself a psychologist, and his theoretical orientations were strongly compatible with those of Redlich. However, although Redlich learned "the basics about social class" in 1942 from John Dollard, they were not able to join hands in research. First, there was Redlich's three-year hiatus from academic medicine to serve in the Army Medical Corps. When he returned in 1948, Redlich was executive officer of the Yale Department of Psychiatry and soon to become chairman in 1951. Inspired by the idea of the IHR, he sought to create in his own department what he called a "merger of the social sciences, psychology, psychoanalysis, and biology." One of the first people he tried to draw into his department was Dollard, but, as he recalls, "Dollard was very involved with his own research and there was no chance of any actual collaboration with him." This forced Redlich to seek someone else; fortuitously, Hollingshead had just arrived on the scene. "He was new . . . and very eager to find a person who would want to work with him. And I was very eager to work with him, so that's how we got together."

Exactly how they made contact is not clear. Hollingshead recalls that Mark May, then the director of the IHR, was the principal broker. Leo Simmons may have played a role, although Redlich was not attracted to Simmons, reporting that the type of sociology Simmons was known for did not appeal to him. Redlich only recalls that "I was told that there is a new man, who's not busy yet, and why don't you talk to him? And I did." The person in question, of course, was Hollingshead.

About Simmons, Redlich said: "Leo Simmons did not appeal to me, because . . . I was looking for an empirical researcher, and Sandy Hollingshead was very much an empirical researcher. Simmons much less so. But I had contact with Simmons. Yes, I did." The setting for this contact was primarily the Department of Psychiatry, not IHR. "The crowd in IHR was," according to Redlich, "actually quite removed from Simmons. Dollard, as well as people like Linton and Murdock, had little to do with Simmons. Simmons was a bit outside, and my contacts were mostly with these other people."[64]

In retrospect, Simmons and Hollingshead can be recognized as representatives of two quite different sociological perspectives, the one descriptive and qualitative and the other analytic and quantitative. Each found a matching colleague in psychiatry. Simmons, using anthropological data in a manner familiar to the clinical, case-oriented psychiatrist, found his sponsor in Eugen Kahn, the German-trained protege of the famous Emil Kraepelin. Hollingshead, a logical positivist in the tradition of the American Midwest, trained at Chicago in the most current quantitative survey methodology, appealed to Redlich, who though also German trained was first exposed to social science when he studied with Paul Lazarsfeld in Vienna.

To this day, Redlich refers to Lazarsfeld as his most important mentor. They met in Redlich's middle school,[65] where Lazarsfeld was a mathematics teacher. Later, after Lazarsfeld had gone to the university as a teacher of psychology, Redlich was again his student. Redlich recalls:

> It was more or less on his [Lazarsfeld's] advice that I shifted to medicine and went later into psychiatry. . . . He thought I would have more access to things if I would be in psychiatry, which at that time probably was true. Opportunities for research in psychiatry were better, particularly compared to European psychology and sociology, which were extremely theoretically oriented.[66]

These events occurred in the late twenties and early thirties. Redlich graduated from the university in 1935, just three years before he was forced to emigrate to the United States.

The collaboration between Redlich and Hollingshead was not always easy, but it was extremely productive and long-lasting. "Sandy and I," Redlich said, "were very different people."

> I was more an idea man, and Sandy was very much a methodologist. So we complemented each other, but it wasn't easy to work together. Sandy could be—well, quite gruff. Actually, we were very different people. Sandy, in spite of the impact he had in the social science field, was very conservative—was very politically conservative. I was more leaning towards the left. Less so today, I would say, but that's a question of age. Sandy, as a matter of fact, was a Goldwater Republican, and we always thought how strange, this man who in a way sort of really blew the inequities in education and in medicine sky-high was such a conservative person. Also, Sandy was a bit on the anti-Semitic side. Which caused occasionally some

problems. . . . It put a certain amount of strain on our relationship, because I was an immigrant and I came from Nazi persecution. But we reached sort of a modus vivendi, where we didn't talk about these matters. But it was there.[67]

Beginning with the Hollingshead-Redlich meeting in 1948, events followed swiftly that were to make Yale the most important gathering place for the launching of medical sociology during the immediate postwar period. The major credit is usually given to Hollingshead, seen as the conceptualizer of both teaching and research and as the source of attraction for both federal and private financial support. However, Redlich was a vital and essential contributor to the success of social science in medicine at Yale. The strength of his commitment was not only tested by the personal strains in his relationship with Hollingshead; he also was forced to stand up to strong opposition from his own psychiatric colleagues. In his own words: "There was, even in our own department, a great deal of resistance against the social science concepts. Psychiatrists in general were [at] first very annoyed and skeptical with it."

A curious twist in this part of Redlich's story is the opposition of the psychoanalysts in his department. Because many sociologists are schooled in the Freudian writings that are strongly sympathetic to the social sciences and because of the fact that in Europe social scientists played a significant role in the history of psychoanalysis, the opposition of psychoanalysis to social science in the United States is surprising. Yet Redlich's testimony to this fact is striking: "The old analysts, who were very powerful in the department, people like Kubie, Lowenstein, and Kris, they had no use whatsoever for social science. They thought these were alien and, if anything, dangerous concepts." Nor was this opposition limited to intellectual discourse. Sometimes individuals were active in attempts to stop Redlich.

Kubie, who was a close friend of mine, and in general very helpful, and he is one of the people to whom I owe a great deal—he thought I was absolutely misled doing research in this particular area. He once wrote a letter to one of the donors who was interested in the department and said: "They are wrong. They are absolutely wrong in what they are doing here."[68]

None of this opposition, however, stopped Redlich. He persisted, both in his own research activities, in his efforts to attract younger psychiatrists to similar inquiry, and in attempts to build social science into the teaching of psychiatry as part of the undergraduate medical education at Yale. However, though Redlich himself remained active throughout his life as a collaborator in research and as an advocate of the integration of social behavioral science in medical education, it was not in psychiatry that medical sociology achieved institutionalization at Yale. The roll call of individuals who worked in the psychiatry department at this time is very distinguished: Edward Stainbrook, Ernst Gruenberg, Eugene Brody, William Caudill. Their achievements, however, emerged more as of the individuals than of a program. Brody, who was an important member of the Yale group, credits Redlich with being the leader of both important theoretical developments and of institutionalized programs. However, as one would expect, the emphasis was on psychiatry rather than the social sciences. Indeed, a new field, "social psychiatry," emerged at this time, and Brody considers Redlich one of its important founders.

On the other hand, medical sociology was not part of social psychiatry's vocabulary and did not become so for at least another decade.

When Hollingshead and Redlich came together in 1948, both psychiatry and sociology at Yale were emerging, each from its own kind of isolation. Fortunately, to catch up neither had to start from scratch. The IHR, previously neglected by both departments, had prepared the way.

As Gene Brody recalls, most impressive was the way Yale psychiatry's previous isolation from other departments of the IHR gave way to open communication. This allowed staff and residents to know people who worked in the same buildings, such as John Dollard, Irvin Child, Ralph Linton, and others in the then burgeoning culture-personality research area.[69] For Brody, it was Redlich who played the key role:

> Fritz Redlich, very much the bridging person, who connected the newly vibrant social, biological and psychoanalytic streams in the department, was fond of an expression which I have plagiarized from time to time. Psychiatry, he said, rests on a tripod. One leg is made up of the medical and biological sciences; one of what we learned from psychoanalysis and psychotherapy; the third, of experimental psychology and the sciences of social structure and culture, such as sociology and anthropology. I don't remember if he then used the term, "behavioral sciences" . . . but as I look back it seems that our developing concept of social psychiatry was very much concerned with the relationships between clinical concepts and the behavioral science disciplines basic to them. . . . The message, it seems to me, is clear: The study of man as a social creature cannot be separated from understanding him as a reflective, introspective one. Nor can it be pretended that he exists outside of an evolving physical body.[70]

In the final analysis, Yale was not able to institutionalize a sustained, continuous collaborative enterprise that joined social science and psychiatry. Only individual partnerships, such as those of Hollingshead with Redlich and later with Raymond Duff or Myers with Roberts and Brody with Caudill, were successful. "Interdisciplinary" never was more than an orientation at Yale; it found no expression in the operational restructuring of intellectual relationships. Even the IHR, so promising and to individual careers so influential, died and was not replaced. Psychiatry, meanwhile, created "social psychiatry" as the expression of the theoretical perspectives represented by Redlich. For sociology, it was to be "medical sociology."

In 1948, of course, medical sociology was not yet even used as a descriptive name. During the period just described, from 1930 to 1950, Yale, through its own internal intellectual development, played a central role in the launching of pilot programs for medical sociology as a subspecialty. During the next stage of its history, however, although Yale continued to be a center of activity, the growth of medical sociology was only possible through another type of institution, NIMH, which was created as a new federal agency in legislation passed by Congress in 1946.

8

The Role of NIMH, 1946–1975

> The path of medical sociology was not a
> smooth and easy one.
> —Robert H. Felix,
> first director of NIMH

At midcentury, the institutions responsible for higher education in the United States were poised for a radical transformation. The changes that followed the war appear at first to pick up and continue the prewar trends, but they were both more fundamental and more diverse. For example, the scientific function of the medical school that Abraham Flexner had recommended in 1910 had been gradually realized during the next two decades. By 1930, as Stevens has so clearly documented, "the faculties in the best schools had become scientific investigators."[1] However, the role of such faculty investigators did not radically change during the thirties. Support for research projects occasionally received earmarked foundation grants, but "in large part, medical schools made no distinction between teaching and research."[2] Following the war, the research function became dominant, reflecting a structural change that altered the social environment of medical schools in a way that no one had predicted, not even the ubiquitous Flexner.

Most obvious was the replacement of private foundation grants by the federal government as the main outside source of research support, but the significance of the change went beyond that. The primary sources were the National Institutes of Health (NIH). Some trace the origins of NIH to 1887 when a laboratory for bacteriological studies was created within the PHS. However, the contemporary model began only in 1930, and it was not until a congressional act in 1937 that NIH developed "specialist research programs focused on specific conditions or diseases."[3] At first these were predominantly on-site research and training at the national capital, but gradually extramural research grants to individuals and institutions were added. The latter grew rapidly to change the balance between the medical school functions of teaching, research, and service. This process started during the war: "An accelerated, focused program of medical research, sponsored both by private organizations and by various governmental departments for wartime needs, led to *separate accounting for research in the schools*, and thus to *a separation of the research function* from the regular expected role of teaching."[4]

By 1948, almost all medical schools budgeted research separately and by so doing set off a chain of major effects. The nominally independent medical schools became dependent for their continued existence on federal research grants. Within the medical schools and the medical centers of which they were part, the role of the scientist became dominant, and inevitably teaching and service became less important. Faculties grew in size, even when student bodies remained stable, but *the balance among functions was skewed to science* because of its contribution to the medical school budget.

While these changes were occurring in medical education, sociology followed what appeared to be a similar growth pattern, but on a much smaller scale. Until World War II, there was virtually no separation of roles between teaching and research, and sociology's main locus in the university was in the college of arts and sciences. Whatever external funding there was came almost totally from private foundations. Except for the contributions of individual scholars to special commissions like the Ogburn Committee on Social Trends, sociologists played virtually no role in the inner circles of government science, except for a small presence in the Department of Agriculture.[5]

The development of medical sociology as a subspecialty began not so much within departments of its own parent discipline or with the creation of a new academic department but, as described earlier, as part of particular interdisciplinary programs in the university, like those in Yale's IHR, or by direct funding from foundations. The Russell Sage Foundation, the Milbank Memorial Fund, and the Rockefeller foundations were the main sources of such support.

Sociologists in general, despite their extensive wartime participation in government war-related research, returned after the war to traditional university roles.[6] One outstanding exception was in the armed forces, where, apparently convinced by wartime experience, the military's use of science, including the social sciences, was increased.[7] In 1947, Congress passed an act creating the Research and Development Board of the Office of the Secretary of Defense. Within this Board, a Committee on Human Resources was established, composed of social scientists.[8]

In the universities, meanwhile, following the trend of wartime experience, research quickly took on greater importance, and like other sciences sociology turned to the federal government for support. Medical sociology, as it grew toward full identification as an intellectual activity in its own right, epitomized this shift, no doubt speeded in this direction by a growing association with medical institutions that always had higher priority for government support than the social sciences. Although private sources of support remained important, medical sociology's development at this stage was closely associated with the NIMH, then the newest federal institute.

In my opinion, NIMH, created in 1946, was the single institution that, more than any other, was responsible for the emergence of medical sociology as we now know it. In the background there was, of course, the postwar increase of the government's role in all of science in the United States, and the development of medical sociology was part of that process. In one sense, NIMH is only an instrument of broad socioeconomic and political forces. Close examination, however, shows that Robert H. Felix, the founding director of NIMH, and a few of his closest associates played critical roles in how medical sociology developed. The NIMH was instrumental in both the training of social scientists and in the financing of research about social factors in health and illness. On the surface, it is not immediately evident that Felix himself, or any social scientists, made a special contribution beyond responding to the requests for proposals that eventually appeared. However, unpublished testimony from Robert Felix tells a very different story about his own very deep interest and the influence of sociologists like Raymond Bowers, August Hollingshead, and John Clausen. The policies that they conceived and set in motion fit the needs of the postwar university, and within it medical sociology found its place.

The Origins and Early History of NIMH

Created by the National Mental Health Act of 1946, the NIMH appeared to be a direct result of the war. At the first meeting of its National Advisory Mental Health Council, for example, the minutes report the following:

> The Chairman then called upon Mrs. Albert Lasker, Secretary of the National Committee for Mental Hygiene, to address the meeting. . . . The growth of citizen interest in the new Mental Health Act, Mrs. Lasker felt, was due to the increasing awareness . . . of the prevalence of mental disease. She mentioned that 1,875,000 men had been prevented from fighting in the recent war because of mental problems, and that 500,000 men who had been fighting had to be released from the armed services for the same reasons.[9]

As Mrs. Lasker turned to discussion of the country's current mental health needs, she quoted Dr. George Stevenson, the medical director of the National Committee for Mental Hygiene, to the effect that fifteen thousand additional psychiatrists were needed to take care of even the minimum needs of American civilians and contrasted this with the fact that Congress had for years been appropriating millions of dollars for research in the care of plants and animals. Fifty-one million dollars was allotted for the latter purpose in 1946, she said, and an additional seven million to fight white pine blister rust. Caustically, she added that Congress had not thought much about the "blisters on the human mind" until the passage of this act.[10]

It was on the basis of the same facts and arguments that the wartime Office of Scientific Research and Development, in its Vannevar Bush report of 1945, urged the federal government to become more active in the support of research, including the problem of mental illness. A twenty-page memorandum by Dr. Robert H. Felix, "Outline of a Comprehensive Community-Based Mental Health Program," written in 1944, became the working paper of the National Mental Health Act. Felix, at the time, had just succeeded Dr. Lawrence Kolb, Sr., as the medical officer in charge of the Federal Narcotics Hospital in Lexington, Kentucky. This hospital, within the Public Health Service, had become part of the Division of Mental Hygiene, and Felix was its head. The Felix program was based on a vision of Kolb, who saw the need for a national neuropsychiatric institute and had generated considerable support for the idea prior to the war.[11]

More than a reaction to the war, the National Mental Health Act should be seen as the culmination of several decades of planning and preparation by a handful of professional and lay persons devoted to improving the treatment of the mentally ill.[12] Until midcentury, however, these efforts were led by voluntary organizations. The most active of these groups was the National Committee for

Mental Hygiene, founded by Clifford Beers in 1909 and merged in 1950 with two other organizations—the National Mental Health Foundation and the Psychiatric Foundation—to form the National Association of Mental Health.[13] These efforts, however, tended to be either limited to particular mental health problems such as drug addiction or to muckraking, consciousness-raising public campaigns to call attention to the abuses of the mentally ill. Clifford Beers's book in 1905 set the pattern.[14] An autobiography, it told the story of Beers's illness and his experiences in the mental institutions of the United States at the turn of the century; it took forty years to achieve effective reform. Only with the National Mental Health Act was a comprehensive approach taken by the federal government to the kinds of problems that Beers and others had lobbied for. The creation of the NIMH as the central agency for research and training was the culmination of this development.

The programs enacted in 1946, however, were not funded until 1947 (i.e., fiscal year 1948). Robert H. Felix, who was to be the first director of the NIMH when it was activated in 1949, decided not to wait. As he himself tells the story,[15]:

> The law passed, and then I was authorized to start to work, but I had no money. Truman signed the law on July 3, 1946, and Congress recessed that day for the summer. The law said that I should convene a National Advisory Mental Health Council which should consist of six people to help us set policy for the program. It said how much we should pay them, but I had no money. So I went to New York and I beat the pavements for a couple of weeks. Everybody was busy, and everybody said, "Well, the government shouldn't be getting money from us—we should be getting money from the government." But finally I ran into the Greentree Foundation, and they made this grant of fifteen thousand dollars to us. That paid for convening the Mental Health Council, getting it started.[15]

Felix added that this was the last grant that foundation gave before it went out of business. Thus the NIMH was able to get started immediately after the National Mental Health Act was signed.

Felix immediately appointed the six-member National Advisory Mental Health Council authorized by Congress, so that they were able to begin to discuss plans for the new agency. Without the necessary appropriation, of course, they acted technically within the Mental Hygiene Division of the PHS, of which Felix was the chief. On April 1, 1949, the Division was abolished, and the NIMH took its place. In 1950, the Council was expanded by law to include twelve appointed members.

NIMH, in the record of its first years, shows little evidence of the importance it was to give to a role for the social sciences. It was an institutional expression primarily of the recognition that psychiatry achieved during the war. It has also been described as a reaction to the public scandal that erupted after the war over the conditions in state mental hospitals. On the one hand, Starr gives credit to conscientious objectors who, during the war, had been sent to work as aides in mental institutions.[16] Their story was picked up after the war by newspapers and magazines and even became the subject of a best-selling novel, *The Snakepit*.[17] In one of the most widely read exposés, *The Shame of the States*,[18] based on visits to two dozen institutions, the historian and journalist Albert Deutsch reported scenes rivaling the horrors of Nazi concentration camps: half-starved mental patients herded into filthy, barnlike wards and stripped of every vestige of human decency. Like others of the time, Deutsch believed that mental hospitals needed closer relations with medicine as well as more resources. In a typical expression of the growing faith in psychiatry, Deutsch wrote: "It is because modern psychiatry is a stranger to so many mental hospital wards that many more patients don't return to their communities as cured."[19]

Out of these origins, the emphasis in the early very rapid expansion of NIMH appears to have been entirely on psychiatry, on the creation of medical research and training programs related to mental health, and on the improvement of psychiatric clinical service. All of the National Advisory Mental Health Council members, for example, were psychiatrists. The original Council was composed of the following doctors:[20]

- Dr. William C. Menninger, medical director, Menninger Clinic, Topeka, Kansas (psychiatrist)
- Dr. John Romano, professor of psychiatry, School of Medicine, University of Rochester, Rochester, New York
- Dr. George S. Stevenson, medical director, National Committee for Mental Hygiene, New York, New York
- Dr. Edward A. Strecker, professor and chairman of the Department of Psychiatry, University of Pennsylvania, Philadelphia, Pennsylvania
- Dr. Frank F. Tallman, commissioner of mental diseases, State of Ohio, Columbus, Ohio (psychiatrist)
- Dr. David Levy, assistant professor of psychiatry, Columbia University, New York, New York

This pattern continued until 1950. All but one of the sixteen appointed in this period were psychiatrists. In 1950 the pattern was broken; six lay people were appointed.[21]

Behind the scenes, in the staff operations of the NIMH, the story was different. Social science was given an important role to play from the very beginning. What the official record of the NIMH does not reveal is that Felix, before his appointment as the first director, had been converted to the importance of social science in medicine at Johns Hopkins, where he was sent by the Public Health Service in 1941 to study public health. At the time, Felix was a medical officer in the Division of Mental Hygiene at the United States Narcotics Hospital in Lexington, Kentucky. When the PHS sent him to Johns Hopkins in 1941, he recalls,

I just became entranced with what I was learning about epidemiology of diseases. And they were concerned at that time about the epidemiology of so-called chronic medical conditions. From this I extrapolated that there must be something we could do to understand in the area of mental diseases. But there were no epidemiologists interested. The people who were most nearly what I was looking for were sociologists. And this is why I turned to sociologists.[22]

During the years 1946–49, while he was shaping the institution that was to become NIMH, Felix maintained this interest. Raymond V. Bowers was the first sociologist who worked with him.

Bowers never thought of himself as a medical sociologist or any other type of specialist. When asked if he was aware of a field called medical sociology at that time, he answered: "Not really, because I never had been interested in these special sociologies. I was a sociologist. And quantitatively oriented . . . And I still have a hard time—I gulp when I think of some of these specialties."[23] In general, he seemed to regard his time with Felix as a kind of happy accident. When asked about the work he did at NIMH, he said: "Well, it was sort of [an] . . . oh, unspecified kind of job. They just wanted somebody in the social sciences. They had a psychologist there, [Joseph Bobbitt], but all the rest of them were medical people."[24] Asked if the social sciences were important at NIMH at that time, he did not think so. "I mean," he explained, "We were the only two people in the whole darn thing. But Bob Felix, you know, was an exceptional kind of person, and he brought us in, I am sure. In fact, I felt kind of out of place with all those doctors around there looking down my throat [laughing]." When told about Felix's own testimony about how important he regarded sociology, Bowers said: "Yes, but you see, I didn't do it. It was John Clausen [his successor] who did it."

Despite the brief period of their association—and Bowers's own disclaimers—Bowers was ideal for Felix's purpose, to create a psychiatric epidemiological research effort. Their combined vision was described in 1948.[25] "The impact of the social environment on the life history," they wrote, "and the relevance of the life history to mental illness, are no longer in serious question as clinical and research findings. But, even though we have come a considerable distance in our systematic understanding of the symptomology and psycho-dynamics of mental disorders, such understanding does not extend to any extent to the role played by socio-environmental factors." What followed became the blueprint for NIMH policy on the social sciences for at least two decades:

> The growing recognition of the seriousness of this gap on the etiology and treatment of mental disorders serves also to point to its seriousness for case-finding and prevention, equally important segments of a national mental hygiene program. Thus it seems well to attempt to define the dimensions of the problem, survey its present research status and outline some important areas of needed research for the future. In so doing we shall also be defining the role of the social sciences in the mental hygiene movement, a matter too long postponed for the benefit of each.[26]

They very clearly defined the problems in question and reviewed a broad range of research findings, including the experiences of the armed services during war. In the article's summary, a bold and unqualified assumption of social responsibility was proposed:

> We need to learn from past success and failure. Then we should support well-designed experiments combining the skills of the clinician and the social scientist, and aimed to discover the most economical and efficient methods of preventing the wasting of human resources incident to personality malfunction. It may be a fifty-year quest, but we should begin now.[27]

Today it is just over fifty years since Felix and Bowers wrote that statement. The program for NIMH that they charted was implemented, introducing a new era of partnership between sociology and the mental health and medical professions. "The separation of the medical and social sciences," they concluded, "has been too long a crippling force in the progress of our field, as has the separation of academic researcher and practitioner. The traditions and status differentials of the past cannot be allowed to shackle the opportunities of the present."

To avoid confusion, it is important to note that Felix and Bowers speak of "the social sciences" when they chart the need for collaboration with the medical professions, even though there is evidence that Felix specifically singled out "sociology" during his experience at Johns Hopkins. Already in 1947, when he began to plan the future of NIMH,[28] he was aware of porous boundaries of anthropology, social psychology, and sometimes clinical and personality psychology with sociology. The late 1940s were markedly a time of belief in the unity and not the diversity of the behavioral disciplines. The use of "behavioral science" was not only defensive against the misplaced confusion with political meanings of the term "social"; it also reflected a hope for an advance toward a unified science of behavior.[29] Medical sociology, in this discussion, refers to a unity of three disciplines—sociology, anthropology, and social psychology—in the effort to find the relations between social factors and health and illness. The social and behavioral sciences are more inclusive, joining political science, economics, general psychology, and related biological inquiry into their meaning. As this discussion of Felix and NIMH proceeds, therefore, there is unavoidable overlap in the use of the terms. "Social science" has the broader meaning;[30] "medical sociology" is more specific.

Bowers, though only thirty-nine years old when he joined Felix in 1946, was already identified as a highly skilled social researcher, especially in experimental sociology and statistics. Born and raised in Victoria, British Columbia, Bowers received his Ph.D. at Minnesota, studying with Stuart Chapin and Malcolm Wiley. From there he went to Yale with a postdoctoral fellowship at the IHR, where he worked with Dorothy Thomas, who was an outstanding pioneer in population research, and statistics.[31] After a few years in his first faculty position at the University of Rochester, he went to the Selective Service headquarters in Washington in 1942. He was still there in 1946 when Felix recruited him for NIMH. One year later, in 1947, he was appointed the director of the newly created Committee on Human Resources, described by him as an interdisciplinary team of social scientists. The Committee was part of the Research and Development Board of the Office of the Secretary of Defense. He remained in the government for another ten years, moving to the Air Force to set up research programs in the latter years of his service. Deciding that "my old age ought to be spent back in the university," he went to the University of Georgia as chairman of the Sociology Department and finished his career as chairman of sociology at the University of Arizona. Although he never thought of himself as a medical sociologist, his contribution to that field was unquestionably significant.

The beginning, however, was not easy. Although Felix chose unusually talented and effective social scientists, the social climate of the country made his task difficult. His first problem was with the name. He had to deal with Congress: "I had to keep in mind that I didn't have any money if I didn't please Congress," he reported, and some members of Congress advised him to be careful about names. "When I first set up, I wanted to set up a branch on sociology, but I was advised against it because they would consider that socialism. Sociology was socialism. So I . . . dreamed up a name that I borrowed from public health, and I developed a laboratory of socioenvironmental studies." He explained further: "As long as I was talking about environment, that went along with fodder, and sewage, and so forth. Socioenvironmental. I could get by with the 'socio' because I had the 'environmental' in it. And that's how I got things started, and through that we developed grant programs both intramural and outside."[32] When asked about the term "behavioral sciences," Felix dated its creation to later, "sometime in the fifties." Its origin, however, was similar, in Felix's view. It was a way to avoid the association between "social" and "socialism." In his words: "Behavior was something they could understand. Kids behave, and misbehave. And I'll never forget, someone was asking me about it one time, and I said, 'Well, everything is behavior. Even misbehavior is behavior.' And they said, 'Well, I guess you're right.' And I said, 'So I can call anything behavioral studies.' "[33]

Unfortunately, the name strategy was not enough to mute the associations with political deviationism. Congress attacked his support of specific early research grants, calling them "communistic." For dealing with this issue Felix gives credit to John Clausen.

John Clausen, described by Felix as "a young Ph.D. from Ithaca," replaced Bowers in 1948. He was, in fact, an assistant professor of sociology at Cornell when Felix recruited him, but his Ph.D. was from the University of Chicago. After undergraduate work at Cornell, in 1936 he went to Chicago. After completing all but the dissertation, he took a job in 1940, and then, from 1942 to 1946, joined Stouffer's research group in the armed forces. He was involved in various aspects of the *American Soldier* research, particularly the study of the postwar plans of American soldiers. In what was to be the core of his dissertation, he wrote the chapters on prediction in the fourth volume.[34] Felix appointed him social science consultant to the director in 1948; more precisely, his appointment was to the Professional Services Branch, Felix's consortium of expert advisors. There he immediately launched a program of research. In 1951, when the intramural research program was founded, he became the first chief of the Laboratory of Socioenvironmental Studies at NIMH, remaining in that position until 1960, when he went to the University of California at Berkeley. In Felix's opinion, Clausen made "a tremendous contribution to the program."[35] Others have said the same.[36] But the formal measure of his importance, indicated by programs and research, does not do justice to the informal advice and support he gave Felix, who said:

> I think it's due to him [Clausen] as much as anything else that I didn't get discouraged when I was trying to develop the whole area of medical sociology as far as mental illness was concerned. And people didn't think this was such a smart thing to do. They thought this was a lot of boondoggle. You know the path of medical sociology was not a smooth and easy one.

Explaining what he meant, Felix referred to two studies, the research on the Hutterites by Eaton and Weil[37] and a study of "complementary needs."[38] Both the general public and particularly some members of Congress "raised unmitigated hell with us." The Hutterite study was "viewed as trying to promote communism," and the other (on complementary needs in marriage) led to the claim "that we were trying to find out how we could get laws passed so we could control who got married to who, to breed a master race." "Need complementarity" is a theory developed by Winch that set the stage for investigation of the hypothesis that "opposites attract"—that persons of dissimilar values or personality traits would marry.[39] I have not been able to find data about why Congress objected to this study, but there is a suggestion that Congress found the research somehow not hard enough "science" to justify government support. The objection to the Hutterite research is even more difficult to imagine. Now considered a classic in the epidemiology of mental illness, it contained a rarely used methodology, total prevalence study, which is difficult to execute and time-consuming but necessary for the uncovering of rates of untreated illness. How Congress could have perceived it as "promoting communism" is truly a mystery, even if allowance is made for the distortions that were the hallmark of the McCarthyism that dominated the period Felix is describing.

The design of the Hutterite study fits exactly into the category Felix and his advisors chose as the first of the kinds of research that were needed to understand the social and cultural correlates of mental illness: "[s]tudies attempting to assess the total or true prevalence of severe mental disorders in delimited populations, specified culturally, geographically, or genetically."[40] The Hutterites are a Christian Anabaptist sect who live mainly in the Dakotas, Montana, and Manitoba. Originally from the Black Forest region of Germany, they are a tightly organized, exclusionist society, who live in thriving agricultural villages with almost no relations to the surrounding American and Canadian societies. Modern medicine is the outstanding exception in their rejection of modern secular life. The Hutterites sought and accepted treatment for illness by physicians from the secular towns near their communities. The same physicians had noted the fact that the Hutterites seemed to be free of mental illness. To test the hypothesis that, for unknown reasons, the Hutterites did not have mental illness, Joseph Eaton, a sociologist, and Robert J. Weil, a psychiatrist, proposed that NIMH support a study of the entire group, involving direct examination of the whole population. The census numbered 8,542 Hutterites in that region in 1950.

Eaton and Weil found that, among the Hutterites, some cases of both psychosis and psychoneurosis did exist. Although the rate of incidence was relatively low compared with other cultures, it was not among the lowest known rates. Notable was the rarity of schizophrenia and that no diagnosis of psychopathic personality was found. The manic depressive symptomatology was most frequent. The reason for their reputation as a group free of mental illness was found in the culture. Hutterites did not define symptoms in the same way as their neighbors. When the symptoms of mental illness appear, the Hutterites do not take them as cues to stop the normal rhythm of the sick individual's life. Rather,

the onset of a symptom serves as a signal to the entire community to demonstrate support and love for the patient. Hutterites do not approve of the removal of any member to a "strange" hospital. . . . All patients are looked after by the immediate family. . . . They are encouraged to participate in the normal life of their family and community, and most are able to do some useful work. . . . No permanent stigma is attached to patients after recovery. The traumatic social consequences which a mental disorder usually brings to the patient, his family and sometimes his community are kept to a minimum by the patience and tolerance with which most Hutterites regard these conditions.[41]

Fortunately, what Congress saw as boondoggle was recognized by Felix and Clausen as basic psychiatric epidemiology, and they persisted on the course that had been set by Felix with Bowers.[42] The direction they chose, though dominated by the goal of increased research, included a heavy investment in training. Here, again, it is valuable to consider Felix's own words: "From the very beginning . . . we decided there were three generic areas in which we should be active: training, both basic and clinical, research, also both basic and clinical, and assistance, including consultation, to the States. Well, we figured the place we had to put our emphasis first was training."[43] Here Felix was referring mainly to psychiatry. His criticism of previous psychiatric research was caustic. Not only were there too few psychiatrists trained for research, he said, but "the research they had done was a very unsophisticated kind of nose-counting: we had so many patients, and we did such-and-such, and so many of them got better, and that makes the conclusions such-and-such. . . . You talk to these people about a controlled study, and they don't know what you are talking about. And," he added, "I wasn't sure I knew either, as far as that was concerned at that time." And so, in order to promote research on mental illness, Felix concluded that he must begin to train researchers.

The training of researchers with NIMH support began in 1948 when nineteen fellowships were awarded, seventeen of which had been transferred from the NIH general research fund. They were made at three levels: predoctoral, postdoctoral, and special (for the experienced investigator). For the more stable development of research scientists, the institute added career investigator grants in 1954. The latter allowed young scientists three to five years of full-time research and additional training. Although these programs were conceived first with psychiatrists in mind, they were actually awarded to all types of professionals who could contribute to research that in any way related to mental health. Such support grew slowly at first, expanded dramatically between 1956 and 1965 as Congress became more approving, stabilized in the midsixties, and began to decline in the late sixties. The record shows that, over the years, fellowships tended to concentrate at the predoctoral level, and the majority of them have been awarded in the field of psychology.[44]

It is important to note that, in spite of the early priority Felix gave to training, sociology and anthropology were not included at first. Not until 1957 was the training program broadened to support them. Why this selective delay? It is hard to document the reasons. One knows, of course, from Felix and others, that the values of the early stages of the Cold War created part of the problem. There were still the misconceptions in Congress about sociology. For others, there were questions about its academic legitimacy. We know that when the bill to found the National Science Foundation (NSF) was brought before Congress on July 3, 1946, the Senate voted by forty-six to twenty-six, with twenty-four members not voting, to exclude the social sciences.[45] The reason given by Senator Thomas C. Hart, Republican of Connecticut, was that "no agreement has been reached with reference to what social science really means." Social science was also attacked because it was an "applied science," and the NSF was intended to support "pure science." Like other objects of prejudice, the sociologists were attacked, as they say, "coming and going."

There were many negative forces at work, and no matter how contradictory they were, Felix was aware of them. We know that he acted with these facts in mind, but he believed in social science. To express this belief, at least in the first decade of NIMH, he supported a social science role that was not as visible as that of the disciplines more clearly relevant to mental health, psychiatry and psychology. Perhaps the most important assignments were behind the scenes, especially in his staff. More publicly, and at times with great courage, Felix supported sociological research, but even here he began by hedging his bets with support for studies in which the sociologists were co–principal investigators with psychiatrists.

For his staff, Felix's method was to pick very strong, competent people, regardless of discipline, and at the same time to keep psychiatry in the forefront of his formal policy-making groups, like the National Advisory Mental Heath Council. As a result, in the working center of his charter members of the NIMH staff, he always kept social scientists in important roles. For example, the social psychologist M. Brewster Smith was a favored advisor.[46] Felix remembered him as someone who, in his own words, "helped us to introduce some rigor into some of [the] sociologic research we supported." Yet, Felix added,

> Even at that early date, I knew that the place we were going to find the most sophisticated investigators in a field as nearly akin to ours as you could find existent at that time was in the field of medical sociology. Now there were medical sociologists who were far afield from us, so it wasn't all medical sociologists. It was a certain group. John Clausen represented this group pretty well. So I first developed a unit in the Institute right after it was formed called the Professional Service Branch.

As it turned out, Felix was defining medical sociology very broadly. It would be more accurate to call the group he recruited scientists trained to study social behavior who were brought together to work on problems of mental health. To ensure their collaboration, Felix said, "I put them into a large bay—deliberately did not give them each a private office. They worked together and they were to pool their information." It was a multidisciplinary team, including Clausen, the psychologists Joe Bobbitt and David Shakow,[47] Daniel Keep from social work, and two psychiatrists, Lawrence Kolb, Jr., and Mabel Ross. Felix used this group as his major advisors. "Whatever anybody wanted to do," Felix said, "in the area of training, research, or whatnot, they had to discuss it with this group, as a group, to see how it fit into what we were trying to do and to get a critique of the soundness of the proposal."

For Felix, the value of the work of social science in the NIMH during the period of his direction (1946–64) was very positive. Asked what he thought of the way medical sociology developed, he answered:

> I thought it developed soundly and well. I was very pleased with the people I was working with, both intramurally and extramurally. They were helpful. They knew what we were trying to do. They were dedicated people. And I thought we made tremendous progress. *As a matter of fact, I think we made more solid progress in the area of sociology than we did in the area of physiology, for the first ten years.* (my emphasis)

The Major Research Trends

Hollingshead was one of the first major research sociologists to be supported by NIMH. His relationship with NIMH began in 1949, when, together with the psychiatrist Frederic C. Redlich, he made his first proposal for an epidemiological study of mental illness in New Haven. This was in the second year of grant support by NIMH, and the Advisory Council served as a review panel for all grant proposals. Hollingshead and Redlich were turned down on that first application, but in 1950 they reapplied and were funded.[48]

In the ensuing research, Hollingshead and Redlich's work is often compared in importance with that of the Chicago ecological studies. Not only were both concerned with the relation between mental illness and social class, but both produced findings that clarified the issue and stimulated other investigators.[49] Freeman, writing in the 1969 *Handbook of Social Psychology*, estimated that the Yale study contributed perhaps "the most definitive data on the distribution of mental disorders by social class"[50] since the Chicago research two decades earlier. Unlike the dominantly incidence data collected by the preceding studies, Hollingshead and Redlich focused on prevalence (the number of cases under treatment at a given point in time), but their findings were consistent with the social ecology researchers of Chicago. They found schizophrenia concentrated in the lower social classes and neuroses and depression more characteristic of the higher classes. Because the findings are based on treated cases, just as most earlier studies, questions about incidence were unanswerable, they decided. They found also that neither the kind of treatment nor the length of hospitalization are independent of social class. A ten-year follow-up study supported particularly the relationship between social class and length of hospitalization.[51] A genuinely landmark study, the New Haven research lacked only data from untreated populations, and that would be the importance of the parallel epidemiological research supported by NIMH, particularly the Hutterite and Midtown studies.

Less well known is Hollingshead's role as an advisor to NIMH. He was appointed to the first NIMH study section in 1950. At that point, this was the only review panel for research proposals to NIMH. From his work on this panel, Hollingshead reported, "It was clear to me [from the research proposals coming in] that there were sociological and anthropological issues that needed to be studied, and that there was going to be a need for trained people."[52] However, when he sought training support from NIMH, he was turned down. As will be seen, he turned to private foundations and was more successful, but this experience demonstrates the selective policy of Felix to support sociology only in research and research consultation in the early years.

Although Hollingshead was the first sociologist to serve on a study section, he was not the only advisor. John Clausen, soon after his appointment to NIMH in 1948, sought the advice of a number of prominent sociologists, including Hollingshead. Among them were Leonard Cottrell, Jr., Kingsley Davis, H. Warren Dunham, Clifford Shaw, and Robin M. Williams, Jr.[53] This is further evidence that Felix quietly but consistently relied heavily on the help of sociologists in his leadership of NIMH. In his formal appointments, Felix always kept someone like Hollingshead to represent sociology, but in the beginning the numbers were small. Robin Williams replaced Hollingshead on the Mental Health Study Section, and in 1956 William Sewell replaced him—still the only sociologist; the others were all psychiatrists and psychologists. Although they did approve studies like that of Eaton and Weil and Hollingshead's proposal, Sewell felt that the extramural program, unlike Clausen's intramural research in the socioenvironmental laboratory, did not appreciate the potential contribution of sociology to mental health. "Immediately I began advocating," wrote Sewell, "a broader definition of mental health relevance and the need for greater representation of sociology and anthropology in the study section."[54] Soon, two such members were added, and the volume of proposals from these disciplines increased. NIMH responded by creating in 1959 a Behavioral Science Study Section to review all social science proposals relevant to mental health other than those in psychiatry and experimental psychology. Sewell chaired this new group. He reported:

> In its first year of existence, over 300 research proposals were evaluated, of which 125 were funded. These included several studies that have become classics in their fields. The section continued to be a major source of support for social science projects until the Reagan administration's insistence on a very restricted definition of mental health relevance crippled it.[55]

Such development, however, could hardly have been predicted in 1949 when Hollingshead and Redlich made their first proposal to study mental health in its relation to social class.

Hollingshead's NIMH-funded research was the culmination of the research planning that began when he and Redlich met in 1948.[56] Notable, however, is the fact that despite the success of their first research collaboration,[57] they separated immediately afterward. Not only in research but also in their intellectual affiliation they diverged, Hollingshead as a pioneer in medical sociology, Redlich as a leader of what came to be called "social psychiatry." Why, one must ask, was it necessary for these two disciplines to so carefully separate their professional identities, even in the full flush of successful research collaboration? Or what, in substance, is the defining difference between the mental health research of medical sociologists and the inquiry of social psychiatry? The question is all the more compelling when one considers that there were, at the same time, a substantial number of similar collaborations that, in a like manner, flourished and then stopped.

Although Hollingshead and Redlich found each other independently, Felix already had a model of interdisciplinary research that he brought to NIMH. His belief in the need for basic studies in psychiatric epidemiology as the foundation for research on the etiology and treatment of mental illness included the conviction that such work should be conducted collaboratively by clinical investigators and social scientists. Hollingshead and Redlich, therefore, were a perfect fit, as were Joseph Eaton and Robert Weil of the Hutterite study and Leo Srole and Thomas Rennie, the directors of the Midtown Manhattan study, another landmark research on the epidemiology of mental illness, which NIMH funded in 1951.[58] In these examples there appeared to be equal contributions from psychiatry and sociology, as Felix intended.[59]

NIMH was not alone in its interest in this kind of research. In the immediate aftermath of the war, there was an unusual confluence of concern among both private foundations and the government about mental illness. In 1949 and 1952, for example, the Milbank Memorial Fund conducted conferences on the epidemiology of mental disorders.[60] In 1950, the SSRC brought together two conferences of social scientists and psychiatrists "to consider the common ground in the fields of their interest."[61] At the same time, a longitudinal study of mental illness in Stirling County of Nova Scotia was sponsored by a consortium of government, universities, and private foundations in Canada and the United States. This was explained by the recognition that until that time, just following World

War II, the amount of mental illness in the United States was usually judged from the number of persons in mental hospitals (see chapter 4). There were almost no studies of untreated mental illness in the community. Now, in the decade 1945–55, an extraordinary research effort occurred to remedy this problem, and the NIMH made a major contribution. The Midtown Manhattan project is one of the outstanding examples.

Thomas Rennie, deputy chairman of the Cornell Department of Psychiatry at New York Hospital, was the originator of the Midtown Manhattan project. Although circumstances made him a minor figure in the actual work of the study, he completed the proposal that was approved by NIMH in 1951, working essentially on his own. He was assisted by consultants, especially Harry Alpert and John Clausen. It was Alpert, a sociologist at Yale, who recommended Leo Srole, whom Rennie recruited in 1952. At the time, Srole was research director of the Anti-Defamation League in the New York offices of the American Jewish Committee. Forty-three years old, Srole already was an established social scientist, with his Ph.D. in anthropology from the University of Chicago, was the senior author of a volume of the Yankee City Series, a six-volume report on a New England city, and had extensive research experience.[62]

The study by Srole and Rennie fulfilled the promise of total prevalence study in a different way from the Hutterite research. The population involved were in a diverse neighborhood of the most modern of cities, New York's Yorkville. While one of the purposes was to replicate the major findings about social class of the Hollingshead-Redlich New Haven research, there was a refinement particularly in the categories of illness and, most important, the method provided for the study of the untreated population; the latter was found to have an unexpectedly high level of mental impairment. Fully 80 percent of the sample reported some symptoms of psychiatric illness. In reading these results, however, it is necessary to look closely at the data, taking account of the way interpretations of impairment were made.

Srole, taking over primary responsibility for the research when Rennie became ill at the very beginning of their work, reviewed exhaustively the methodology of total prevalence study, leading to the choice of a combination of psychiatric and sociologic techniques. To assess psychopathology, a two-part interview, including structured scales, were rated independently by two psychiatrists. "Traditional diagnostic categories were abandoned and in their place the respondents were categorized according to generalized anxiety symptoms, specific symptom constellations, gross typology, and severity of disturbance."[63] According to the data collected and analyzed in this way, the conclusion of the Midtown study was that only one out of five people in central New York City qualified for the designation "essentially well."

Considerable public and professional attention was stimulated by this finding. Mental illness, by these criteria, was much more widespread than previously estimated. On closer examination, however, the findings were not as bleak as was suggested by the ratio of "essentially well" to "psychiatrically disabled." Of the latter category, for example, almost 60 percent were judged to be reasonably well adjusted to their life circumstances in spite of some degree of emotional difficulty. Therefore, the percentage who were judged to be "impaired" is 23.5, and only half of these were judged to be severely impaired or incapacitated. This estimate of one out of ten "severely impaired" was soon to be replicated by other total prevalence studies. In the Leightons' Nova Scotia study, for example, using methods similar to those of Srole, the number of individuals judged to have "psychiatric disorder with significant impairment" was virtually identical, 20 percent. Total prevalence, however, was smaller in Nova Scotia: 57 percent. Although more individuals in the rural and small-town environment of Stirling County were judged to be "essentially well" than in the Midtown Manhattan urban population, the same proportion—about one out five—were found to be notably handicapped in their life adjustment, and fewer suffered from severe disorder.[64] These findings were replicated by another total prevalence study in Baltimore by Pasaminick, who added important data about how many of the impaired were untreated.[65]

The Srole-Rennie study also added significantly to the research dialogue about social class:

1. Anxiety was found to be highly prevalent in the entire population and independent of social class.
2. Symptom constellations were most prevalent in the lower class and least prevalent in the upper.
3. Among the gross typologies the prevalence varied inversely with status, with the exception of the simple neurotic type, which was found to be significantly associated with the upper class.
4. When a general mental health rating was made, more severe disturbance was found in the lower class, and significantly more of the symptom-free were found in the middle and upper classes. Additional data were also presented relating social class to physical conditions presumed to be psychosomatic. . . . Overall, prevalence of psychosomatic conditions was not associated with class.[66]

The hopes of Felix, Bowers, and Clausen for total prevalence methods were more than fulfilled. During the first decade of NIMH-supported research, the scientific debate about the epidemiology of mental illness was advanced in a remarkable way. Rates of severe mental illness proved to be stable, associations with social class were clarified, and the amount of untreated serious psychiatric illness was found to be high.

On the surface, Srole and Rennie appear to fit Felix's model of collaborative research between clinical psychiatry and sociology, and the results testify to its success. However, at Cornell School of Medicine, the site of the Midtown research, the path of medical sociology, again, was not "smooth and easy."

From the beginning, Tom Rennie and Srole faced internal opposition to their work at the Cornell Psychiatry Department. Oscar Diethelm, the chairman of the department, was against the research. Diethelm's commitment to clinical psychiatry with a classical European focus on nosology clashed with this kind of sociological research. He decided that it did not fit in his department. The resulting internal conflict was similar in form to the resistance of Yale's psychiatrists to Hollingshead and Redlich and may be seen as just another sign of the constant struggle that sociological research experienced within psychiatry. One can speculate that psychiatry, struggling already for legitimacy within medicine because its own framework was distinctive from the rest of medicine, could not tolerate another approach, the sociological. Diethelm did not directly attack what Rennie was doing. He simply insisted that Rennie, who was his deputy chairman, must continue with all his clinical and teaching duties without relief. In effect, this allowed Rennie no more than two hours a day for the research.

In this situation, Srole assumed most of the responsibility. Within a few years, Rennie became terminally ill. Even then, Diethelm did not relent. By 1956, Leighton was appointed to succeed Rennie, even though Leighton was preoccupied with the Stirling County study. Srole, as the first stage of the research was completed, began to talk of a follow-up. Leighton was not interested, and Srole, now the principal investigator of the Midtown Manhattan project, left Cornell. In his own words, he was fired.[67]

John Clausen recognized the difficulties for sociologists but approached the problem pragmatically. He accepted the need, writing that the roles for sociologists within the mental health field require a large measure of collaboration with professionals, especially psychiatrists and other personnel who provide direct services to the mentally ill. Such sociologists may be surprised, he said, at the highly organized interdependence of several of the mental health specialties.

> It is a well-integrated group, usually in close agreement on value premises relating to the effectiveness of a particular therapeutic approach, with clearly established patterns of deference and responsibility and, quite often, a substantial unconcern with the objective social situations and social structure. . . . The strangeness of this subculture . . . and the focus upon feelings and emotions rather than upon variables which sociologists are more familiar with, may incline the sociologists to a somewhat critical attitude.[68]

In these remarks, Clausen could have been describing the experiences of Hollingshead and Srole. Curiously, at that very moment in research time, a parallel series of studies were being conducted by sociologists and anthropologists in mental hospitals, demonstrating *the power of the culture and social structure of these institutions to shape the therapeutic results* and also all behavior within them, including the research roles. The epidemiological studies similarly showed the importance of culture, whether it was in the religious precepts of the Hutterites or in the class stratifications so important in both the New Haven and Midtown Manhattan inquiries. Redlich was instrumental in bringing William Caudill, then a young anthropologist from the University of Chicago, to study from the inside the culture of Yale's own psychoanalytically oriented mental hospital.[69] And at St. Elizabeth's in Washington, D.C., Erving Goffman, working under the auspices of Clausen's socioenvironmental lab, told a story of hospital culture in which the boundaries between professional and patient subcultures were high and the status of patients was low. Goffman's graphic description of life in such a "total institution" caused a sensation beyond the medical and academic professions about the implications of such cultures for patients.[70]

If, as Clausen warned, the entry of sociologists into the world of mental health professionals started with the discomfort of *the stranger entering a tightly organized culture,* the sociologists themselves held the keys to understanding by their own theories and inquiries. After all, they should have expected that, as Clausen said further,

> He [the sociologist] is not likely to be immediately accepted into the subculture, even though the mental health specialists may have the friendliest

personal feelings and a strong desire for collaboration on a poject. As a scientist, he may find it difficult to accept some of the assumptions that clinicians make about therapeutic practices which have not been systematically validated. As he becomes more comfortable with the specialists, better able to share his perplexities, and as they become more comfortable with him, better able to share their own doubts, the possibilities of fruitful collaboration will often lead to a very satisfying team relationship.[71]

Clausen's hope became a reality, at least for the first two decades after the war. Remarkably productive collaborations proliferated. For example, at Harvard as well as at Yale, investigations by Stanton and Schwartz and by Milton Greenblatt, Daniel J. Levinson, and Richard H. Williams contributed important findings about the social structure, culture, and behavior in mental hospitals.[72] In addition, under the aegis of private foundations other fields drew sociologists together with physicians, as in the research on the sociology of medical education by sociologists at Columbia and Chicago universities.[73]

At the NIMH, soon after its beginnings, research questions were also raised about the alternatives to the hospital, especially the family. Initially, the focus was on the hospital. The scandals about psychiatric hospital conditions, the experiences of wartime treatment, and the data about the extent and distribution of psychiatric illness in the community were foremost in professional and public consciousness. Soon, however, studies were proposed about the effects of the mentally ill on those who normally assumed responsibility for them outside the hospital. Clausen himself, pursuing this question in the newly formed intramural facility at NIMH, was a major figure in this effort. It was not enough, he argued, to have a firm grasp of the extent of mental illness as indicated by hospital admissions, outpatient statistics, and from studies of total prevalence that revealed the untreated. What about the stresses caused by the severe illness of individuals on others? The family, for example, had been studied, prior to this time, with a focus on the contribution of the family or family members to the emotional breakdown of the individual. Little research attention had been paid to the question: What does illness or the ill person do to the family?[74]

"The consequences of mental illness in the family," Clausen said, "manifest themselves not only in the removal of one member, but also in changes in the structure and functioning of the whole family, both during the illness and afterward."[75] Especially if there is hospitalization, changes must be expected in the settings where the patients have lived. In their primary relationships, the family and work situation, the effects are significant for everyone involved. "One might anticipate," Clausen wrote, "that so substantial a practical problem, with so many aspects of significance for understanding the dynamics of human relationships, would have been thoroughly studied by social scientists. Unfortunately," he found, "this was not at all the case. With the exception of a few papers, primarily by psychiatric social workers who have drawn upon an intimate experience with the problems of families of mental patients rather than upon systematic data, there is no research literature on the impact of mental illness upon the family."[76]

When the Laboratory of Socio-environmental Studies was founded in 1951 and Clausen was appointed the first director, its specific mission was to "develop a research program bearing upon significant sociological and social-psychological issues relating to the cause, treatment and consequences of mental illness and aimed at increasing understanding of the cultural and social systems whereby mental illness is defined and dealt with."[77] Clausen was apparently fully aware of how Felix was forced, when he named the laboratory, to keep the word "sociological" in the closet. He proceeded to act with both caution and boldness. In a recent obituary, one of his successors at the Laboratory wrote:

> John thought he had to prove both himself and social science to NIMH, NIH, and the Public Health Service. He accomplished this with notable success, employing a complex combination of cautious tactics and audacious strategy. He cautiously undertook a not very exciting evaluation of some early polio vaccine trials, to prove to the Surgeon General that social science can be useful to public health. But he also encouraged Erving Goffman to confront organized psychiatry with the reality of the mental hospital being what Erv termed "a total institution," far different from anything that psychiatry cared to acknowledge. John was going to prove the Lab useful, but on his own terms.[78]

The founding of the Laboratory signaled the rapid diversification of research supported by NIMH. With the epidemiological research agenda strongly launched, Clausen personally committed himself to the study of the impact of mental illness on the family. An intensive longitudinal study was conducted of families from which the husband was hospitalized for mental illness. By 1955, the project was able to report, in a special issue of the *Journal of Social Issues*, on a wide range of types of influence that mental illness exerts on the family.[79]

As the first decade of the National Mental Health Act ended, Congress in 1955 passed the Mental Health Study Act, authorizing $1,250,000 for "an objective, thorough nationwide analysis and reevaluation of the human and economic problems of mental Illness." This was a far cry from the beginning in 1946. In 1948, after its first two years without a budget, NIMH was up and running, with thirty-eight research grants totalling $373,226. Seven years later, the Mental Health Study Act was a strong indicator that Congress no longer was being sidetracked by questions of legitimacy, political or scientific, in its willingness to support mental health research, even when it was done by sociologists. The Joint Commission on Mental Illness that it created was directed by a social psychologist, Marie Jahoda, and M. Brewster Smith was one of its officers. With what was at the time a huge budget, the Joint Commission represented a highly significant juncture in the federal government's commitment to both mental health research and the participation of social scientists. Shortly after the Joint Commission legislation was passed, the annual NIMH budget was almost doubled, from $3,890,631 to $7,326,311 in 1957.[80] Ten years after that, in 1967, the NIMH budget was $303,000,000.

It is tempting to believe that the rapidly growing acceptance of NIMH by Congress, and especially its creation of the Joint Commission, was due to the success of the NIMH research program. To some extent, that was probably true. There were, however, other important influences at work. Clausen himself credits the lobbying of voluntary organizations like the National Association for Mental Health and the manpower shortages in mental hospitals.[81] Clark Vincent, who became the first executive secretary of the social science subcommittee of the NIMH Training and Manpower Resources Branch, believed that a variety of influences were at work:

Many interlocking factors . . . combined and converged to stimulate the federal government's initial assumption of major responsibility for mental health. Some of the factors were the rejectees of World War II, the VA programs, the shortage of psychiatric manpower and hospital beds, drug research, and the spiraling costs of confining increasing numbers of patients in institutional facilities that were fast wearing out.[82]

In any event, most important in the development of medical sociology, the NIMH, after supporting important research by social scientists for a decade but reserving its training funds for the clinical professions—psychiatry, pschology, social work, and nursing—recognized the need to train social scientists in 1957. In that year, NIMH sponsored two pilot training programs for social scientists.

Research Training in the Social Sciences

Felix, as quoted earlier, concluded that during the early years of NIMH medical sociology made "more solid progress" than any other discipline. However, he must have been referring entirely to research because, in its early years, NIMH supported social science only in research. In spite of the piority Felix gave to training, its application in fact was selective. In its first decade, NIMH training support focused on the research training of psychiatrists and psychologists but also to some extent in related clinical fields (as mentioned earlier). Not until 1957 was the research training broadened to include social sciences. It was as though research was required first to demonstrate the need for social science training related to mental health. At least that was the judgment of Kenneth Lutterman, who was the third executive secretary of the Social Science Research Training Committee.[83] "It became apparent from the work of Hollingshead and Redlich and others," Lutterman wrote, "that much greater knowledge of the social determinants of mental illness and of the behavioral science context underlying deviant behavior was required for both effective treatment and prevention."[84] At Harvard University Medical School and the University of North Carolina Institute for Research in Social Science, NIMH gave pilot program support for mental health–relevant research training in 1957. A third pilot program was awarded in 1958 to the Social Science Institute at Washington University in St. Louis, Missouri.

Another explanation for the additional funds from Congress for the new training program in 1957 is more simple. An NIMH Research Task Force said:

This [the award of funding to NIMH for the research training of social scientists] was begun in 1957—not coincidentally the year the first manmade satellite was orbited by the Russians. Under this program, NIMH has awarded grants to public and private nonprofit institutions to provide financial assistance to students in the behavioral sciences who are preparing for service or research in fields related to mental health.[85]

Whatever the reasons were, in the fall of 1958, a brochure was sent to chairs of sociology and anthropology departments announcing the availability of grant support for two broad categories of doctoral and postdoctoral training: "(1) [t]raining of social scientists for research in mental health areas, and (2) training of professional personnel from the mental health disciplines in the research methods of the social sciences." Twenty-two applications were received and reviewed by an ad hoc committee in the fall of 1959; four of these were awarded five-year grants with activation dates of July 1, 1960, and the three grants previously awarded as pilot programs were reclassified as regular programs.[86]

In 1960, the first full-time administrator for the social science training program, Clark Vincent, was appointed, and the Social Sciences Subcommittee was started with six members. Within a decade, the budget for this program grew from $314,128 for seven programs to $4,664,400 for seventy-six programs.[87] The growth of this program was extraordinary, as if they were attempting to catch up for the delay before 1960. Until 1965, the concentration of this support was in sociology: 80 percent of both the monies and the doctoral trainees were for sociology and social psychology, about 11 percent in anthropology.

A brief definition is inserted here to clarify the fields that are being discussed as the subjects of NIMH grants and that together make up the behavioral sciences of medicine. Misconceptions are most likely about social psychology. First, as Gordon Allport wrote, "no sharp boundaries demarcate social psychology from other social sciences. . . . It overlaps political and economic science, cultural anthropology, and in many respects is indistinguishable from general psychology. Likewise, its tie with sociology is close."[88] The confusion is increased, Allport adds, by the fact that the writers of textbooks in the subject are almost equally divided between sociologists and psychologists. Nevertheless, social psychology has its own core of theory and data and its own special viewpoint.

> Its focus of interest is upon the social nature of the individual person. By contrast, political science, sociology, and cultural anthropology take as their starting points the political, social, or cultural systems in which an individual person lives. . . . They seek inclusive laws of social structure, social change, cultural patterning. . . . By contrast social psychology wishes to know how any given member of a society is affected by all the social stimuli that surround him.[89]

The NIMH was able somehow to maneuver among these confusions and to treat social psychology, correctly, as an independent field.

The rapid growth of support for research training in the social sciences during the early 1960s coincided with manpower shortages in new and expanding universities. The annual supply of Ph.D.s in sociology and anthropology was considered too low to meet the growing demand. More specifically, in 1965, Clark Vincent estimated that 185 Ph.D.s in sociology and about 70 in anthropology graduated in the United States. He regarded these numbers as "critically low to meet the demand for new and replacement faculty in existing departments of these two disciplines, much less to supply the needs of new and expanding universities."[90] The NIMH program proved to be influential on a much wider academic base than the originally planned mental health relevance.

Initially, "mental health relevance" was defined to mean that the research training would take place in a medical or clinical setting or involve active participation of psychology. The first three pilot programs were in medical settings, and social psychology was accepted, Clark Vincent reported, on the basis that psychology was one of the core mental health disciplines.[91] As early as 1962, the members of the Social Science Subcommittee became concerned about the narrowness of this definition. They feared that (1) it could result in turning out "mental health technicians" rather than well-trained sociologists or anthropologists; (2) the growing demand for social scientists from schools of medicine, public health, social work, and nursing might deplete the faculty within sociology and anthropology departments; and (3) the potential contributions of any one social science to the mental health field would be limited by the pressure to adhere to models and research questions that were only appropriate to clinical and mental health disciplines.[92] As a result, and with the approval of the National Advisory Mental Health Council, a broad interpretation of mental health relevance became operational. After 1963 this interpretation prevailed, and the training program operated on the principle that a well-trained research professional in any of the social sciences was the most effective potential recruit for mental health–relevant research. As Lutterman wrote, looking back at the history of the program, "[q]uality training was what was needed, and the by-products of the process would feed into manpower and research of the mental health effort. Programs that looked at deviant behavior, social disorganization, social organization, the family, aging, and so forth, were all regarded as reasonable content areas for support, and the scope of relevance became virtually all inclusive."[93]

The emergence of this inclusive philosophy can be interpreted either as a response to market forces or as a deliberate value-based decision. Supporting the former explanation, manpower shortages did exist, from 1955 to 1975, both for medical sociology and for sociology more broadly. In medical institutions and in the expanding university departments, positions were available. At the same time, this was also the preferred policy of Clark Vincent, Nathaniel Siegal, and Kenneth Lutterman, who served as the first three executive secretaries to the Social Science Subcommittee at NIMH.[94] This is reflected in their choices for the membership of the Social Science Subcommittee, whose first appointees were Orville Brim, Jr., John Honigman, Ronald Lippit, Edward Stainbrook, Robert Straus, and Edmund Volkart. Only Straus and Volkart could be considered full-time medical sociologists at that time, and Stainbrook, a psychiatrist, was a pioneer of behavioral science. The others had no specific association with medicine or mental health research. The next round of the Subcommittee membership included Peter Rossi (chairman), Edgar Borgatta, Donald Cressey, and Raymond Sletto, all outstanding mainstream sociologists; Kimball Romney (anthropologist); and John Spiegel; only Spiegel, a psychiatrist, could be considered an active scholar in subjects of medical social science. Throughout its history, the subcommittee membership represented a broad, inclusive definition of manpower needs.

The rapid expansion during the 1960s of support for social science by NIMH in both research and training spilled over to other federal agencies. At the National Institute of General Medical Sciences (GMS), individual research grants with sociologists as principal investigators appeared, and some special training program grants were awarded. GMS supported a research training program at Brown University and another at the University of Michigan School of Public Health. These types of grants were reassigned to the NCHSR, an agency created in 1968.[95]

The NCHSR can be interpreted as the high point of interest in the social and behavioral aspects of health. With a specific interest in promoting research about the delivery of health care services, its first director, Paul Sanazarro, created an office of research training, headed by Allan Mayers, a sociologist. The various individual grants from GMS were transferred to the NCHSR Training Committee, and a full range of training program and career fellowship grants was pursued with generous funding. Frank Caffee, the first deputy director of the Office of Training of the NCHSR, estimated that fully five million dollars was allocated for doctoral trainees, postdoctoral fellowships, and career fellowship awards.[96]

The emergence of NCHSR was further evidence of the increase of government interest in applied social research. Among the factors that fueled this development the Joint Commission on Mental Illness and Health must be considered. Its report in 1961[97] was used as a basis for proposed federal action by a cabinet-level committee. Their recommendations were the main source for President Kennedy's message to Congress on February 5, 1963, and the result was the Community Mental Health Centers Construcion Act (P.L.88-164), signed into law by President Kennedy on October 31, 1963. This direction of the government's interest in mental health and retardation caused both the expansion of the market for social scientists and the broadening of the definition of what kinds of programs would be supported. Such areas as urban studies, the economics of human resources, history, social science, and various types of interdisciplinary research were increasingly welcomed by the Social Science Research Training Committee of the NIMH,[98] and the NCHSR focused on training for research that could be applied to problems of health care delivery and to the social problems that interfered with equitable systems of health care.

From its modest beginnings in 1957 at NIMH, the subcommittee for social science research training by 1972 was awarding one thousand five hundred stipends at a cost of thirteen million dollars. Then suddenly the Nixon administration, in connection with the amended budgets of fiscal years 1973 and 1974, announced its decision to phase out federal support for categorical professional training programs. This included all programs, affecting the NCHSR as well. At the same time, the Public Health Service reached the apex of reorganization that had begun during the middle 1960s. The net effect was to reduce both research and training support, with a focus on the social sciences in the 1970s. There seems no question that the purpose of administration actions from 1972 to 1974 was to phase out federal support for much of the social science programs, but especially training. Fortunately, that goal was never reached, but the levels of support that were achieved during the decade of the 1960s were gone and did not return.

A full description of the organizational changes that occurred in the NIMH and NCHSR are detailed in a report of the Task Force of the NIMH that was published in 1975.[99] Further discussion of health services research and the relation between NIMH and social science will be included later, after summary assessment of this period, 1950 to 1970, and how it effected the institutionalization of medical sociology.

Summary and Additional Biographical Notes

For the better part of a century after the Civil War, as I have shown, there was active research about how social factors influence problems of health and illness. Yet the participation of sociologists was episodic, and the research, often outstanding in quality, was not preserved in the way that is necessary for the building of a scientific field. To achieve such a goal, medical sociology needed the continuous accumulation of knowledge. Prior to the Second World War, this did not occur. Soon after the war it did, and more than anything else the support of IMH made this important step possible. First in research and later in research training, federal funds were channeled through NIMH to sociologists who were primarily major investigators of mental health problems at the beginning and of a broader spectrum of research later.

Sociologists also, from the outset, functioned as part of the policy-making staff of the NIMH. Robert Felix, the first director, decided that sociology in particular and social sciences more generally should be a vital part of the new institute, and in spite of resistance from Congress and some of his medical colleagues, he made it happen. The individual people who emerged during this part of medical sociology's history were from various backgrounds, representative of the parent discipline and not distinctive in any way that can be attributed to medicine as a separate interest.

Hollingshead, whose contributions are noted by virtually everyone who participated in this period, is more typical of the early sociologists who dominated American sociology from the late nineteenth and early twentieth century. His personal roots are in the American heartland, where his formative years were in the West and Midwest, a classic Protestant background. Born in Wyoming, his sociological training was at the University of California at Berkeley and the University of Nebraska at Lincoln, where he received his Ph.D. At the University of Chicago, he did a postdoctoral fellowship with W. Lloyd Warner. His first major book, *Elmtown's Youth*,[100] was a community study on the model that was developed by his mentor, W. Lloyd Warner.

Leo Srole, on the other hand, was representative of the influx of what Shils called "a different type of recruit to sociology."[101] The son of immigrants from Lithuania, he grew up in Chicago. Although he shared midwestern boyhood with Hollingshead, his background otherwise could not have been more different. In a curious way these two landmark studies, now regarded as classics, paired unlikely partners. Both involved men from traditional American Protestant backgrounds, Hollingshead and Rennie, each working in tandem with first- or second-generation European Jews, Redlich and Srole.

Srole's career was unorthodox from the start.[102] Born in 1909, he went directly from high school to Northwestern, "hated it," and quit almost immediately, going to work as a collection manager for a furniture credit house. After working a few years, he resumed his schooling at Harvard. "Harvard," he said, "was as far away to me at the time as Oxford—a rich man's school—and my father barely made a living." A close high school friend who was at Harvard recommended it, and Srole, although he had not "even remotely considered it," decided, "why not." When asked about it, he added: "Mind you, when I was admitted in 1930, Lowell was still president[103] and quotas were still very much in effect. That was the atmosphere, and my being there was quite accidental."

Srole's undergraduate years at Harvard coincided with the beginning of the school's department of sociology. In 1931 the Faculty of Arts and Sciences established a Division of Sociology, with Pitirim Sorokin as chair.[104] Srole, still a maverick, began as a philosophy major but again, repeating his Northwestern experience, was dissatisfied. During his second academic year, however, he found what he wanted working with W. Lloyd Warner, a social anthropologist, who had just arrived at Harvard from Australia, where he had done the research for *Black Civilization*.[105] By February 1932, although still an undergraduate, he started field work in Newburyport, New Hampshire, the site of the Yankee City Series.[106] Eventually, Srole became one of the senior authors in the Warner study,[107] his first major publication.

These were, as Srole remembered many years later, "heady" years for sociology at Harvard. A starting point was the Pareto seminar of Lawrence J. Henderson. Srole's entry into the seminar was through Warner, coinciding with his joining the Newburyport staff:

> My first assignment was to study the Jewish community. Various partici-
> pants—Connie Arensberg,[108] for example, studied the Irish, and Alison Da-
> vis studied the blacks, and so on—We would give reports, and when I gave
> a report on the Jewish community, Elton Mayo came. He became a bridge
> to the Harvard Business School group, and Warner was a consultant to the
> Western Electric Research. That was how I met Henderson.[109]

Srole's impression of Henderson is, typically, very much his own, contrasting with the generally very admiring reminiscences of people like George Homans and Bernard Barber (see chapter 5).[110] Srole recalls:

> He was such a vivid guy. First of all he was on the short side, maybe five
> feet six inches, rather full-bodied, and had this magnificent red beard which
> made him look sort of jovial. But in manner, he was a mandarin: everyone
> sitting at his feet, speaking with great authority. . . . He was an opinionated
> son-of-a-bitch, but everyone, of course, had great respect for him.

Srole was duly impressed with the wide range of outstanding intellectuals who attended the Henderson seminar and who in some cases were Henderson's de-voted followers.[111] In the end, however, Srole turned away from the Henderson group. In spite of his great respect for Alfred North Whitehead and others in the seminar, he "was turned off by Pareto." For Srole, Pareto "seemed to me to be kind of a root of Italian Fascism." Srole was careful to add that he did not see Henderson himself as a Fascist or even an admirer of European Fascism. He saw him only as a Yankee conservative.

Srole graduated in 1933 and continued as a graduate student at Harvard until 1935. Essentially he was continuing as part of the Yankee City research. When Warner went to Chicago in 1935, he asked Srole to go with him, so Srole com-pleted his doctorate in anthropology in 1940 at Chicago.[112] Until the interruption of the war, Srole's focus was on ethnic relations and on community study. His shift to medically related research occurred during his military service. There, two types of experience placed their stamp on the remainder of his career. First, in the Air Force, he was assigned to work with psychologists responsible for the selection of air crews and later with psychiatrists treating air crews who had cracked up in combat. He learned quantitative skills that were to serve him well in his epidemiologic research, and he saw mental illness firsthand. Second, in early 1945, when the concentration camps were opened by the allied troops, he volunteered for the refugee agency that was just getting started. Discharged "in the national interest" from the Air Force, Srole went to Germany, where for a year he worked with displaced persons. Working with survivors of Dachau, Bu-chenwald, and other camps, he returned from the experience "so burned out" that he could not return to academic life. He spent another year lecturing about the DP camps all over the United States, and then joined the Jewish Anti-defamation League as research director. In 1952 Tom Rennie recruited him to the Midtown Manhattan study.

Hollingshead and Srole, and the two landmark studies they directed, are outstanding in the first postwar cohort of researchers, who, in effect, demonstrated the value of social science research on mental illness, preparing the way for the large-scale support of federal funds that came in the second decade of NIMH. Bowers, Clausen, Sewell, Eaton, Caudill, Goffman, Schwartz, and others joined in this path, until congressional resistance was completely eliminated and large-scale support flowed, not only from NIMH but also from other government agencies. However, although much of the story as told here centers on the function of NIMH in the emergence of medical sociology as a subdiscipline, there is also the reciprocal story of how sociology influenced the early development of NIMH. It is a story of both methodology and substance. The public concern about mental illness, intensified by the experience of war, created government support for research that would identify the extent of the problem and clinical programs that would attempt to more effectively prevent and treat mental illness. In the beginning, sociology functioned mainly for research consultation. Robert Felix recruited people like Bowers, Clausen, Hollingshead, and Sewell for their methodological abilities, using them to recruit and direct research that, at first through epidemiological study, provided a more valid portrait of the nature and extent of the problem.

As I have shown, this was not an easy task; barriers like the stereotypes of Cold War politics and interprofessional prejudice were encountered. Even the support of total prevalence research was blocked when first proposed. In the case of Hollingshead and Redlich, for example, their first effort at a community population study, similar in its sampling to the subsequent Midtown Manhattan research, was rejected on the basis of arguments by a social scientist in the review process of the first NIMH Council. As a result, when they reapplied, the Yale group used a more traditional hospital-based sample.[113]

Nevertheless, Felix and his staff persisted and were successful in stimulating an era of remarkable research that provided data for dramatic changes in public policy on the treatment of mental illness. The stage was being set for the deinstitutionalization of the mentally ill, a policy that was to take full root two decades after the war during the Kennedy and Johnson administrations. As part of this process, Felix again played a significant role in recruiting sociologists to a new research task. This came about in 1963 when Felix turned his attention to the policy directions that followed from the Mental Health Study Act of 1955. In that Act, Congress created the Joint Commission on Mental Illness and Health, and its final report, *Action for Mental Health*, was released in 1961.[114] The Joint Commission produced a multidisciplinary effort that can be compared to such policy-oriented groups as the CCMC and the Ogburn Committee on Social Trends (see chapter 3). Thirty-six national agencies participated in the Joint Commission's work. "They ranged from the American Legion to the American Psychiatric Association, the American Medical Association, the Council of State Governments and the Veterans Administration," wrote Bertram M. Brown, M.D., who was the chief of the Community Mental Health Facilities Branch of NIMH and later became Felix's successor.[115] "The very comprehensiveness of the range of organizations involved assured that the report would receive major attention."

Between 1961 and 1963, a cabinet-level committee analyzed the Joint Commission's work, and on February 5, 1963, President Kennedy gave a special message to Congress on mental illness and retardation. On October 31, 1963, Congress passed Public Law 88–164; Title II of that law was the Community Mental Health Centers Act. This was to usher in a major new direction for federally sponsored social science research, but in preparation, immediately after the February presidential message to Congress, Felix acted.

Robert Straus tells how this occurred in an autobiographical memoir.[116] "One day in March 1963," Straus wrote,

> a call came from Dr. Robert Felix . . . requesting a "drop everything" trip to Washington. There he had assembled seven men (four psychiatrists and three social scientists) coincidental with President Kennedy's message to Congress calling for nation-wide programs in comprehensive community mental health. Dr. Felix asked this group, under the chairmanship of Dr. Francis Braceland, to recommend guidelines for the implementation of a national program of support for community mental health centers. In thirteen months, we met nineteen times in a most exciting adventure in planning for social policy.[117]

After setting in motion these new directions of NIMH research, Dr. Felix left Washington in 1964 to become dean of the Medical school at St. Louis University. Without any question, he was a major figure in the development of modern medical sociology.

9

Becoming a Profession

The Role of
the Private Foundations

Medical sociology, to establish itself, required conditions of intellectual interest, of social demand, of sponsorship, and of resources. Although the federal government, particularly NIMH, was instrumental in the professional development of medical sociology, private foundations prepared the way—especially in training, in introducing the social sciences into medical education, and in directly stimulating and supporting professional organization. Both before and after federal agencies became involved, private foundations continued to play a vital function. The Commonwealth Fund, the Milbank Memorial Fund, and the Rockefeller Foundations deserve special mention, but the Russell Sage Foundation played the most singular role. It set directions of research, recruited already established social scientists, and trained a cadre of sociologists who were to be among the most influential of the early medical sociologists.

The Russell Sage Foundation

Medicine was not targeted in the Foundation's program[1] until Donald Young became its president[2] in 1948, but one can trace related interests much earlier. In 1907, when Margaret Olivia Sage established the Russell Sage Foundation, the goal of the new organization was defined as "the improvement of social and living conditions in the United States of America."[3] Toward this end the Foundation's initial program embraced two complementary efforts: "to professionalize social work and to eliminate deleterious environmental conditions."[4] For the next forty years it supported the field of social work, both its organizations and its research. This did not mean the professional practice of social work. Margaret Sage chose research as the means whereby the Foundation should be a national "center of charitable and philanthropic information,"[5] and in the process it became a leading source of social welfare data. Eric Wanner, the current president of the Russell Sage Foundation, recently recalled the ten years after its founding as a time when a thriving research enterprise was established.[6] However, as a policy research institution, it was also a prototype for subsequent "policy think tanks."[7]

Even as the Foundation was seen as engaged primarily in the effort to professionalize social work, it was also fully involved in an array of other programs that sought to alleviate poverty, improve the conditions of children, prevent tuberculosis and aid other forms of public health, and relieve social inequities for industial workers and women. Therefore, Hammack recently argued, although the Foundation's support of social work has received the most attention, the Foundation played a signal role in the development of a variety of fields. He views the change of policy that occurred in 1947 as a break with its past but not as radical a change as it might appear. These facts notwithstanding, Russell Sage was identified with the field of social work and general purpose charitable issues until soon after the Second World War, when the Foundation changed its course. "It emerged as one of the few organizations specifically committed to social and behavioral sciences."[8]

Signaling this shift of focus was the change of its leadership. Donald R. Young was the choice as the new general director. Young, immediately before his appointment, was the executive director of the SSRC. Before that he was a professor of sociology at the University of Pennsylvania, and during World War II he helped to organize the research branch of the U.S. army, the famous I and E Research Branch directed by Samuel Stouffer. Very much in the forefront of Young's plans for the Foundation was the introduction of social science in the professions, and Esther Lucile Brown, already established as a senior staff person, was seen as a key figure in this program. Brown, in turn, was closely associated with the Foundation's premier statistician, Ralph G. Hurlin. A member of the Foundation's staff for forty-three years beginning in 1920, Hurlin specialized in community surveys and the development of the field of social statistics.[9]

Hurlin and Brown together played a key role in President Herbert Hoover's commission, the Ogburn study of social trends, for which Hurlin was asked to write the chapter on occupations.[10] This was in 1930, the year Esther Lucile Brown applied to the Russell Sage Foundation for a job. Two years earlier, she was the first woman to receive a Ph.D. in anthropology from Yale, followed by a year as a SSRC fellow studying in France. Hurlin welcomed her as a consultant in his work for Ogburn. In her own words:

> He [Hurlin] said to me that he would be very happy to have a social scientist as a consultant in connection to the chapter on occupations because he came through a biological background to statistics. When I told him I had no statistics, he said the one thing he did not need was statistics. He was extremely busy at the time, and I said to him, "While you are getting ready to see what you want to do in the way of discussion, would you like me to collect material on professions which would constitute one small portion of the chapter on occupations?" And he said, "Wonderful idea." At the end of six months, I had enough material for a comparative look at several professions, so the Foundation said, "Oh, we must continue this. We must bring out material that has been more fully developed as individual publications, because the chapter on occupations could not exceed seventy pages." Dr. Hurlin thought he could allot ten pages to the professions.[11]

Although she remained in Hurlin's Department of Statistics, Brown continued to work on the professions essentially on her own. Beginning with what was still the focus of the Foundation, her first study, *Social Work as a Profession*, was published in 1935.[12] Almost immediately afterward she turned to the other professions, publishing, in rapid succession, books on engineering (1936), nursing (1936), physicians (1937), and lawyers (1938).[13] Finally, after almost fifteen years, the anomaly of such work being conducted under the aegis of a department of statistics was recognized. In October 1944 the Department of Studies in the Professions was created in the Foundation, and Brown was appointed as its head. Her own recall was that Hurlin turned to her one day and said: "It's just ridiculous for us to be publishing the books on professions from the Department of Statistics." A department of professions was then formally created.

Within a few years, the Foundation was reorganized, and Brown and Hurlin were essentially the only members of the prior senior staff who continued when the new president joined the Foundation. They represented both the social science and policy interests that were chosen, a sharp change from what had prevailed before.[14]

To a degree, the immediate effect appeared to favor the study of the professions generally. Certainly for Esther Lucile Brown, these new auspices were associated with a broad range of studies. She published another book on lawyers in 1948 and in the same year a book on nursing based on a study for the National Nursing Council, financed by the Carnegie Corporation and Russell Sage. She was co-author in 1955 of a book on mental health care that was to have a powerful influence on psychiatry.[15] After her retirement in 1963, she continued research and writing on nursing, conducting a study requested and financed by the National League for Nursing.[16]

Young, however, asked Brown to concentrate her work on the health field as part of a strategic decision to turn away from the Foundation's former association with social work.[17] "Although Dr. Young had respect for some practitioners in the field of social work," Hammack wrote,

> he thought the field as a whole was rather soft and poorly developed. Perhaps even more important, in the prestige rankings of the professions, social work fell far below medicine. If the Russell Sage Foundation could bring social science to bear in an important way on medical practice, the world of practitioners and scholars would sit up and listen. The same effect in social work would not be seen as such an accomplishment. And among the professions of a status higher than that of social work, medicine, unlike law, had a research tradition.[18]

In this way, medical sociology became a major beneficiary of Young's policy.

Young and Brown were well aware that, within medicine, the fields most receptive to social science at that time were public health and psychiatry, so they started there. At the suggestion of Dr. Hugh R. Leavell of the Harvard University School of Public Health, the Foundation funded the full-time services of Dr. Benjamin D. Paul "for the purpose of developing a series of fully documented cases that could be used in teaching the sociological and psychological factors involved in problems commonly encountered by public health personnel, together with the methods of social science that might be of help in resolving such problems."[19] As Dr. Leavell said at the time, "[p]ublic health in the past has depended primarily on the biological and physical sciences. It now needs to draw heavily on the social sciences as well."[20] Paul used this experience to create a teaching casebook that became one of the Foundation's best-selling books, widely used to teach medical anthropology and sociology.[21] Psychiatry similarly received support. Otto von Mering, an anthropologist, was sent to do research at the University of Pittsburgh Department of Psychiatry, recruited from the Boston Psychopathic Hospital, where he had been doing research with Paul S. Barrabee on the incompatibilities between ethnic cultural values and those of the wider community. Von Mering, together with Stanley King, later published with Russell Sage a study of their attempts to utilize anthropological concepts in a new action treatment program called "social remotivation."[22]

But Donald Young wanted to penetrate the more standard and resistant parts of medicine as well. As described earlier,[23] Brown was already in contact with Harold G. Wolff, the professor of medicine and neurology at Cornell University Medical College, and knew of his interest in having a social scientist join him in both research and teaching. Brown convinced both Wolff and Leo W. Simmons, a sociologist at Yale, that they should work together. In 1949, Simmons took a leave from Yale to join Dr. Wolff at Cornell. This was the initial collaboration that resulted from Young's new approach to social science and the professions.[24] Others soon followed.

Young did not commit the Foundation to any one profession, however, without a disciplined scholarly exploration of the potentials. For this purpose, he turned to Columbia University in 1949, where he gave a grant to create a University Seminar on the Professions in Modern Society. It was composed of representatives of the University's several professional schools, its social science faculties, and the Foundation staff. The seminar was designed to provide "a forum at which members report on the function, development and present status of the professions represented; on social science theories and studies relevant to professional problems; and on the utilization of social science content and methodology by the professions."[25] Presiding at this seminar was Professor Robert K. Merton of Columbia's Department of Sociology, and William J. Goode was brought from Michigan State University to act as staff to the seminar. Merton and Goode examined the literature and condensed the seminar discussions, creating a document that Russell Sage expected to become a general casebook on social science and the professions. Within two years, however, the focus of this seminar's work was on medicine. Out of this seminar, perhaps the most important result was the research on the sociology of medical education directed by Professor Merton and Patricia Kendall in collaboration with Dr. George G. Reader, professor of medicine at Cornell University School of Medicine. The latter study, started in 1953, became a path-breaking contribution to studies of the socialization of physicians that were supported by the Commonwealth Fund.[26]

In 1950, Dr. Harvey L. Smith joined the staff of the Foundation to make a two-year study of psychiatry. In addition, research on interpersonal relations started by Leo Simmons at New York Hospital–Cornell Medical Center yielded research on nursing and patient care. At the same time, the Russell Sage Department on the Professions arranged in the late summer of 1951 for social science assistance to health services for Spanish-speaking patients. Professor Lyle Saunders was supported to take a two-year leave of absence from the Department of Sociology of the University of New Mexico to go to Denver "to assist the University of Colorado Medical Center in individualizing therapeutic and health services for Spanish-speaking persons, who constitute a large proportion of the patients of the Denver General Hospital and its associated clinics and public health services."[27]

These early efforts of Young and Brown almost immediately produced teaching programs at medical schools and schools of public health, as well as research. In effect they helped to create a new academic market, setting up a demand for social scientists to work in medical institutions. To meet the demand, the Foundation created a program of Health Service Residencies for Social Scientists. The plan for these residencies was completed by 1950, and the first appointment was made. "The demand for social scientists," the Foundation wrote,

> within medical centers, public health agencies, and professional associations interested in promoting medical and health services is already larger than can be met by drawing upon university faculties of the behavior sciences. There is also a need for more specialized knowledge and experience in dealing with questions of sickness and therapeutic and preventive services than now possessed by most academic social scientists if any distinctive contributions are to be made."[28]

Accordingly, residencies were created for young Ph.D.s to train in institutions requesting such services. The Foundation provided comparable university salaries for two-year appointments. The first appointment was of Albert F. Wessen, a recent Yale Ph.D. in sociology, to work in the Department of Pediatrics of the Yale Medical School, studying the impact of health service residencies for social sciences on the sick child and its family. With this program, Russell Sage anticipated by a full decade the training programs of NIMH, which were not to be fully implemented until 1960.

By 1953, there were six Russell Sage crossdisciplinary residencies.[29] Wessen continued at Yale and received a two-year extension of his appointment. Carol F. Creedon, a psychologist, trained with the Family Health Maintenance Demonstration Program at Montefiore Hospital in New York City. Richard W. Boyd, a psychologist, was studying the relationships between social behavior and physiologic reactions at the Boston Psychopathic Hospital. Stanley H. King, a clinical psychologist, received an appointment for work involving sociology and physiology at the Boston Psychopathic Hospital. Harold D. McDowell, a sociologist, explored the usefulness of sociological knowledge for problems of medicine and its practice at Vanderbilt University School of Medicine. Harriet Linton, a psychologist, studied the precipitating events in mental illness and ward behavior at Rockland State Hospital in Orangeburg, New York.

The Foundation also decided that "because of the difficulty in finding individuals well trained in [both] social science and in a specific area of professional practice, encouragement of experimental programs for such dual training in strong graduate schools seemed desirable."[30] Virtually the identical conclusion had been drawn by Hollingshead when he sat on the first study section of NIMH in 1950. It was fitting, therefore, that Russell Sage gave the first grant of this type to the Department of Sociology at Yale University to establish a faculty seminar "to facilitate communication across disciplinary lines, develop a systematic program of cooperation between the social and medical sciences, and plan a student training program."[31] In this way the Foundation helped to start what was to be the first formal training program in medical sociology. Russell Sage was interested in Yale's plan to conduct a four-year course of training in sociology in cooperation with the School of Medicine and the Department of Public Health. With this start-up support, the Yale sociology department developed a training plan for a proposal that was made to the Commonwealth Fund in 1953, and in 1955, the program was started. In the same year, an announcement was circulated offering one thousand five hundred dollars per year and tuition for predoctoral fellows in medical sociology. The first four Yale Commonwealth fellows included Ray H. Elling and Leonard Syme, who both went on to become major contributors to the field. The other two fellows in this first graduate class did not complete the program.[32]

Very quickly, however, problems emerged. During the year 1952–53, Russell Sage reflected on its decision, five years earlier, to devote primary attention to the relationship between the social sciences and the practicing professions. Although they found much evidence of success, they also identified "a variety of limiting factors." At a two-day conference of twenty-one participants in the Foundation's programs, held in the Department of Social Relations of Harvard University, some of the problems were uncovered. From the social science standpoint, the most serious problem appeared to be the result of "conflicting aspects of the prevailing ideas and work habits of the research and practicing professions involved."[33] Virtually all the participating social scientists expressed uncertainty about how to work with the practicing professions. Misunderstandings led to feelings of threat or disappointment on both sides. Diverse institutional traditions and operating patterns troubled the collaborations. The clinicians tended to be impatient about the time and money required for related research; the research-oriented social scientists were likely to be reluctant to recommend changes in how things are done without strong data to support such changes. There were also different orientations toward research. Psychiatrists, for example, seemed to be more ready to accept the interviewing techniques of anthropologists than the complicated statistical data of experimental psychologists or survey sociologists. There were career anxieties. Social scientists particularly feared a loss of status in the eyes of their academic peers as a result of their focus on applied problems of practice, especially when extended affiliation with nonacademic institutions were required.

In most instances, these problems mirrored those (described in chapter 8) of the social scientists who served on the staffs of NIMH and of the early recipients of federal grants where collaboration with medical professionals was required. Yet, just as those problems did not stop the growth of such collaborative work, so too the Russell Sage programs were not deterred. The Foundation, however, recognized what was judged to be "a very real danger for social scientists who move into applied fields that they may inadvertently reduce their contacts with social science because of an almost exclusive association with and identification with a practicing profession."[34] Therefore, every effort was made to see that some formal association was maintained with social science colleagues.

In the final evaluation, it was not concern for the problems encountered that was emphasized; rather it was the shortage of suitably trained and experienced personnel and the "poverty of materials available giving form and substance to the research-practice relationship . . . prepared by individuals who are intimately acquainted with the problems in definite areas of practice."[35] These conclusions gave new vitality and direction to the continuation of the Foundation's program in social science and the professions.

During the next two years, 1953–55, the program of the Russell Sage Foundation expanded, with increased activity in the other professions: law, theology, social work, education, and government. At the same time, all of the initiatives involving social science and health services were continued and in two areas were expanded: the development of social science teaching in schools of the health professions and the cross-disciplinary residencies. At Yale, Leo Simmons returned from his work at Cornell–New York Hospital to chair the Committee on the Social Aspects of Medicine,[36] an activity that was financially supported by Russell Sage. A joint venture of the School of Medicine and the Department of Sociology, this committee functioned as a study unit and planning group. Three faculty members from the School of Medicine and three from the Department of Sociology held monthly meetings.[37] Simmons's book, coauthored with Harold G. Wolff, was published by the Foundation in 1954, and although its main focus was on the sociocultural links between stress and disease, it offered much to students of medical and social sciences. Simmons's new role as the chairman of the Yale Committee was to plan for the medical school, the school of public health, and the graduate students in sociology concerning research collaboration in the social aspects of medicine. Also at Yale, Albert F. Wessen offered an undergraduate course in 1954 on the social aspects of health and medicine to over forty students, most of whom were premedical. Continuation of this project was assured in 1954 by a generous grant from the Commonwealth Fund.

Social science teaching for students in the health professions expanded rapidly in the Foundation's program. At the University of North Carolina, Harvey Smith created for fourth-year medical students instruction in social and cultural environmental factors in health and illness. Sociology graduate students were engaged in this program. Similarly at the Cornell–New York Hospital School of Nursing, Frances C. Macgregor, a sociologist, introduced social science perspectives in teaching. At the Boston University School of Nursing, Dorian Apple, a sociologist, was appointed to explore the literature and methodology of social science to provide teaching materials to undergraduate schools of nursing. Benjamin Paul at the Harvard School of Public Health and Lyle Saunders at the University of Colorado Medical Center continued their work and added significant teaching programs. All of these programs produced books within a remarkably short span of time from 1954 to 1962, which proved to be of strategic value for the establishment of medical sociology as a young field in its early stages, especially in its role as one of the basic sciences of medicine and nursing.[38]

During 1954–55, five new residents in social science and medicine were appointed. Included were Eliot Freidson to work with the Family Health Maintenance Program of the Montefieore Hospital in the Bronx,[39] and Edward Wellin, an anthropologist, at the Harvard University School of Public Health. Both were to become outstanding scholars of medical sociology. In 1955, the Ford Foundation made a grant to Russell Sage Foundation of $731,000, to be used over the next five years to expand the program in training and development in the health and welfare professions. This made possible the appointment of seven new residents each year in addition to those appointed on the Foundation's own funds.

By 1956, the Foundation, in addition to the activities just described, was supporting two substantial training programs in schools of public health, at Harvard and Pittsburgh. Both had been given previous grants to bridge the relation between social science and public health. Now the decision was to help them develop broader programs. Ben Paul's work at Harvard was granted $223,000 to implement a five-year program involving teaching, research planning, and other functions. Paul was joined by Sol Levine, a social psychologist, and later by Norman Scotch, a sociologist. This program was to become a model for the field, and the subsequent careers of all its senior members are notable. Paul, as described earlier, went to Stanford. Levine, at Boston University, the Kaiser Foundation, and Harvard, continued his contributions to medical sociology.[40] Scotch became professor of behavioral sciences and dean of the School of Public Health of Boston University. Meanwhile, Stanley King was supported at the University of Pittsburgh School of Public Health in a plan to extend his program of social science and public health.

Beyond these programs, there were now ten new crossdisciplinary residents in 1955–56, eight of whom were in the health professions, joining Edward Wellin, who continued into his second year at the Harvard School of Public Health.[41]

The next group of nine new residents of 1956–57 included five who were in health settings. Robin Badgley was to work at the Yale University School of Medicine; Aaron V. Cicourel at the University of California, Los Angeles, School of Nursing; Ray H. Elling at the Academy of Medicine in Dusseldorf, Germany; Lawrence Kohlberg at Children's Hospital, Boston; and Victor Sanua at Cornell University Medical College and the Albert Einstein College of Medicine. In the next year, 1957–58, nine new appointments were made. Of these six were in health, but most notable in terms of his future career was Howard B. Kaplan, who joined the Department of Psychiatry at Baylor University College of Medicine in Houston, Texas. Similarly, among the residents appointed in 1958 and 1959, William A. Glaser joined Columbia University to work on problems of sociology and nursing; George L. Maddox, Jr., went to Duke University to work on problems of sociology and medicine; Norman A. Scotch joined the program at the Harvard School of Public Health; and Robert A. Scott began a residency at Stanford in sociology and medicine.

During the decade after Young's appointment, the Foundation, in addition to its program for social science in the health professions, maintained its tradition of active research, both by members of its own staff and through grants. It also expanded its programs in the other professions. The period, however, is remarkable for the outstanding service the Foundation performed in establishing medical sociology through the training of social scientists who became leaders in the field, in supporting experiments in teaching social science to future health professionals, and in research. Moreover, the Foundation seemed almost casual about claiming any credit. Instead, it readily shared with other foundations and sometimes gave anonymously. As just one example, consider the University Seminar on the Professions in Modern Society at Columbia University.

The University Seminar is a formal institution at Columbia University that is designed for the faculty and for the exploration of questions on an interdisciplinary basis. It is not a teaching device and generally is invoked only for professorial level inquiry. The Seminar on the Professions was one of the earliest grants in Young's regime at the Russell Sage Foundation, and it was one of the most important for medical sociology. Although the Foundation's official record shows only that an award was given to the Columbia University Seminar, "chaired by Professor Elliott E. Cheatham of the School of Law," the seminar was actually an invention of Robert K. Merton in 1949.[42] Constituted to represent eight professions—medicine, law, architecture, engineering, social work, ministry, nursing, and education—the seminar included at least two members of each profession and attracted the most distinguished members of Columbia's professional school faculties. In medicine, for example, Dana Atchley,[43] a world-renowned internist, was one of the members. After the Seminar began and an outline for procedure was prepared, Merton invited William J. Goode to come from the Wayne State University sociology department to take part as its executive secretary. The Russell Sage Foundation paid Goode's full-time faculty salary for two years to allow him to devote himself to the seminar.[44]

Young was interested mainly in the efforts of Merton and Goode "to view the subject of professions generically and in a more systematic and dynamic manner than [had] hitherto been done in [the] United States."[45] Young's expectation was that the product of the Columbia seminar would be a major book that would apply social science perspectives to the professions.[46] Instead, the seminar became the source of a proposal for the sociological study of medical schools that was submitted to the Commonwealth Fund in June 1952.[47] Reading like a detailed outline of the book that was originally expected, the proposal became the basis of one of the landmark research projects of its time: a study of socialization in the medical profession involving three medical schools, Cornell, the University of Pennsylvania, and Western Reserve. Over the next ten years, the research produced one book reporting the findings,[48] seven doctoral dissertations, and twenty-eight published articles.[49] The influence of Russell Sage did not end here. In their support for Lyle Saunders at the University of Colorado Medical School in Denver, the Foundation was also part of the origins of another large-scale research study about an educational experiment similar to the Cornell Comprehensive Care and Teaching Program. The General Medical Clinic at Colorado was also based on comprehensive care, and the study of this clinic's role in the medical school produced a major book from research support by the Commonwealth Fund.[50] Nor was that the end. Other important books followed, and the model of the Columbia Bureau of Applied Social Research (BASR) project influenced additional detailed institutional case studies.[51] Yet it is usually the Commonwealth Fund that is credited for supporting these studies, whereas, especially in the starter role, the Russell Sage Foundation was the catalyst.

The Russell Sage also played an important role in the creation of the first professional organization of medical sociologists, the Committee on Medical Sociology, which, in turn, became the Section on Medical Sociology of the ASA. In this case, Donald Young showed how foundations need not wait for requests before acting to commit resources. Initially, A. B. Hollingshead convened a small group of medical sociologists at the 1955 annual meeting of the American Sociological Society (later changed in name to the American Sociological Association) in order "to explore ways of exchanging experiences and better identifying common interests."[52] When an informal committee was formed, ready to use their own meager resources, Donald Young approached them and offered a small amount of discretionary funds from Russell Sage to help them get started. In this way, the Committee on Medical Sociology began.

From my own experience, I can testify that there was nothing distant or impersonal about the Russell Sage Foundation during Donald Young's tenure. In 1957, the Foundation assigned a postdoctoral fellowship[53] to my Division of Behavioral Science in the Psychiatry Department of the Baylor University College of Medicine. This allowed me to advertise the position, and, in the fall of 1957,

Howard B. Kaplan[54] came to work with me in Houston. In 1958, I received another grant from Russell Sage to assist in a teaching program in behavioral science and psychiatry.

I never applied formally for either the fellowship or the grant. Both were initiated by the representatives of the Foundation. At a national meeting, I was approached by Leonard S. Cottrell, the secretary of the Russell Sage Foundation. I did not know "Slats," as everyone called Cottrell. He introduced himself and told me someone had sent him a set of notes that I handed out in a course I was teaching to medical students at Baylor. He started to talk about the course and asked some questions. He was very easy to talk with, and I, as an admirer of his writings, was delighted to have the opportunity. Later at the same meeting, he asked me to join him so that I could meet Donald Young. I found Young very different from "Slats." A gray-haired, bulky man, Donald Young reminded me of my high school principal, a stern, no-nonsense Pennsylvania German with whom I did not get along. As it turns out, Young was himself from a Pennsylvania German background,[55] but the comparison ended there. After a brief recap of my talk with Cottrell, he asked me if the Foundation could help me with my teaching program. My first choice was the chance to hire a Russell Sage Fellow, because I was then the only social scientist at Baylor and I decided that what I most needed was a colleague. A few months later, Young asked me if there was any way he could help directly with the course outline that he and Cottrell read and discussed. I laughingly said that money would help, and soon thereafter I received my first grant, six thousand dollars to support the creation of teaching materials. Another six thousand dollars was sent subsequently to help me write what would become the book *The Doctor and His Patient: A Sociological Interpretation*. Esther Lucile Brown became my chief editor for the book, and it was published in 1963.[56]

There is no question that this was one of the highlight experiences of my life. The Russell Sage staff were more than benefactors; they were my friends. I very specially cherished my friendship with Esther Brown. When I last saw her, at the 1989 annual meeting of the ASA in San Francisco,[57] she was, in her ninety-second year, only slightly less imposing than when I first met her in 1958. The circumstances of that first meeting were auspicious for me but ordinary for her. Cottrell, who until then was my primary contact at the Foundation, asked me to meet Dr. Brown and to think of her as one of the editors of my book. I will never forget the first author-editor lunch that we had.

Tall and strongly built, Esther Lucile Brown was, in her own way, elegantly fashionable. There was about her an imposing strength that put a younger person on the mark, as though in the presence of an admired teacher who, though brooking no nonsense, was clearly your friend. She possessed an old-fashioned dignity that I associated with myths of frontier women and New England "ladies," but her conversation was a delight—challengingly intelligent and leavened with good humor. She was a tough but immensely helpful editor. She, Cottrell, and Young were a team at the Foundation. They created a resource that contributed something very special to medical sociology in its most critical years of development.

The Sociology of Medical Education

The research on medical education by the BASR at Columbia University was the first sociological study of socialization in a medical school. It was not only a first in the field of sociology but represented a major departure for medicine in its efforts to understand and improve the education of physicians. By the testimony of its principal investigators, it was a direct outgrowth of the Columbia University Seminar on the Professions in Modern Society. However, given that the Seminar included members from eight professions, how was medicine chosen for its first intensive and systematic scrutiny?

In the proposal submitted by BASR, there were two reasons given for the choice of medicine. First, "the Seminar concluded that the professional school represents the single most critical phase in the making of the professional man." Second, "growing out of these considerations, it was felt that sociological study of the medical school, as a social organization and an environment of learning, would afford a prototype for comparable studies in the other professions."[58]

As finally constituted, this research had sources other than the Columbia Seminar. Most important was the Department of Medicine of Cornell University Medical College and its educational experiment in comprehensive care. Concerning the latter, it is fortunate that detailed testimony is available from George G. Reader, who became the physician collaborator in the BASR research.[59] Dr. Reader was then an instructor and special assistant to Dr. David P. Barr, the chairman of the Department of Medicine at Cornell. As early as 1947, well before the Columbia University seminar on the professions began, Reader and Barr approached the Commonwealth Fund, requesting support for the Comprehensive Care and Teaching Program (CC&TP), the experimental program at Cornell. How these two programs, the BASR study of medical education and the Cornell CC&TP, converged is a key incident in this stage of the development of medical sociology.

In the 1952 proposal, Robert Merton, speaking for the Columbia BASR, wrote that in modern medicine there appeared to be what he called "a slowly but clearly emerging interest in exploring actual and potential connections between the medical and the social sciences." This idea was given a broad interpretation: "Just as the laboratory sciences played their essential part in radically modifying medical education and practice in the first part of the century, so the social and psychological sciences, in their own necessarily modest fashion, bid further to modify medical teaching and practice during the second part of the century."[60] There were, however, specific events that illustrated the validity of this observation. One was the preparation at Western Reserve for the radical transformation of the traditional medical curriculum; another was the comprehensive care movement, especially as it would be developed at the medical schools of Cornell and Colorado. At Cornell, Reader describes a lengthy process of preparation, including support from the Commonwealth Fund. The "Medicine Aid Clinic," a product of Dr. Harold Wolff and Dr. Stuart Wolff, preceded the Comprehensive Care Clinic that was created by Barr and Reader in 1949. The Wolffs were interested in psychosomatic medicine, and for years Cornell's departments of medicine and psychiatry followed that lead. As described earlier, Harold Wolff brought the sociologist Leo Simmons to Cornell with the help of the Russell Sage Foundation. But Barr and Reader became disillusioned with the psychosomatic emphasis, and even as their attraction to social science grew, Simmons was not their choice as a collaborator.

Dr. Reader was himself a graduate of Cornell Medical School. A member of the class of 1943, he continued at Cornell as an intern until, in 1944, he entered the navy. He returned to a Cornell residency in 1946 and in 1949 became an instructor in medicine. Immediately after his military service and during his residency he became a special assistant to Dr. Barr, in charge of teaching fourth-year medical students in the medical clinic. The clinic, with Reader as its head, became the vehicle for what Barr saw as a revolutionary approach to clinical hospital care and medical education, called comprehensive care.

Comprehensive care was conceived both as a corrective device and as a contribution in its own right to advance the healing power of clinical medicine. Correctively, it was a reaction against the reductionist influence of specialization. Self-conscious about the tendency to view each patient as a "disease entity," something that had grown in the high-technology medical centers, clinical teachers sought methods of reorienting medicine to a more holistic view. The introduction of future physicians to medicine by long years in premedical and preclinical laboratories were increasingly regarded as dehumanizing. Medical students, despite evidence that showed they began their medical studies with motivation to help people, were believed to suffer losses in humanitarianism in the process of becoming physicians. To counteract the "emotional calluses" that scientific medicine seemed to produce as a defense against emotional involvement, it was hoped that comprehensive care would establish in the doctor-patient relationship the patient's position as a "whole person."

Basically, the method of comprehensive care was to reintegrate the several dimensions of human behavior that had first been separated by the sciences for heuristic purposes and then frozen in their separateness by the process of clinical specialization. The biomedical, the psychological, and the social aspects of illness had become tightly compartmentalized, and within the biological further subdivisions proliferated. Comprehensive care sought to restore the unity of the human organism by reasserting the centrality of the patient and his family as the focus of health care. To do this, the specialty clinic was subordinated to the general or comprehensive care clinic, where a generalist, usually an internist, assumed responsibility for each patient, calling on the specialists as needed but not "referring" each patient into what often became a journey through series of specialty workups, each disconnected from the other, with no one continuously responsible for putting all the pieces together in a coherent analysis of the patient's problems and a treatment plan.

Among the earliest and best-known expressions of this approach were the Cornell CC&TP[61] and the Colorado General Medical Clinic (GMC).[62] Both described themselves as educational experiments and were committed from the start to evaluating the outcomes of the programs. These two programs reached a point where they were secure enough to seek evaluation at the same time, about five years after the Second World War and it was at that point that the convergence between Cornell and the BASR occurred. At first, support was solicited from the Commonwealth Fund only for the introduction of comprehensive care to medical education. Later, additional support was requested to evaluate the achievements of the programs. The outcomes were defined as attitudinal, and both were drawn to sociologists because they recognized that the medical school had become a changing environment in which the cognitive increments of learning were not adequate measures of their goals. At both Colorado and Columbia, Russell Sage had helped set the stage for the evaluation research that the Commonwealth Fund sponsored. These two research efforts constitute one of the success stories of the movement to join social scientists and the practicing professions in common effort. Especially at Cornell, the dominant voice in the study of outcomes was to be sociological; at Colorado, it was more in the tradition of psychology, through Hammond. The Colorado team did include Lyle Saunders, a sociologist, but he functioned outside of the main study and published a separate book focused on the Spanish-speaking patients.

Very early, the distinguishing feature of the Cornell approach to the evaluation of CC&TP was the decision that the study of attitudinal effects could not be limited to the specific time period of the comprehensive care teaching-learning experience. The researchers reasoned that the whole medical school experience needed to be studied as "socialization for the professional role," an approach to inquiry that was to become one of the major types of research in medical sociology and one of its main contributions to the field. How this came about, according to Reader, dates back to 1947, when Dr. Barr,[63] acting to correct his disappointment with the Medicine Aid Clinic, approached the Commonwealth Fund to help him take a new approach.[64]

Relations with the Commonwealth Fund, at that time, were typically interactive, with the Fund staff initiating contacts and ideas with chosen individuals and institutions. Long interested in Cornell, Lester Evans and Geddes-Smith at the Fund, after sponsoring the Wolffs and their psychosomatic approach, became sympathetic to Dr. Barr's plans for a comprehensive clinic. This fitted in with their more general interest in comprehensive care, expressed first at the Case Western Reserve University School of Medicine. Comprehensive care became the central theme of the Commonwealth Fund's program in the postwar years, dominating its attention until 1960 and remaining as a subcategory of its concern for two decades thereafter. In fact, as Reader described it, negotiations with the Fund were typically "long, drawn-out discussions with the staff," not a formal process. Involved were mainly Lester Evans and Geddes-Smith for the Commonwealth Fund and Dr. Barr. By the time Reader saw the proposal, he found only a very small amount of money was designated for evaluation, about three thousand dollars. He immediately went back to the Fund to ask for a bigger budget to study the effects of the new program.

At the same time, Fred Kern was asked to do a similar job at the University of Colorado, also with the backing of Commonwealth. Before he actually moved out West, he and George Reader visited a number of places in search of expertise in evaluation. At the Educational Testing Service (ETS) in Princeton, New Jersey, they thought they found what they needed, and signed a contract. ETS, the outstanding national organization for educational testing and research, saw the comprehensive care clinics as something they wanted to learn more about, but Reader, initially enthusiastic, was quickly disillusioned. ETS decided the task required much the same techniques they used in other educational situations and presented a plan for tests to measure what Reader understood to be personality structure. He, on the other hand, was more interested in what kind of social situation he could create that would "mold students, or at least turn them in the direction he wanted."[65]

Seeking a better approach and aware only that his interests were not being met by the psychologists, Reader turned to the sociologists at his own university in Ithaca. He spoke to Robin Williams, the chairman of sociology, who recommended Edward Suchman of the same department. Although Suchman was an outstanding social researcher, he was too busy at the time and was unable to send anyone to reconnoiter. As Reader recalled: "Suchman was pretty awe-inspiring. I just didn't think we would work well together. Williams I could see getting along with . . . but Suchman was in a phase where he was really setting the world on fire. Even when sitting . . . I felt too much tension, so I was sort of relieved that I had made my overture and they had turned it down."[66] After following such a logical path in his search, Reader now stumbled accidentally on what he was looking for. At his church he met a young graduate student who was studying with Robert Merton at Columbia. He discussed his problems with this new acquaintance,[67] telling him that he was still looking around for the right kind of help. "The only place to go," he was told, "is to the Bureau of Applied Social Research." Reader promptly went to the BASR and spoke with Charles Glock, the director. At first, after an on-site visit and discussion with Dr. Barr, Glock was not sure this was the Bureau's kind of thing. In the meantime, however, Reader was contacted by Lester Evans of the Commonwealth Fund, who told him that Robert Merton, acting for the BASR, had applied for a grant from the Fund. This was the preliminary proposal that emanated from the Columbia University Seminar on the Professions, late in 1951.[68] When Merton was informed by Lester Evans of the activities at Cornell, a quick about-face occurred at BASR. Glock made what Reader calls a one-hundred-and-eighty-degree turn and told Cornell that the Bureau would like nothing better than to do the evaluation of Cornell's comprehensive care program. When Glock and Reader reviewed the existing budget, of course, they agreed that it was inadequate, and Patricia Kendall was recruited as codirector of the research to rewrite the proposal. They also agreed that a fieldworker was required so as to gain for the BASR a firsthand view of the Medical School and to coordinate the two sites. Mary W. Goss was appointed to this position and was introduced to Reader.[69]

Dr. Goss, at the time still a graduate student at Columbia, went on to have a distinguished career on the Cornell Medical School faculty. At the time, however, because of the experience with Leo Simmons,[70] she was introduced very cautiously. "There was, at that point, a lot of paranoia about having social scientists in your midst who betrayed you," says Reader. The way Goss was introduced, therefore, was carefully thought through at the Bureau, even to the way she dressed. As described by Reader, she appeared in her Smith College girl's outfit, skirt, sweater, and saddle shoes, very demure and playing it very low profile.[71] All of this activity was by way of feasibility study, prior to the final proposal and the formal beginning of the research. Even later, however, after the research actually started, there was continued sensitivity to the potential conflicts between the collaborators, coming as they did from such different academic worlds. Immediately after the grant was approved, Merton invited Reader to a seminar on socialization held at the Bureau for the project staff. Before long, early in 1953, Renee Fox[72] joined the Cornell field team, and with as many as six graduate assistants conducting studies at the same time, the social scientists blended in without difficulty.

In June 1952 the final proposal was submitted by the BASR to the Commonwealth Fund, and it included the evaluation study of the Cornell CC&TP. The overall conception was a study of the full four-year medical student experience; the specific evaluation of CC&TP was included, but the larger context was seen as required for understanding the fourth year. The historical and intellectual sources of the conception of medical education as socialization for the profession were described in detail.[73] Although the request was for five years of support, the first year was designated as a preliminary year. In fact, one year later, the research was expanded to include two other medical schools, but the central focus remained on Cornell.

The collaboration between the Cornell CC&TP and the Columbia BASR can be cited as the model of what Donald Young had in mind when he started his program for social sciences and the practicing professions at the Russell Sage Foundation. This became a case of reciprocal effects, whereby both parties were influenced by the other. On the medical side, George Reader, whose major research had been in hematology, became so deeply involved in medical sociology that, to this day, he is a regular contributor to the professional journals and meetings of sociology nationally and internationally. Sociologists like Mary Goss and Renee Fox, in a parallel way, have become well known in the medical profession, both as scholars and educators.[74]

The conception of socialization for the profession, to some extent, replaced professional training as the central paradigm of medical education. The latter was based on the idea that the core of the medical profession was composed of knowledge and skills. Accordingly, the job of medical educators was to communicate that core effectively, keeping up with the changes that were demonstrated by research to be effective. The task of students, in this view, was to master what the faculty gave them. Professional socialization, on the other hand, expanded the arena of education to include the medical school as a social environment. All the members of this environment shared an institutional culture, and learning included the effects of social interaction among all the members. Students, for example, were seen to learn from the norms of the school and medical center community, transmitted directly and indirectly. They learned from each other and from all the types of people involved, not just from the faculty. At the time, these ideas were truly revolutionary in medicine. It was, as Reader recalls, a period of great ferment about innovation in medical education. Even today, fifty years later, although many leading medical educators embrace the view of medical education as socialization for the profession, there is also widely held opinion that medical education is essentially training in the mastery of knowledge and skill, a view much the same as in 1940.[75]

The role of a private foundation like the Commonweath Fund was particularly felicitous. The Fund allowed great power to staff members like Geddes Smith and Lester Evans. Both these men were dedicated to the idea that medicine was an instrument of society and had a basic responsibility for promoting its well-being. "Medicine and health," Evans said, "however you define this complex, is a function of society and not a prerogative of the health professions. They are only its agents. . . . Society arranges the circumstances under which the technologies, the professions, the facilities and all—which are instruments of medicine—are brought into play."[76] Evans, himself, was a critically influential figure in promoting this very progressive philosophy of the social responsibility of medicine through the programs he convinced the Foundation to support.

Lester Evans first joined the Commonwealth Fund in the 1920s when, as a pediatrician, he worked on a program to improve rural health care. Geddes Smith developed the idea that the main reason there were so few doctors in rural areas was the lack of hospitals. The Fund consequently set up some experimental hospitals in selected rural communities around the country. Such hospitals were viewed as a community institution. The Commonwealth Fund invested the basic capital and the community the rest. "We viewed the hospital as being run by the community," Evans reported, "with a lay board of directors, with no medical men on the Board. We set up postgraduate opportunities, fellowships for the rural practitioners, and so on. Quite a diverse group of hospitals were established. The first one was in Murphysboro, Tennessee." The program continued until World War II, when the Hill-Burton Act took over similar responsibilities.

"We expected the hospitals to operate at a deficit," said Evans. "That was our definition of a community hospital. If it didn't operate at a deficit, it was a proprietary hospital. If it made a profit, it was not a community hospital." He contined:

> All the services available in the hospital were controlled by the hospital. X-ray, clinical laboratory, pathology, were all hospital functions. They were not functions of private practice. At one time, we tried to set up a flat rate for hospitals. If you were a surgical case, you went in and so much was charged for the first few days, which was more than for a medical case, let's say, and then so much per day for the next days or weeks. On the theory that the patient goes to the hospital for what a hospital is and therefore should not be charged individually and should not be charged for the separate charges of the hospital.

Although a medical theme dominated the policy of the Commonwealth Fund from the beginning, the first director, Barry Smith, was a social worker, and there were always key staff members, like Geddes Smith, who were not physicians. Anna M Harkness, widow of Stephen V. Harkness,[77] established the Fund wth a broad charge to enhance the common good, and her son, Edward Stephen Harkness, led the Fund during its first two decades. An important part of the Foundation's method was the direct staff solicitation of work that they decided was important and the rapid turnaround of funds. These characteristics persisted into the postwar period when the Columbia project on the sociology of medical education was started.

In the 1950s, the Commonwealth Fund defined the major problem of medicine as the undue emphasis on specialization. "Increased government spending, particularly in biomedical research," they believed, "was encouraging the growth of specialized medicine and . . . creating an oversupply of physicians expert in specific diseases but untrained to treat the patient as a whole."[78] To address this issue, the Fund saw itself as one of the founders of the concept of comprehensive medicine in medical education, and without any doubt they were the major source of its implementation. The complete revision of the curriculum at Case Western Reserve was the first experiment in comprehensive medicine that they supported. Other educational experiments for the same purpose were backed at Cornell, Colorado, Pennsylvania, North Carolina, Massachusetts, Vermont, and elsewhere.

For medical sociology, starting from what appears at first to be a different intellectual ground, the comprehensive care movement was an ideal place to join hands with medical educators. It provided a logical follow-up to the earlier postwar invitation from psychiatry to join interdisciplinary teaching in the medical school. As part of the team charged with creating a basic science of behavior, sociologists joined in the development of a "biopsychosocial" view of disease. This was what George Engel has called "a unified concept of health and disease,"[79] and comprehensive care was interpreted as its appropriate application in health care delivery. The concept asserts the importance of the human organism as a whole, defining health as a state of the organism when it is functioning effectively, fulfilling needs, successfully responding to the requirements or demands of the environment, whether internal or external, and pursuing its biological destiny, including growth and reproduction. Disease, on the other hand, corresponds to failures and disturbances in the growth, development, functions and adjustments of the organism as a whole or of any of its systems.[80]

This definition contrasts with "the cellular concept of disease which, by focusing primarily on changes within the cell as the basic component of disease, is reductionistic and tends to restrict attention to only one aspect of disease."[81] The unified concept was a perspective intended to correct for the basically "primitive and prescientific views of disease" as something bad that is external and gets into the body and causes disease. Furthermore, it substitutes "process" for "cause" and finds all single factor theories of illness to be defective whether based on the causality of germs, anatomical defect, biochemical defect, or mechanistic "breakdowns of the body machine." All such concepts share the idea of a "discrete 'thing' inside the body, an entity having an existence of its own, apart from the patient, who not so incidentally is represented as the victim."[82]

The unified concept of health and disease is a system theory, based on premises of functional life processes that assert adaptive equilibrium (or homeostasis) as a dynamic, ever present principle. Engel's interpretation fits with what was, at that time, the dominant paradigm of sociology: functionalism, or social system theory. As expressed in comprehensive care, sociology was therefore able to join and help to articulate this approach. Especially when this framework was applied to medical education, sociology, with its theories of the influence of the social environment on learning, particularly the learning of attitudes and values, was relevant.

Comprehensive care also challenged the hegemony of the hospital inpatient service in the clinical training of medical students. It anticipated later efforts to shift the emphasis of training from the secondary-tertiary focus of the teaching hospital to that of primary care. There were limitations, however. Too often the teaching was located in the hospital, the very organization that it sought to reorient, and its leaders were specialists who, despite their commitment to a holistic type of patient care, were themselves role models of specialization. Thus critics have charged that the comprehensive care movement rearranged the immediate physical contours of ambulatory medicine but did not alter basically the roles of the participants. Not the least of its handicaps was its position in the sequence of professional education. Students at both Cornell and Colorado were exposed to comprehensive care only at the end of their medical school experiences.

The sociologists who participated in the comprehensive care movement were there precisely to observe and report its deficiencies as well as its achievements. Evaluations of the attitudinal effects of the Cornell CC&TP raised serious question about the efficacy of so limited and so late an exposure to a framework that was intended to persist and deeply influence subsequent professional behavior.[83] The results at Colorado were even more problematic.[84] Moreover, the trends of career choice showed an unbroken intensification of interest in specialization as the students moved through medical school. Caplovitz, in his study of student attitudes toward the faculty at Cornell, revealed a pattern of role modeling in which students judged very accurately the value priorities of the institution, priorities that led to greater rewards for the specialist and the academic scientist.[85]

The signal program in the Commonwealth Fund's support of comprehensive care was at Case Western Reserve School of Medicine. Guided by much the same objectives as Cornell and Colorado, Hale Ham and his colleagues at Western Reserve made the hard decision to revise the entire four-year experience of medical school.[86] Beginning in the late forties, they conceived, over several years of study and negotiation within the faculty, a plan with the following general principles:

- *Growth and development.* The standard curriculum at midcentury was focused on the adult human organism, a static approach that neglects knowledge about growth and development. Therefore, in all aspects of learning, from anatomy to the clinical sciences, learning should be oriented to a view that includes the dynamic course of human development from birth to old age.
- *The unity of knowledge.* Knowledge for understanding requires a unified, multifactorial view. The tendency to specialize by basic science discipline and clinical specialty is inherently opposed to such unification. Education, therefore, must include integration, both horizontal across the basic disciplines and vertical to join the basic sciences with the clinical subjects.
- *The behavioral sciences.* Advances in psychology, anthropology, and sociology offered an opportunity to medical education to teach a more rigorous, skilled, and understanding approach to the human relations of medicine, from the doctor-patient relationship to the social structure of health care delivery. Thus the emphasis on biomedical sciences needs to be balanced with the study of human behavior.

In 1953, when Western Reserve launched its new curriculum, the medical schools of the United States were virtually identical in structure and sequence of education. During the first two years, a block system prevailed, in which attention was concentrated on one or two subjects at a time. The order of the major subjects was anatomy, physiology, biochemistry, pathology, microbiology, pathology, and pharmacology. Toward the end of the second year, as a preparation for clinical study, history-taking and physical examination were introduced but mainly on a theoretical basis and thus still removed from actual patients. In the third year, rotating in small groups, clerkships at the bedside were given by all the clinical departments, with the largest blocks in surgery and internal medicine. In the fourth year, the clinical rotations were duplicated but now in the outpatient department and clinics of each specialty. This was the curriculum that evolved within two decades of the Flexner report,[87] and it became a universal standard throughout the country. It was rigorous, keeping the student in lectures and laboratories for eight hours daily from Monday through Friday and for four hours on Saturday. In the clinical years, at least the same amount of time was required in the hospital, sometimes more. There were few electives, and memorization was the primary intellectual demand.

At Western Reserve, the changes took several forms. First, the hard lines between basic science and clinical subjects were broken by introducing patient contact from the very beginning of the medical school experience as well as by carrying the basic sciences beyond the second year. Second, the subjects were subordinated to problems that allowed interdisciplinary teaching. Instead of studying each discipline in blocks, organ systems like the musculoskeletal, the cardiovascular, and the neurophysiological were presented. Within each teaching problem, the human organism was presented as it grows and develops and not only in adult cross-section. In the clinical studies, patients were looked at in their social context, especially as members of families, in order to acquaint students with the contributions of the behavioral sciences.

In these ways the Western Reserve Curriculum was an expression of the comprehensive care philosophy in the whole curriculum rather than in the clinical studies alone. It also attempted to convey the unified concept of health and disease by infusing the whole of medical education with an integrated, multidimensional approach to human biology.

Medical sociology cannot be considered part of the determining source of the comprehensive care movement. Rather, comprehensive care represented in the postwar academic environment a framework of thought that was more compatible with sociology than in previous years. Both as a contributing intellectual source and as a research partner for evaluation, sociology at this time found a niche in the comprehensive care movement. Looking more specifically at Western Reserve and the other comprehensive care experiments, all developed with the help of the Commonwealth Fund. About the influence of medical sociology, it is difficult to document, but nevertheless much can be said.

First, the actual participation by sociologists was very uneven. Lyle Saunders was a major participant throughout the Colorado experience, from conception to implementation, but the main nonmedical collaboration was from psychology.[88] At Cornell, the early stages were dominated by internists, but from the time that the Columbia BASR was first contacted in 1952, a close partnership between sociology and medicine was formed and persisted for decades.[89] Indeed, George Reader, the physician who was the single most important conceptual and operational leader of C C & T P, has been recognized over time as a major medical sociologist in his own right.[90] At Western Reserve, on the other hand, where the utilization of concepts directly related to sociology appears to have been greatest, sociologists were employed only in minor roles, except in the evaluation, where again the Columbia University BASR played an important role.

In effect, it was in the study and evaluation of the comprehensive care teaching programs that sociologists played their most substantial direct role, and this was to be the case in the sociology of medical education generally. What they achieved, however, transcended the usual consultant role. They translated from the unitary theory of disease a perspective that was to be applied to the health professions themselves. Especially important was their impact on the idea of medical education as a developmental process.

Prior to 1945, the recruitment and training of health professionals, especially doctors in the United States, was based upon a conception of "traits" that was a close analogue of disease theory. That is, it was assumed that recruitment was essentially a task of selecting individuals who had "good" traits for professional behavior and of screening out those with "bad" traits. The good traits came to be defined as the cognitive capabilities of quantification and a demonstrated ability to succeed (achieve high examination grades) in science. These traits were emphasized in the construction of the general qualifying examination called the Medical College Admission Test (MCAT). Admission procedures from about 1930 heavily weighted the MCAT score and prior performance in college as shown by the grade point average (GPA).

The "bad" traits were social qualities, most often informally screened by personal interview. They included gender—women were thought to be poor risks because of marriage and child-bearing and were therefore discouraged except in token numbers—and social background. The latter standard emphasized conformity—good appearance and manners—and was often used to discriminate against the immigrant minorities who pressed very aggressively for entrance into the professions at that time.

The overall result in American medicine between the two world wars was to consolidate a gatekeeper approach, epitomized in the Flexner injunction:

> It is necessary to install a doorkeeper who will, by critical scrutiny, ascertain the fitness of the applicant: a necessity suggested in the first place by consideration for the candidate whose time and talents will serve him better in some other vocation, if he be unfit for this; and in the second, by consideration for a public entitled to protection from those whom the very boldness of modern medical strategy equips with instruments that, tremendously effective for good when rightly used, are all the more terrible for harm if ignorantly employed.[91]

In actual fact, Flexner's concern was with the ethics, intelligence, and skill of doctors and not with social background. The elitism of white males was an unanticipated consequence.

Sociology provided the knowledge base for the shift of perspective away from gatekeeping to the view that professional education is a continuous, long-term process of growth and development. Merton's concept of "socialization for the profession," fitted the functional paradigm in that it described each individual in dynamic adaptation with his social environment. The medical school came into focus as a community-in-itself, a small society, complete with its own culture. Instead of the more mechanistic "trait" theory, whereby the proper type of person was selected and then "trained"—given the knowledge and skills necessary for the profession—the student now was conceived as part of a distinctive social ecology. The medical school, in the latter view, was assigned new significance as the source of values and attitudes, communicated both in the way skill and knowledge are taught and as part of a life experience in school-culture. Signalling this change was the special conference held by the AAMC in 1957 entitled "The Ecology of the Medical Student."[92] At that conference, sociologists like Merton were given a prominent place.

A new language grew out of the sociology of medical education. Role attributes like "detached concern"[93] and "training for uncertainty"[94] were recognized as intrinsic objectives of professional learning. The potential conflicts inherent in the status differences between the participants in education were evoked in the descriptive analysis of what Becker and his associates called "boys in white."[95] The Becker study described a secret subsociety of medical students, where students preserved their own identities while at the same time they defined survival as requiring that they present a very different face to their faculty. It was a description that was seen as a mirror by many other medical schools. The study of similar phenomena was extended into the postgraduate experiences of internship and residency.[96]

Evidence of the continuing vitality of these concepts can be seen in the re-sistance of educators as well as in their efforts to apply them. A statement by physician-educator Daniel Funkenstein written in 1971 is still applicable today:

> Many faculty members [demand] that [medical] schools remain institutions whose chief goals are basic biomedical research and the care of hospitalized patients whose illness is biological in nature. Some charge that they are not conscious of their social responsibilities. This is not true. They see them differently. In interviews with faculty members at a number of medical schools, they state that the problems of the delivery of medical care and the education of new types of family physicians should be the concern of "other schools"; they firmly believe that through biomedical research all the problems of health care eventually will be solved. . . . They cannot seem to grasp that all illness may not be susceptible to biological approaches. . . . They seriously question whether medical schools can or should take on social factors that breed disease.[97]

Even though current trends are strongly directed toward an emphasis on primary care and the integration of preclinical and clinical study, the conflict of views persists between the two polar points described by Engel, the disease-centered biomedical on the one hand and the unified functional theories of behavior on the other. The cycle of opinion seems always poised to swing backward toward the traditional Flexnerian mode. What does this tell us about the influence and performance of sociologists and other social scientists in medical education?

George Reader and Rosemary Soave, reviewing the history of comprehensive care in medical education, give good marks, on balance, to the sociologists who played so important a role in the comprehensive care movement.[98] In their thoughtful, unsparingly self-critical essay, sociologists are judged to have done what they were asked to: to study the processes of education and their outcomes with reference to the goals of comprehensive care. What they found, however, in spite of its acknowledged scientific validity, had surprisingly little impact.[99] Two factors seem to be critical in the process of teaching the values and attitudes necessary for the comprehensive care approach:

1. *The full professional context in which teaching occurs:* That is, if these values and attitudes, and their associated clinical skills, are taught sep-arate from what the students see as the mainstream of professional work, the effects are only temporary. This holds both for the nature of the set-ting, the general clinic with its comprehensive approach, as compared with the specialty-oriented teaching hospital that is its dominant envi-ronment, and for the time sequence—the comprehensive clinic experi-ence sandwiched between the specialty departments of medical school and the specialty-oriented postgraduate experiences of internship and residency.

2. *The attitudes of the general medical school faculty:* As Reader and Soave comment, citing the findings of a review of primary education by Alpert and Charney[100] that included programs like the Cornell CC&TP, "The programs succeeded as experiments but failed because the majority of the faculty never recognized them as more than that. . . . The programs

were too isolated, indicating the principles were not widely accepted."
They (Alpert and Charney) also suggested that the fourth year of medical
school may be too late to introduce students to such programs, and cited
the lack of role models and the inevitable conflict between the goals of
primary care and hospital medicine.[101]

Our own interpretation suggests two possible explanations. One is that the
comprehensive care movement—and perhaps its successsors, family medicine
and primary care—were embraced by the leaders of medical education cynically
and only as experiments in order to defuse the underlying social forces that produced them. The second is that the educators sincerely accepted and put them
in place, but the groundwork for their continuing viability was withdrawn by the
political decisions of external forces like the federal Department of Health Education and Welfare. In the plurality and independence of United States institutions, of course, both explanations may be correct.

The story does include certain immutable facts. The problem addressed by
comprehensive care combined intellectual imperatives and social realities. The
goal was to change clinical practice in the so-called real world. This translation
of knowledge to policy was caught in unfavorable circumstances. American medicine at that time was highly specialized, and the prevailing health insurance
system reinforced a delivery system structure that preserved a division of medical
labor based on specialization. As a result, the highly successful marriage between
clinical medicine and sociology in the comprehensive care movement was contained in a minority of medical schools attracted to educational experiments, of
which Western Reserve was the most extensive. The lesson was that education
requires continuity. Socialization for professional roles must be seen as closely
interdependent with the structure of the situation in which it occurs and, equally,
for which it is preparatory.

In the final analysis, comprehensive care, given strong thrust by the generous
support of the Commonwealth Fund, tested educational approaches that survive
today, such as problem-based and student-centered methods of teaching/learning
and teaching teams that integrate biological with psychosocial knowledge and
skills, to name just two. It was an ideal ground for building a legacy of participation by medical sociology in medical education. The current curricula of the
University of New Mexico, Harvard University, McMasters University, and many
programs in medical schools in the United States and internationally all revive
and implement ideas that were forged in the comprehensive care movement of
the fifties.[102]

The Milbank Memorial Fund

The Milbank Memorial Fund, much like the Russell Sage Foundation and the
Commonwealth Fund, was founded by a wealthy heiress in the early years of this
century.[103] Elizabeth Milbank Anderson, like Anna M. Harkness and Margaret
Olivia Sage, believed that the millions she inherited should be used for the benefit
of society and especially for the "constructive and preventive treatment of human
suffering."[104] Throughout most of its history, the Fund has been guided by chairmen of its board who are descendants of Samuel Milbank, the grandfather of
Elizabeth Milbank Anderson. At the same time, the Fund's staff has been led by

remarkably progressive individuals, each quite different from the other. The result has been that the Fund's policies have been in the forefront of public health and medical education. Integral to that policy has been leadership in supporting the contributions of sociology to problems of health and illness.

From its beginning in 1905, when it was known as the Memorial Fund Association,[105] the Milbank Memorial Fund was characterized by the twin themes of public health and preventive medicine. Elizabeth Milbank Anderson herself devoted much of her charity to child welfare and to the poor and was among the earliest supporters of the National Committee for Mental Hygiene,[106] but, as her cousin Albert G. Milbank tells, her own personal history guided the direction of the Fund's future major policy:

> As often happens in human affairs a shattering personal loss had a profound effect upon Mrs. Anderson's attitude toward philanthropy. Her only son died of diphtheria when he was still a little boy. As her brave spirit rose to meet the most crushing blow that fate could have dealt her, she . . . [organized] a charitable corporation with which to explore the possibilities of constructive and preventive treatment of human suffering in contrast to the . . . palliative measures which were generally in vogue.[107]

This was very much at the outset of the large-scale, organized philanthropy, which, "embodied in the notion of 'scientific giving' and in the institution of foundations, is a uniquely American phenomenon."[108] This development represented what Arnove has called "a confluence of economic, political, and social forces at the beginning of the twentieth century, [including] the amassing of great industrial fortunes, the industrial processes and social relations of production that led to both great wealth in the hands of a few and to poverty and discontent on the part of many."[109] The Milbank Memorial Fund emerged as one of only a handful of general purpose foundations at the time, soon to grow in numbers, which represented "a vehicle for proposing and implementing programs of social remediation at a time when the federal government was greatly limited by law or by what the public was willing to support."[110] Moreover, the need was intensified by the poor health conditions of the time. Although the great epidemics of cholera, yellow fever, and smallpox had been ended, tuberculosis was rampant among the poor, and the childhood diseases of dysentery, diphtheria, measles, and whooping cough were widespread, especially in the overcrowded ghettos like New York City's Lower East Side.

In this situation, the first sixteen years of the Milbank charity was characterized by the personal decisions of Elizabeth Milbank Anderson, her cousin Albert Milbank, and her closest advisors, a small group of lawyers, doctors, and investment bankers. After her death in 1921, however, striking changes took place. The name was changed to the Milbank Memorial Fund, honoring her grandfather's family. The Fund was made the beneficiary of new assets, and a reorganization created a more professional approach, specifying the goal of preventive and public health. The immediate result was the creation of a set of three health demonstrations for the control of tuberculosis, which became textbook cases for public health and gave the Fund national prominence.

In connection with these demonstrations, the Fund made the decision to add statistical expertise to its staff, both for the more rigorous selection of areas of study and to evaluate the effectiveness of their programs. Among the members of the Fund's Advisory Council was Dr. Hugh Cumming, surgeon general of the United States Public Health Service. Late in 1925, Dr. Cumming arranged for Dr. Edgar Sydenstricker, public health statistician of the United States Public Health Service, to be appointed the statistical consultant of the Fund. Sydenstricker[111] had a profound effect on the character of the Fund.

From the time he joined Goldberger's study of pellagra in 1914, Sydenstricker focused on the importance of culture and social factors in the analysis of his survey and statistical data. A rigorous scholar, he was an ideal collaborator for John Kingsbury, the social worker and activist who had been special consultant to the Fund in 1921 and became its secretary in 1922. Kingsbury, in effect, was the head of the staff of the Milbank Fund at the time. Sydenstricker, in turn, set a high standard as the director of the Division of Research, which he created. From that time forward, the Fund became known for the excellence of the social epidemiological research that it sponsored in the service of its public health and prevention goals. Through Sydenstricker's influence and representation, the Fund became an active supporter of the CCMC, which was created in 1927. By the end of CCMC's work in 1932, the Milbank Memorial Fund had appropriated $260,000 toward the research of the Committee. Yet, as strong as the Fund's support was for the work of the Committee, Sydenstricker, speaking for the Technical Board, dissented from the Committee's final recommendations.[112] Through Sydenstricker, the Fund became identified with early spokesmen for universal health insurance, castigating the Committee for failing to provide a "comprehensive plan on a nation-wide basis" to ensure the health care of the nation's population.[113]

Early in 1933, Dr. I. S. Falk, who had been associate director of the research staff of the CCMC, joined the staff of the Milbank Memorial Fund. The three staff members, Kingsbury, Sydenstricker, and Falk, were a powerful team dedicated to carrying forward what they saw as the incomplete work of the CCMC.[114] At the same time, close connections between this team and the new administration of Franklin D. Roosevelt were becoming clear. Two men who had been close to the work of the Milbank Memorial Fund were important figures in the new administration. Harry L. Hopkins, a former protege of John Kingsbury, became the head of the Works Progress Administration and one of Roosevelt's closest advisors; and Thomas Parran, a member of the Milbank Technical Board and commissioner of health of New York State, became the surgeon general of the PHS in 1936. Parran has been described as "perhaps the most influential surgeon general in the history of the Public Health Service."[115] Kingsbury himself had been appointed by Roosevelt to membership in the New York State Health Commission for 1930–32. Kingsbury also traveled to Russia in the summer of 1932 and wrote a book on medicine in the U.S.S.R. in 1933.[116]

During 1932 and 1933, the staff of the Fund moved vigorously, both in research and activities related to policy-making, to follow up on their interpretations of the CCMC report. Kingsbury conferred with members of the cabinet like Harold Ickes and Frances Perkins; Sydenstricker and Falk were assisting the President's Committee on Economic Security to study programs of medical care and public health. By the time of the 1934 June meeting of the Milbank Board, however, some members had become uneasy. Although the participation of the Fund's staff was defended by Dr. Livingston Farrand, Chairman of the Technical Board, complaints were made by leaders of the AMA, who, as they did with portions of the CCMC report, charged that the New Deal was promoting "socialized medicine."[117] Albert G. Milbank acted in 1935 to defuse this situation, addressing a group of county medical societies, appealing to physicians not to prejudge honest efforts to address difficult questions or to repeat previous mistakes about the public health movement. Nevertheless, John Kingsbury, acting on the differences between some members of the board and himself, resigned in April 1935.[118] Shortly thereafter Sydenstricker was named the scientific director of the Fund.

Falk, in the meantime, was completing his studies for the Fund on medical care, which were published in 1936.[119] Controversy continued on the Milbank board, led by its physician members. Therefore, when his close friend, Dr. Frank G. Boudreau, was appointed to the new position of medical director in March 1936, Sydenstricker was clearly relieved. He was able to shed the overall administrative responsibility that he felt had kept him from his scientific work. Also, in the meantime, he had become deeply involved in the National Health Survey. He also helped to establish the Office of Population Research within the Woodrow Wilson School of Princeton University, of which Frank W. Notestein, of the Fund staff, was appointed director. Unfortunately, Sydenstricker had a stroke and died suddenly in March 1936. Dr. Boudreau succeeded him as director of the Milbank Memorial Fund.

Without doubt, the Milbank Fund went through a crisis during this period that highlighted ideological differences between the staff and members of the board. The team of Kingsbury, Sydenstricker, and Falk were out front in the struggle to take public health and preventive medicine in the direction of universal health insurance. Physician members of the Milbank board, on the other hand, were reluctant to endorse this move completely, mirroring the concerns of official medical bodies like the AMA. Albert G. Milbank defended his staff, but the crisis persisted. In the end, Frank Boudreau, a physician trained in Canada with extensive experience in international health,[120] was given leadership responsibility. As a physician he may well have been more acceptable to some of the critics of Kingsbury and Sydenstricker on the Fund's board. Boudreau himself was a progressive on policy and a distinguished public health scientist who, in the end, was able to provide continuity with the major research directions pioneered by his predecessors, with the exception of medical care.

Boudreau added nutrition and the public health aspects of housing as subjects of research at the Milbank Memorial Fund and continued the previous work on population and fertility. His experience in international health found expression in the important roles he took after the war in the establishment of the Food and Agriculture Organization of the United Nations and the World Health Organization (WHO). In 1948, responding to the passage in Congress of the 1946 Mental Health Act, he led the Fund in progressive policies on mental health. This was a renewal of the policy of Elizabeth Milbank Anderson in the earliest years of the Fund, when she had befriended Clifford W. Beers[121] and made several grants to the National Committee on Mental Hygiene. Boudreau was responsible, in significant part, for including the phrase "physical, mental and social well-being" in the charter of WHO, laying the foundation for many governments to include mental health equally in their health programs.[122]

Thomas Parran, as the surgeon general, also was instrumental in the reform of government policies toward mental health. Grob, in his history of mental health policy in modern America, tells how Robert Felix, among other young career officers in the PHS at the time, was supported by Parran. It was Parran who urged Felix to update the Kolb memorandum for a new institute, thereby setting into motion the steps toward the National Mental Health Act of 1946 and the creation of NIMH.[123] This helped to set the stage for the Milbank Memorial Fund to play a role in the developments of medical sociology in association with NIMH that I described in chapter 8.

Like Dr. Robert H. Felix, Boudreau believed that "epidemiology forms the scientific foundation for all disease control forms."[124] Applying this principle to mental health, he organized the first of what were to be annual conferences on mental disorder, bringing together leading epidemiologists and pyschiatrists. The monograph that emerged in 1949, *Epidemiology of Mental Disorder*, was the first ever published on this topic, thereby influencing the direction of developments in both social science and medicine. At this meeting, Dr. Alexander Leighton presented the proposal that later developed into his Stirling County study of Nova Scotia, and the Milbank Fund supplied the initial funding. Ernest Gruenberg, then of Yale's departments of psychiatry and public health, began his long association with the Fund at this meeting and joined the Milbank staff in 1955 to direct its work in mental health. The 1949 meeting launched an increasingly intense effort by the Fund in both research and demonstration projects in communities that pioneered in open ward mental hospital treatment and community mental health services. Bertram Brown, who succeeded Robert Felix as director of NIMH, wrote of the Milbank Memorial Fund's effect on the 1963 message of President John F. Kennedy to Congress and on the legislation that followed, opening the wards of mental hospitals and providing community services to the mentally ill.[125]

Boudreau, however, did more than foster large-scale research and demonstration programs in the United States and abroad. Like other foundation leaders discussed here, he used his influence in an informal, personal way. David Willis tells how his career was affected by this side of Boudreau, allowing him to move from a highly individual and unorthodox early training to a distinguished career in the social science of medicine and public health.

Willis, who in 1970 became vice-president for program development and evaluation at the Milbank Memorial Fund and editor-in-chief of the *Milbank Quarterly,* was born in New York, raised in Long Island and Boston, and went to Haverford College, where he majored in sociology, studying with Ira Reed, a well-known black sociologist.[126] On a Danforth Fellowship he studied at the University of Pennsylvania, beginning in 1952, focusing on demography with Dorothy Thomas.[127] Always oriented toward an active career in public policy, Willis, after completing his M.A. in demography and sociology, joined the Philadelphia City Planning Commission as their first social scientist. Assigned as liaison to the city health department, he moved into active work with local hospitals, joining a network, "very informal but highly sophisticated, of communication and sharing among all of the Jewish-sponsored hospitals around the country." It was in this network that he came to know people like Cecil Sheps and Sid Lee of Beth Israel in Boston and Martin Cherkowsky of Montefiore in New York. This was a group that "was perhaps more highly focused on social aspects of medical care than were any of the other hospital-related professional groups." It led him to become part of the American Public Health Association, the American Hospital Association, and the New York Academy of Medicine. Willis concluded that "the real frontiers in social medicine were really in that informal network of the Jewish-sponsored hospitals. . . . The entire push for social medicine, which included the movements toward long-term care, home care, and so on came from the roots it had in Jewish community organization." After three years, he decided that, to stay in the health field, he needed additional professional training. His choice was to study for a Master's in Public Health (M.P.H).

At the time, however, his most trusted advisor, Sid Lee of Boston Beth Israel, told him there were no schools of public health that were going to be intellectually challenging. Willis therefore set about finding a place where he could be with at least one congenial person with whom he could work and where there were opportunities outside of school to absorb his energies. He chose the University of Pittsburgh, where Thomas J. Parran, Jr., M.D., was the dean. Willis was also attracted because the school provided active teaching roles for people from the labor movement; members of the United Mine Workers, Leslie Falk and some others, were in active teaching and research roles in the school.

There were, however, some drawbacks. Willis found the school dull, as he had been warned. In addition, at the time, it was not possible to get any of the degrees offered at the school of public health unless one came with a medical or related degree in the biomedical sciences. In negotiations with Dr. Parran before he entered, Willis was able to secure Parran's reluctant agreement to allow him to receive an MPH if he took some summer courses in microbiology, spent a second year in residence doing a special piece of research, and wrote a dissertation. He would be allowed, as he said, "to get the same degree that nurses, doctors, dentists, veterinary scientists could do in one year." In any event, he graduated second in his class, and with the extra courses and second year, he was awarded the M.P.H.

For the final qualification, however, one was also required to do a residency. Since he was interested in hospital social organization and health care, ("that was in the days when 'hospital' was not a pejorative term") he arranged to be a student trainee at the Massachusetts General Hospital in Boston. His access to the hospital was through Dean Clark, the general director, whose work with miners and the health needs of Appalachia attracted him. As Willis describes it,

> When I negotiated with Dean Clark, he was absolutely delighted to have a new, unspoiled person with some training, because he was convinced that 1956 was the right time to organize a hospital-based, comprehensive, prepaid group practice. . . . He had just recruited someone who had been a business manager for the Health Insurance Plan (HIP) in New York, but he needed someone who knew more about the organization of the medical end, and who could do some work in the community. . . . He was very concerned that whatever was planned by the hospital . . . must bear some relationship to the needs of the community.[128]

Willis also had the unique experience at Massachusetts General of living with the interns and residents. As an M.P.H. resident, Dean Clark offered him the same salary and status as a medical resident. In future years, Willis was to regard this as an invaluable part of his training, giving him experiential insight into hospital life:

> I was not just a casual observer because part of my duties in learning how that hospital ran was to participate in the running of it. And to be in charge of the emergency department, on twenty-four-hour shifts. . . . One begins to understand slowly why doctors are as they are, when you share. . . . It was very important to me, and I learned a great deal.

Willis found himself a participant in the type of situation that sociologists like Renee Fox, William Caudill, Ivan Belknap, and others studied by the method of participant-observation. Using the experience as training primarily rather than research, he was able to utilize the special conditions of the time. This was in the early days of health insurance as we know it, and Willis was responsible for finding ways to efficiently administer a new system of financing the hospital health care. As a result, he became intensely involved in what he recognized as the political-economic aspects of health care, and he saw England as a place where, with its different system, he might learn to understand more about this problem. A team from England visited the hospital, a Mr. Pierce, head of the King Edward's Fund of London, and Joe Bennett, who was head of a regional hospital board. They invited Willis to come and do a work-study year in England, if he could find the resources. It was at that point that he first encountered the Milbank Memorial Fund.

With Dean Clark's encouragement, Willis wrote a proposal to take advantage of the invitation from England. Clark was on the Technical Board of the Milbank Fund, and, on his recommendation, Willis sent the proposal to Milbank, requesting five thousand dollars to support a year of work and study. By return mail, he received the award. Before going, he visited Dr. Boudreau to thank him and to ask what sort of a product he should provide at the end, expecting at least to be required to send a report. Dr. Boudreau anwered:

> We don't want any reports from you. If we really wanted a detailed and analytic report on the National Health Service, we wouldn't pick a young unknown, inexperienced person like you. We'd have picked an expert. We are investing in you as a person, because you seem to have interest, to have done a bit of homework, and want you to have the chance to experience and to develop. And to take advantage of the serendipitous opportunity that [this] might be. Therefore, we don't want you to be encumbered; that will constrain you in a dysfunctional way. So go, and let your career when you come back be your report to us.

Willis did just that. After a year serving in various capacities in the National Health Service, he returned with a unique combination of experience and skills for a future in hospital planning and health policy. In England, he was able to arrange to be mentored by Brian Abel-Smith and Richard Titmus, two of England's outstanding social scientists working in health.[129] Both represented the English brand of social science, vested in the discipline called "social administration." Willis saw it as "an intellectual base in social welfare which pulled together sociology, economics and the medical care system" in a way that he found more systematic than he had seen before. Its "Fabian intellectual tradition [was] very compatible." This experience, so remarkable in its informal auspices from Boudreau, was a launching pad for Willis's career.

Willis clearly saw social science as a tool both of advocacy and of rigorous inquiry. His point of view may be seen as more English than American in both its ambivalences and its activism. He returned from England and soon moved again, now back to the University of Pittsburgh School of Public Health to work with Rufus Rorem, an economist who had been one of the original key staff of the CCMC. Rorem, in Willis's view, was always somewhat dubious about the utility of sociology. He had the view that sociologists tend to make things complicated. Willis, on the other hand, saw the situation as one where much that goes on in health care today has an "unpaid debt" to sociology. Willis was here referring to survey methodology, a technique that he sees as a specific and valuable technique that comes from sociology but in its adaptation to health care is usually interpreted as emerging essentially from statistics. This was a difference of opinion between Rorem and Willis as they introduced surveys of the needs, especially those unmet, of the consumers of health care. Willis, with the assistance of Lowell Levin, who was then at the University of Pittsburgh, sought to introduce the most rigorous social scientific methods, while Rorem thought they were being unnecessarily complicated.

After three years with Rorem, Willis, with a growing reputation as a hospital planning specialist, went to Rochester and then to Temple University Medical School in Philadelphia, where he joined Dr. L. E. Burney, former surgeon general of the PHS, as his assistant vice-president for program and community planning. There his unique preparation found its most fertile medium. With major new building programs required to modernize the Temple University hospital, medical education, and health care complex, he was put in charge of bringing the surrounding community into partnership in this effort. As a lower-income and racially diverse setting, this was a tinder-box situation, especially in the highly charged civil rights urban atmosphere of the 1960s. One should recall that this was the period of the massive race riots in major cities like Detroit and Los Angeles, triggered by just the kind of innovations that Burney sought to introduce. One of the causes for such events was the perception by the communities themselves that high-handed and insensitive approaches to achieving goals that were shared caused frustration and anger. "Colonialism" was the term that came into vogue in this situation.

Willis's first response was to hire a social worker, Betty Reichert, who had experience with this type of problem. His second appointment was more unusual and was controversial: he hired a local black community leader named Harold Haskins. Haskins was a high school dropout who had become a community organizer for Mobilization for Youth and was a specialist on black street gangs. He had studied one gang and was able to trace its basic social structure, finding it to be closely similar to the hierarchies and differentialization of function in modern business corporations. Haskins had organized this gang into a film-making enterprise, and their first film, *The Jungle,* was a documentary about the natural history of a street gang in Philadelphia. Willis sought out Haskins after he saw the film and decided that "[a]nyone who had the sensitivity, insight, and ability to carry out this . . . is somebody I have to meet." Consequently, after finding him and talking with him at length, he offered Haskins a job in the University's planning program.

Willis reports that Haskins was at first confused "and a little put off about why a university would want to hire a high school dropout at what seemed an indecently high salary." He finally agreed after several long talks. As Willis tells it, their final agreement came about as follows:

> At our final meeting, we clinched the deal, and I remember well we were standing on a street corner and I said, "Harold (looking up to him, because Harold was about six feet four inches), you've got to be on guard about one thing. You know that this has been an institution that has not had the most enviable racial record." He said, "I know." And I said, "The danger that you

and I have to protect against is that you must not become our house nigger." Harold looked down at me, and, as he did many times later on, he grabbed me by both shoulders, lifted me off the ground, and said, "Baby, don't worry about that!"

The experiment with Haskins proved to be highly successful, much to the satisfaction of both Willis and Burney. When in 1970 the Milbank Memorial Fund invited Burney to become its executive director, he brought Willis with him as senior associate of the technical staff, and later as vice-president for program planning and development.

When assessing Willis's contributions to medical sociology while he was at Milbank, it is important to note that the groundwork had been laid by Dr. Alexander Robertson, who succeeded Dr. Boudreau as executive director in July 1962, together with Robin Badgley as senior member of the technical staff. They were responsible for introducing the most clear and pointed contributions by the Fund to medical sociology.

Dr. Robertson grew up in Scotland, where his father was a physician, and studied medicine at the University of Edinburgh, finishing in 1949. From there he went to the London School of Hygiene and Tropical Medicine, graduated with a diploma in public health, and continued there on the faculty until he went to the University of Saskatchewan in Canada as chairman of the Department of Social and Preventive Medicine. He succeeded Dr. Boudreau as executive director of the Milbank Memorial Fund in July 1962.

One of his innovations at Saskatchewan had been the development of the social and behavioral sciences in preventive medicine. This interest persisted when he came to the Milbank Fund, and he strengthened it by appointing Robin Badgley, a Yale-trained medical sociologist,[130] as senior member of the technical staff. For the first time, medical sociologists appeared on the technical board. In general, the Fund's policies shifted to an emphasis on medical education and to the support of Latin America, but throughout, the importance of the social sciences remained fundamental. Even when he was still in England, Dr. Robertson sought contact with medical sociologists and joined the Committee on Medical Sociology, as one of its first international members, in 1957. Early in his leadership of the Milbank Fund, he offered support to the newly formed Section on Medical Sociology of the ASA. This became the first such grant to any section of the ASA and was a significant factor in the institutionalization of medical sociology.

Changes in Orientation after 1980

Until about 1980, all three of the foundations maintained policies that functioned consistently to enhance the development of medical sociology. Afterward, although they continued to favor social science, there was a distinct shift toward a focus on health care policy that involved emphasis on economic and political questions. Even their leadership reflected this change. Currently, for example, the Commonwealth Fund is headed by Karen Davis, a renowned scholar of health economics. Daniel J. Fox, a social historian whose work focuses on public health policy, is the operational leader of the Milbank Memorial Fund. Eric Wanner, a political scientist, is president of the Russell Sage Foundation. They all maintain some interest and support for sociology, including medical sociology, but economic and political questions are dominant in their programs.

The history of relations between medical sociology and the private family foundations can be interpreted as a part of a more general movement to establish the social sciences during the postwar era. Just as, in medicine, social science grew under the rubric of "behavioral science," so also was there a movement to sweep all of social science into the behavioral sciences. Between 1951 and 1957, the Behavioral Science Division of the Ford Foundation granted over twenty-three million dollars for support of the behavioral science movement. The intention was to buttress the basic science research requirement of social research while, at the same time, encouraging its efforts to select and study problems where policy applications would be a high priority.[131]

It can be argued that the private foundations provided the crucial and necessary ingredient for the social sciences to establish themselves during the period immediately after the Second World War, when the government did not yet support either their training or their research. Such private support continued, parallel but less critical, beyond 1960 when the federal government's involvement took hold. Two decades later, however, the situation changed. The United States entered a period when all of the social sciences were placed on the defensive, and the focus and priorities of both private and public support changed.

Summary

Hammack's interpretation of Donald Young's early choices as the leader of a major foundation is perhaps the key to understanding this part of medical sociology's history: "He [Donald Young] thought . . . if the Russell Sage Foundation could bring social science to bear in an important way on medical practice, the world of practitioners and scholars would sit up and listen."[132] From this view, the twin themes of advocacy and objectivity should be equally served. Social science research had proved its value in the service of World War II and now should serve the needs of society in peacetime. The way to fulfil its promise was not to retire to the seclusion of the academy but to engage directly in both the development of knowledge and its applications to effective practice; and medicine was the setting in which to demonstrate both.

These goals fit well in the three foundations that have played a special role in medical sociology. All were founded by women, the heirs to great private fortunes, and each began with similar devotion to goals of active engagement in helping child welfare and poverty. The eventual concerns with medicine that engaged these foundations were in public health and prevention, thereby maintaining the emphasis on social betterment, and not in individual scientific disciplines or basic science. Notwithstanding their strong advocacy, however, they also concluded early that, within the range of their financial ability, they would not support professional practice as such but would make more long-term and important contributions by supporting demonstration programs for new ideas and selected research. In terms of current attitudes toward gender, it is notable that these foundations, notwithstanding their founders, were largely run by men. Significant contributions by a woman like those of Esther Lucile Brown at Russell Sage were the exception until very recently.

In the institutional development of medical sociology, the role of private foundations was to both anticipate and complement the demand for social science in the medical profession. Such demand occurred in both research and education, and, as it grew, required an increasing supply of social scientists who were able to perform in situations concerned with problems of health and illness. As a result, special training programs were needed. The foundations supported such programs when public sources did not and, in research, stimulated inquiry in selected problems, like socialization for the profession.

In my description of the origins of NIMH, for example, it was clear that the first director, Dr. Robert Felix, in spite of his convictions about the importance of sociology and the other social sciences for the field of mental health, made the decision to support research but not training in those fields during the early years of NIMH. Thus, when Hollingshead recognized the need for "trained people to study the sociological and anthropological issues so important in mental illness,"[133] his application for training support was turned down at the same time that his request for research support was approved. Both requests were in 1950. When he turned to the Commonwealth Fund, however, they supported what became the model for medical sociology training programs that, in 1957, began to attract large-scale support from NIMH. Similarly, years before the federal government did, the Russell Sage Foundation provided postdoctoral trainees who were to be invaluable to the rapidly growing demands for medical sociologists.

This was a time of palpable promise for sociology. There was a climate of optimism that the study of both human emotions and social relations would find a common and binding ground in a science of behavior. Medicine, already deeply committed to psychosomatic explanations for diseases like ulcerative colitis, and opening its education to psychoanalytic theory, was poised to give access in education and research to social scientists. Demand for such social scientists emerged from various sources. Individuals like Frederick Redlich, Thomas Rennie, Alexander Leighton, and Ernest Gruenberg, all psychiatrists interested in psychiatric epidemiology, sought and found skilled social researchers and made them equal research partners. These efforts found support from both the private and public sectors. Schools of public health were already converts to the importance of basic knowledge from the social sciences and were ready to try experiments in teaching. For these efforts, the private foundations provided strategic support impossible to get elsewhere. New theoretical conceptions about critical problems of the medical profession, like socialization for the profession and comprehensive care, found expression that, at the outset, was almost entirely based on support from their own universities or the private foundations, especially the Commonwealth Fund.

Very few careers in medical sociology during the postwar period were unaffected by the efforts of these three family foundations: the Russell Sage Foundation, the Commonwealth Fund, and the Milbank Memorial Fund. In the earliest stage, from 1946 to 1953, they responded mainly to requests that depended on the leadership and participation of established figures like Robert K. Merton, Everett Hughes, Leo Simmons, and August Hollingshead. Within a short time, they were helping the youngest recruits, such as Eliot Freidson, Harvey Smith, Edmund Volkart, Renee Fox, Mary Goss, Robin Badgley, Ray Elling, Leonard Syme, and others. One can argue that the attitudes and policies of large government organizations like the NIMH did catch up and very well might have ended up where they eventually did, influenced primarily by the large-scale social and political forces of the time. On the other hand, the historical fact is that the private foundations acted to encourage and help shape the pathways of social science in medicine. Moreover, in one vital step in the institutionalization of medical sociology, the creation and advancement of professional associations and journals, it was again private foundation support that proved to be crucial. Specifically, I refer here to the creation of the Section of Medical Sociology, the subject of the next chapter.

10

From Ad Hoc Committee to Professional Association

The Section on Medical Sociology,
1955–1980

The Section on Medical Sociology of the ASA is the first and most widely known professional association for social scientists with interests in problems of health and illness. The Section was formally created in 1959, but it developed from an unaffiliated organization, the Committee on Medical Sociology, started in 1955. The Committee was founded by sociologists but included the full range of social scientists, anthropologists, social psychologists, social workers, and physicians. Even after it evolved into an official Section, it continued as a multidisciplinary group.

According to the Ben-David model of the institutionalization of an intellectual activity,[1] such professional organization was the fourth and final step. Medical sociology needed first to be differentiated in subject matter and method from other fields; second, to move from a peripheral position to become a meaningful part of sociology; and third, to follow an increasing pattern of recruitment, gaining in numbers, resources, and stature. The fourth stage[2] consists of "the successful consolidation of a distinct scientific community with its own subculture, a broad operational base, a communications network, publications, and scientific associations."[3] In earlier chapters, the first three stages were described in detail. How was this final step achieved?

The Sociology of Medical Sociology

The Ben-David model is misleading in its orderly structuring of reality. The stages of institutionalization do not occur in succession, each waiting its turn. In the period from 1946 to 1960 there was such intense intellectual turmoil and growth that medical sociology, much the same as sociology more generally, grew in all the different ways that intellectual activity can. It is only after the fact that rational

215

patterns can be traced, much like trend lines on a statistical graph. Perhaps for this reason most reviews of the field—and there are many[4]—are more histories of ideas than studies in the sociology of knowledge. The reconstruction of how the sociologists in this new field went about creating professional organizations overlaps with the stories of how the first steps of development occurred.

Hollingshead, whose pioneering work in both medical sociology training and research was described earlier,[5] was also quick to grasp the need for professional organization. In 1954 he convened a group at the annual meeting of the American Sociological Society, inviting anyone who had some interest in problems of health or illness. At the end of this first meeting, the group decided to meet more formally in 1955 and thereby became the source of what, in five years, would be a full-fledged professional organization.

At the meeting in 1955, Hollingshead's group began to call itself "The Committee on Medical Sociology." The organization of this group was completely informal; that is, the customary paraphernalia of officers, by-laws, and so on, were sidestepped in favor of what was then thought to be a more functional form. Robert Straus, who served as Hollingshead's coleader, reported that this meeting led to agreement on two specific goals: the designation of time on the program of the American Sociological Society annual meeting for the presentation of research papers in medical sociology and the facilitation of communication among interested persons.[6]

The first objective was quickly achieved. The number of contributed papers that fit the definition of medical sociology was sufficient to establish a regular and important place on the annual program. Toward the second goal, Straus was designated to act as the group's secretary, the sole office of the organization. He compiled a tentative list of people working in the field and distributed a questionnaire to make the list more complete. He also created a newsletter to be distributed annually to the members. Absorbing the costs in his own SUNY-Syracuse office at the time, Straus began the biannual publication of a census of individuals who were either teaching or doing research in medical settings. This list was the membership of the Committee. No formal requirements for membership were specified, and at no time during its history did the Committee charge dues.

In 1957, Bob Straus asked me to take over the office of secretary, and the Committee accordingly changed its address from Bob's office, then at the University of Kentucky, to mine at the Baylor University School of Medicine. As it had been for Straus, this was strictly a voluntary labor. The Committee, as it developed, was the improvised product of a few people's imagination, a device primarily for creating what we now call a "network" of people who were, in one way or another, working in the sociology of medicine. We were doing something that, in both sociology and in medicine, had the feel of a new intellectual enterprise, and the guidelines were unclear. The Committee filled a need to share the experience and to provide mutual support. As the only officeholder, my address became a conduit for the sharing among members of course outlines, bibliography, and lecture notes. Soon, because the costs quickly grew beyond my departmental resources, the American Sociological Society agreed to provide its facilities for the biannual census of medical sociologists and the annual newsletter and to underwrite the cost of its mailings. Behind the scenes, and unknown to anyone on the Committee, Donald Young of the Russell Sage Foundation provided the necessary funds.[7]

When, in 1958, the American Sociological Society approved new bylaws authorizing sections,[8] there were 280 participants in the Committee on Medical Sociology. Of these, 71 percent were sociologists; the remainder were anthropologists, psychologists, physicians, and social workers. The majority thought that joining the national society as a section would be little more than a formalization of a relationship already in existence and, in addition, a means of stabilizing the Committee's structure, both financially and professionally. There was a dissenting group, however, that asked to be heard. According to the bylaw, at least two hundred members were required to formally file for the creation of a section. Before the final vote, therefore, the newsletter invited letters to argue for and against the change from independence to affiliation with the national organization of sociologists.[9]

A vocally militant group, led by Bernard Kutner, a psychologist[10] working then at the Albert Einstein Medical School in New York, argued that the field would thrive better in an independent status, unafilliated with any discipline. The essence of the objection appeared to be the belief that there is no such thing as "medical sociology." More accurately, this opinion asserted, the field is interdisciplinary and should be called "behavioral science in medicine." The Committee on Medical Sociology, in spite of its informal and largely sociological origins, had become identified as the representative organization for all of the social science of medicine at this time. Therefore, the argument continued, it has responsibilities to its membership from all the various subdisciplines, whereas a formal affiliation with the American Sociological Society would favor sociologists and be discriminatory toward members from the other social sciences. Special concern was expressed about qualifications for the officers of the Section. Would nonmembers of the Society be excluded from election to leadership?[11]

Kutner recommended what he felt were more democratic steps. First, create a new organization of "behavioral scientists in medicine"; then, postpone the affiliation for two years until the new group could complete its organization. This statement represented the major concerns of the opposition, repeated in various statements and all published in the newsletter. They feared a loss of multidisciplinary cast in the membership and consequent discrimination. They wanted a free-standing, independent organization of behavioral scientists to represent what had started and thrived under what they considered a more restrictive name. Another interpretation is that they were arguing in favor of an identification that was problem-centered and interdisciplinary and against primary identification by academic discipline.

In answer to these arguments, the national society was asked to rule on who qualified to be officers of the section. The answer was that voting membership in the parent society was not required for sections but only for officers of the Society itself. Up to that point, the nonsociologists from both the United States and more than a dozen foreign countries had participated in the Committee without restrictions. When the vote was taken, the membership decided overwhelmingly in favor of becoming part of the American Sociological Society. When the Council of the Society, in September 1959, voted to approve the formation of the Section on Medical Sociology, it repeated for the record the ruling that members who do not have active or fellowship status, that is, nonvoting members of the Society, would have both voting and officeholding privileges in the Section. Medical sociology thus became the second section to be created, following social psychology.

In January 1960, only four months after the Section was formed, its paid membership numbered 407. In April 1961, the membership had risen beyond seven hundred. As shown in table 10-1, the membership continued to be large, increasing in its proportion of the ASA membership, except for dips in numbers and percent of the total membership during the 1990s. These variations appear to be associated with the creation of the Section on Mental Health in 1991 which, to some extent, competed for members.

In spite of the Section's success in maintaining a broad social science identity, the argument for more specialized identity never went away. In 1970, the Association for the Behavioral Sciences and Medical Education (ABSAME) was formed, with the objective of "bringing together behavioral scientists and professionals from medicine, nursing, and other health care fields around issues of enhancing the teaching of the behavioral sciences in medical (health) education."[14] There is also the Academy of Behavioral Medicine Research, concerned with "the integration of biological and behavioral knowledge in a multidisciplinary approach," and the Society for Behavioral Medicine, which has as its major focus the application of biobehavioral knowledge.[15] Other new organizations were formed on the basis of both loyalty to academic discipline and problem-focus. The former found expression in groups like the Society for Medical Anthropology[16] and the Division of Health Psychology of the American Psychological Association.[17] Within the ASA, the Section on Mental Health was created in 1991 to express a focus on problems of mental health.[18] The federal science establishment increasingly has favored the use of the more inclusive term "behavioral science." Most recently, the National Research Council published a report on biomedical and behavioral scientists, defining the latter to include "psychology, sociology, anthropology and speech and hearing sciences."[19] Although this does not, in any way, adjudicate the issue, it bears mentioning that no separate analysis is included in the Council report for each discipline but only for the whole, and medical schools generally favor behavioral science as the name for faculty engaged in research or teaching involving psychosocial problems.

Table 10-1 Membership of Medical Sociology Section and ASA

Year	Section	ASA	% of ASA
1970[12]	693	14,156	4.9%
1975	928	14,387	6.7%
1980	1,018	12,868	7.9%
1985	993	11,485	8.6%
1990	1,080	12,841	8.4%
1995	980	13,254	7.4%
1996	948	13,134	7.2%
1997	970	13,108	7.4%
1998	1,015	13,273	7.6%
1999	1,025	13,056	7.8%
2000	1,019	12,854	7.9%
2001[13]	1,007	12,388	8.1%

The Early Membership of the Section

In 1959, the records of the Committee on Medical Sociology were analyzed just prior to its transition into the new Section. It was found that 309 individuals defined themselves as engaged to some extent in medical sociology. Of these 224 were sociologists, including eleven who were both sociologists and psychologists and one physician-sociologist. The remainder were anthropologists, psychologists, physicians, and social workers.

For the most part, the members were part of academic departments of universities, with a small but growing number in health-related professional schools. It was not always possible from the records to identify the type or amount of activity they devoted to either research or teaching. However, the following findings were compiled for those individuals who were primarily indentifiable as sociologists: nineteen were full-time members of fourteen different medical school faculties; in significant measure, they were directly responsible for teaching medical students. In addition, nine sociologists were members of the teaching faculties of five graduate schools of public health and one school of nursing. Full-time research appointments in medical schools were listed by thirteen sociologists. In four graduate schools of public health, nine sociologists had full-time research appointments. The remaining 174 sociologists on the Committee's list were engaged only part-time in medical sociology. Of the latter, seventeen described some responsibility for teaching medical students. Another fifty-seven did some teaching of other medical personnel. The other one hundred sociologists were engaged in part-time research with no function as teachers of medical personnel.

As a basis for comparison, Anderson and Seacat, in a national study conducted in 1957,[20] were able to identify 216 behavioral scientists who were engaged in research in the health field full-time or part-time. Of these, 193 responded to a mailed questionnaire. It was found that 63 percent were working full-time and 37 percent part-time on research. The largest proportion were primarily affiliated with a university department of sociology and anthropology. About 20 percent (forty-four individuals) were affiliated with medical schools, mainly in departments of preventive medicine and psychiatry. On the whole, their attitudes toward their work were "satisfied" and "hopeful," with a notable lack of serious concern about the problems of working in a new area of inquiry and in collaboration with health professionals.

As the Section on Medical Sociology began, there were, at its meetings and in the journals, both factual evaluations and lively discussions of the role of medical sociology. Similar to the earlier concerns expressed by the Russell Sage crossdisciplinary residents, particularly at their meetings in 1952–1953, there was anxiety about the risk of too much involvement in the world of medicine at the cost of alienation from social science colleagues.[21] One expression of this view asserted the primacy of basic sociological theory with the warning that medicine was no more than a secondary interest for the sociologist. Oswald Hall and Talcott Parsons are examples. "Medicine has no unique interest for sociology," wrote Hall. "When the sociologist studies medicine, he is studying work. . . . The justification for its study lies in the light it throws on more general forms of social organization."[22] Parsons argued in terms of the tension between advocacy and objectivity for sociology generally. "The problem of differentiation from applied interest," said Parsons, "was particularly acute in the American case. . . . Only within the last generation . . . [has] sociology . . . reached what is perhaps a first level of maturity as a scientific discipline."[23] He argued that sociology should maintain a full commitment to basic research and training and that the formulation of social policy is not and should not become its responsibility.

Although these polemics were intense, the members of the Section on Medical Sociology moved forward and, once organized, quickly became engaged in all the usual aspects of professionalism, seeking support, creating a journal, and rapidly growing into the national association's largest and most active section.

The Early Years of the Section

The first organizational meeting of the Section on Medical Sociology, at the annual ASA meeting of September 1959, committed the Section to continue the major functions of the Committee that preceded it. Once a year a directory of members would be published and twice a year a newsletter. For the first time, a nominating committee created a full slate of officers for a mail vote conducted by the Executive Office of the ASA in October, 1959. The following ballot was sent (the names of those elected are in italics):

Chairman: *A. B. Hollingshead* and Robert Straus

Chairman-elect: *Odin Anderson* and H. Warren Dunham

Secretary-treasurer: *Samuel W. Bloom* and Albert Wessen

Council (six nominees, elect three): *Everett Hughes*, Lyle Saunders, *Benjamin Paul, George Reader*, Howard Becker, and Richard Williams

With reference to the concern about the risk of exclusion of the nonsociologists in the Section, it should be noted that Reader, a physician, and Paul, an anthropologist, were elected to the three-person council.

At the 1959 Section meeting, a section day was created, when, at the Annual Meeting of the ASA, following the scheduled section business meeting, a special program would be arranged by the current chairman. Hollingshead invited the following panel to discuss, on August 28, 1960, at the ASA meeting in New York City, "The Training of Medical Sociologists":

Rodger L. Buck, M.D.	Harvard University
Raymond S. Duff, M.D.	Yale University
Saxon L. Graham	Roswell Park Memorial Institute
Leon Lezer, M.D.	University of Vermont
Robert Straus	University of Kentucky

Eliot Freidson was appointed as program chairman to select four sessions of scientific articles on the sociology of medicine.

The chairman's panel reflected Hollingshead's continuing focus on the need to prepare sociologists for a role as scientist-educator in medical sociology.[24] When, almost a decade earlier, he had first attempted to establish a training program for medical sociologists at Yale, the situation included deep uncertainties in the medical school as well as resistance and lack of interest among sociologists. Before any active steps could be taken, Hollingshead reported,

I had to clear the situation here at Yale. I couldn't get any place because the School of Medicine was in a disorganized state as part of the university. There was a serious question whether the medical school would be continued because it was expensive and the university was in a stringent financial situation. The university was also looking for a new dean of the School of Medicine. I was told in no uncertain terms that nothing would be done until the new dean was on the ground.

A dramatic and favorable change occurred with the appointment of Vernon Lippard as the new dean. Lippard was an outstanding and progressive medical educator, under whom Yale's medical school thrived. As a result, Hollingshead was able to create a model for the training programs that the NIMH, after a long delay, began to support on a pilot basis in 1957. In 1960, Clark Vincent, the first full-time administrator for the social science training program of NIMH, was appointed, together with six members to conduct peer review of proposals.[25] These developments dramatically changed the institutional character of medical sociology.

Against this background, the first chairman's session of the Section was particularly strategic.

Who Is a Medical Sociologist? 1961

When the decision was made to create a section, the controversy about whether to join the national organization of sociologists or to remain independent would seem to have been resolved. Underlying the debate, however, was another question: Who is a medical sociologist? This question did not go away; it became instead the second major issue for the Section. What are the criteria, it was asked, for designating who is a medical sociologist? Should there be established formal criteria? The second chairman, Odin Anderson, prepared a background paper on this question for discussion at the annual meeting of the ASA in St. Louis, Missouri, August 29–September 2, 1961. This seemed all the more important as George Reader reported that the International Sociological Association was intending to form a Subcommittee on Medical Sociology at its Fifth Congress in 1962.

Anderson began by describing the background of concern.[26] "Behavioral scientists," he wrote,

> have been entering the [health] field in increasing numbers in recent years. ... They work under, in association with, and [at times] in a supervisory capacity over the health professionals in interdisciplinary research projects. ... Working with essentially biological and physical science oriented health professionals who have inherited a well-developed and accepted hierarchy of titles, statuses, and duties and prerogatives mainly as daily practitioners has created problems as to where and how behavioral scientists fit into this imposing structure.

In this situation, Anderson continued, there arise problems such as the "stranger" role, where the behavioral scientist enters without the same recognized role as health professionals. There is also the risk of people being engaged as social researchers in health who have no knowledge of substantive problems in the health field, and even some who have no solid claim to be social scientists.

These conditions, Anderson said, suggest a need for behavioral science to adapt to "some of the hierarchical designations of the health professionals" so that both will feel more comfortable and know what to expect of each other. Anderson did not argue for criteria like licensure and specialty board examinations that were clearly protections for the general public because of the direct relations the clinical professionals and the public must have. He recognized that behavioral scientists (with the exception of clinical psychologists) have no direct therapeutic relationship with the public. Instead he cited "classical reasons":

> The criteria that may be desirable for medical sociologists are self-imposed by a professional group seeking identity and status in the presumed larger interest of standards. There are the classical reasons for the establishment of criteria by a developing profession in western society; a profession setting up its own standards to keep out charlatans and incompetents aside from state regulations if there be any such at all.[27]

On these bases, he recommended that the "common sense criteria for medical sociologists could be all or a combination of some of the following:

1. Ph.D. in sociology, anthropology, social psychology.
2. Evidence of research, teaching and publications using the health field as source of data and Ph.D.
3. M.D. plus evidence of research in health field of a social science nature.
4. Formal courses in public health, medicine, hospital administration, etc., in addition to degree in a social science.
5. B.A. and/or M.A. in behavioral science.
6. B.A. and/or M.A. in behavioral science plus experience in health field."[28]

Although he knew that a formal procedure would be necessary to provide and enforce such certification, and he was fully aware of the attendant difficulties involved, Anderson nevertheless went on record in favor of certification and believed that the Section on Medical Sociology should be the agent of the process. At the very least, he argued, the Section should use such criteria as qualifications for membership, thereby creating a professional validation that could be used by those who need to recruit medical sociologists.

Anderson's memorandum came at a time when the demand curve for sociologists in general and for medical sociologists in particular was at the early stage of a rapid rise.[29] As both Lutterman[30] and Freeman[31] concluded fifteen years later, the rapid expansion of American universities that began in the fifties and carried into the midseventies created a demand for sociologists that exceeded the supply. Within this manpower pattern, medical sociologists chose most often to work in university settings, primarily as teachers. Even research in medical sociology, more often than not, was conducted from a university liberal arts department base in preference to medical organizations. These conditions are part of the explanation why, although Anderson and others represented the case for certification with both clarity and passion, Anderson's memorandum was not presented by the Section Council to the membership. Its substance was described in the newsletter, and the Council's negative reaction was reported. Beyond that, the question seemed to die at that point, rising again only decades later when the general membership of the ASA became engaged in the question of whether the identity of the general sociologist needed certification.

Certification was not a new issue in the ASA. As early as 1956, there was action by the Association to protect the profession from "exclusionary provisions of state laws being promoted by psychologists to license or certify psychologists and social psychologists."[32] Rhoades describes this as probably the most intense organizational effort ever made by the Association. The source was a report by the Ad Hoc Committee on Implications of Legislation that Licenses or Certifies Psychologists, composed of Theodore Newcomb, Elbridge Sibley, and Guy Swanson, chair, in 1956. They wrote:

> The American Psychological Association and its state affiliates have faced the problem of professional self-regulation by establishing a code of ethics and by working for the enactment of state legislation to insure that the public receives a high quality of professional service. The American Psychological Association, in the letter and the spirit of its policy recommendations for such state legislation, has sought to protect the legitimate interests of other professions.

They added that "some unintended consequences resulted that might limit sociologists trained in social psychology from performing their normal activities in teaching, research or consultation without violating the state code."[33] In 1957, Amos H. Hawley was appointed by the ASA to chair the Committee on the Implications of Certification Legislation. On the Committee were Edgar Borgatta, Philip Hauser, Alex Inkeles, Saul Mendlovitz, Gideon Sjoberg, and Ralph Turner. They succeeded in negotiating protections for sociologists in forty-seven states. This was reinforced by Talcott Parsons, acting for the Committee on the Profession in 1959, in an agreement with the American Psychological Association to protect the rights of social psychologists who were not certified psychologists. The latter, however, did say that "the American Sociological Society undertakes on its part, through its newly organized Section on Social Psychology, to set standards for the certification of sociologists entitled to this privilege."[34]

Odin Anderson, therefore, was expressing a concern that was not limited to medical sociologists. There was also, however, a deep resistance among sociologists to certification. One can only speculate that, as a scholarly profession and not a client-directed consulting profession,[35] sociologists were protective about the less formal professional requirements, most particularly vested in educational and experience criteria in preference to government-sponsored examinations. Nevertheless, certification again became an issue more than twenty years later, this time stimulated by federal government requirements for the employment of social scientists.[36] Again, a manpower market condition was created in which psychologists whose profession provided certification were advantaged in situations where sociologists had equivalent research qualifications. Under these conditions, the ASA reacted by offering certification procedures for those who wanted them or felt they would benefit. Nevertheless and notwithstanding the emergence of a new Section of Applied Sociology, the demand for certification among sociologists remained modest.

There was, however, one notable outcome of the Anderson memorandum for the Section on Medical Sociology. A survey of the Section membership was commissioned in 1962 to find out more about who were the individuals who identified themselves as medical sociologists. The survey was conducted by Rose Laub Coser, who became in 1962 the second secretary-treasurer, aided by Janice Hopper of the ASA central office. Out of 854 dues-paying members in 1962, 382 filled out a questionnaire. Among the respondents, 82 percent (312) were sociologists, although some of these, fifty-three individuals, had a double identification with either anthropology, medicine, or psychology, and twelve had triple identification. Research was the dominant activity, with 85 percent of the total sample engaged in some form of health-related research, either part-time or full-time. Teaching was reported by 55 percent of the population.[37]

The Creation of an Official Journal

At the sixth meeting of the Council of the Section, August 31, 1964, in Miami Beach, a formal proposal was made by E. Gartly Jaco, the editor and publisher of the *Journal of Health and Human Behavior*, requesting that the Section take over its publication. At the time, no section sponsored its own journal. In fact, until 1954, there was only one official journal of the ASA, the *American Sociological Review* (*ASR*), created in 1936. When the American Sociological Society was founded in 1905, it took over the *American Journal of Sociology* (AJS), which had been started in 1895 as the first sociology journal published in the United States.[38] In 1936, the *AJS* was separated from official sponsorship and returned to the University of Chicago when the *ASR* was founded. Not until 1954 was another journal sponsored by *ASA*: in that year, *Sociometry* was donated by J. L. Moreno and was officially published by the Association in 1956 under the editorship of Leonard S. Cottrell, Jr. In 1958, the *Journal of Educational Sociology* became the third. However, none of these journals were presented to the ASA by sections. It was the policy of the ASA that no journal could be officially sponsored by a section, even though there might be, as was the case with medical sociology, a close association between a section and its related journal.

When Jaco came to the Section with his proposal, he was director of research at the Cleveland Psychiatric Institute and Hospital and associate professor of sociology at Western Reserve University. The editor of the first book-length collection of articles about medical sociology[39] and author of an epidemiological study of mental disorders in Texas sponsored by the Russell Sage Foundation,[40] he had started his career in medical sociology on the faculty of the Departments of Neuropsychiatry and Preventive Medicine at the University of Texas Medical Branch, Galveston, Texas. In 1960, he and Austin L. Porterfield started to publish the *Journal of Health and Human Behavior* as a free-standing publication, the first journal in modern times devoted entirely to medical sociology. "Jake," as he was universally known by his friends, although at first listed as the coeditor, was the real force behind the journal. He was, on the surface, a larger-than-life Texas caricature, tall and rangy, gregarious, and funny, a real "good old boy." Actually, he was born in New York City, had worked after the army as a publicist in New York, and was professionally a superbly qualified social researcher and one of medical sociology's most distinguished pioneers. His journal, aside from being the first, had an editorial board that read like a Who's Who of the social science of medicine, including anthropologists, physicians, and nurses.[41]

In 1964, the *Journal of Health and Human Behavior* was in its fifth volume. Jake had begun its publication with the financial support of the Potishman Foundation, a small Texas organization that was directed by Austin Porterfield, chairman of the Department of Sociology at Texas Christian University. Although it was very much a one-man operation, Jake had managed to gain a worldwide audience and a list of high-quality articles. By 1962, however, the responsibility for the journal had become burdensome. Porterfield had been forced to withdraw because of health, and, as a result, the journal was operating without the Potishman Foundation's financial support. Nevertheless, when Jake began to negotiate with the Section, there were twelve hundred subscribers, and the journal was still self-sufficient, albeit with some debts. Legally, Jake owned the journal. When in 1962 he moved to the University of Minnesota, he was promised an annual subsidy for it of three thousand dollars, but a challenge from the Internal Revenue Service forced his new employers to withdraw the offer. When he approached the Section, therefore, there was only enough money in the *Journal's* bank account to pay for one issue out of the three still due in the fifth volume. This, however, proved to be only one of the problems to be surmounted before the journal could become an official publication of the ASA.

In October 1964, the Council of the Section formally accepted Jaco's request that the *Journal of Health and Human Behavior* be sponsored by the Section on Medical Sociology. Preliminary discussions with the ASA indicated that, if the journal were accepted by the national organization, the final authority rested with the ASA Publications Committee, not with the Section. It was also clear that the annual deficit projected from past performance might prevent the ASA from accepting the publication. Nevertheless, the Section agreed to go forward with the request. On August 30, 1965, at the meeting of the ASA Publications Committee, it was formally proposed that the *Journal* should become an official journal of the ASA, sponsored by the Section. The request was tabled until the meeting of the following year.

In the background of these negotiations, the influence of the Section leadership's relationship with the Milbank Memorial Fund was critical. In July 1962, Dr. Alexander Robertson was appointed executive director of the Fund, and in May 1963 Robin F. Badgley became senior member of the technical staff. Robertson was interested in social science from the earliest stages of his career as an academic physician in public health and preventive medicine in Scotland, London, and Saskatchewan. He joined the Committee on Medical Sociology and later the Section prior to coming to New York. Badgley, a Yale-trained sociologist and Russell Sage postdoctoral fellow, had joined forces with Robertson in Saskatoon, and Robertson brought him to Milbank to spearhead new policies at Milbank in support of the behavioral sciences in medicine. As the Section grew, it was evident that financial support beyond that available from the ASA would allow more imaginative policy initiatives. Not the least of these was the opportunity to sponsor a journal. When Jaco offered his journal to the Section, therefore, it was decided to propose to the Milbank Fund that it support general professional development of the Section, with funds specifically allocated to undertake the publication of the *Journal of Health and Human Behavior*, under the aegis of the ASA. An annual budget of fifty-one hundred dollars was requested, and in December of 1964, a grant of twenty-five thousand dollars was approved covering three years of the Section's activities.

This is, in my opinion, another case where the strategic support of a private foundation, especially from individual foundation leaders like Donald Young,[42] Lester Evans,[43] and Robertson, made a vital difference in the history of medical sociology. I was, during 1964–65, the chairman of the Section and, together with Robin Badgley, represented the Section in its request to the ASA. We were surprised to find the Publications Committee generally hostile to our request. Specifically, they focused on questions about the financial viability of the *Journal*. Close to the surface, however, was their resentment of an upstart young group to which they hesitated to give the imprimatur of the national organization. For them, medical sociology was "applied," not real sociology, and they were worried about opening the door to specialized journals. We had anticipated the financial questions but not the professional hostility. I remember that the atmosphere became heated, forcing Robin and me to fight hard against the Committee. As it was, the timing of the Milbank proposal saved the day. The grant's budget named a sum for the *Journal*. Without that promised financial source, I think the Publications Committee would have rejected outright the Section's request. Even with the financial backup, they postponed a decision, tabling the question till their next meeting.

Badgley and I, fearing that the Publications Committee was going to reject our request, approached the incoming president of the ASA, Wilbert Moore. Speaking to what we saw as the major objections raised in the Committee, we asked Moore to present our views before the business meeting of the Association in September 1965. At that meeting, Moore presented the Section's request, and the ASA formally approved the acquisition of the *Journal* for a trial period of three years. Even so, the formal transfer did not occur until March 1966. Between 1964, when Jaco first made his request, and 1966, when the ASA formally took over responsibility, the *Journal* could not have survived without the Milbank grant.

Questions of authority and finances still remained. About authority there was no confusion. The rules of the ASA were that all their official journals were subject to the overarching authority of the ASA Council, acting through the Publications Committee. Therefore, the Section on Medical Sociology functioned only in an advisory capacity. The finances were more complicated. The terms of the ASA's approval were that the *Journal* must be self-sufficient at the end of three years; but how would self-sufficient be defined? The accounting methods of the ASA were not very clear. Their estimate was that the *Journal* would have an annual cost of $10,500. Lengthy negotiations with Edmund Volkart, the ASA executive secretary, were still required to determine what, exactly, would be the obligations of the two parties for the *Journal's* expenses.

In the end, the *Journal's* success made all the questions groundless. The name was changed to the *Journal of Health and Social Behavior* (*JHSB*). Eliot Freidson was chosen by the ASA as the first editor, and his already distinguished reputation as a sociological theorist blunted the professional reservations of the ASA's Publication Committee. There need not have been any concern. The minutes of the Section Council of December 15–16, 1965, reveal a remarkable list of nominations for editor of the journal, including Ozzie Simmons, Robert Wilson, Robert Straus, Jerome K. Myers, Sol Levine, and Jaco. None of these men were narrowly specialized. All had already established reputations in mainstream sociology. Recommendations for the editorial board were similar. In addition to those named as potential editors-in-chief, the list included Harvey Smith, Edward Suchman, Albert Wessen, Howard Freeman, David Mechanic, Charles Kadushin, Robert Scott, Charles Wright, and Patricia Kendall.[44]

In March 1966, when the ASA began publishing the *JHSB*, there were one thousand subscribers, 80 percent of which were institutions. The institutional rate was ten dollars, and the subscription rate for members was five dollars. The rejection rate was 90 percent. By August 1967, Freidson reported a sharp increase of submitted manuscripts, increased quality, and a rejection rate of 83 percent. In December 1967, the number of subscriptions was up to sixteen hundred and the number and quality of manuscripts was up substantially. Freidson now was concerned about the time lag between receipt and publication of twelve months.[45] In a report to the Milbank Fund on October 1, 1967, the expenditures for the *JHSB* were listed as $17,514.26. However, there was also income from the *Journal* listed for subscriptions, reprint permissions, and back issues of $12,189.19. Thus the actual subsidy from the Milbank grant was $5,325, and it was clear that the Section retained major fiscal responsibility for the journal. This soon changed, and the *JHSB* became an accepted official journal.

Records of the ASA on its publications only go back to 1979. At that point, the *JHSB* had the third-highest subcription rate of all the official journals, ranked behind *ASR* and *Contemporary Sociology*. More precisely, there were 4,203 total subscriptions, 2,339 individual members and 1,254 nonmembers, including institutions. This rank remained constant, although by 1995, the total subscription rate had fallen to 3,702. Similar reductions were experienced by the two higher-ranked journals. As expressed to me by the ASA executive office, *JHSB* is more than self-sufficient and has been from very early in its history.

In 1967, a new social science quarterly, *Social Science and Medicine: An International Journal*, began publication in the United Kingdom under the editorship of Peter McEwan. Since then other journals have appeared that specialize in medical sociology or the social sciences of medicine.[46] The *JHSB* has continued to be a leading publication in the field.

As a final comment on the story of *JHSB*, I was struck by Jaco's announcement in the original *Journal of Health and Human Behavior* (Volume 7, number 2, 1966) telling of the transfer in the next issue to the ASA. Speaking for Professor Porterfield and himself, he expressed pride at what they had accomplished and warned that he intended "to keep a close and concerned eye on the behavior of this journal in its new home."[47] And well he might. Looking back at the seven volumes that Jaco edited, it is clear that he attracted contributions from the most outstanding medical sociologists of the time. Ranging from Parsons[48] to Roemer, Fox, Rosen, Falk, Mechanic, Leonard Syme, and Robert Straus,[49] to name only some of the best-known, these were a very select group of scholars indeed. History has proved Jaco's pride to be justified.

The Leadership of the Section

The officers of the Section in its first decade were a mix of established sociologists out of the mainstream of the discipline and relatively young scholars whose achievements were more focused in medical sociology. Hollingshead, Everett Hughes, and Edward Suchman were well-known senior professors in leading sociology departments. Hughes received his degree at the University of Chicago in

1928, returning to teach there ten years later. He was a man of broad interests, most intensely concerned about the effects of industrialization on modern cities. He also coedited, with his wife Helen, the *American Journal of Sociology* and was president of the ASA in 1962–63, immediately after he was chairman of the Section on Medical Sociology. His interest in medicine probably began with his study of work and occupations and started with nurses. That was in the late 1940s.[50] He was the mentor and partner of medical sociologists such as Howard Becker, Anselm Strauss, and Blanche Geer.[51] Anderson represents a very different type of career. Although he started and ended his working life in academia, he was the research director of a privately funded organization, the Health Information Foundation, for almost thirty years. He was the first sociologist to work in a school of public health, at the University of Michigan, in 1942–49, and the first full-time sociologist in a medical school, at the University of Ontario in 1949–52. He is one of the outstanding pioneers in the policy-oriented field of health services research.[52]

Although it was fitting that these trailblazers should be the first elected to the top office of the Section, younger people were not forced to wait long. As table 10-2 shows, by 1963, when Harvey Smith, from the University of North Carolina, was elected chairman, the pattern shifted to the younger, though still broadly trained, medical sociologists.

The offices of the Section very quickly became identified with specific functions. The chair represented the section with the ASA and presided at business Council meetings, but, perhaps most important, organized a special session at the annual meetings, with invited participants. Anderson presided over discussion about the criteria of membership. Hughes created the first session that honored and celebrated the work of an early pioneer in the field, Michael M. Davis. Freidson and I, in 1964 and 1965, turned to questions related to conceptions of research, respectively, the meaning of professions and socialization for the profession. Suchman, in 1966, invited Milton Roemer, a leader in the field of public health, to present a paper, "The Future of Social Medicine in the United States." This position paper assessed the current status of the field in the nation and outlined the directions in which it appeared to be going. The discussants were from both medicine and sociology: Mervyn Susser, Leslie Falk, Robert Wilson, and Jack Elinson.

The secretary-treasurer was the sustaining office of the Section, responsible during a three-year term for the day-to-day running of affairs. It was in this office that the early negotiations for the *Journal of Health and Human Affairs* were managed and the request for funding from the Milbank Memorial Fund was conceived and negotiated. There was a change, however, in the division of labor whereby the newsletter was separated from the secretary-treasurer's office and allocated to an editor appointed by the Council. The updating and publication of the census of medical sociologists was shared by the secretary-treasurer and the editor of the newsletter and instrumented through the executive offices of the ASA.

From the Council, a variety of functions emerged. Most central was the role of the Section in the program of the ASA's annual meeting. The Council decided that the Section should assume authority for the selection and running of the sessions of scientific papers dealing with medical sociology, and, after negotiations, the ASA agreed. From the start, the dominant theme of relations with the ASA was the Section's role in advancing the intellectual responsibilities of the

Table 10-2 Chairmen of Section on Medical Sociology, 1960–1970

Name	Affiliation	Year
August B. Hollingshead	Yale University	1960
Odin W. Anderson	Center for Health Administration Studies, University of Chicago	1961
Everett C. Hughes	University of Chicago	1962
Harvey L. Smith	University of North Carolina	1963
Eliot Freidson	New York University	1964
Samuel W. Bloom	Downstate Medical School-SUNY	1965
Edward A. Suchman	Cornell University	1966
Howard E. Freeman	Brandeis University	1967
Robert Straus	University of Kentucky School of Medicine	1968
Sol Levine	Harvard School of Public Health	1969
David Mechanic	University of Wisconsin	1970

field. Even before joining the ASA, the Committee on Medical Sociology published in the *ASR* an article based on a panel discussion on the sociologist as medical educator, sponsored at the 1968 annual meeting of the ASA.[53] This particular panel became a model for the chair's sessions, and it became a regular practice to publish the presentations of these programs. As examples, the papers presented in 1965 about socialization by John Clausen and in 1966 by Daniel J. Levinson were published together in *JHSB,* with a comment by Howard Becker and Blanche Geer.[54] These articles became the centerpiece of scholarly discussion of socialization for the profession at the time. When the Reeder Lecture was initiated in 1978, the practice of publishing the annual address in *JHSB* was established.[55]

Another important function of the Council that developed during the first years was the establishment of liaison with related professional groups. George Reader, in 1961, proposed that the Section form a subcommittee on medical sociology at the Fifth World Congress of the International Sociological Association (ISA) in 1962. Charles Loomis and Eliot Freidson joined with Reader to document the importance of such a group in the ISA. Reader also functioned as liaison with the American Public Health Association (APHA). Ozzie Simmons was nominated to act as liaison for social sciences with the American Psychiatric Association. Peter New represented the Section with the American Society of Applied Anthropology. Similarly, contributions to the ASA liaison with the American Association for the Advancement of Science (AAAS) were arranged. For example, Vincent Whitney, when he was responsible for two sessions on sociological research at the AAAS program, requested contributions from medical sociology. Arrangements were also made for relations between the Section and the regional professional sociology associations.

The minutes of the early years of the Section reveal that certain members were particularly active. George Reader, as already indicated, and Eliot Freidson deserve particular mention as the Section's representatives to the ISA, and together they attended the planning meeting of the ISA in Uppsala, Sweden, in May 1965, preparing for the meeting in Evian, France, in 1966. They found the ISA "a baffling structure" but were able, nevertheless, to establish a place for medical sociology on the ISA program. They followed up with proposals to various government and private funding sources to finance the participation of American sociologists at the Evian meeting. Eventually a Section on Medical Sociology was established in the ISA and, with representatives from East Germany, Yugoslavia, South America, and the United Kingdom, organized a one-day symposium at the Evian meeting on "Illness and Social Conditions," and another session on medical education. Reader also became the informal representative of the Medical Sociology Section in the Section on Medical Care of the APHA, which he regarded as a more activist policy-oriented group with very similar interests. As time progressed, both these organizational ties remained strong.

In 1966, a Committee on International Medical Sociology was created,[56] and an ambitious set of joint activities with medical sociologists abroad was launched. In 1965, a request came from the International Organization for Social Psychiatry for closer relations with the Section, and Rose Coser became the delegate of the Section to this organization.

In general, the minutes of the Section's first fifteen years reveal a close relation between the main scholarly themes in the field and the activities that can be identified specifically with the institutionalization processes of its social history. For anyone who has worked as a scholar in the field, the minutes read like a bibliography of its major investigators. In addition to those already mentioned, Norman Bell, Marvin Sussman, Erving Goffman, Irving Zola, Hans Mauksch, Joseph Eaton, Anselm Strauss, Elaine Cumming, Ray Elling, Kerr White, Fred Davis, Howard Freeman, Sol Levine, Leo Reeder, Edward Suchman, Joseph Eaton, George Maddox, Jack Elinson, Rod Coe, Rue Bucher, Thomas Scheff, William Rosengren, and Benjamin Paul were among the notably active members in the early years. At the same time, the key players of the training and research programs of the federal agencies, especially NIMH and NCHSR were equally active. Clark Vincent and Nathaniel Siegel of NIMH and Fred Chaffee and Paul Sanazaro of NCHSR appear repeatedly in the early Section records.

Attention was paid to each of the facets of professionalization, including the supply of and demand for manpower. In 1964, the Committee for the Study of Social Science in the Curricula for Education of the Health Professions was created, with Peter New responsible for its operation. In 1967, New reviewed the content of courses taught by behavioral sciences in professional schools and also sponsored a series of summer institutes. Subsidized by a Milbank grant, New completed a report that reviewed current curricula and course syllabi. Chaired by Sydney Croog, the Committee included Joseph Eaton, Peter New, Paul Sanazaro, Nathaniel Siegal, Marvin Sussman, and myself. Also active was the Committee on Graduate Students in Medical Sociology, chaired by Ray Elling, with Eliot Freidson, Howard Freeman, and Edward Suchman. These formal structures expressed the Section's concern for the role of medical sociologists in education, both in their traditional settings as teachers in the college of arts and sciences and as part of medical school education.

The Committee on Issues of Public Policy was created, chaired by Albert Wessen, with Robin Badgley, Joseph Eaton, Lowell Levin, Milton Roemer, Howard Freeman, and Robert Straus. Questions of relationship between federal agencies and research investigators, particularly the freedom and integrity of researchers, were high on its agenda. There was agreement that the committee should be very active and aggressive, especially in its liaison with national agencies like NIMH.

Discussion of the role of the Section in public policy dominated the annual business meeting of 1967 at San Francisco. The field was criticized for a lack of interest in how medical sociology should act in public policy. The following is extracted from the minutes:

> Robert Straus asked the members present (approximately 80) how many were personally involved in studies dealing with questions relevant to the formulation of public policy. About half responded in a show of hands. The distinction between involvement by an individual and by the Section was raised by Howard Freeman. George G. Reader suggested that it would be useful to make an inventory of the extent to which members of the Section were dealing with matters of public policy. . . . He drew an analogy to the paucity of information about current research on medical care in New York City. During the summer, he had hired a graduate student to make an inventory of such studies. He had found that $14 million was already being used to support studies in this field and an additional $48 million was to be allocated within a year. Albert F. Wessen concurred with the recommendation of conducting an inventory. He rejected the recommendation to develop resolutions to present to the public and contended that the appropriate role for the Section should be to clarify findings relevant to questions of public policy.[57]

Thus, in the familiar debate of objectivity versus advocacy, the Section appeared to be taking the position that an intellectual field should be the arbiter of knowledge in public policy and not an advocate of specific types of action.

By 1970, the institutionalization of medical sociology was complete. A distinct scientific community, identified with its name, had consolidated its own subculture. A broad operational base had been established with a communications network, publications, and professional associations. The criteria of Ben-David and Shils were met.

The Section's Next Phase

As the Section on Medical Sociology entered its second decade, professional goals were pursued with a sense of high purpose. Free of the internal organizational concerns of other sections, medical sociology was engaged in securing the directions of medical sociology as a science, in demonstrating the effectiveness of translating knowledge into public policy, and in forming partnerships with like-minded sociologists throughout the world. Rhoads, in his official history of the ASA, described this period as a time of troubles between Sections and the parent group. "Relations," he wrote, "between Sections and the Association were somewhat strained through a major part of the seventies. The problem centered on the amount of time allocated to Sections during the Annual Meeting and the scheduling of Section Day activities."[58] For the Medical Sociology Section, however, these were not problems. Secure as a large section, it did not need to worry about its share of the annual program for scientific papers. Furthermore, its Section Day activities were established as an occasion when invited presentations consistently met the highest academic standards, were topical, and were usually published in the best available refereed journal.

On the other hand, one important problem presented itself in 1970. The Milbank grant, which had been so important for the organization to launch its professional services, was now ended. The *JHSB* was already self-sufficient and, as Howard Freeman replaced Eliot Freidson as editor in 1970, had already secured a place as one of the ASA's major publications. In the meantime, other important functions had become dependent on external funding, particularly the expanded role of the Committee on International Medical Sociology. The Council and other standing committees also expressed concern about their ability to continue their development without special funding. The first response was to seek additional funds through dues from the ASA. The second and more effective response was to find support from another private foundation.

David Mechanic, during his term as Chair of the Section in 1970, created a development committee to deal with this problem. He did not seek to fill in the holes left by the loss of the Milbank funds, however. Rather, he wanted to break new ground. The means he chose was a proposal to the Carnegie Foundation in which he emphasized a shift in the Section's orientation in the direction of public policy and health services research. The proposal, "Sociological Aspects of Health and Health Services," was funded, and the first meeting of the Carnegie Grant Steering Committee was held on December 29, 1971, at the Center for Health Administration Studies of the University of Chicago. Carnegie granted sixty-nine thousand dollars, as requested, for a three-year period to finance the activities of two new committees: the Committee on Organizational Consequences of Varying National Programs for Providing Health Services, with Odin Anderson as its chairman, and the Committee on Preventive Health and Health Maintenance, led by Sol Levine. The grant also funded related Council activities.

Although this grant did not provide for the prior Section standing committees, there is no question that it gave the Section a general material boost and inspiration to move forward in its development. Unlike that of the earlier Milbank grant, the goal was to study health care delivery problems, specifically "issues relevant to the implementation of a national health insurance program for the United States,"[59] and through a policy-related report "to have some impact on what is happening with respect to the actual delivery of medical care."[60] Care was taken to protect the activities from the more usual Section routine. Ronald Andersen, as the secretary-treasurer of the Section, was formally responsible for monitoring the funds. Interest in this work was immediately expressed by the NCHSR, and the Carnegie Foundation remained involved, asking that the work be interdisciplinary, with representatives particularly from the medical profession, economics, and health education. The Steering Committee, however, acted immediately to ensure that the Section should retain its independence, albeit welcoming representatives of the NCHSR and other disciplines.

It was decided that three subcommittees should divide the labor of each major committee. Under Odin Anderson, the subcommittees and their chairpersons were as follows:

1. Professional Organization and Control, Mary Goss[61]
2. Health Indicators, Jack Elinson[62]
3. Humanization of Medical Care, Jan Howard[63]

Under Sol Levine:

1. Design of Health Service for Health Maintenance and Disease Control, Seymour S. Bellin.[64]
2. Modifications of Patient Behavior for Health Maintenance and Disease Control, Marshall Becker[65]
3. Determinants of Health Levels in addition to Health Services, Monroe Lerner[66]

These subcommittees were instructed at the first meeting of the Steering Committee to "work toward a final report which would be a state of the arts type of paper emphasizing policy implications."[67] As intended, these reports were completed and published in a special supplement of *Medical Care*, edited by David Mechanic and Sol Levine.[68]

In their preface to the published report, Mechanic and Levine argued that there were, in the debate about national health insurance, a variety of issues that were being neglected. The prevailing focus, they said, was on financing. More important were the organizational consequences, preventive health, and health maintenance. In addressing these issues, however, they believed that more than the scientific results were involved. The Carnegie grant was also intended "to stimulate interaction between social scientists interested in these problems and health professionals, policymakers, and other participants in the health arena."[69] In the latter regard, the grant succeeded in extending the activities of the Section beyond the Association itself. The committees prepared articles and other publications but also met with policy-makers and others engaged in program efforts to discuss issues of mutual concern, such as the reorganization of the Alcohol, Drug Abuse, and Mental Health Administration and the Children's Television Workshop series on health. The Committee on Health Indicators organized a continuing seminar at Columbia University on measurement of health, and the Committee on Humanization organized a national interdisciplinary conference at the University of California Medical Center.

Speaking most directly to the mission of the Carnegie grant, in 1972, the Section's Public Policy Committee presented a strong statement, "Principles and Criteria for National Health Insurance," which became the subject of a special symposium at the annual meeting of the ASA in New Orleans. "Based on both professional judgment and commitment to certain humanitarian democratic principles,"[70] the position of the Medical Sociology Section was delineated as follows:

- that the people of the nation have a right to comprehensive health care;
- that such health care should be effective and of high quality;
- that financial and other barriers should not limit its availability;
- that it should be provided at times and places that render it accessible;
- that it should be coordinated with other programs relating to health and the prevention of disease;
- that it should offer continuity of care for individuals and their families;
- that health care, including the production and distribution of drugs and medical supplies, should be regarded as service to the community and to the nation, rather than as profit-making enterprises;

- that people have the right and responsibility to participate in shaping health policies and programs; and
- that the government has the duty to assure that these health rights are fulfilled.

The statement concluded that the present health industry has not provided these necessary components and that a reorganization of the health care system is therefore necessary. This statement, with detailed explanation and comments on the Administration's health care bill (HR 7741), were submitted to the Ways and Means Committee of Congress via a legislative subcommittee of the Society for the Psychological Study of Social Problems.

Without any question, therefore, the Section, stimulated by the Carnegie grant program, acted to accomplish its policy objectives. The nation's policy-makers, however, were not responsive. As a result, the most lasting evidence of the accomplishments of the Section's Carnegie-sponsored work is in its major publications, the special 1977 issue of *Medical Care* and two books published in 1975 and in 1986.[71] The former is essentially the final report to the Carnegie Foundation, consisting of separate articles by each of the subcommittees; the latter are guided by similar goals but are more extensive, with invited contributions from a wider array of scholars, telling about "the uses of social science research, to provide illustrations of how the social sciences have influenced our thinking about health care issues, and to underscore some promising and relevant areas of research for the future."[72] The 1986 volume was made possible by another grant to the Section, this time from the Robert Wood Johnson Foundation.

As one reviews these reports, it is first evident that the underlying conditions and pressures were not new. The article that opened the 1977 report, by Mary Goss and her associates, is an example.[73] They describe an upheaval in health care organization and financing that is a result of increasing pressure for some form of national health insurance. This pressure stems, they believe, from the federal health and poverty legislation of the mid-1960s, from the new forms of organizations spawned by those programs, from the 1975 National Health Planning and Development Act, and from the 1972 legislation that created professional standards review organizations (PSROs). Also significant, they wrote, is the federal allocation of funds for the development of health maintenance organizations (HMOs). Although these types of organization were sponsored largely in the attempt to contain spiraling costs of health care, "their importance for the organization and conduct of professional practice—quite apart from their economic significance—can hardly be overestimated." Fifty years earlier, however, in 1932, the CCMC described very similar conditions and recommendations. At that time, the CCMC, reporting on problems of the social organization of medical institutions, of the relations between psychosocial and sociocultural factors in health and illness, and of professional education, concluded strongly, albeit with some equivocation, in favor of national health insurance. Further, they recommended that group practice and HMO-type payment plans should be allowed to compete equally with individual fee-for-service health care.

Today, just twenty-four years after the Section's Carnegie report and sixty-nine years after the CCMC's report, similar underlying conditions, interpretations, and solutions are again at the front rank of concern for the organization of health care delivery. The HMO has, after a long delay, become the organization of choice for health care. The type of prepaid group practice that has become most prevalent today, however, is not the same as the earlier versions.[74] The current dominant form of HMO or managed care is motivated more by profit and cost control than by the efficiency, prevention, and equitability that were the moving factors for CCMC and again during the early 1970s. The preferred structure for the HMO has become the for-profit, publicly traded corporation that defines health care as a commodity. The effects of these changes on health indicators and on how these types of organization perform have yet to be determined. In the Carnegie report of 1977, the conclusion was:

> Informative sociological studies of physicians and their work have appeared sporadically since the 1940s. But we do not yet have a sufficiently system-atic body of knowledge about social organization and control in medical work in the United States to permit either reasonably accurate predictions or soundly based recommendations for implementation or change in na-tional health care policy.[75]

Although an entire section of the 1986 volume is devoted to discussion of the available data about organization and delivery of health services,[76] much the same kind of conclusion is justified today.

On the social psychology of health behavior, the Section's Carnegie report was particularly informative. Discussing the humanization of health care and the psy-chosocial correlates of individual health-related behaviors, the subcommittee re-ports anticipated some of the most influential research of the next two decades. On the effects of technology and of different forms of health care delivery, Jan Howard's committee provided a framework that influenced the field;[77] and Mar-shall Becker's committee provided an approach to understanding individual and population compliance that, much like his earlier work on the Health Belief Model, found a ready audience among medical educators.[78]

Overall, the Section's 1977 publication was a strong intellectual achievement. Mechanic, nevertheless, was aware that the achievement was limited. His contin-uation of the effort, as represented by the book published ten years later, testified to his and the Section's conviction of the growing importance of policy analysis and social science research. "In almost every aspect of identifying disease, un-derstanding precursors, implementing effective treatment, and controlling risk," he and Aiken argued, "behavioral research is central. In organizing to identify the burdens of ill health and provide an efficient and effective response, the role of social science and policy analysis is an essential ingredient."[79] One could say that the Section's 1977 Carnegie report met the objective of "dealing with important issues relevant to the implementation of a national health insurance program for the United States,"[80] but its influence on the national policy-makers responsible for such a program is another matter. There is no evidence that the Section's efforts went beyond selected representatives of federal agencies like the NCHSR or private foundations, particularly the Robert Wood Johnson Foundation. It needs to be added, however, that no other group or argument succeeded any better. The cyclical path of efforts to create a national health policy in the United States continued, with no noticeable result in either the 1970s or the 1980s. Nev-ertheless, the direction Mechanic sought for the Section during his term of office as chairman in 1970 persisted among his successors over the next decade (see table 10-3).

Table 10-3 Chairs of the Section on Medical Sociology, 1970–1979

Name	Affiliation	Year
David Mechanic	University of Wisconsin	1970
Jerome Myers	Yale University	1971
John Clausen	University of California, Berkeley	1972
Robert Wilson	University of North Carolina	1973
Rose Coser	SUNY–Stony Brook	1974
Renee Fox	University of Pennsylvania	1975
Saxon Graham	University of Buffalo	1976
Jack Elinson	Columbia University–Public Health	1977
Peter K. New	University of Toronto	1978
Virginia Olesen	University of California, San Francisco	1979
Mary Goss	Cornell University School of Medicine	1980

What's in a Name?

It should not be concluded, however, that the affairs of the Section proceeded without a wrinkle or a wave. In 1974, in the middle of a very busy period of the Section's Carnegie grant activities, question was raised again about the name "medical sociology." The question involved was not very different from that of earlier debates about group identity. The discomfort was on several counts. First, the use of "medical" was thought to misrepresent the core identity of the group by suggesting that it was part of, or mainly concerned with, the medical profession. For what was primarily a social science, the name might be misleading. A second problem was the name's connotation of pathology. Disease was not, after all, the main focus of this subspecialty. The earlier remedies were to shift the emphasis from medicine to "behavior" and to attempt in a name change to reassure the multidisciplinary colleagueship that was typical of the beginning period of medical sociology. At this time, however, there was a move to change the name to "the sociology of health."

The name change was part of a more general effort to reorganize the structure of the Section. An ad hoc committee to rewrite the bylaws of the Section was appointed, consisting of Jack Elinson, Peter New, Hans Mauksch, and Betty Coggswell. It was proposed that the Section should be renamed "The Section on the Sociology of Health." The existing bylaws contained the following purpose:

> The purpose of the Section on Medical Sociology is to foster the development of behavioral science in medicine through the organized interchange of ideas, teaching experiences and research programs and results. Encouragement shall be given to the achievement of this general purpose through organized meetings and conferences, publication and such other means as are deemed appropriate by the Council of the Section. The term "medical sociology" shall be interpreted in its broadest sense to include the efforts in both teaching and research to develop the concepts and principles of behavioral science (sociology, anthropology, and social psychology) as they apply to problems of health and illness.

The ad hoc committee proposed, in addition to the name change, to strike the entire definitional statement beginning with "The term." All other bylaws were reviewed and changed accordingly, with all the offices and standing committees reviewed.

Although the revisions of the bylaws and reorganization of the Section committee structure, as proposed by Jack Elinson's committee, was adopted for the most part by the Section, the proposed name change was rejected. Medical sociology, it was argued, had a de facto recognition as the name of the field and as such should be retained. And so it remains today, even though the issue was raised again in the early 1980s and even as recently as 1996 at the annual meeting of the Section in New York.

International Medical Sociology

This was also a time of rapid development of international medical sociology. The early work of Eliot Freidson, George Reader, and Robin Badgley was successful in creating the Research Committee for the Sociology of Medicine of the International Sociological Association. Mark Field, from Boston University and the Harvard University Center for Russian Studies, was the chair, and Magda Sokolowska, from Poland, was the vice-chair. Derek Gill (then at Aberdeen, Scotland), Manfred Pflanz of Germany, Robin Badgley, and George Reader were on the Committee. The working members included members mainly from Europe and the United States, with Judith Shuval and Aron Antonovsky the first of what became a large group from Israel.

Malcom Johnson, acting for the relatively new British Sociological Association Medical Sociology Group, sought in 1973 to link the two groups.[81] Johnson also compiled a register of research and teaching for the British Medical Group that was distributed by the ASA Section on Medical Sociology.

Although the Section, from its outset, was actively engaged in cooperation with international colleagues, the appointment of Albert Wessen to the WHO stimulated intensification of this interest. Wessen, in 1968, took a leave from Washington University at St. Louis, Missouri, where he was professor of sociology, and joined a new social science research organization at WHO.[82] One of his first acts was to commission a study by the Advisory Group on the Sociology of Professional Training and Health Manpower.[83] The Group published a monograph on their findings in 1972.[84]

Wessen returned to Washington University in 1974 and was replaced at WHO by Ray Elling, then secretary-treasurer of the Section. Elling had been one of the most active proponents of closer relations with international colleagues. From this time forward, the ties between the United States and other countries was assured, in no small measure because of the role of the Section on Medical Sociology.

The "Fletcher Report"

In 1968, John Kosa[85] became the chairman of the Section's Committee on Teaching Medical Sociology in Schools of Medicine and Public Health. Drawing from its report of 1967, the Committee made a proposal for a national study of current teaching of behavioral science in schools of the health professions in the United States that was accepted by the National Center for Health Services Research and Development (NCHSRD). However, NCHSRD agreed to a contract rather than a grant; they excluded schools of public health because they were so different from medical schools; and the study was of "behavioral science" so that the fields of anthropology, psychology, and medical education were made equal partners with sociology in the study. The formal contract was with the ASA, for $149,947, funded in June 1969. C. Richard Fletcher, then of Yale University, was selected as the principal investigator, and Mat Weisenberg, a psychologist, represented NCHSRD. The expert committee selected to advise Fletcher was the following: Charles C. Hughes (Michigan State University) and Donald A. Kennedy (Harvard University) represented anthropology; Murray Wexler (University of Southern California) and Carl Eisdorfer (Duke University) represented psychology; the author (Mount Sinai School of Medicine) and Robin Badgley (University of Toronto) represemted sociology; and Evan G. Pattishall (Pennsylvania State University) and Edward J. Stainbrook (University of Southern California) represented medical education. Jack Elinson was the liaison to the ASA. John Kosa was the senior consultant. The contract was for thirty months.

The charge to the project committee was

> to describe current activities and programs in the teaching of behavioral science in schools of medicine and to make recommendations for strengthening this innovation in medical education. Because the NCHSRD's mission focused upon the delivery of health services there was particular interest expressed in the actual and potential interplay between health services delivery, the behavioral sciences, and curriculum changes within the medical schools.[86]

Although this contract was derived from the ASA Section's activities, particularly the Committee on Teaching, it was influenced from the start by the newly formed ABSAME, in which Donald Kennedy and Evan Pattishall were leaders. Also in the winter of 1969, another event in which John Kosa, Kennedy, Pattishall, and Robert Straus played an important part, strengthened the project. The National Board of Medical Examiners (NBME) voted to establish an ad hoc committee to prepare behavioral science test questions for the Part I examination taken by most medical students at the end of their second year. In 1972, formal recognition was granted to this committee as a basic science committee of the NBME of equal status with anatomy, pathology, pharmacology, biochemistry, physiology, and microbiology.

In its four-volume report, the Kosa-Fletcher Teaching Project attempted to present both the basic conceptual frameworks of the several behavioral sciences and concrete examples of how the knowledge of these subjects translated into health skills. The alternative organizational arrangements for including the behavioral sciences in medical schools were also described. The final volume presented the complete behavioral science teaching programs of nine selected medical schools. Although NCHSRD published the full report, wider readership was assured by related books by Kennedy and by Lella.[87] In general, the report came to be known as the "Fletcher report," after its principal investigator. In actuality, Donald Kennedy was responsible for most of the writing, with the project committee sharing the collection and analysis of the data.

The premise of the report was taken from statements by current leaders of medical education to the effect that "medical education in the United States has entered the 1970s confronted with an imperative to concern itself with the problem of the nation's health care enterprise as a primary institutional mission, comparable to its role in the advancement and application of the biomedical sciences."[88] The nine selected cases of behavioral science teaching in medical education were:

- Duke University School of Medicine
- Harvard University Medical School
- University of Kentucky College of Medicine
- Michigan State University College of Medicine
- University of Connecticut School of Medicine
- University of Missouri School of Medicine
- Pennsylvania State University College of Medicine
- Stanford University School of Medicine
- University of Toronto Faculty of Medicine

The result, with its emphasis on health services, was a companion piece for the Carnegie grant report: Carnegie focused on research, and the NCHSRD grant focused on teaching in medical schools.

The recommendations of the Fletcher Report reflected the intellectual climate of the time. In 1972, the behavioral sciences of medicine were in a growth phase. In training, research, and organization, expansion was the watchword. Consequently, the report recommended the following main steps:

1. The establishment of a department of behavioral sciences or human behavior with the full range of responsibilities, support, and prerogatives afforded to other departments of the medical school.[89]
2. A minimum staff of seven full-time faculty for such a department.
3. Joint appointments in the graduate department of arts and sciences or another professional school of the university.

When this report was written, there were only two such departments in the country. Consequently, the project committee was taking a position that was radical, not hesitating to be controversial. In the years that followed, however, very few schools followed these recommendations.

The Leo G. Reeder Award

On September 25, 1978, a commuter plane out of Los Angeles crashed in San Diego. Among the passengers was Leo G. Reeder, professor of public health and of sociology at the University of California at Los Angeles. A Ph.D. graduate of the University of Chicago, he was chair-elect of the Medical Sociology Section at the time of his death. Active in the Section from its earliest days, he was an outstanding pioneer in social epidemiology. A close friend and colleague of the so-called Boston Mafia (Howard Freeman, Sol Levine, Norman Scotch, Sydney Croog), he was coauthor of the *Handbook of Medical Sociology*, which was just being printed in its third edition at the time.[90] Writing of his "gregariousness, warmth, humor, drive, and toughness," Howard Freeman expressed the feelings of many for whom this sudden tragedy was devastating.[91]

Two years earlier, in 1977,[92] the Medical Sociology Section had established an award for distinguished service to the field, the first such award established for ASA sections. Immediately following Leo Reeder's death, the award was named in his honor. In table 10-4, the recipients are listed.

It became the practice for the winners of the Reeder Award to address the business meeting of the Section at the annual meeting of the ASA. Beginning with the award in 1984, these addresses were published in the *JHSB*, each in the first issue of the volume for the next year.[93]

This was also a time when the Section sponsored increased activity in the field of disability and rehabilitation. Building on the published results of the 1965 Carmel conference, "Sociological Theory, Research and Rehabilitation,"[94] a Committee on Disability became active as part of the Decade of Rehabilitation, 1970–

Table 10-4 Leo G. Reeder Award for Distinguished Service to Medical Sociology

Year	Name	Affiliation at Time of Award
1977	August B. Hollingshead	Yale University
1978	Everett Hughes	University of Chicago
1979	Margot Jefferys	Bedford College, London
1980	Odin Anderson	University of Chicago
1981	Anselm Strauss	University of California-San Francisco
1982	Eliot Freidson	New York University
1983	David Mechanic	University of Wisconsin
1984	Renee Fox	University of Pennsylvania
1985	Jack Elinson	Columbia University School of Public Health
1986	Sol Levine	Boston University
1987	John Clausen	University of California-Berkeley
1988	Virginia Olesen	University of California-San Francisco
1989	Samuel W. Bloom	Mt. Sinai School of Medicine/CUNY
1990	Irving Zola	Brandeis University
1991	Leonard Pearlin	University of California-San Francisco
1992	Marshall Becker	University of Michigan
1993	Marie R. Haug	Case Western Reserve
1994	Ronald M. Andersen	University of California-Los Angeles
1995	John B. McKinlay	New England Research I
1996	Rodney M. Coe	University of St. Louis School of Medicine
1997	Howard Waitzkin	University of California-San Diego
1998	Robert Straus	University of Kentucky
1999	Bruce Dohrenwend	Columbia University
2000	Mary E. W. Goss	Cornell University School of Medicine

80. Special sessions were organized at the annual meetings of the ASA in August 1971 and 1972. Peter K. New of the University of Toronto and Richard T. Smith of Johns Hopkins University were the organizers.

Summary and Discussion

The first twenty years after the establishment of the Section on Medical Sociology was, for its members and for the social sciences of health, a period of rapid growth, diversification of activities, and conflict. In some ways, it was a golden age; in others, it was a time of unrequited promise and of disappointment. The expansion of the beginning was replaced by the contraction of demand as 1980 approached.

Throughout this period, the Section represented the field within the ASA and in relations with academic and other constituencies external to the ASA. Its first major achievement was to secure the *Journal of Health and Social Behavior* as one of the official publications of the ASA. It was also the first section to acquire financial support from a private foundation when, in 1964, the Milbank Memorial Fund gave funds for the general development of the Section. This was followed by a contract in 1969 with the NCHSD to study current teaching of behavioral science in schools of the health professions and by a grant in 1971 from the Carnegie Foundation to study sociological aspects of health and health services.

The Section was also successful in establishing linkages with groups like the ISA, the American Public Health Association, the American Psychiatric Association, the AAMC, the American Society of Applied Anthropology, the American Association for the Advancement of Science (AAAS), and ABSAME. Active liaison has continued with these groups, and in some cases parallel subgroups were formed, such as a Medical Sociology Section in the ISA and similar groups in the British Sociological Association and the European Sociological Association.

In 1967, the Section participated in the decision by the NBME to explore the feasibility of including the behavioral sciences in their examinations. By June 1973, a Behavioral Science Test Committee was operating and responsible for including the same number of test items in Part I of the National Boards, with equal weighting, as the six other basic sciences (anatomy, biochemistry, microbiology, pathology, pharmacology, and physiology).

To communicate some of these achievements to a broader public, the Section published two books and a major government monograph.

Thus there is a record of accomplishment to show that the Section played a major part in the consolidation of medical sociology as a fully institutionalized intellectual activity. The Section grew rapidly, from its initial membership in 1959 of 224 social scientists and physicians to 561 by the end of its second year. During most of its history, the Section has been the largest in the ASA, climbing from 4.7 percent of the ASA membership to as high as 9 percent in 1987. After 1980 it stabilized at a level of between 7 and 8 percent of the ASA membership. Currently, its membership is 1,019, compared with 1,121 at its high point.

The context for these developments was the growth of demand for social scientists to work in research, teaching, and the delivery of health services and the development of sources of supply. As described earlier (chapter 9), the training of medical sociologists was limited from 1950 to the end of the decade, supported mainly by private foundations. After that, the federal government, especially the

Social Sciences Research Training Program of NIMH, took over the selection and funding of graduate study in medical sociology and, indeed, the training of sociologists in general.[95] From the two pilot programs funded in 1957, costing $84,916, the NIMH program was formally launched in 1960 with seven schools and thirty-five trainees. By 1964, there were fifty-four schools, 333 trainees, and a budget of over two million dollars. The program doubled in size during the next eight years, when, in 1972, seventy-seven schools trained 570 students, supported by $5,211,684.[96] The expansion was boosted by the creation of the NCHSR in 1968. With a budget of thirty-seven million dollars for 1969, NCHSR added both training and research support for sociologists, among others.

The end of federal support of growth, however, was signaled by the decision of President Nixon in his budget message for fiscal 1973 and 1974, promising to phase out federal support for categorical professional training programs, including all research training programs in NIH/NIMH. Strong protests from the scientific community and Congress led to the restoration of a much smaller research training program.[97] By 1980, even though the extreme negative view of the Nixon administration toward the social sciences had been mitigated, the support of the government for training and research in the social sciences was drastically reduced.

Intellectually, the substantive changes in the directions of interest were equally striking. When the Section began, the primary host for social science in medical education was still psychiatry, and in research this was reflected by emphasis on problems of mental health relevance. Public health and preventive medicine had much longer historical roots for the social sciences, but they were slower to include them as partners during the period immediately following World War II. In the 1960s, the pattern changed. The grand themes of the decade—social welfare, civil rights, and equality of access to education and health care—produced the community medicine movement and with it a special home in medical school departments of community medicine and schools of public health for medical sociologists. At the same time, new therapeutic drugs in psychiatric treatment, the so-called psychomimetic or tranquilizer drugs, began to replace and sometimes eliminate the intense interest that psychiatry had been focusing on the social factors in mental illness. By this generalization, I do not mean that social science was abandoned by psychiatry. NIMH continued as a major source of support. In 1975, NIMH devoted 15 percent of its research funds to studies by social scientists. However, only about one-fifth of the money for the social sciences supported basic research. In actual dollars, this meant that of eleven million dollars spent for extramural programs of social science research, $1,832,000 were spent for basic research in all of the social sciences and $333,000 was specific to sociologists.[98]

To some extent, these patterns of changing interest and therapeutic emphasis helped to upgrade the importance of health services research. What had been a hope that social science would contribute to the theoretical understanding of mental illness, the interpersonal relations of the health professions, the social organization of its major institutions, the social ecology of illness, and other subjects of basic research shifted toward more policy-oriented study of health care—its access, delivery organization, cost, and insurance. The Section was in the forefront of these changes in research interest, mounting a large effort in the 1970s to study and explain the questions about health services that were most urgent.

Throughout the twenty-five years of medical sociology's most intense professional growth, 1955–80, a group of individuals played highly visible roles, as leaders and workers in making the Section the central institutionalizing group of this relatively new subdiscipline. Robert Alan Day has referred to them as the "influentials" of the field, and they fall into two distinct categories.[99] One outstanding group was composed of sociologists who had already achieved positions as leaders of the field more generally and for whom studies in the sociology of medicine were incidental to the main body of their work. Talcott Parsons, for example, was probably the most influential general theorist of the postwar period. In chapter 10 of his best-known book, *The Social System*,[100] he uses medicine as an example of the professions in modern society, illustrating his theory of functionalism. Others were Robert Merton, Everett Hughes, and August Hollingshead. All four were presidents of the ASA. Each of them used medicine as an empirical case to test their more general ideas. Both Merton and Hughes were interested in adult socialization and the role of the professions in society. Medical schools and medicine as an archtypal profession suited their purposes for research. Hollingshead was already deeply involved in the study of social stratification when he teamed up with the psychiatrist Redlich to study the epidemiology of mental illness. While they played influential roles as individual scholars in medical sociology or as the leaders of teams of scholars, they also were mentors to younger people who became influential in the field.

A second category of "influentials" included younger sociologists who became medical sociologists after their training. Like their older associates, most of them only entered the field of medical sociology after they completed their studies. As examples, one thinks of Freidson, Volkart, Sol Levine, Howard Becker, Blanche Geer, Patricia Kendall, Leo Simmons, Howard Freeman, and Robert N. Wilson. A few did dissertations that studied medicine or health—Renee Fox, Robert Straus, David Mechanic, Walter Wardwell, Mary E. W. Goss, Harvey Smith, Mark Field, and Emily Mumford—but they were not part of formal training programs in medical sociology. Only from Yale were there early examples of fully trained people: Robin Badgley, Ray Elling, Leonard Syme. In part this was compensated by the postdoctoral fellowships of the Russell Sage Foundation: Albert Wessen, Howard Kaplan, and many others. However, the training programs at the predoctoral level only began to fully function well into the 1960s.

No matter how they entered the field, they were active in the Section on Medical Sociology. Every one of those named here appears regularly in the minutes of the Section's meetings, and most held some office. Overall, they number about thirty individuals who were truly influential in the institutionalization of the field, as well as playing an active part in its scholarship.

This was also a generation that is unique in another way. With few exceptions, they were participants in World War II. Many came from the kind of modest origins that traditionally did not supply the university faculties of the United States. They were driven to change their own lives and the world, for the most part in the most idealistic of value-terms. The war, the Holocaust, the Cold War, the technological and scientific revolutions of the postwar decades: these were the context of their development into leadership of this emerging intellectual field. Against such a background, public policy and the application of knowledge in the public interest were never far removed from view. Medicine, with its own traditions of the search for knowledge and its use in the service of public good, seemed a most reasonable partner.

But this partnership appeared to shift ground in 1980. A new era appeared at that time, when large-scale social and intellectual changes challenged everyone in the society. For medical sociology, several aspects of these changes were to be specially significant. The women's movement and its expression in academic women's studies has had a profound effect. The changes in the national economy, particularly as represented in the restructuring of the health care industry, is equally if not more important. In the next chapter this next and most recent phase of medical sociology will be discussed.

PART III

THE CURRENT STATUS OF MEDICAL SOCIOLOGY

11

An Era of Change, 1980–2000

Medical sociology, as a general rule, followed a path parallel but slightly behind national trends in science and higher education. At the same time, relations between mainstream science, medicine, and social science were unstable. During the century prior to World War II, there was a certain consistency in the objectives they shared: social science actually played a larger role in medical research than is generally known, and both took it as their overriding objective "to use quantified data to illuminate the relationship between morbidity and mortality patterns . . . and broad environmental factors."[1] From 1945 onward, the pace of research development quickened and diversified. Guided by strong leaders, the relationship between medicine and social science intensified, but the pattern of its interests split the next fifty years in half. The first half was dominated by several quests: for a scientific epidemiology, for a viable theory of the social psychology of interpersonal relations in therapeutic institutions, and for analysis of the sociology of the professions. The second half, beginning in the seventies, turned in focus toward socioeconomic and sociopolitical explanations of health services delivery and the organization of both the traditional and new health care institutions.

For those who were part of these shifting developments, however, the feeling and meaning of what was happening are not captured by such generalizations. Henry Riecken, speaking from his view as the first head of the Office of Social Sciences at the NSF[2] from 1958 to 1965, described how "the winds of change" affected all of science in the postwar's first quarter-century. From its beginning orientation toward basic "pure" science, Riecken wrote, a decided shift occurred toward demands for proof of utility, accompanied by often angry criticism of the purity, even the truthfulness, of the methods and purposes of the scientific establishment. Riecken strikes a nostalgic, sometimes poetic, note about these changes:

The comfortable assumptions of the sixties about federal support for scientific research; about the dedication of professors and graduate students to the life of the mind; about the fundamental importance of the pursuit of truth through pure research—all these and more have been shaken. Instead of being the private business of a select few, science and technology have now become the preoccupation of politicians, of leaders of the ecology movement, young radicals, and old conservatives. The prominence which many scientists yearned for in the fifties and sixties has turned into an unpleasant notoriety in a very perplexing way. Even scientists themselves have begun to raise questions about the legitimacy of some of their work, and have suggested that rather than the eternal search for pure truth, science might well try discriminating between knowledge that is worth having and that which is dangerous to produce.[3]

Riecken, of course, was describing the experience of all science, but he reserved a heavy irony for his own. "One of the grave difficulties of the social sciences," Riecken said, "is that they deal primarily with a subject matter that is 'everybody's business.' Everyone knows something about human behavior and society because he is a participant in it and he believes that his view, his analysis, his image of the way society works and human beings behave is the correct image."[4] As a consequence, social science was forced to fight for its very existence when the postwar support system by the federal government was institutionalized. Once accepted, however, the official expectations of what it could accomplish became unrealistic. When the NSF was formed, the social sciences were kept out at the beginning on the premise that they were not "real" sciences.[5] Once they were accepted and attention turned toward social problems that were often attributed to the results of new technology and science itself, they were challenged to solve those problems with applied science. When they did not rise to those challenges sufficiently to satisfy the policy-makers, they were as often as not punished with the withdrawal of funding by either the executive branch or by Congress.[6]

Despite these obstacles, the federal support for social science increased many-fold from its modest beginnings. The proportion of the federal budget for research in the social sciences, even though small when compared to the total R & D budget, about 3 percent on average, continued to grow, from thirty million dollars in 1956 to $588 million in 1990.[7] Riecken points out that, looked at in the community of science, the place of the social and behavioral sciences displays three outstanding features. "First, the United States literally leads the world in the size, activity, and sophistication of its social science community, and, with a few exceptions, the intellectual leadership and methodological influence of the United States presently dominates the social and behavioral sciences in virtually all parts of the world."[8] Second, within the span of the history of science, the differentiation of the social and behavioral sciences from primarily ethical and moralistic description into empirically grounded sciences is more recent than that of the physical and biological sciences. And third, their achievement of a place in the information and advice structure of the scientific affairs of the United States is still shallow. Even though social scientists serve on the President's Science Advisory Committee and their numbers have increased in the National Academy of Sciences, their place in official government agency networks is not yet secure.[9] Unlike the steady upward curve of federal support for scientific research generally, the flow for social science goes both up and down, declining in most of the years after 1980.

Within this overall picture, if one narrows the focus to medical sociology, the historical pattern is the same: its professional development consistently gained strength after 1945 but with recurring challenges to its basic legitimacy by the official agencies of government science and especially by the Office of Management and the Budget (OMB) in both the Nixon second term and the Reagan administration. Beginning in 1980, although medical sociology continued to build strength institutionally and intellectually, the framework in which it operates is characterized by challenge and change. To document the details of these changes will be the main purpose of this chapter, ending with an assessment of where the field's major identity is today and where it appears to be going.

The Change in Training: A Case Example

Starting with programs of research training, the directions of the changes that were initiated during the 1970s may be illustrated by a case example, called here Urban University.[10] In 1981, Urban was rejected for renewal of its NIMH research training grant, ending twelve years of support for the teaching of both predoctoral and postdoctoral fellows in a joint medical school–graduate school program. Like most NIMH social science training programs—there were seventy-six in 1975—the Urban NIMH program was not limited to health-related research. Sponsored by both the graduate school and the medical school, it was designed to give all students a comprehensive view of the literature of medical sociology and field experience in medical institutions, but always kept within the perspective of mainstream sociology. Only nine of the thirty-five predoctoral fellows wrote dissertations in medical sociology; the others chose topics in other areas of sociology. The nine postdoctoral fellows, on the other hand, were required to select research in the field of health and medicine.

Urban was a typical grantee of the NIMH Social Science Training Program from 1960 through 1980. The policy of the agency, as described earlier,[11] had been to support those applicants who could demonstrate general research excellence as well as specialized research relevance to problems of health and illness. Within the context of rapidly expanding higher education, including both sociology and medical school programs, such a policy was designed to serve the general needs of the university and the special demands of the health field. The guiding motto was: good research training, whatever its subject matter, would supply best the social science needs of medicine. However, in the midseventies, there was a sharp change.

The nature of the change was described by the Health Policy Committee of the ASA Medical Sociology Section in a 1979 report that tracked developments in funding that would affect medical sociologists. They made the following generalizations about training policies:[12]

1. There has been a sustained shift from predoctoral to postdoctoral training.
2. Payback mechanisms are becoming more frequent. Trainees must show evidence of entry into the designated field or pay back the training monies.
3. Dissertation support has increased somewhat. This is interpreted as a federal strategy to limit training monies to those working in certain areas for short periods of time.

4. There is a move away from institutional support for training and greater support to individuals.
5. The Office of Management and the Budget (OMB) is negative about social science training across all agencies, and has been effective in limiting training programs, especially general training programs in the social and behavioral sciences. A possible strategy around this roadblock is for social scientists to:
   A. use the research grant as a training mechanism; and
   B. when applying for training monies[,] to identify a discrete substantive area, i.e., alcoholism, compliance, costs, etc.

In other words, health policy relevance became more important, and the budget was severely cut. The Social Science Training Program was itself put on notice. The Urban University program, whatever its weaknesses or strengths, was caught in the pattern of changes that were occurring, and its demise became just one indicator event in a process that deeply affected the relations between medical sociologists and government agencies.

NIMH was not the only agency involved in these changes. The NCHSR, for example, had provided research training support since its inception in 1968. In 1973, "the Secretary of Health, Education, and Welfare (SHEW) decided to terminate all existing training programs and announced a new training program that emphasized postdoctoral fellowships."[13] After failure to obtain approval from the OMB, all support for research training at NCHSR was terminated by the end of fiscal year 1976. In spite of two congressional acts designed to maintain the continuation of health-related training in the behavioral sciences and a 1976 report by the National Academy of Sciences verifying the need for such research training, funding continued to be denied.

By 1980, it was uncertain that any federal support for training would survive, even the reduced and more focused specialized programs that NIHM had retained while they closed out the bulk of the original social science research training program.

The Reaction of the Section on Medical Sociology

The ASA Medical Sociology Section, in 1980, had reason to expect that the effects of the changes in funding policy were to be deep and continuous. Ever since the beginning of Nixon's second term in 1972, it was clear that social scientists were still linked in the minds of conservative legislators to the economic and social interventionism of the Roosevelt New Deal. Lyons, in his study of the history of social science research in the federal government, shows how this identification of social science with liberal political ideology put the social sciences on the defensive when, immediately after the Second World War, the role of science in the United States was recast from its prior separate and academic autonomy into a central position in the national government.[14] In spite of the eventual success in the struggle to include social science in federal support agencies like the NSF and NIMH, Lyons describes how this defensiveness remained:

In the years since the establishment of the NSF in 1950, social scientists have continued to be on the defensive, not only in debates about government support for research, but also in discussions about the role of the social sciences in American society more generally. This defensiveness has, moreover, often been a protection against the anti-intellectualism of conservative critics.[15]

Such critics, with renewed vitality, surfaced as part of the Nixon administration. Their attack on social science was slowed temporarily by the Watergate scandals only to reappear in 1981, "when the new Reagan administration severely cut the social science budget . . . for fiscal year 1982."[16] The attack was very broad. Kenneth Prewitt documents how the budgetary process was used to focus attention on the

> federal funding and promotion of the behavioral and social sciences. The most dramatic event was a proposal by the Office of Management and Budget to reduce funding for the social science program in the National Science Foundation by perhaps as much as 75 percent, and to eliminate most social science funding from the National Institute of Mental Health. The budgetary arm of the Reagan administration seemed to suggest that the social sciences are of such marginal importance that they can safely be eliminated from the federal support system for the sciences. Other parts of the Reagan administration were less concerned about the budgetary implications than about the putative ideological coloration of the social sciences, which they viewed as arrayed against their own policies. In this view, the social sciences were to have their funding reduced because they were influential, not because they were only marginally effective.[17]

In other ways, the social sciences found it necessary to return to old battles, thought to be part of a thirty-year-old past. The old fear of "socialism," a plague of the early fifties, reappeared in new guises, and its companion was the question whether the social—even when renamed the behavioral—sciences could "prove that regularities in human and social behavior could be objectively identified and, once identified, used as a basis for effective public programs."[18] In their answer to these challenges, the top officers of the SSRC wrote in 1981: "One of the most disturbing aspects of the Administration's treatment of the social sciences was the implicit accusation that they are lesser sciences than the physical and natural sciences—if indeed they are sciences at all."[19] But whether challenged as being marginally important or too influential, the social sciences, at this point in time, were not as vulnerable as they were in 1950.

A policy shift was underway that went beyond health, including the political, economic, and educational life of the country, seeking to move the country away from the progressive welfare state policies of the previous half-century with its expansionist approach to public policy and replacing it with a retreat from active government on all fronts except defense.[20] Medical sociology was no less affected by these changes than any other segment of the national life. In response, the Section on Medical Sociology assumed a more proactive stance.

The Section's Health Policy Committee, in 1979 and again in 1980, submitted testimony to the National Academy of Sciences' Committee on a Study of National Needs for Biomedical and Behavioral Research Personnel, which, annually since 1976, had recommended increased funding for training programs in health services research. They were not acting alone. In 1977, the Office of Science and

Technology Policy of the Office of the President of the United States commissioned the Institute of Medicine (IOM) to undertake an assessment of the field of health services research that would clarify the boundaries of the field and improve its contribution to decisions affecting health care. Tom Bice, a member of the Section on Medical Sociology, was a major author of the IOM report. David Mechanic, Bob Eichhorn, and others put together information to be used by Russell Dynes, the executive officer of the ASA, in his testimony at the public hearings cn March 8, 1979, before the Committee on a Study of National Needs for Biomedical and Behavioral Research Personnel.

Such reactions, however, targeting the executives of federal agencies and the Congress, seemed to miss the mark entirely at the appropriations level. The OMB consistently, at this time in history, rebuffed the recommendations of the expert committees, whether they came from the prestigious National Academy of Sciences or the IOM. Dynes, who, as the full-time Washington representative of sociology, became the primary lobbyist for the discipline at that time, recalls the influence of both political ideology and leadership.[21]

Dynes[22], the Executive Secretary of ASA from 1977 to 1982, reports that when he first came to Washington he worked closely with NIMH, where he found a "more or less behavioral science–friendly situation; [but] there was a shift somewhat suddenly in philosophy at NIMH and more broadly." He attributed the change to the leadership on the one hand and to the political climate on the other. Dynes turned for help to other social scientists in Washington, including the Consortium of Social Science Associations (COSSA), and to Otto Larsen, who became the NSF director of the division of social and economic research in 1980 just before Reagan became president.[23] From that time on, Dynes says, he was occupied with "trying to save anything in social science."

"Anything in social science," of course, meant more than medical sociology. To fully grasp the implications for the subdiscipline, therefore, it is necessary to study the full organizational context and its leadership.

The Organizational Context

Although NIMH has played the most important role in relations between the federal government and medical sociology, the NSF is the central agency in the postwar federal support system for social science more generally. In fact, the problems of NSF reflected those of all the social sciences and have been the subject of the most detailed critical analysis of national policy.[24]

The origins of NSF were similar to those of NIMH. World War II was the major catalyst. The blueprint was provided by the "Bush report": a document commissioned by President Roosevelt in November 1944 and written and submitted to President Truman in July 1945 by Dr. Vannevar Bush, a former vice-president of the Massachusetts Institute of Technology, who went to Washington in 1938 as head of the Carnegie Institution and became chairman of the National Advisory Committee for Aeronautics (NACA) in 1939. Lyons describes how Bush, both in the prewar and war years,

"working closely with scientists in the NACA and the National Academy [of Sciences], worked out a plan in 1940 for the establishment of a National Defense Research Committee (NDRC) to coordinate, supervise, and conduct scientific research on the problems underlying warfare. Approved by the president on June 27, 1940, the NDRC became the central base for the scientific organization that was to develop during the war.[25]

Bush also created the Office of Scientific Research and Development (OSRD) within NDRC, and although still wholly a creation of physical scientists, it was there that social scientists became involved, often in association with the National Research Council. Therefore, when Bush, as a "distinguished scientist and wartime research leader, [was commissioned] to advise on means of consolidating the mobilization of science for public purposes during peacetime,"[26] there was a precedent for him to include cooperation between social science and the physical sciences.

Earlier in this discussion, the influence of the Bush report on the founding of NIMH was described, and it was equally important in the first days of NSF. Bush, at the time, was the chief scientific advisor to the president. Less well known is the Steelman report, which was commissioned at almost the same time by President Truman and submitted in 1947.[27] John Steelman, a special assistant to President Truman, was trained in sociology and economics. The full weight of representation for social science in the formation of NSF, however, fell to the SSRC, which was invited by Senator Magnussen to explain why social science should be included in the new government agency for scientific research that was recommended by the Bush report.[28]

The Bush report was interpreted "to view science as an end in itself."[29] The Steelman report took a different approach:

The Steelman Report applied to it [science] a political prism, placing more emphasis on the role of *science as a means to an end,* the end being the public welfare. The Truman Administration, by publishing its own survey of postwar science practically on the heels of the Bush Report, brought into focus a philosophic dichotomy on the subject that, coming to view at intervals in the future, would run through the story of the National Foundation like a leitmotif in a Wagnerian opera.[30]

Larsen sees the competition between these orientations, basic versus applied research, as a constant factor in entire history of NSF. "The manner in which commitment to these modes of inquiry oscillate," he writes, "provides one key for understanding what has and what has not happened to social science at NSF."[31]

It is also a fact that the SSRC, when given the opportunity to testify on this issue, added more confusion than clarity. In the beginning, their contribution was promising. They were represented by Wesley C. Mitchell, the economist and director of research for the National Bureau of Economic Research; he, in 1945 before a congressional committee, argued the case for including the social sciences in the proposed NSF. Mitchell, from a position of professional prestige almost as formidable as that of Vannevar Bush, was poised to exert powerful influence on the outcome of the debate, and at first his performance did just that. However, he was joined in testimony by a distinguished group of colleagues, and although Mitchell, like Bush appeared to favor the view of basic science, there was a division of opinion among the social scientists themselves.

Klausner and Lidz report that

the community of social scientists was not of one mind regarding its role in a National Science Foundation. Each discipline had both scientific and humanistic wings. There were distinctions both of methodology and of attitude to the politics of scholarship. Indeed, the failure of political scientists to support the Committee for a National Science Foundation in large numbers reflects some discomfort in being "packaged" as one among several social sciences.[32]

Among those who testified, in addition to Wesley Mitchell, were William Ogburn, professor of sociology at the University of Chicago, Robert M. Yerkes, professor of psychobiology at Yale, E. G. Nourse, vice-president of the Brookings Institution, and Monsignor John M. Cooper, professor of anthropology at the Catholic University of America. Donald Young, then the executive director of SSRC, was also involved. It is impossible to discount the effects of the ambivalence of the social scientists themselves on the conclusion of the Senate. Senator Thomas C. Hart, Republican from Connecticut, speaking to the Kilgore Committee about the proposed Foundation, said he would seek to exclude the social sciences because "no agreement has been reached with reference to what social science really means."[33]

On July 3, 1946, the Senate voted to exclude the social sciences from the support specified under the proposed NSF. There was, however, a qualification allowing social science to enter by a side door. On the same day, the Senate voted also on a formula that would allow social science research in NSF but not to give it division status. The formula was: NSF was not to be told to accept or to exclude the social sciences; it had the option of doing either. Thus there were no social scientists on the staff when NSF began operations in 1950, but two years later, Harry Alpert,[34] a sociologist who had analyzed public opinion and statistics for the Office of War Information, the Office of Price Administration, and the Budget Bureau, was borrowed from the Budget Bureau to fill a specific need on a project as a program analyst. However, the assignment was only part-time, and to fill the other part of his time, Alpert was assigned to the NSF Biological Sciences Division, which began to support physical anthropology, cultural anthropology, archeology, and areas of social science "that impinged rather closely on the biological sciences."[35] Alpert continued, with great effectiveness, in this role. In 1954, he and his assistant, Bertha W. Rubinstein, issued a report, "The Role of the Foundation with Respect to Social Science Research." Based on that report, he also addressed the social sciences themselves in their various professional journals concerning what he thought was needed for them to achieve acceptance and support.[36] Only four years later, in 1958, approval was won for the creation of a social science division in NSF, to be activated in 1960.

A similar pattern occurred at NIMH. In the beginning, despite the support of key leaders, controversy and ambiguity forced social science into compromised positions where formal equality was either denied or sidestepped. The controversies included:

1. The validity of social science as "real" science; put another way, were the social sciences "sufficiently rigorous intellectually to be included in the community of science?"[37]
2. The related question of whether the social sciences are basic or applied sciences

The ambiguity was definitional. What exactly is social science, Congress asked, and within the question was a challenge to its legitimacy as an objective science. In a corollary way, there was suspicion about its association with political ideology: specifically, social science was identified with radical left-wing advocacy. In the end, the momentum of wartime research of all types was not to be denied, whether basic or applied, pure or as a means to an end, and in all its forms: physical, biological, and social. In spite of the controversies and the legal qualifications of the laws that instituted both NIMH and NSF, social science was, in fact, included, even as it was sometimes forced to enter surreptitiously. By the late 1950s, full legitimacy was won.

The answers to some of these definitional questions were in the charter for the NSF. For example, social science was defined as follows:

> Social sciences are directed toward an understanding of the behavior of social institutions and groups and of individuals as members of a group. Social sciences included anthropology, economics, political science, sociology, and social sciences not elsewhere classified.[38] Psychology is a separate category and is not included. Its definitions include distinctions between biological and social aspects. The latter include social psychology; educational personnel; vocational psychology, and testing; industrial and engineering psychology; development and personality.[39]

The NSF charter also defined basic and applied science:

> In *basic research* the objective of the sponsoring agency is to gain fuller knowledge or understanding of phenomena and observable facts without specific applications toward processes or products in mind.
>
> In *applied research* the objective . . . is to gain knowledge or understanding necessary for determining the means by which a recognized and specific need may be met.
>
> *Development* is the systematic use of knowledge or understanding gained from research, directed toward the production of useful materials, devices, systems or methods, including design and development of prototypes and processes.[40]

My own interpretation is that, in medical sociology, the intellectual product of the first two decades following the war was mainly in basic research and that, by 1960, the controversies surrounding the introduction of NSF and NIMH as major institutions were muted. The panic that greeted the appearance of the Russian *Sputnik* in 1957 swept social science into the general effort to upgrade American science education. The expansion of government support for the next twenty years was explosive. Not until the late 1970s was there a reaction, and in 1980 it struck with full force. Much of the early controversy was revived. Again the questions of legitimacy and purpose that marked the beginnings of 1945 were raised. Is social science the equivalent of "real" science? And is it fulfilling the purposes of "useful" science?

"In the 1970s," Larsen wrote, "social science had difficulty sustaining a positive image. . . . It was in double jeopardy: basic research was deemed a waste of money and applied research did not apply."[41] Nevertheless, the National Science

Board directed that the budget for *basic* social and behavioral science be accelerated for 1977, 1978, and 1979, and president Carter's budget for 1979 proposed a 22 percent increase for social science. It was at that time, however, that the full strength of the attack by its opponents struck and put social science on the defensive ever since. Social science survived but in a different form. Once again, strategies of survival were required. Social science, unlike the physical and natural sciences, was not allowed the autonomy of accepted intellectual activity, the right to be "pure" and to follow step-by-step the intrinsic development of knowledge about social behavior defined by and for social science.

Such strategies were required from the start at both NSF and NIMH. I cannot improve on the description by Larsen as he summarized the history of social science at the NSF. About the debates at NSF, he wrote:

> Two distinct views were expressed. One would exclude the social sciences because they were not considered to be sufficiently rigorous intellectually. The other would include them because of their prospective social utility. Neither view prevailed. A compromise was adopted. . . . The NSF found it prudent to defend its enlarging role for social science in terms of its responsibility for basic research; it did not claim much immediate practical relevance for the work it supported. By supporting projects convergent with the interests and philosophy of physical science, social science gradually gained respect inside the foundation.[42]

This was the strategy of convergence identified with Alpert's role in establishing a place for social science in NSF during its first decade, in spite of the very strong opposition from both Congress and the physical sciences. A second and related strategy was to separate the social sciences into two categories: the social and the behavioral. The former included sociology and economics, the latter anthropology, psychology, and social psychology. During the formative years, the 1950s, all these disciplines were able to assume a collective identity. "In the 1960s and 1970s, with growth and differentiation, it grew harder to sustain."[43] Anthropology, from the beginning, was aided by affinities to medicine. Psychology became over time closer in interest with biological science. Economics, as it developed methods of quantitative modeling, achieved prominence on its own. Sociology, more at risk for association with political ideology, was squeezed between the success of what was seen as a highly relevant economics and medically connected behavioral science.

Medical sociology also required such strategies. Until its formal acceptance in the NIMH training program in 1957, medical sociology was dependent on the sponsorship of psychiatry. At first, the interest was in a basic behavioral science, broadly defined but encompassing classic sociological concerns with culture, socialization, and interpersonal relations, together with anthropology and social psychology. Economics was low in priority until the 1970s and became increasingly valued from then on, eventually overtaking and going on to dominate NIMH support of social research on health issues in the 1990s. Overall, the support of basic research yielded to problem-specific inquiry, beginning with mental health broadly conceived and eventually focusing on specific illnesses such as drug and alcohol abuse and AIDS. As the 1980s produced more and more serious threats to social science, strategies of response gained importance.

Reorganization of Federal Agencies

Although the most dramatic evidence of change was revealed after 1980, there were indications earlier. Most obvious were the changed policies that occurred as a result of reorganization in all the federal agencies during the 1970s.[44] Until then, one could track the types and amount of support with reasonable clarity. After 1975, the diversification of the structure made it difficult to draw a portrait of training and research for any particular discipline, especially in medical sociology.

The process began in 1967 when NIMH was separated from NIH and raised to bureau status in the PHS. The NIMH Intramural Research Program continued at NIH under an agreement for joint administration between NIH and NIMH. At the same time, St. Elizabeth's Hospital, the federal government's only civilian psychiatric hospital, was transferred to NIMH. In 1968, NIMH became a component of the PHS's Health Services and Mental Health Administration (HSMHA). In 1972, the Drug Abuse Office and Treatment Act established a National Institute on Drug Abuse (NIDA) within the NIMH. In the next year, 1973, these organizations were combined as the Alcohol, Drug Abuse, and Mental Health Administration (ADAMHA), formally authorized by P.L.93–282 in 1974. Instead of being concentrated in NIMH, social and behavioral science research and training were now distributed among at least seven federal agencies: the NICHD, which had been founded in 1963, the NIA, founded in 1974, NIMH as part of ADAMHA, NSF, the NIDA, and the National Institute on Alcohol Abuse and Alcoholism (NIAAA). In 1987, the National Institute of Allergy and Infectious Diseases (NIAID) established centers for AIDS treatment and evaluation that also were to become important sites of social science collaborative research with medicine.[45]

The situation was further complicated in 1981, when President Reagan signed the Omnibus Budget Reconciliation Act. This act repealed the Mental Health Systems Act of 1980, which was based on the Report to the President (Carter) from the President's Commission on Mental Health and was intended to improve services for the mentally ill. Reagan instead consolidated ADAMHA's treatment and rehabilitation service programs into a single block grant that enabled each state to administer its allocated funds. "With the repeal of the community mental health legislation and the establishment of block grants the federal role in services to mentally ill became one of providing technical assistance to increase the capacity of State and local providers of mental health services."[46] This shifted the federal climate toward applied research and in general created an atmosphere of uncertainty, especially for social science.

In 1985, another major reorganization began, culminating in 1992 when ADAMHA was abolished and the research components of NIAAA, NIDA, and NIMH rejoined NIH. The services components of the institutes became part of a new PHS agency, Substance Abuse and Mental Health Services Administration (SAMSHA).

What all these changes meant for social science is not easy to assess. One place to start is by looking at the leadership, particularly at NIMH.

The Leadership of NIMH

As already mentioned, Russell Dynes, when he came to Washington as the executive secretary of the ASA, found a "behavioral science–friendly situation" that, he said, changed in a less friendly direction soon afterward. The shift was attributed specifically to Herbert Pardes, who was appointed director of NIMH in 1978, replacing Bertram Brown. Dynes contrasted Pardes, whom he regarded as "pretty much biologically oriented, not too interested in social behavioral sciences," with Gerald Klerman, head of ADAMHA, the parent agency of NIMH at that time. He saw Klerman as "much more social behaviorally oriented. . . . And then, after Reagan won, the whole nature of the structure, the orientation, the philosophy changed radically."[47] Closer examination, however, casts some doubt on Dynes's interpretation of the effects of the leadership.

Pardes was the fourth director of NIMH, as shown in table 11-1. Unlike his predecessors, all of whom were veterans of government service when appointed to the top office of NIMH, Pardes was appointed directly from academic psychiatry. Only forty-four years old, he was a graduate of the SUNY College of Medicine, Downstate Medical Center, in Brooklyn, where he also completed a psychiatric residency and joined the faculty, rising to become chairman of psychiatry. He then went to the University of Colorado, where he was head of the Psychiatry Department from 1975–78 just before joining NIMH.

Dr. Pardes's exposure to social science was substantial. He was a graduate fellow in a research training program at Downstate that was directed by an outstanding research psychologist and studied with other social scientists in that program.[48] While he was chairman of psychiatry at both Downstate and Colorado, he appointed Emily Rumford, a sociologist, to full professor and collaborated with her in training and research activities. Pardes describes a sociology teacher at Rutgers as one of the most influential of all his teachers.[49] Later, as a faculty member at Downstate, he was part of the team that taught a large course in behavioral science, serving as both a lecturer and small group leader. It follows, then, that Pardes was well informed about the social sciences, and he described favorable experiences working with sociologists in medical education. This makes Dynes's negative assessment of his attitude toward social science surprising. Officially, NIMH documents describe Pardes as a director who reinvigorated the neuroscience research efforts.[50] From his own description, his attitudes about the relative importance of behavioral sciences are more complicated.

Asked for his perception of the role of social science, particularly medical sociology, in medicine and medical education, he answered:

> When I think of powerful concepts that I use as an approach to understanding any problem, some of the most powerful ones I find come from physiology. Some of them came from what I would consider dynamic psychology. But I am not as taken with the knowledge base of sociology as much as perhaps the perspective of the sociologist. For example, one of the people I worked with most closely is Emily [Mumford]. I think Emily has a way of taking in the entire culture of a setting, an educational environment, a health care facility, which I would have thought is one of the strengths of what somebody does in sociology. But if you said to me, write out a chapter of basic sociological concepts, I'd probably have great difficulty doing it.

As he elaborated these views, Pardes used case illustrations that he believed were essential to communicate sociological ideas to physicians and medical students. As difficult as he found the concepts to communicate, he endorsed their importance. "My feeling about behavioral science," he said, "is that there are many

Table 11-1 Directors of NIMH

Name	Date of Birth	Dates of Office
Robert H. Felix	1904	1949–1964
Stanley F. Yolles	1919	1964–1970
Bertram S. Brown	1931	1970–1977
Herbert Pardes	1934	1978–1984
Shervert Frazier	1921	1984–1986
Lewis L. Judd	1930	1988–1992
Frederick K. Goodwin	1936	1992–1994
Rex William Cowdry (Acting)	1947	1994–1996
Steven E. Hyman	1952	1996–Present

people in medicine who are oblivious of it, to a disastrous degree. And so I have always felt that the teaching of medical students about behavioral issues . . . was a central and essential part of their education." From various books and teaching films, he chose illustrative cases. The mistake "many people have made" is in the way it is taught. One must begin, Pardes believed, with clinical problems and develop the ideas from them. When he went to Colorado, he developed a course that he saw as "a prototype of that kind of teaching, because it is very much run by clinicians, with [the] inclusion of an array of biological and social scientists." From that course he coedited a textbook that became a popular requirement for the teaching of behavioral science by psychiatrists.[51] Pardes's teaching philosophy, focused on behavioral science, is expressed in the preface to the First Edition:

> There have been many different approaches to the study of human behavior. In some medical schools a group of behavioral scientists without immediate and ongoing clinical experience have attempted to teach human behavior to medical students. These attempts have, in general, not succeeded in involving the students, and the most typical complaint has been the remoteness of many of these areas of study to the immediate concerns of the medical student and the practicing physician. This book is the ougrowth of a course that attempts a close integration between the many clinical aspects of human behavior and the behavioral sciences.[52]

As far as the policy of the NIMH toward teaching, Pardes took a strong stand, both on the importance of the support of education generally and specifically in social science.

It seems clear, therefore, that Pardes does not fit Dynes's description of a leadership figure unfriendly to social and behavioral science. That he had reservations about the effectiveness of social scientists in medical education is also clear, but his attitude was sympathetic. What concerned him most was the trend toward reduced support for training. In general, he felt that teaching was losing ground at NIMH, and he did not feel able to change that through his own influence. "I think the economic squeeze is going to jeopardize the incorporation of a broad enough perspective in either the delivery of, the teaching of, or the researching of medical care." Sociology, he feared, might be a casualty, driven in large part by major changes that were occurring in medicine.

The second major leader mentioned by Russell Dynes was Gerald Klerman, who, in 1978, shortly after Pardes came to Washington, became the first full-time administrator of ADAMHA, the umbrella organization of NIMH. Characterized by Dynes as "much more social behaviorally oriented," Klerman was indeed deeply involved with social science from early in his education and career. After graduating from the Bronx High School of Science in New York, he went to Cornell University, where, in his first year, he took a sociology course taught by John Clausen.[53] Drawn to Clausen, Robin Williams, Edward Suchman, and other sociologists at Cornell, Klerman was a sociology major. Because he was also a premedical student, his faculty advisor was Alexander Leighton,[54] who at that time was in Ithaca as part of the Cornell School of Industrial Relations.[55] It was Leighton "who introduced me to the possibility of psychiatry as a career," reported Klerman.

Klerman retained a membership in the ASA throughout his career and regularly attended their professional meetings. I remember first meeting him in the 1960s at a meeting of the Eastern Sociological Society, where he introduced himself and commented on a paper that I had just presented. He was a friendly, modest man who communicated a fine intelligence and professional commitment. Even though he was very practical about the advantages of being a doctor, which he described as "a conventional status and solid foundation,"[56] he saw himself as part of an important but marginal academic pathway. There was a familiar irony to his story about his parents' attitude: "My mother and father," he told me, "always kept asking me when I was going to open an office with an x-ray machine like a real doctor. They never understood what I was doing." This story was a mirror image of my own parents' attitudes: they never came to terms with how a sociologist could be on the faculty of a medical school, asking the same question: Why couldn't I be a real doctor?

Klerman went to New York University School of Medicine and found it "intellectually a barren period, so much rote memory." For relief he took courses at the New School for Social Research. This was in 1950–54, a time when the New School had a distinguished faculty of refugee scholars from Europe, offering an exciting and unique experience to social science students. Klerman was particularly interested in Alfred Schutz, a phenomenologist philosopher and economist. Against the background of the preclinical years, which were so "intellectually barren" that he was "very unhappy," he used the New School and new friendships with George Reader and Renee Fox[57] to keep himself going. Although he in fact received very high grades in the first two years, it was not until the clinical years that medical school captured his interest. Just before that, in the summer of 1952, John Clausen arranged for him to spend four months at the NIMH Laboratory of Socio-environmental Studies. In his own words:

> I worked with him [Clausen] on the study about the wives of schizophrenics. They were in the planning stage, and I had a rather dull task . . . to go through the records at St. Elizabeth's Hospital to get some idea of the characteristics of first-admission schizophrenics. [Nevertheless] that was an intellectual high point. Mel Kohn was there,[58] and I met a lot of interesting people.

This was obviously a very formative period for Klerman, his first experience in government research: "NIMH was just getting started. The Clinical Center had not yet been built. There were a lot of bright young people, [and] a sense of excitement, high hopes for the future, most of which were realized over the next twenty years. . . . I worked as a sort of junior research assistant and it was fun."

After medical school, Klerman joined a two-year residency in internal medicine and neurology at the Massachusetts Mental Health Center. He was following what he called "his fascination with the drama of taking care of patients." He reports a "socialization" experience that is common in medical settings: "When I said I was interested in psychiatry or social science, everybody laughed at me. My supervisor kept saying, how could a good doctor like you want to do that kind of stuff? So there was a lot of joking, but very clear socialization pressure for me to stay in internal medicine." At first he did continue, spending an extra year working at the Columbia Division of Bellevue in the cardiac catheterization laboratory, where the chief of service was Richards,[59] who won the Nobel Prize. Then he visited friends at the Boston Psychopathic of Harvard, where he met Daniel Levinson, Milton Greenblatt, Elvin Semrad, and Myron (Mickey) Sharaf. Again, Klerman was smitten: "We hit it off instantly, a sort of meeting of the minds. I felt, boy, this is really an exciting place, interesting ideas." And these were people that he remained in close touch with for the rest of his life. Moreover, they were an outstanding group whose intellectual contribution to both psychiatry and the behavioral sciences was substantial.[60] From that time forward, when he went to Yale, ADAMHA, and later to Cornell Medical College, Klerman sought to maintain his connections to the psychodynamic approach to psychiatry and to social science.

Despite the evidence of his interest and commitment to the social sciences, however, Klerman's judgment of their influence was not very favorable, much like the judgment of Pardes. "In medical education," Klerman said, "I don't think sociology has had much impact. One of the most common complaints [of patients] about the practice of medicine is that physicians don't treat them enough as individuals . . . the sensitivity of practitioners to cultural and class differences, gender, and background is lacking." Nor was he optimistic about the effectiveness of curriculum change. "I think the main determinant is the structure of practice," he said.

> Ideally, we would like to have practicing physicians infuse their humanism with some scientific understanding of things like social class or role differences based on gender or ethnic backgrounds or the nature of the social organization of the hospital. That's no more than requiring, as doctors make decisions about what drug to use, that they know a little bit about the pharmacology or biochemistry or physiology involved. But I do not feel we have made much progress.

Klerman is very specific in differentiating the intellectual from the applied effects of medical sociology. "If one of the goals of sociology in medicine is to make physicians more aware, appreciative, [and] sophisticated about the transactions and their interactions with patients," he said, "[its] effect is limited, and little change has occurred. But intellectually, medical sociology has had a tremendous impact on research and on theory in psychiatry, epidemiology, and public health, but not on the practice of medicine." Klerman spontaneously cited a wide range of illustrations from sociological research. He mentioned virtually all the major studies that have been discussed in this book. He was particularly impressed with the spirit of collaboration between social science and psychiatry during the fifties, naming the major studies of the sociology of social class and of the social organization of the hospital. But, he added, the spirit of that collaboration has been lost.

The change, Klerman believes, was caused by the community mental health movement as it responded to the urban crisis and the racial minorities civil rights movement of the 1960s. There was a great weakening of the intellectual developments, he feels, as the effort intensified to provide services. At the same time, there was a body of research in the social sciences that was critical of psychiatry, especially by Goffman and the labeling theorists, and psychiatry reacted defensively. But perhaps more than anything else, the "tremendous explosion of biological knowledge" has changed the situation at NIMH, in Klerman's view:

> In psychiatry, the advent of the drugs changed clinical practice, and the new biology has had an intellectual momentum, in genetics and pharmacology, that the social sciences don't seem to be able to deal with. There is not a sense in the social sciences of building upon previous knowledge in a cumulative way. . . . For example, I went to a meeting at Palo Alto, on reviewing the relationship between social class and schizophrenia. John Clausen, Mel Cohen, Fritz Redlich, and others were there. Clausen pointed out that with the relationship observed by Hollingshead and Redlich, there is still a debate: Is it social drift or social causation? Is it truly incidence and prevalence or is it help-seeking behavior? So there you have a finding, but we are no further along in understanding its generalizability or the mechanism producing it than almost twenty years ago. [Similarly,] there is nobody now doing any work on the sociology of hospitals.

Klerman, as he said this, obviously had feelings of reluctance about the negativity of his statements. "I am very sympathetic to the social scientist," he added. "But there is something missing. There is a lack of a sense of movement, progress, momentum."

In his efforts to clarify his own views about the role of the social sciences in psychiatry, Klerman asked, "Have you interviewed Mel Sabshin? He has an interesting theory about why social psychiatry has not kept up with its intellectual vigor past the 1960s. His theory," Klerman added, "is that it gave way to the community mental health center movement, and got caught up in community mental health practice." He was referring to Melvin Sabshin, the medical director of the American Psychiatric Association, who certainly qualified as one of the most influential medical leaders in 1980.

Sabshin, like Klerman, was attracted to the social sciences in college.[61] The son of a general practitioner in the Bronx, Sabshin remembers that from an early age it was clear that he was going into medicine, but his interests in psychology and the humanities in college at the University of Florida at Gainesville directed him toward a career in psychiatry. After graduating from Tulane University School of Medicine in 1948 and completing his psychiatric graduate training at Tulane in 1955, he began his academic career at the University of Illinois School of Medicine in Chicago. There he became the leader of a team that studied the social organization of hospitals. The team included the sociologists Anselm Strauss, Rue Bucher, and Leonard Schatzman.[62] Eventually, he became the chairman of psychiatry and then dean of Abraham Lincoln School of Medicine of the University of Illinois School of Medicine. During that time, after first publishing a variety of studies in psychosomatic medicine, he was the coauthor of several of the same studies of the social organization of the hospital that Klerman admired so much. In 1974, he became the medical director of the American Psychiatric Association.

Like Klerman, Sabshin began his medical career with his concerns centered on the psychophysiological variables, and only after almost ten years did he return to his earlier involvement in the psychosocial. "One piece of work that I had done on the relationship of the social setting to the use of drugs . . . made me convinced. . . . Unless you looked at the ideology and social context, you would miss the point." As a result, Sabshin said:

> I was interested in how social variables affected what I saw clinically and was reported clinically. I was also interested in evolving concepts of social psychiatry, especially in the 1950s. This was, I thought, a period of conceptual and practical developments, and I was active in trying to change services as a reflection of the theory and saw community psychiatry as a way to achieve that.

But Sabshin was disappointed and watched social psychiatry "get lost" in the 1960s. Community development, he said, became based on expediency and crisis after the 1960s and lost its theoretical boundaries and respect for science. "I saw social psychiatry as a theoretical field, not as a field of practice. One would look at how independent social variables affected the whole sequence, pathogenesis . . . of the kinds of illnesses or maladaptations or disability that we saw. Also how such variables affected institutions where psychiatry was practiced, especially in hospitals." Although he admired many of the same classic works on hospitals, social epidemiology, and transcultural psychiatry that Klerman did, Sabshin, like Klerman, was disappointed in how the field of medical sociology developed and believed that it had not been notably successful in medical education. He said:

> As chair of the department at Illinois, I was eager to see social science play an active role, and fostered it. . . . I believed very strongly that social science theory was important for medical education. But I think it has never quite made it as an important part of medical education. The reasons for it are complicated. They are similar in some ways to the problems of psychiatric education in the medical school. It goes against the tide and the basic kinds of forces and learning experiences the students have. . . . I think only a small minority of medical students are able to continue to perceive the importance of social science.

The essence of his explanation is that social science has not yet demonstrated its importance to the career aspirations and expectations of the medical students. It tends to be presented, he said, as an isolated experience. "I think the same thing is true of public health and preventive medicine." Social science also suffers from its frequent placement in a psychiatric context. None of these are seen as "a core experience in medical school."

Pardes, Klerman, and Sabshin served during the late 1970s through the early 1980s, when the attack on social science was most pointed and intense. All three were in favor of medical sociology. It does not seem reasonable, therefore, to assign responsibility for the attack on social science to the medical professionals who were the operational leaders of the federal agencies. It was the structural change that occurred in NIMH, both in training and research, that caused the major challenges to the adaptation strategies of medical sociology. The sources of those changes, however, include the fact that NIMH was different from the other institutes of NIH. In their analysis of organizational change at NIH, Berkowitz and LaMountain note that

> other institutes acted as mechanisms that filtered federal funds to medical school researchers in well-defined medical specialties. The NIMH, by way of contrast, assumed a social mission from the very beginning. . . . Its medical research agenda . . . enabled the NIMH to remain in the NIH family for many years. Ultimately, however, the social and medical research missions proved incompatible and forced the NIMH to leave the other institutes.[63]

The Social Mission of NIMH

Although the NIMH was constituted on the model of the other institutes of NIH, it contained from the start striking differences. The goal of research was shared, but "unlike the leaders of the other institutes, the leaders of the NIMH openly expressed an interest in public health and the provision of care."[64] NIMH also stressed the importance of training and treatment to a degree that made it very different from the other institutes. These aspects tied it "inextricably with broad social concerns . . . [so that] opponents of the National Mental Health Act [of 1946] . . . tied it to socialized medicine."[65] Social science has been labeled and identified with radical politics persistently since the end of World War II, but psychiatry, as a major clinical medical specialty, was less vulnerable to such attacks. Nevertheless, during the hearings on the National Mental Health Act, Congressman Frederick C. Smith, Republican of Ohio, said: "This is piecemeal legislation to socialize medicine. Dr. Parran [surgeon general of the PHS] and those who want to see the same system of medicine established in this country as in Russia need not worry about attaining their end so long as they can get Congress to continue passing legislation such as this."[66] Despite such opposition, the need was so evident from the experience of wartime that the legislation passed and NIMH was created. At the same time, its identity as an agency dedicated to a social mission persisted.

NIMH was an expression of the coming-of-age of psychiatry, which had lagged behind in the development of medical specialization during the 1930s. At the beginning of the war, for example, only thirty-five hundred doctors practiced psychiatry in America, and most of them were in the extensive public mental hospital system. Gerald Grob, in his masterful history of the care of the mentally ill in the United States,[67] documented a century of changes in mental health policies and their causes. As he explains, before World War II, psychiatry was linked with a comprehensive system of institutions, mainly state hospitals that provided services to the mentally ill and although at no financial cost to the patients, kept them languishing for long periods of time with little or no treatment. During the 1940s, the wartime experiences created a model that emphasized the superiority of community-based over mental hospital systems, and the specialty of psychiatry was transformed. The National Mental Health Act of 1946 made the federal government the vehicle of change. Postwar psychiatry substituted psychotherapy for the custodial emphasis of institutional care and created an optimism that scientific research and social and preventive approaches to care would fulfil the therapeutic promise of psychoanalytic theory.[68] Within this framework, the social sciences were embraced as partners in medical education and as basic scientists of behavior in terms similar to those of the incorporation of the basic preclinical biological sciences into general medicine. This period, from 1946 to 1965, was the golden age of the partnership between social science and psychiatry. As Berkowitz and LaMountain concluded, "[n]o other component of the National Institutes of Health featured such a close relationship between practitioners of social sciences and medical doctors."[69]

Another distinguishing feature of the first phase of NIMH history was its emphasis on training. As discussed earlier, Robert Felix, the first director, believed that psychiatry was deficient both in research and clinical training. NIMH created an ambitious program to remedy these deficiencies. By the close of the 1950s, psychiatry was a different specialty, and, as Grob argues, the foundation for a new policy of mental health care appeared to have been laid. "The introduction of psychotropic drugs and rediscovery of milieu therapy held out the hope that large numbers of mentally ill persons might be able to live more or less normal lives in the community."[70]

The Mental Retardation and Community Mental Health Centers Construction Act of 1963 was a large next step in the radical transformation of psychiatry. It coincided, however, with the Vietnam War, and with all of the war's social and political conflicts and antiorganizational and community empowerment ideologies. This was also the period when Medicare and Medicaid were introduced, further changing the role of the federal government in medical care.[71] The effect of these changes was to shift the emphasis of federal support from the basic research that characterized the immediate postwar decades to more applied service-related research.

The 1970s, as the testimony of Pardes, Klerman, and Sabshin strongly suggests, witnessed a growing disillusionment with psychosocial and psychodynamic explanations of mental illness. Grob draws the same conclusions, reporting how biological psychiatry gradually replaced the psychosocial paradigm. Crediting a powerful bipartisan health lobby with maintaining a strong federal agenda of biomedical research and the dissemination of the benefits of modern medicine to the entire population, Grob writes that the election of Nixon marked the end of such policies:

> Unlike his predecessors, Nixon had an uneasy relationship with the specialty of psychiatry. Psychodynamic practitioners, who still dominated the specialty, were generally associated with a liberal political ideology and committed to a variety of social programs. Moreover, some community mental health centers—particularly those in urban areas—were associated with a radical political agenda. Given Nixon's conservative political base and outlook, it was perhaps inevitable that conflict over both the proper shape of mental health policy and the role of the federal government would follow.[72]

Preoccupied with the Vietnam War, Nixon did not act on these sentiments immediately. In 1970, however, open conflict broke out when Stanley Yolles, successor at NIMH to Robert Felix, was forced out. From that time on, the Administration fought with Congress to cut NIMH programs. Although Grob saw "no one of stature" in the replacements to Robert Felix, it seems to me that Bertram Brown, Pardes, and Klerman were strong leaders who represented much the same values as Felix. All contributed to the Mental Health Systems Act that became law in October 1980 just before the election—legislation that, despite many compromises, continued the main policy outlines of previous years. It was Reagan's election that led to an immediate reversal of these policies.

The new administration acted swiftly. Preoccupied with reducing both taxes and federal expenditures, Reagan proposed a 25 percent cut in federal funding. Included was the conversion of federal mental health programs into a single block grant to the states carrying few restrictions and without policy guidelines. In the summer of 1981 the Omnibus Budget Reconciliation Act was signed into law. Included were not only the block grant but also the repeal of most of the provisions of the Mental Health Systems Act. The new legislation did more than reduce federal funding; it reversed nearly three decades of federal involvement and leadership.[73]

The 1980s, therefore, began with a formidable challenge to social science generally and to medical sociology in particular. The major supporter of its training and research, the NIMH, was under attack from the executive branch of government, which viewed NIMH itself as suspect for being too liberal in its policies. Psychiatry, as the dominant professional group in NIMH and ADAMHA and SAMSHA, changed its scientific orientation in favor of biological research and in the process reduced its support of social research. This intellectual change was reflected in its leadership. Pardes, who remained as NIMH director until 1984, was, in effect, the last strong supporter of social science in that office. His immediate successor, Shervert Frazier, leaned still toward a psychodynamic orientation, but after 1986, the frame of reference changed. (See table 11–1). The current leader of NIMH, Steven E. Hyman, M.D., appointed in 1996, is a good example.

Hyman, a graduate of Harvard Medical School in 1980, became the director of Harvard's interfaculty initiative in mind/brain behavior. His research has focused "on how drugs of abuse, neurotransmitters, and cytokines produce long-term changes in brain function by activating or suppressing the expression of genes within nerve cells. In recent years, his main focus has been on brain regions involved in the control of motivated behavior."[74] His predecessor, Frederick K. Goodwin, M.D., was a researcher with a similarly biological focus, studying the efficacy of lithium as a treatment for the depressive phase of manic depressive illness. Both Goodwin and Hyman were leaders of NIMH during a time when the main support for social science research was from the Division of Neuroscience and Behavioral Science, where the emphasis is on cognitive, personality, emotional, and social processes research. In other words, the major interests have turned to the biological and the psychological aspects of behavior.

How have sociologists managed their training and research needs as their funding milieus have changed? Larsen at the NSF wrote about the beginning of the 1980s: "For social science, harsh cuts threatened a drift toward disaster."[75] As part of the reaction, an expanded debate occurred about the relative merits of basic versus applied research.[76] Soon after Reagan's entrance, the *Wall Street Jour-*

nal and the *New York Times,* each according to its own point of view, summarized the effects on social science. The *Wall Street Journal* said:

> Reagan's Ax—Cuts Raise a New Social-Science Query: Does Anyone Appreciate Social Science?

> President Reagan is clipping the wings of the sociologists, psychologists, anthropologists, even economists, who study how people behave and why. The social scientists have been flying high ever since Lyndon Johnson's Great Society began ladling out millions of dollars to study everything from day care to the death penalty. They have come to rely almost exclusively on federal contracts. Now the Reagan administration has started slashing social-research funds sharply, and Congress is expected to approve most of the cuts with little fuss.[77]

A few days later, the *New York Times* reported about the same budget cuts:

> The ax is falling also at the National Institute of Mental Health, injuring studies in rape, divorce, racism, sexism, family life and aggression. Such glib judgments probably betray a conviction that "social" science somehow attacks mostly conservative values. And that is merely a foolish prejudice. Sound public policy, whether conservative or liberal, has to be grounded in social reality. Good social science research helps to protect Government and all society against error, above all the error being made here: assuming that in facing difficult choices, politicians really know what they're doing.[78]

Such perceptions bounced back and forth throughout the 1980s. The question here is: How did sociology fare in supporting its training and research needs? And, within its parent discipline, what can be said about the level of support of medical sociology?

General Sociology: Its Current Status

In its total support for research and development (R & D), the United States spends more than Japan, West Germany, France, and the United Kingdom combined.[79]

> From 1960 to 1989, U. S. expenditure increased in current dollars from $13.5 billion to 132.4 billion. On a regular annual basis this represents around 2.7 percent of the gross national product (GNP). Also, rather consistently, about one-third of this total national investment has been for research and two-thirds for the development part of R & D. In turn, monies for research also split, with about one-third for basic and two-thirds for applied research.[80]

Contributing to the national investment, in addition to the federal government, are industry, private foundations, universities, and state and local government. Since 1980, the federal government is no longer the foremost supplier of funds. From 1960 to 1989, the percentage of its total contribution dropped from 65 percent to 47 percent, although its share of basic research increased from 60 to 65 percent. The federal government continues to be the major supplier of academic R & D, but for the social sciences it is not. Overall, "after the mid-1970s, the climate for social science chilled, [and] the decline in the social science share of the rising science budget was particularly sharp during the Reagan decade."[81]

Within the social science budget, sociology during the years 1962–90 received $1,789,064,000 for research from the federal government, an average of $61.7 million per year. Although this is less than 1 percent of the total research allocation for all science, "it is a formidable investment."[82] Psychology received about three times as much and economics twice as much so that the three disciplines received 5.3 percent of the total federal obligation to research over those three decades. Unexpectedly, given the trends, sociology, like science in general but not like social science overall, shifted away from applied research. "By 1990, basic research received 54 percent of the $117 million federal obligation to sociology, an even greater proportion than noted for all science. . . . In 1972, 83 percent of the total went to applied research."[83]

Does this mean that there was a real change in the research behavior of sociologists? Larsen thinks not. Rather, "sociologists seem to have learned how to thrive, or at least survive, in changing funding milieus."[84] Instead of focusing on one agency, like NIMH or NSF, the researcher learns to work his way through layers of organizations, NICHD, NIA, and others, and though these are known as mission agencies because of the substantive focus of their concerns, the research can retain its original purpose. At least, this is the judgment of expert observers when evaluating large research outlays for social science research programs by NIA, NIMH, NICHD, and NSF.[85]

Research training is a different story. Although the National Academy of Sciences (NAS) consistently recommended the retention and increasing of training programs in regular reports from 1978 to 1994,[86] predoctoral training for sociologists was virtually eliminated. Postdoctoral training continued and in some cases thrived; but overall the training support shifted to psychology and economics.

The Current Status of Medical Sociology

Within the generic framework of social science and as a subdiscipline, how did medical sociology adjust to the attacks of the 1980s? Did it follow the same strategies, expanding its grant support base from NIMH to various alternative agencies like NIA and NICHD? To answer these questions about the specific experience of medical sociology, I will draw from the testimony both of members of the federal agencies responsible for financial support and of individual medical sociologists.

Ronald Manderscheid, for example, was for twenty years an official of NIMH, and since 1992 has been in the Center for Mental Health Services (CMHS), where he is chief of the Survey and Analysis Branch.[87] The CMHS emerged as part of the 1992 reorganization that abolished ADAMHA. The research components of NIAAA, NIDA, and NIMH rejoined NIH, while the service components became part of a new PHS agency, SAMSHA. Within SAMSHA the CMHS was created.

Manderscheid received his graduate training in sociology at the University of Maryland at College Park, doing a dissertation with data from the Mental Health Study Center, the last community laboratory of NIMH. His work ever since has been focused on mental health, and he has been an active member of the ASA Section on Medical Sociology.

The 1992 reorganization, in Manderscheid's view, made NIMH a vastly reduced organization. In his own words:

The organization that you knew at NIMH as of 1975–80, when it was a very dynamic, vibrant organization that was multidimensional, no longer exists. It's [now] a very unidimensional operation, intending to be almost pure neuroscience. . . . A new director [in 1996], Steven E. Hyman, is a neuroscientist, fairly narrow, and the programs are becoming progressively more narrow. Just recently, NIMH did away with, eliminated its epidemiology branch, . . . [and] it no longer has a recognized population epidemiology program.[88]

Considering that psychiatric epidemiology was the major goal of Robert Felix, the first director of NIMH, this is indeed a startling change.

About training, Manderscheid tells a similar story. Clinical training programs, another of Felix's highest priorities, has also been virtually eliminated. A budget that grew to $117 million in 1972 receded to $3 million in 1993 and by 1995 went to zero. Social science research training, on the other hand, has survived, but in very different terms. Only the training of minorities was strongly favored.

The value climate at the federal government, Manderscheid says, is

entrepreneurial. . . . We have moved out of what, I would say, is a role of social construction in this society. . . . This is a result of being downsized; we have fewer staff, we have less money. . . . The Clinton administration has had a vast impact on the federal bureaucracy in terms of driving it to be more entrepreneurial. They want us to be more like the private sector. . . . The consequence, in my mind, [is that] we are less socially oriented. We are less concerned in saying "We are here to represent the people of the United States" than we were fifteen or twenty years ago.

Speaking specifically about medical sociology, Manderscheid says that, at the ASA meetings in 1997, the program did not reflect a concern about the social reorganization of health care that is occurring, what he calls a "major, major thing."

To take something that essentially is a social good and turn it very dramatically into a commodity will have [great] impact. How it is organized, how the people [enter] who enter, what their motivations are. Very few people are studying any of this. And its a vast, trillion-dollar social experiment that is going on. It is not being chronicled by anybody.

Some of the other issues, the training of providers—there used to be a very big focus on professions. [Now] there's very little focus on providers or on the evolution of the consumer movement.

Manderscheid feels that medical sociologists have abandoned such issues and speculates that the funding entities are conservative. He includes the peer review committees themselves.

Training in sociological research has survived, Manderscheid says, but has changed. With some exceptions, he feels, we are training people who are not going to make major contributions intellectually. They are people who are going to go out and be "the hired hand researchers." If you need somebody to work on an evaluation, they will design your instrument, collect the data, crank it out, and give you an answer. These are a much more technologically oriented group of people than they are intellectuals. Among the exceptions are "five or six centers," among which the unit at Rutgers University directed by David Mechanic is an outstanding example, financed for almost two decades mainly by the NIMH Services Research Branch.

Mechanic, one of the most eminent medical sociologists today, looks at the field in terms much like those of Manderscheid. Although he agrees that training continues—his own program still supports ten postdoctoral fellows a year—it is changed. "When Reagan came into office . . . everything got redefined, and you had to be working on disease, not on just basic ideas. There is a lot of hostility to social science and anything with 'social' in it."[89] Mechanic's extensive research and training program at Rutgers dates to 1979–80 and continues to the present. Although it started with both predoctoral and postdoctoral fellowships, currently it only grants postdoctoral awards. The core of his program is a Center Grant from NIMH, called the Center for Research on the Organization and Financing of Care for the Severely Mentally Ill, providing about half a million dollars each year. This is supplemented with grants from the Robert Wood Johnson Foundation and other foundations as well as individual research grants from NIA or other agencies.

The Rutgers program is a model of today's most successful medical sociology academic operations. It is multidisciplinary, with a strong health services research theme.[90] Other such centers are at the University of Michigan, Indiana University, Johns Hopkins University, the University of North Carolina's Sheps Center, and the University of California–San Francisco's Aging and Health Policy Center. These units all tend to be multidisciplinary and concerned with a variety of health care financing, measurement, and policy problems. Despite these signs of strength in the funding of medical sociology, Mechanic decries what he sees as a basic intellectual loss:

> One of the things that has really hurt medical sociology is that, in the golden days, we had strong programs in the best sociology departments; at Wisconsin, Yale, North Carolina, and Columbia. All of these programs pretty much shut down, and we are not really training the next generation at the major universities. There are exceptions, like Michigan.

Also, Mechanic notes, in the 1950s and 1960s

> we had all the action to ourselves, but now there is health economics, which has become very powerful and influential, and health psychology has come into its own. Medical anthropology has developed. Political science has moved into the health field. We have much more competition than we used to have, and I think that is good. The field as a whole is prospering, but medical sociology relative to all the other participants isn't quite as compelling as it used to be.

Although the social science of medicine is thriving, both institutionally and intellectually, very often it is not in sociology departments. "It is in schools of public health, in health services research centers. That is where the action is."

Although there is a lot of support federally, Mechanic credits the private foundations with continuing to make a major contribution to the field. However, the preeminence of Russell Sage, Milbank, and Commonwealth has been replaced by that of the Robert Wood Johnson Foundation (RWJ). This foundation has, for example, a fellowship program for policy investigators that provides substantial stipends to mature investigators like Mechanic himself, Bruce Link of the Columbia School of Public Health, and Richard Scott at Stanford. They also fund training programs at Yale, Berkeley, and Michigan for postdoctoral fellows in sociology, economics, and political science, offering fifty-five thousand dollars annually for two years to attract talented people into the health field. Other foundations like the Lilly Foundation and Hughes are offering similar support.

Concerning the leaders of the field today, Mechanic seems inconsistent. On the one hand, he looks at figures like Renee Fox and Eliot Freidson as part of an earlier time and sees them as not replaced in kind. On the other he finds strong hope in the work of people like Ronald Kessler, Paul Cleary, and Mary Jo Good at the Harvard Medical School Department of Health Care Policy, Bernice Pescosolido of Indiana, Theda Skocpol of the Harvard Department of Sociology, and others.

Professionally, in 1980, medical sociology appeared to be at the crest of its development.[91] The ASA Section on Medical Sociology had grown from 407 members in 1960 to 1,018, 8 percent of the ASA membership and the largest of the twenty existing sections.[92] Sociologists were on the faculties of most of the 143 medical schools of the United States and Canada, in full-time or part-time roles.[93] Of the 228 university graduate departments of sociology, 226 were offering specialization in medical sociology,[94] an impressive accomplishment that must be qualified by the fact that only a handful are significant teaching centers. Sociologists were also employed by all kinds of medical and health care organizations, in health-related policy-oriented roles in government and in research positions directed toward the evaluation of the health care system.[95] The attitude of the medical profession found expression in the editorial of the official AMA journal, the *Journal of the American Medical Association,* of March 8, 1981: "The question should no longer be: Should the social sciences have a role in undergraduate medical education? Rather, it should be: How can we more effectively bring the lessons and insights of the relevant social and behavioral sciences to the students?"[96] This opinion was matched by Sol Levine, probably the premier medical sociologist of the time, who said: "It is time to start thinking of sociology *with* medicine."[97] The same view was shared by the opinion leaders of medical education: they joined in public support for the behavioral sciences in general and medical sociology specifically.[98] Moreover, these endorsements continued to the present day, gaining strength as they were repeated. The major educational report of the eighties, the "General Professional Education of the Physician," (GPEP) Report,[99] was followed during the next decade by a series of commissions, all unanimous in the recommendation that the teaching of the social behavioral sciences should be a basic part of the education of physicians.[100] Even the Liaison Committee for Medical Education, in its most recent certification procedures, requires that a teaching program in behavioral sciences should be in place in all the medical schools of the United States.

Similar status was also evident in Europe. Thirty-two of the thirty-four medical schools in the United Kingdom were teaching medical sociology.[101] The same was true for other countries.[102]

Thus, in both medical institutions and in the university, a consistent demand for medical sociology existed in 1980. Medical school faculty positions, sociology department programs, and financial support from private foundations and government agencies seemed, despite the cutbacks of certain federal agencies, to assure the structural foundations of its training and research. Professional associations and scholarly journals provided for the communication of its theoretical and research analyses.[103]

From 1980 until today, however, the environment for sociology, and medical sociology in particular, has changed. In funding policies, severe cuts and demands for relevancy were introduced. This was true for the United Kingdom as well as the United States; in both countries, the changes were in the form of attacks on the prior programs of the Democratic Party in the United States and the Labor Government in Great Britain, with the attempt to replace them with policies more ideologically compatible with the conservative philosophies of the Reagan and Thatcher governments.[104] Although some damage was done, however, medical sociology was not left penniless, but it is difficult to track the effects precisely. We know that at the peak of the Social Science Training Program in 1972–73, five million dollars supported 77 program grants and 570 stipends, primarily earmarked for sociology and anthropology with only a small number of interdisciplinary programs included. By 1980, structural and definitional changes occurred that made "behavioral science" the preferred category in official reports and distributed the support in a variety of institutions, as described earlier. Included under "behavioral science" as the single umbrella term are sociology, anthropology, and psychology, as well as speech and hearing sciences. Psychology is the major recipient, and predoctoral awards for sociologists have yielded in importance to postdoctoral. One can only conclude that training support continues but at a much reduced level and a different form from two decades ago.[105] In research, on the other hand, funding is available in all areas of basic and clinical research on health and disease throughout NIH, so that medical sociology's share of relevant R & D has been maintained.

The Section on Medical Sociology, from 1980 to the present, follows closely the pattern of its parent professional association. Both the Section and the ASA were unstable during this period, bouncing up and down until 1991. After 1980, both ASA and the Section lost members until 1984, when yearly increases began again. The Medical Sociology Section reached 1,166 members in 1991, 9 percent of the ASA, which itself had also gained members. In 1992, another decline in the Section on Medical Sociology occurred, to less than nine hundred members, 7 percent of the ASA membership, which, during the latter years, remained stable at close to thirteen thousand. Some of the Section's decline, however, was probably a result of the creation in 1991 of a new overlapping Section on Mental Health, which in May 1997 contained 355 members.[106]

However, this description, as impressive as it is in some ways and sobering in other ways, has been concerned mainly about the social history of medical sociology. What can be said about medical sociology's major intellectual mission, contribution to the development of knowledge, current professional identity, and the trends of its institutional development?

Current Institutional and Intellectual Trends

Medical sociology's path has been primarily within academic institutions.[107] From origins in university sociology departments, it began, during the 1950s, to add another place alongside the basic (or preclinical) sciences in the university med-ical school. It did not develop out of attempts to explore conditions of health and disease per se in the way pathology and biochemistry did. Instead, like physiol-ogy, "it arose in an effort to describe human functioning, but as this occurs in the social group rather than in the individual organism."[108] Accordingly, medical so-ciology does not include a role of clinical practice; however, the practice of med-icine itself has been one of its major subjects of inquiry, including both its core relationships and the health care system's organizational structures. Pressures to apply sociology's skills to the understanding of health services and health care policies have always existed and in recent years are a dominating force, associ-ated with the transformation of American medicine into a corporate form. Sixty years ago, the dominant form of medical practice was the opposite. It is not by chance, therefore, that L. J. Henderson, in the thirties, studied the doctor-patient relationship, defining the human dyad as a social system, and Talcott Parsons and Robert K. Merton focused their attention on the doctor when they analyzed the place of medicine in the social system of the Western world. The dominance of the doctor was the preeminent characteristic of medicine at that time, just as the corporate organization of medicine highlights the present.

The point I wish to make is that medical sociology has developed in a trajec-tory that follows its parent discipline but with reference always to the changing institutional dynamics of medicine. In a time when doctors practiced primarily in solo or small group private offices and patient choice and fee-for-service pay-ment characterized the system, medical sociologists perceived the doctor and pa-tient as the major roles for analysis. Since then, however, the rapid growth of specialized clinical practice and the explosion of knowledge and technology have elevated the importance of a different set of organizations, especially university teaching hospitals, and the focus of sociological inquiry accordingly has changed, just as today the dramatically altered economics of medicine are forcing another shift, this time to health services research and the study of the commercial models of health care delivery that now prevail.

The institutional trends of medical sociology, therefore, can only be under-stood against the background of sociology and medicine as academic professions and within the context of historical changes to both professions and the health care system. Turning toward speculation about the future, what can be said, drawn from the story I have told so far? I am hardly alone, of course, as a fore-caster. A number of my colleagues have tried the same, with fascinating but widely diverse results.

Freidson, for example, has suggested that "medical sociology as a field is in decline, and may even vanish."[109] Elinson, at the same time, is exuberantly op-timistic. "Evidence[s] that medical sociology is alive and well are all about us," he wrote.[110] Renee Fox added a third view: alive, even vital, but parochial. She described the paradoxical way the field of medical sociology developed:

> Its sphere is potentially vast; the number of social scientists it has drawn into its orbit is impressively large; the literature it has generated is sizeable. And yet, on closer inspection, the phenomena, milieux, and themes with which sociologists of medicine have been concerned are relatively restricted and selective.[111]

Freeman added yet another critical perspective. Like sociology in general, he said, medical sociologists cling to a conventional professional ideology that restricts their primary role to "teaching undergraduates, training future faculty replace-ments, and contributing by their writing and research to an understanding of social phenomena."[112] The result, he concluded, neglects sociology's potential for applied research and introduces the risk of giving up work opportunities to other types of social scientists. Economists, for example, but also public administrators, health services specialists, social planners, and managers are doing the work that, "from a craft-union perspective, should be undertaken by a sociologist."[113] Haf-ferty and Pescosolido take a similar view, calling attention to the

> massive changes in the provision of medical care as well as the rise of new health problems [that] challenge current knowledge, medical practice and social policy. . . . The field of Medical Sociology has not kept pace with the development of social policy . . . the importance of this field has dimin-ished, and . . . its parent discipline of Sociology has lost its taste for ad-dressing the most pressing social and policy problems."[114]

Donald Light, on the other hand, was more upbeat. In 1991, while he was organ-izing a scientific meeting on the sociology of American medicine, he expressed surprise "to discover many papers that took fresh approaches to old topics, recast theories that had pervaded the field for twenty years, or mapped entirely new territory." Light wrote:

> The sociology of medicine, it appeared, was undergoing one of those gen-erative periods when fresh gales blow through a specialty, uprooting old plants and bringing in new seed. For too long, it seemed to me, this large and fertile field had been working off old plantings, and further inquiry convinced me that younger scholars and a few established ones were doing more original work than one normally sees. . . . A new body of work was being produced that drew upon and contributed to the discipline as a whole.[115]

Most recently, Sol Levine saw the field much as Light described it. Looking back from 1995, Levine made the comment: "It is impossible to survey the field of medical sociology without being impressed by its remarkable growth in the United States and in many other parts of the world."[116] At the same time, Levine described a parallel tendency by medical sociologists toward parochialism and "the presence of opposing intellectual camps that ignore and even impugn each other's work." He identified two large clusters of "structure seekers" and "mean-ing seekers."[117] Levine's purpose was to convince these competing groups that each was a legitimate approach but that their common purpose and therefore the integration of their views was the more important goal.

Each of the opinions just cited, with the possible exception of Levine and Light, speaks to a selected aspect of the field. Their approaches all focus on in-tellectual history. Only Freidson gives equal weight to the field's social character, describing medical sociology's institutional structure as a "learned" profession that functions in the environment of a "practicing" profession, and that, like all professions, is a combination of achieved, highly developed knowledge and an organized professional social organization.[118] It is with a similar full view, bal-ancing knowledge and social development, that I seek here to appraise the state of the field.

One of the greatest hopes for medical sociology as it emerged fifty years ago was that it would create a place for sociologists in a new academic role in medical schools. The university college of arts and sciences has tended to be the main venue of the sociologist. Commenting on this fact, Lutterman, in 1975, estimated that 88 percent of sociologists were employed in their traditional academic departments. He wrote:

> If we want to understand the sociology of knowledge, the sociology of sociology, we must see the discipline for what it is. At the present time, sociology is almost entirely a teaching discipline. Most sociologists spend the vast bulk of their time teaching rather than doing research. They get paid for teaching and writing textbooks. . . . When they do research, and many do not, it is typically on the individual scholar basis as a part-time researcher.[119]

After 1975, the success of two decades of government-sponsored training programs resulted in a surplus of Ph.D. sociologists relative to the conventional academic demand, and federal support changed to place explicit emphasis on training for research careers in applied situations "such as community mental health centers and state, federal and private research settings."[120] The response of the discipline, however, appeared to do little to accommodate to the new manpower situation. Lutterman, writing a decade later in the mideighties, found no reason to alter his earlier observations about the barriers to change in most sociology departments:

> A major concern of the seventies was the delivery of mental health services and the evaluation of service programs. By 1980, about half the programs [NIMH-supported training] concerned services research and evaluation research and involved training for applied settings. Faculty members with experience in applied research are hard to find, and often departments are unenthusiastic or hostile to developing training programs with an applied focus. It is much easier and less threatening to deal with problems of the discipline rather than the problems of the client; it is simpler to reproduce one's self . . . than to train students to work in applied settings.[121]

Lutterman was speaking from his position as associate director of Mental Health Services Planning Research and Research Training in the Division of Biometry and Epidemiology at NIMH, giving him a nationwide view of the field. He acknowledged that some of the resistance was structural. "Unlike schools of public health and public policy," he said, "sociology departments generally lack strong ties to agencies or other nonacademic research settings. Thus it is difficult to place students as interns, to supervise their research, and to help them find jobs in nonacademic settings." Nevertheless, he added, "intellectual snobbery often dictates what kinds of research are important and worthwhile, and applied research is usually seen as less respectable, unless perhaps performed by a Paul Lazarsfeld, a James Coleman, or a Peter Rossi."[122] This view of Lutterman, written in 1983, was contradicted by his colleague Manderscheid in 1998. Manderscheid, as quoted earlier, argues that the research training of medical sociologists has become what Lutterman hoped for: they now are trained to do applied research.

The result, however, at least in Manderscheid's view, is "hired hand researchers" who are expert technologically but narrow intellectually.

Medical sociology, because of its association with a service profession, was expected to escape from the opportunity limits described by Lutterman, and to some extent it has. In health-related research organizations, including the intramural programs of NIMH and other government organizations, sociologists found their place, including prominent and leadership roles.[123] Similarly, in the government bureaucracies devoted to various types of health sciences research, they were included. But the high expectations for academic medicine were not fulfilled. There was the attempt, starting in the fifties, to create a new department to house medical sociologists and other behavioral scientists in the medical school. The University of Kentucky, in its formative years as a new medical school, recruited Robert Straus for this purpose, and today, fully forty years later, that Department of Behavioral Science is still thriving.[124] Time has proven Kentucky to be an exception, however. The only departments with a similar name are not mainly for the social science of medicine but usually for psychiatry. Although most medical schools today do employ sociologists and other behavioral scientists, they are mainly the guests of existing departments, selected mainly for their research skills; their teaching, like their research, is in teams, part of broad problem-defined subjects, like the Harvard Medical School Patient-Doctor course.[125] But there is not a stable institutionalized faculty role.

The early promise of a partnership with psychiatry, which appeared so strong fifty years ago, was not fulfilled. Different reasons are offered. First, there is the charge that sociologists were destructive critics. When labeling theorists like Goffman,[126] Scheff,[127] and others observed how mental hospitals stripped patients of their identities and basic human rights, public reactions against psychiatry were stimulated. Although the most sensational findings were highlighted by the media, these were only part of a series of outstanding research reports on mental hospitals that were welcomed and admired by most psychiatrists.[128] Nevertheless, in retrospect, they are regarded as the cause of a backlash by psychiatry against sociology.[129] This was a situation in which the outsider was seen as violating the rules of the host. Like Leo Simmons's first public reports after he joined Harold G. Wolff in the Cornell Medical School faculty,[130] Goffman's publications were seen as a betrayal even as they were admired. This type of "insider-outsider" ambiguity was part of the sociologists' experience from the start of their work in medical settings, especially in their relations with psychiatry.[131]

A second reason for the aborted faculty role of sociologists in medical schools was in their type of knowledge base. Interpersonal human relations, especially the doctor-patient relationship and the interprofessional relations of the modern hospital, at first appealed to medical educators as an essential ingredient of the training of future physicians. Combined with the basic skills developed by sociologists, such as interviewing, survey methods, statistics, and organizational analysis, curriculum models were created as early as 1951 that were widely adopted.[132] At the same time, medical educators accepted the conception of medical education as socialization for the profession, replacing the more limited view of the medical school as a training ground primarily for knowledge and skills. This was an educational paradigm that emerged from sociological research on medical education, and it effectively established the perception of the medical school as a social culture and environment, as opposed to the more limited training school.[133] The Western Reserve curriculum reform of the 1950s was built on this intellectual foundation, as other major reform efforts have been to this day. Current problem-based learning programs, including those at McMasters, the University of New Mexico, and Harvard University, are arguably the product of social science fundamentals.[134] Below the surface of this favorable consensus for medical sociology, however, were barriers. Whether it was the persistence of sociology's identity as an outsider, the qualifications about the effectiveness for medical education of sociological thinking as expressed by friendly leadership figures such as Pardes, Klerman, and Sabshin, or the resistance of medicine's biological preoccupation, the fact remains that the acceptance of a social science of medicine as one of the basic sciences of medical education, so promising during the golden age of the fifties and sixties, did not occur.

Psychiatry, in medical education and at NIMH, has come to be dominated by a biological and psychopharmacologic frame of reference. To a degree, so have community medicine, public health, and preventive medicine departments of the medical school. Certainly, advances in brain physiology and psychomimetic drugs are major contributing factors. But whether it was from the biological preference or the insider-outsider tension, a secure role in psychiatry departments for medical sociology in the medical school has not been achieved.

The strongest institutional role for the medical sociologist has been in the traditional sociology department of the college of arts and sciences. Teaching of medical sociology is an established part of most undergraduate and graduate college curricula. Thus, most medical sociologists appear to be working outside of medical institutions, except as guest researchers. The single exception is the school of public health. In the nation's specialized schools of public health, medical sociology has achieved its place. The Department of Sociomedical Sciences at Columbia University is an outstanding model, matched by other major schools such as Boston University, the University of Michigan, and the University of North Carolina.

In sum, the major roles that have emerged for medical sociologists are:

- University teacher in sociology department, in undergraduate and graduate college curricula
- Adjunct teaching collaborator with physician colleagues in medical school
- Basic scientist of behavior in collaborative situations in medical school
- Full-time faculty in social science–oriented department of school of public health
- Policy analyst and consultant

These are the structurally determined positions of contemporary medical sociologists. What of the intellectual achievements?

My own reading is that the intellectual side of medical sociology is thriving independently of its position in the social structure. On the other hand, the subjects of inquiry are influenced by the greater sociopolitical climate. For example, twenty years ago, asking a similar set of questions, I wrote: "When one charts the patterns of research emphasis in medical sociology's growing body of knowledge, there is a reflection of the increasing demand for applied research, and of the changing nature of medicine itself in this postmedicare and medicaid health care environment. The following broad intellectual trends in medical sociological inquiry can be traced:" (see table 11-2).[135]

Table 11-2 Trends in Medical Sociological Inquiry

From	To
A social psychological frame of reference	Institutional analysis
Small-scale social relations as subject of research	Large social systems
Role analysis in specifically limited settings	Complex organizational analysis
Basic theoretical concerns with classic social analysis of behavior	Policy science directed toward systematic translation of basic knowledge into decision-making
A perspective of human relations and communications	Power structure analysis

The attempt in table 11-2 to abstract patterns of inquiry was not meant to indicate that research stopped or lacked importance in the left ("From") column. That was not true then nor is it now. Some examples are studies of socialization,[136] on interpersonal relations in limited settings,[137] and on doctor-patient relations.[138] Nevertheless, the trended emphasis appears to be in the directions that are charted. These trends, however, refer to knowledge development based on theoretical questions. By 1972, Richard Williams was able to show how basic and applied questions were being joined in medical sociology. For example, studies of the social ecology of disease are shown to contribute to the knowledge of cancer and rheumatoid arthritis. In a similar way, Williams shows how basic sociological research relates to other specific problems of health and disease.[139]

What Williams makes clear, it seems to me, is that the demand for more applied research by medical sociology that characterized the period since 1980 was already being richly served at the beginning. Yet, as *Science* reported in March 1981, Congress was ready to withdraw support for both training and research in social science.[140] Although the attack was heavily weighted on the conservative side, even such liberals as Senator Edward M. Kennedy, chairman of the Senate Health Subcommittee, were challenging the research community to be more responsive to its social obligations.[141] Most striking is the disjunction between the facts and the demands of the representatives of the public. Social science knowledge had been used to frame important health policies such as the Neighborhood Health Center Program of the "War on Poverty," and, within medicine itself, such knowledge was basic to the conception of the therapeutic community approach of mental hospitals, the development of community mental health centers, and the deinstitutionalization of a large proportion of hospitalized mental patients. The identification of patient-consumers as particular ethnic, racial, or gender groups and the conception of the neighborhood as the natural environment of urban life have been particularly useful in the development of a more responsive health movement and the expansion of environmental and occupational health.

If we study medical sociology as a case example of the effects of increasing dependence on the fiscal policies of the federal government, we see in 1980 a discipline that is small but increasingly visible among university-based professions because its subject and methods are relevant to problems of health and illness. As it responded to medicine, it was caught in the tides of medical manpower development, sharing the experience of institutional changes and becoming almost totally dependent on federal subsidy. In 1980, it found itself threatened with the withdrawal of those federal funds in both training and research. But this was a threat that, under one or another changing circumstance, had happened before and would repeat itself again. Each time, as I have shown, medical sociology survived these challenges. The survival strategy was just that: a strategy. Medical sociology, in effect, continued much as always, succeeding in the intellectual side of its activities while institutionally it adapted to the structure of the various situations in which it conducted its work. After 1980, that situation, more and more, downgraded the importance of sociological inquiry about education and professionalization and about the social organization of the profession, demanding cost-related health services research because the dominance of medical education as the site of a research-focused medical center yielded to a form of practice organization whose major mission was to control costs within the boundaries of commercial markets.

The Current Situation

Managed care has become the defining term of the current health care system of the United States. As such, no discussion of medicine today is possible without attention to its transforming effects. According to the American Association of Health Plans (AAHP), the most recent available figures (as of the end of 2000) estimate that 92 percent of employed workers are in managed care programs, or 70 percent of the total population,[142] and 94 percent of the nation's physicians have some type of managed care contract.[143] More precisely, managed care is defined as

> [h]ealth insurance plans intended to reduce unnecessary health care costs through a variety of mechanisms, including: economic incentives for physicians and patients to select less costly forms of care; programs for reviewing the medical necessity of specific services, increased beneficiary cost sharing; controls on inpatient admissions and lengths of stay; the establishment of cost-sharing incentives for outpatient surgery; selective contracting with health care providers; and the intensive management of high-cost health care cases.[144]

This definition includes HMOs and preferred provider organizations (PPOs).[145]

Without question, managed care has radically changed the institutional structure of medicine. Instead of the dominance and autonomy of physicians and voluntary hospitals that characterized medicine from the beginning of the twentieth century, power has been transferred to the huge health care conglomerates that increasingly represent managed care programs. The irony is that prepaid, capitated medical care for broad-based populations originated in the 1920s and was represented by nonprofit organizations like Kaiser-Permanente (1945) and Group Health Cooperative of Puget Sound (1947). The major objectives of these early variants of the HMO were to increase access to quality health care at a low price, based on a strong emphasis on primary care and prevention. The profit potential of this type of organization, however, after a long intervening period, attracted the establishment of publicly traded, for-profit corporations in a marketplace that has grown phenomenally in recent years.[146] Paul Starr made the prediction in 1982 that

> medical care in America now appears to be in the early stages of a major transformation in its institutional structure, comparable to the rise of professional sovereignty at the opening of the twentieth century. . . . Corporations have begun to integrate a hitherto decentralized hospital system, enter a variety of other health care businesses, and consolidate ownership and control in what may eventually become an industry dominated by huge health care conglomerates.[147]

Managed care is the fulfillment of that prediction.

The risk in this process has been described as "turning medicine into a product rather than a social service."[148] When the Healthcare Company (HCA), a huge private hospital chain, attempted to buy Harvard's prestigious McLean Hospital and make it part of a for-profit corporation, Harvard's chairman of medicine, Arnold Relman, argued that the qualities that make medicine a profession will be lost if patient care is dominated by the for-profit motive.[149] The values of the university teaching hospital were jeopardized. More broadly, Starr argued that the coming dominance of for-profit corporations in medicine could send the United States back to a two-tier system of medical care. The wealthy and the well-insured and those with "profitable" illnesses would have easy access to the system. The poor would not.[150] Just how accurate this prediction was can be seen in the front-page account by the *New York Times* on July 6, 1998, telling how most of the health care corporations have dropped coverage for the elderly and the poor by severing Medicare and Medicaid enrollees.[151]

What this represents is the emergence of "the medical-industrial complex," as identified by both *Fortune* and the Ehrenreichs in 1970.[152] The managed care revolution, therefore, is the culmination of at least a three-decade process, based on ideas that first surfaced more than sixty years ago. In significant terms, it mirrors the way in which commercial insurance companies took over hospital insurance in the 1930s.[153] In essence, it is a story that began when a feasible hospital insurance plan was first developed in the United States by Dr. Justin Ford Kimball of Baylor University Hospital in Dallas, Texas, in 1929. This plan was community rated; that is, payments reflected the average cost of care for all subscribers. The amount paid by a group or individual did not depend on age, gender, health status, or the previous or anticipated use of health services. This strategy implied a subsidy from younger, healthier members of the population to its older, sicker members. Buyers considered the subsidy, a form of risk averaging, one of the desired attributes of insurance. This was the early approach of the first "Blues," Blue Cross and Blue Shield, and was based on nonprofit organizational structure. However, private insurance companies, which prior to this had regarded health insurance as unprofitable, now perceived in this plan the opportunity for new markets. To compete with the community-rated nonprofits, however,

> they based their premiums on the health care costs incurred by specific sub-groups of subscribers. This approach became known as *experience rating*, and it encouraged insurers to look for lower-risk individuals or groups, including employees of particular firms, and to offer them reduced rates.

Such a tactic had two unfortunate consequences: it became advantageous for persons or groups with people at lower risk to dissociate from persons with higher risk, and groups with people at higher risk, such as the elderly, found that their premiums increased.[154]

Nevertheless, these private, so-called indemnity insurers elbowed the community-rated nonprofits to the margins and became the basic form of the health insurance industry that dominated American health care for the next half-century. This movement was also the basis of a cost structure that made the United States the country with the highest percentage of its gross national product going to health care.

Managed care has been chosen as the method of containing those costs. Unlike indemnity insurance, however, which did not touch the autonomy of the doctor-provider, managed care forces the doctor into roles that are intrinsic to an industry. The managed care doctor is an amalgam of worker, manager, and clerk. His or her prior professional autonomy is, at best, severely compromised; his or her professional dominance is leveled.[155] What Relman feared corporate medicine would do to the values of the Harvard University Medical School managed care is doing to the structure of the medical profession. It undermines the foundations of a delicate balance of privileges and responsibilities that was forged over centuries between Western medicine and the societies it served. As Sigerist so carefully documented,[156] the key difference between a profession and a craft is based on trust that allows the profession to do the best it can for its clients without fear of punishment for making the attempt as long as it could be defended as based on the best available knowledge. Without that agreement, it was impossible, between Hippocrates and the Renaissance, to effectively base medical practice on science. Instead, doctors were forced to avoid cases where they were not sure of success.

As Parsons correctly observed, commercial relations depend on the principle of *Caveat emptor* "Let the buyer beware."[157] Medicine in this century scrupulously avoided adopting this principle and in the process was granted the right to generous material rewards. The structure of modern medicine has preserved as its most fundamental requirement the license to offer what are arguably the best solutions available; otherwise, it was claimed, there can be no joint effort between professional and client to solve problems of health and disease. With all the risks that are part of such a precarious bargain, there is no comparison with those of the commercial marketplace. My judgment, in other words, is that if medicine in the United States continues on its present course toward control by publicly traded corporate health care organizations, the consequences will include corruption of a precious, even essential, basis for the core human relations of medicine. Moreover, I am fully aware that there is disagreement among scholars about such a conclusion.

Harry Nelson, in his valuable review of this question for the Milbank Memorial Fund, marshaled available data and arguments on both sides of this question.[158] Clarke and Estes reported on data that they believe tested both sociological and economic theories of markets and nonprofits.[159] Mechanic, most recently, addressed the issue of trust.[160] Mechanic reformulates the argument so that "effective communication" is presented as a definably separate but essential attribute of health care relationships. He believes that current structural changes jeopardize such communication; but the underlying assumption seems to be that if measures are created to maintain and improve effective communication, the essentials of high-level professional quality of care may be preserved. In other words, by another strategy, medicine can survive as a profession even as its structural foundations are turned upside down. Mechanic, in this way, has joined a venerable theoretical question in sociology: Can values transcend the material factors that inherently are contradictory? Or, put another way, can technological imperatives be withheld in favor of practices designed to serve ideology?

Briefly to recapitulate Mechanic's argument, effective communication, he writes, allows the physician to understand the patient's expectations and concerns; to obtain accurate information, thereby facilitating diagnosis; to plan and manage the course of treatment; and to gain the patient's understanding, cooperation, and adherence to treatment. Although the importance of this fact is universally recognized, he adds, it is jeopardized by several more pressing medical and economic concerns. Among the latter are barriers to effective communication specifically associated with managed care, including the reduction of sufficient time and continuity of care by pressuring physicians to see more patients and the increasing of responsibility for allocating care and the perverse financial incentives that are associated with such allocation.[161] Mechanic finds that widespread recognition of both the importance of and barriers to effective communication has produced

> impressive innovative programs for teaching communication skills to clinicians, for developing empathy and leadership in patient-oriented care, and for helping patients to become better-informed and more effective participants in their treatment. [Yet,] most innovators remain invisible, isolated in their efforts, with few career rewards in this difficult and underfunded area. Those who pursue it, enter an uncertain and precarious trajectory in academic settings.[162]

Mechanic seems to be saying that it is possible to block the negative effects of corporate medicine on the doctor-patient relationship and that it is essential to do so because it is so important. At the same time, although he is impressed by the widespread programs to educate and facilitate effective communication in patient care and by their creativity, these efforts are not strongly endorsed by the medical profession and their sources of fiscal support.

My own reading of this debate is unequivocal: the current trends in the organization of health care are overwhelming the human relations of medicine. The defense of the importance of the psychosocial dimensions of health care by various innovative programs, in spite of their validity and excellence, is puny compared to the massive structural pressures for commodifying medicine. Universal health care is inherently a human right and needs to be institutionalized as such. To fail in that endeavor is both costly and impractical within the framework of modern democratic nations. This is not a debate about the tax status of organizations, as some investigators have framed it.[163] There are deeper questions about the social effects of the current trend toward publicly traded corporate medicine. It is affecting all the basic institutions of medicine: medical education, the basic sciences of medicine and the research structures that house them, and clinical medicine with the various settings, including hospitals, where it is practiced.

Medical sociology, in this book, has been shown in a wide range of functions and activities. Overall, I agree with those who judge the intellectual achievements of the sociology of health and medicine to be very strong. Most medical sociologists, however, appear to have settled into institutional roles mainly outside medical settings but very actively engaged in research about problems of health and illness and the organizations that deal with them. Although they are engaged more as welcome guests than as strangers in those organizations, sociologists are still outsiders. As such, their function as critical analysts has been one of the most important, as attested to by the work of Goffman, Freidson, and Waitzkin, to name just a few.[164] At the same time, they have increased the technical skills that brought them into medical institutions in the first place, allowing them to better serve the applied aspects of their work. Fifteen years ago, I made the observation that, at heart, sociology is a scholarly profession and, as such, requires a work environment that protects and nurtures free, intellectual inquiry. There is a natural tension between independent intellectual analysis and the controlled knowledge enterprise of "targeted" research. The latter, increasingly, is demanded of medical sociology in the form of evaluation research. The threat is that, to survive in the current climate created by scarce resources for an expanded high-skill social science manpower, we will become the "hired guns"[165] of government agencies and special interest groups, charged with producing research results that fit preconceived policies. In the process, we may lose the traditional heart of our enterprise.[166] This comment is even more valid today than it was then. It places us in equal jeopardy with medicine, both struggling to retain the independence of science on the one hand and of trusted service on the other. In our histories, we can hope, we will find the strength to sustain the inherent values of our contract with society to continue in mutual benefit.

Notes

Introduction

1. Felix Marti-Ibanez, ed., *Henry E. Sigerist on the History of Medicine* (New York: MD Publications, 1960), 14–15.

2. Norman Cameron, "Human Ecology and Personality in the Training of Physicians," in *Psychiatry and Medical Education: Report of the 1951 Conference on Psychiatric Education.* Association of American Medical Colleges (AAMC). (Washington, D.C.: American Psychiatric Association, 1952), 64.

3. Although psychology attracted similar interest a generation earlier, it was only in that part of it that closely paralleled the natural sciences. Approval to teach in terms that more fully expressed the complete range of content in psychology was held back until midcentury. Sheppard Ivory Franz, "On Psychology and Medical Education," *Science* 38 (1913): 555–566; John B. Watson, "Content of a Course in Psychology for Medical Students," *Journal of the American Medical Association* 58 (1912): 916–918.

4. Samuel W. Bloom, "Sociology of Medical Education: Some Comments on the State of the Field," *Milbank Memorial Fund Quarterly* 43 (1965): 143–184. Samuel W. Bloom, "Socialization for the Physician's Role: A Review of Some Contributions of Research to Theory," in E. C. Shapiro and L. M. Lowenstein, eds., *Becoming a Physician* (Cambridge, Mass.: Ballinger, 1979), 3–52. Samuel W. Bloom and Ruth E. Zambrana, "Trends and Developments in the Sociology of Medicine," in Julio L. Ruffini, ed., *Advances in Medical Social Science* (New York: Gordon and Breach, 1983), 1:73–122.

5. Robert K. Merton, "The Sociology of Science: An Episodic Memoir," in Robert K. Merton and Jerry Gaston, ed., *The Sociology of Science in Europe* (Carbondale, Ill.: Southern Illinois University Press), 5.

6. Joseph Ben-David and Randall Collins, "Social Factors in the Origin of a New Science," *American Sociological Review* 31, 4 (August 1966): 451–465. Edward Shils, "Tradition, Ecology and Institution in the History of Sociology," *Daedalus* 99, 4 (1970): 760–825.

7. See Robert K. Merton, George G. Reader, and Patricia L. Kendall, *The Student-Physician: Introductory Studies in the Sociology of Medical Education* (Cambridge: Harvard University Press, 1957. For a summary and complete bibliography of the studies associated with the Columbia University Research team, see Samuel W. Bloom, "The Sociology of Medical Education."

8. William Caudill, "Applied Anthropology in Medicine," in A. J. Kroeber, ed., *Anthropology Today* (Chicago: University of Chicago Press, 1953). John A. Clausen, "Mental Disorders," in Howard Freeman, Sol Levine, and Leo G. Reeder, eds., *Hand-*

book of Medical Sociology, 3rd ed. (Englewood Cliffs, N.J.: Prentice Hall, 1979); Renee C. Fox, "Advanced Medical Technology: Social and Ethical Implications," in *Annual Review of Sociology*, vol. 2 (Palo Alto: Annual Reviews, 1976); Howard E. Freeman and Leo G. Reeder, "Medical Sociology: A Review of the Literature," *American Sociological Review* 22 (1957): 73–81; Saxon Graham, "Sociological Aspects of Health and Illness," in Robert E. L. Faris, ed., *Handbook of Modern Sociology* (Chicago: Rand McNally, 1964), 319–347; Martin Hyman, "Medicine," in Paul F. Lazarsfeld, William H. Sewell, and Harold L. Wilensky, eds., *The Uses of Sociology* (New York: Basic Books, 1967), 119–155; Patricia L. Kendall and George G. Reader, "Contributions of Sociology to Medicine," in Freeman, Levine, and Reeder, *Handbook of Medical Sociology*, 1–22; Sol Levine, "Time for Creative Integration in Medical Sociology," in *Journal of Health and Social Behavior*, extra issue, *Forty Years of Medical Sociology: The State of the Art and Directions for the Future* (1995): 1–4.

9. Sharon N. Barnartt, "A Review of Medical Sociology Textbooks," *Teaching Sociology 18, 3,* special issue on medical sociology (1990): 372–376, lists the special textbooks currently available as follows: W. C. Cockerham, *Medical Sociology,* 7th ed. (Englewood Cliffs, N.J.: Prentice Hall, 1998); R. A. Kurtz and H. P. Chalfant, *Sociology of Medicine and Illness* (Boston: Allyn and Bacon, 1984); E. Mumford, *Medical Sociology* (New York: Random House, 1983); A. C. Twaddle and R. M. Hessler, *A Sociology of Health,* 2nd ed. (New York: Macmillan, 1987); F. D. Wolinsky, *The Sociology of Health,* 2nd ed. (Belmont, Calif.: Wadsworth, 1988). Readers also used for teaching are: Phil Brown, ed., *Perspectives in Medical Sociology* (Belmont, Calif.: Wadsworth, 1989): Peter Conrad and Rochelle Kern, eds., *The Sociology of Health and Illness: Critical Perspectives,* 3rd ed. (New York: St. Martin's Press, 1990); Howard D. Schwartz and Cary S. Kart ed., *Dominant Issues in Medical Sociology* (Reading, Mass.:Addison-Wesley, 1978); Linda Aiken and David Mechanic, eds., *Applications of Social Science to Clinical Medicine and Health Policy* (New Brunswick, N.J.: Rutgers University Press, 1986); Chloe Bird, Peter Conrad, and Allen Fremont, eds., *Handbook of Medical Sociology,* 5th ed. (Englewood Cliffs, N.J.: Prentice Hall, 2000). See Steven P. Wallace, "Institutionalizing Divergent Approaches in the Sociology of Health and Healing: A Review of Medical Sociology Readers," *Teaching Sociology* 18 (1990): 377–384. Reports on the field include Donald A. Kennedy, Evan G. Pattishall, Jr., and DeWitt C. Baldwin, Jr., *Medical Education and the Behavioral Sciences* (Boulder, Colo.: Westview Press, 1983).

10. Robert Lynd expressed the same feeling in a way I cannot improve: "No one is wise enough or informed enough to venture with assurance upon the large task here undertaken. The only reason for attempting it is that such efforts at appraisal of the present work and potentialities of the social sciences, however faulty in detail, seem clearly to be needed at the present stage in the development of social science and of American culture. And if it was to be undertaken at all, it seemed desirable to push the analysis straight through the network of diffidence and respect for one's colleagues that tends to shackle frankness within an academic fraternity." Robert S. Lynd, *Knowledge for What?* (Princeton: Princeton University Press, 1939; reprint, New York: Grove Press, 1964), ix.

11. Harry Stack Sullivan, "Social Psychiatric Research: Its Implications for the Schizophrenia Problem and for Mental Hygiene," *American Journal of Psychiatry* 10 (1931): 977–991, and "The Modified Psychoanalytic Treatment of Schizophrenia," *American Journal of Psychiatry* 11 (1931): 518–540.

12. Lawrence J. Henderson, "Physician and Patient as a Social System," *New England Journal of Medicine* 212 (1935): 819–823.

13. The Henderson-Hesselbach theorem has been familiar to every medical school graduate for more than a half century. It formulates in precise mathematical terms the acid-base equilibrium and sets the pattern for Henderson's lifetime efforts to demonstrate functional theories of first physiochemical and later social systems. "In the late 1920s," Bernard Barber writes, "Henderson was encouraged to read Pareto's *Sociologie*

Generale (1917) by his Harvard colleague William Morton Wheeler, whose own classic studies of insect societies had led him to become interested in Pareto's analysis of human societies. Henderson was immediately and enormously impressed; it was just what he had been looking for. He became an enthusiast of Pareto, and for the rest of his life he devoted more and more of his time and activities to Pareto and to social science." *L. J. Henderson on the Social System* (Chicago: University of Chicago Press, 1970), 5. In 1933 the Society of Fellows was started at Harvard and one year earlier, a seminar on Pareto, in both of which Henderson was the originator, and which became the cultural settings for his influence in social science. The Society of Fellows, in his time, produced George Homans, William F. Whyte, and Conrad Arensberg, all of whom testify to his important influence. The Pareto seminar consisted mainly of his colleagues such as Schumpeter, Parsons, Crane Brinton, Clyde Kluckhohn, and Henry Murray, but some advanced graduate students attended and Robert K. Merton was one. In 1938, Henderson started his course, Sociology 23, and this widened the scope of his influence to include, among others, Bernard Barber and Leo Srole. For descriptions of Henderson's teaching, see especially Barber, *L. J. Henderson on the Social System*, 1970); Parsons, *The Social System* (Glencoe, Ill.: Free Press, 1951), 828–833; Alvin W. Gouldner, *The Coming Crisis of Western Sociology* (New York: Basic Books, 1970), 149.

Chapter 1

1. The best source I have found for the early period of medical sociology is George Rosen, "The Evolution of Social Medicine," in Howard Freeman, Sol Levine, and Leo G. Reeder, eds., *Handbook of Medical Sociology*, 3rd ed. (Englewood Cliffs, N.J.: Prentice Hall, 1979), 23–52. Also by Rosen, *From Medical Police to Social Medicine* (New York: Watson Academic, 1974). Another excellent source is Bernhard Stern, *Historical Sociology: The Selected Papers of Bernhard J. Stern* (New York: Citadel Press, 1959).

2. Edwin Chadwick, *Report on the Sanitary Condition of the Labouring Population of Great Britain,* edited with an introduction by M. W. Flinn (Edinburgh: University Press, 1842). See also Anthony Oberschall, ed., *The Establishment of Empirical Sociology: Studies in Continuity, Discontinuity, and Institutionalization* (New York: Harper and Row, 1972). Oberschall gives a thorough description of the French social hygienists of the 1830s. For the early German contributions, see Erwin Ackerknecht, *Rudolph Virchow: Doctor, Statesman, Anthropologist* (Madison: University of Wisconsin Press, 1953), and Salomon Neumann, *Die Offentliche Gesundheitspfege und das Eigenthum: Kritisches und positives mit Bezug auf die preussische Medizinalverfassungsfrage* (Berlin: Adolf Riess, 1847), 64–65, 84, as cited in Rosen, *From Medical Police to Social Medicine*, 63.

3. Rosen, *From Medical Police to Social Medicine*, 60.

4. Virchow is better known as the father of modern pathology. The quotation is from Ackerknecht, *Rudolph Virchow.* Also Rosen, "Evolution of Social Medicine," 62.

5. Neumann, *Die Offentliche Gesundheitspfege und das Eigenthum,* 64–65, 84, as cited in Rosen, "Evolution of Social Medicine," 62.

6. This was, of course, the time when social science was just beginning its development toward professional status in the modern sense. In the United States, this was a post–Civil War development, often dated to 1865 when the American Social Science Association (ASSA) was formed. The first professional organization of social science, the ASSA began with a social-problem, reform-minded agenda. Its members included at first probably more amateurs than professionals. Only gradually did competition between the amateur reformers and the academic professionals emerge. When it did, the ASSA no longer served as a common ground, and the new academics formed their own professional associations of economics, political science, and finally (in 1905),

sociology. Virchow and Neumann, therefore, and their historical counterparts in social science were contemporary allies. See Mary O. Furner, *Advocacy and Objectivity: A Crisis in the Professionalization of American Social Science, 1865–1905* (Lexington: University Press of Kentucky, 1975), 4–5.

7. Owsei Temkin, *The Double Face of Janus, and Other Essays in the History of Medicine* (Baltimore: Johns Hopkins University Press, 1977), 423. "Epidemics," Virchow wrote, "resemble large warning tables in which the statesman of great style can read that a disturbance has appeared in the development of his people which even indifferent politics must no longer be allowed to overlook."

8. Milton I. Roemer, Leslie A. Falk, and Theodore M. Brown, "Sociological Vision and Pedagogic Mission: Henry Sigerist's Medical Sociology," in Elizabeth Fee and Theodore M. Brown, ed., *Making Medical History: The Life and Times of Henry E. Sigerist* (Baltimore: Johns Hopkins University Press, 1997), 18.

9. Roemer, Falk, and Brown, "Sociological Vision and Pedagogic Mission," 315. They cite as support for this statement Albert J. Reiss, "Sociology: The Field," in David L. Sills, ed., *International Encyclopedia of the Social Sciences* (New York: Macmillan, 1968), and Wold Lepenies, *Between Literature and Science: The Rise of Sociology* (Cambridge, England: Cambridge University Press, 1988); Dorothy Ross, *The Origins of American Social Science* (Cambridge, England: Cambridge University Press, 1991); Thomas L. Haskell, *The Emergence of Professional Social Science* (Urbana: University of Illinois Press, 1977); Furner, *Advocacy and Objectivity*; Robert C. Bannister, *Sociology and Science* (Chapel Hill: University of North Carolina Press, 1987), Cecil E. Greek, *The Religious Origins of American Sociology* (New York: Garland, 1992).

10. Temkin, *The Double Face of Janus,* 42.

11. Ibid., 42; also Ludwig Edelstein, "Motives and Incentives for Science in Antiquity," in A. C. Crombe, *Scientific Change* (New York: Basic Books, 1963), 15–41.

12. Temkin, *The Double Face of Janus,* 43; and Louis Cohn-Haft, *The Public Physicians of Ancient Greece*, Smith College Studies in History, vol. 42 (Northampton, Mass.: Department of History, Smith College, 1956).

13. Cecil Sheps, *Higher Education for Public Health*, A Report of the Milbank Memorial Fund Commission (New York: Prodist, 1976), 3.

14. Ibid., 3.

15. Rosen, "Evolution of Social Medicine," 23.

16. Rosen, *From Medical Police to Social Medicine,* 165.

17. Ibid., 166.

18. Rosen, "Evolution of Social Medicine," 1974.

19. This development of medicine in the interests of the state found its fullest expression in the work of Johann Peter Frank (1745–1821). Frank detailed a plan for the "measures to be taken by government for the protection of individual and group health." This work, "pervaded by a spirit of enlightenment and humanitarianism," is described as "the work of a public medical official who spent his life in the service of absolute rulers, great and small: the exposition is meant less to instruct the people— or even physicians—than it is to guide the officials who are supposed to regulate and supervise all the spheres of human activity, for the benefit of society" (see Rosen, "Evolution of Social Medicine," 24, and Rosen, *From Medical Police to Social Medicine,* 121).

20. Rosen, *From Medical Police to Social Medicine,* 121.

21. Rosen, "Evolution of Social Medicine," 24.

22. Irving Louis Horowitz, *Professing Sociology: Studies in the Life Cycle of Social Science* (Chicago: Aldine, 1968), 32.

23. Rosen, "Evolution of Social Medicine," 31.

24. Oberschall, *The Establishment of Empirical Sociology*. Also see Rosen, *From Medical Police to Social Medicine*, 74.

25. Rosen, *From Medical Police to Social Medicine,* 72–76.

26. See ibid., 92.

27. This idea has been challenged recently by Bonner: "Scholars working in American medicine have overstated the weaknesses of medical schools in the nineteenth century United States"; Thomas Neville Bonner, *Becoming a Physician: Medical Education in Great Britain, France, Germany, and the United States, 1750–1945* (New York: Oxford University Press, 1995), 9.

28. John Duffy, *The Healers* (New York: McGraw-Hill, 1976), 190.

29. Ibid., 190; Charles E. Rosenberg, *The Cholera Years: The United States in 1832, 1849, and 1866* (Chicago: University of Chicago Press, 1962), 43.

30. Duffy, *The Healers*, 206–207.

31. Ibid., 202; Barbara G. Rosenkrantz, *Public Health and the State: Changing Views in Massachusetts, 1842–1936* (Cambridge: Harvard University Press, 1972).

32. Duffy, *The Healers*, 210.

33. Ibid., 223.

34. Rosen, *From Medical Police to Social Medicine*, 70.

35. Ibid., 70.

36. Alfred Grotjahn and F. Kreigel, *Soziale Pathologie*, 2nd ed. (Berlin: August Hirschw ald Verlag, 1915), 9–18, as cited by Rosen, "Evolution of Social Medicine," 34.

37. Rosen, *From Medical Police to Social Medicine*, 112. Also Edward T. Devine, *When Social Work Was Young* (New York: Macmillan, 1939).

38. Rosalie A. Kane, "Social Work as a Health Profession," in David Mechanic, ed., *Handbook of Health, Health Care, and the Health Professions* (New York: Free Press, 1983), 499.

39. Lawrence T. Nichols, "The Establishment of Sociology at Harvard: A Case of Organizational Ambivalence and Scientific Vulnerability," in Clark A. Elliott and Margaret W. Rossitter, eds., *Science at Harvard University: Historical Perspectives* (Bethlehem, Pa.: Lehigh University Press, 1992), 204.

40. James Ford, cited in ibid., 205.

41. Fielding H. Garrison, *Contributions to the History of Medicine* (New York: Hafner, 1966).

42. Thomas M. Brown and Elizabeth Fee, " 'Anything but Amabilis': Henry Sigerist's Impact on the History of Medicine in America," in Fee and Brown, *Making Medical History*, 335.

43. Charles McIntire, "The Importance of the Study of Medical Sociology," *Bulletin of the American Academy of Medicine* 1 (1894): 425–434.

44. Elizabeth Blackwell was the first woman graduate of a medical school. After being turned down by many, she was accepted in a small upper New York State school, Geneva Medical School, where she got her M.D. in 1849. After studying in France and Germany, she pioneered in medical practice as a woman, overcoming great prejudice against female doctors.

45. Published by D. Appleton (New York).

Chapter 2

1. Ellen W. Schrecker, *No Ivory Tower: McCarthyism in the Universities* (New York: Oxford University Press, 1986), 14.

2. The best source for this subject continues to be Laurence R. Veysey, *The Emergence of the American University* (Chicago: University of Chicago Press, 1965; reprint of Chicago: First Phoenix, 1970). Also very helpful for this discussion was Donald Light, "The Development of Professional Schools in America," in Konrad H. Jarausch, ed., *The Transformation of Higher Learning: 1860–1930* (Stuttgart: Klett-Cotta, 1982), 345–366.

3. This rather bleak portrait of nineteenth-century American medical education is contested by Bonner, who argues that the physicians in the United States were trained as well or sometimes better than their European counterparts. See Thomas Neville Bonner, *Becoming a Physician: Medical Education in Great Britain, France, Germany and the United States: 1750–1945.* (New York: Oxford University Press, 1995).

4. Robert Straus, "The Nature and Status of Medical Sociology," *American Sociological Review* 22 (1957): 200–204.

5. Frederick Fox Cartwright, *A Social History of Medicine* (London: Longman, 1977), 1.

6. For elaboration of these ideas, see Samuel W. Bloom, "Institutional Trends in Medical Sociology," *Journal of Health and Social Behavior* 27 (1986): 265–276.

7. Most recently, this is the case for what is called "clinical sociology."

8. See Robert K. Merton, "Insiders and Outsiders: A Chapter in the Sociology of Knowledge," in *The Sociology of Science: Theoretical and Empirical Investigations,* edited with an introduction by Norman W. Storer (Chicago: University of Chicago Press, 1973), 99–138.

9. Paul F. Lazarsfeld and Jeffrey G. Reitz, *An Introduction to Applied Sociology* (New York: Elsevier, 1975), 1; Howard W. Odum, *American Sociology: The Story of Sociology in the United States through 1950* (New York: Longman Green, 1951); L. L. Bernard and Jessie Bernard, *Origins of American Sociology*, New York: Thomas Y. Crowell, 1943); Anthony Oberschall, ed., *The Establishment of Empirical Sociology: Studies in Continuity, Discontinuity, and Institutionalization* (New York: Harper and Row, 1972); Mary O. Furner, *Advocacy and Objectivity: A Crisis in the Professionalization of American Social Science, 1865–1905* (Lexington: University of Kentucky Press, 1975).

10. Lazarsfeld and Reitz, *Introduction to Applied Sociology*, 1; Oberschall, *Establishment of Empirical Sociology.*

11. Furner, *Advocacy and Objectivity*, 1.

12. Ibid., 2.

13. Ibid. See also Veysey, *Emergence of the American University.*

14. Prominent among such critics was William Welch, founding dean of the Johns Hopkins University School of Medicine. William G. Rothstein, *American Medical Schools and the Practice of Medicine* (New York: Oxford University Press, 1987), 89.

15. Gerald L. Markowitz and David Rosner, "Doctors in Crisis: Medical Education and Medical Reform during the Progressive Era, 1895–1915," in Susan Reverby and David Rosner, eds., *Health Care in America: Essays in Social History* (Philadelphia: Temple University Press, 1979), 190.

16. Veysey, *Emergence of the American University*, 2.

17. Light, "Development of Professional Schools," 351–352.

18. John Duffy, *The Healers* (New York: McGraw-Hill, 1976), 173.

19. Abraham Flexner, *Medical Education in the United States and Canada* (New York: Carnegie Foundation for the Advancement of Teaching, 1910), 5.

20. Ibid., 6.

21. Ibid.

22. Bernard and Bernard, *Origins of American Sociology,* 835.

23. Odum, *American Sociology,* 27–28.

24. Ibid., 10.

25. Lazarsfeld and Reitz, *Introduction to Applied Sociology.*

26. For current figures, see table 10–1.

27. Fred H. Mathews, *Quest for an American Sociology: Robert E. Park and the Chicago School* (Montreal: McGill-Queens University Press, 1977).

28. Roscoe Hinkle and Gisella J. Hinkle, *The Development of Modern Sociology.* (New York: Random House, 1954), 3.

29. Ibid.

30. Ibid.

31. Albert J. Reiss, "Sociology," in *International Encyclopedia of the Social Sciences*, 2nd ed. (New York: Macmillan, 1968).

32. Hinkle and Hinkle, *Development of Modern Sociology*, 7–10.

33. Charles Booth, *Life and Labour of the People in London* (London: Macmillan, 1892).

34. Sidney and Beatrice Webb, *English Local Government: English Poor Law History, pt. II, The Last Hundred Years*, vol. 2 (London: Longmans Green, 1929). See also Sidney and Beatrice Webb, *The State and the Doctor* (London: Longmans Green, 1910).

35. David Elesh, "The Manchester Statistical Society: A Case Study of Failure," in Oberschall, *Establishment of Empirical Sociology*, 31–73.

36. Furner, *Advocacy and Objectivity*, 291.

37. Ibid., 291.

38. Ibid., 292. Furner is citing Small to Walter A. Payne, April 30, 1908, sociology folder, President's Collection, University of Chicago.

39. Ira W. Howerth, "Present Condition of Sociology in the United States," *Annals of the American Academy of Political and Social Science* 5 (1894): 112–121.

40. Reiss, "Sociology," 813.

41. I do not count the sociology departments in Russia that taught only so-called Marxist sociology.

42. Richard Hofstadter, *Social Darwinism in America*, rev. ed. (Boston: Beacon Press, 1955).

43. Edward Shils, "Tradition, Ecology, and Institution in the History of Sociology," *Daedalus* 99 (1970): 760–825; and Edward Shils, *The Calling of Sociology* (Chicago: University of Chicago Press, 1980).

44. Reiss, "Sociology," 814.

45. Ibid. 814.

46. Ibid., 813.

47. E. Richard Brown, *Rockefeller Medicine Men: Medicine and Capitalism in America* (Berkeley: University of California Press, 1979).

48. Rosemary Stevens, *American Medicine and the Public Interest* (New Haven: Yale University Press, 1971), 69.

49. Robert Alan Day, *Toward the Development of a Critical, Sociohistorically Grounded Sociology of Sociology: The Case of Medical Sociology* (Ann Arbor, Mich.: UMI Dissertation Services, 1981).

50. David C. Hammack and Stanton Wheeler, *Social Science in the Making: Essays on the Russell Sage Foundation, 1907–1972* (New York: Russell Sage Foundation, 1994).

51. Oberschall, *Establishment of Empirical Sociology*, 218.

52. See chapter 9, where the role of the Russell Sage Foundation is fully explored.

53. Lazarsfeld and Reitz, *Introduction to Applied Sociology*, 2.

54. Reiss, "*Sociology*," 817.

55. Odum, *American Sociology*, 438–439; James L. McCartney, "Medical Sociology: A Case Study of a Special Area Receiving Much Support," in "The Support of Sociological Research: Trends and Consequences," Ph.D. diss., University of Minnesota, 142–157.

56. Ibid.

57. Lazarsfeld and Reitz, *Introduction to Applied Sociology*, 2.

Chapter 3

1. Bernhard J. Stern, *Historical Sociology: the Selected Papers of Bernhard J. Stern* (New York: Citadel Press, 1959). See also Samuel W. Bloom, "The Intellectual in a

Time of Crisis: The Case of Bernhard J. Stern, 1894–1956," *Journal of the History of the Behavioral Sciences* 26 (1990): 17–37.

2. Barbara S. Heyl, "The Harvard 'Pareto Circle,' " *Journal of the History of Behavioral Science* 4, 41 (1968): 316–334. Alvin W. Gouldner, *The Coming Crisis of Western Sociology* (New York: Basic Books, 1970), 149.

3. The theory was developed in the 1930s, but the substantive illustrations were not published until after the Second World War.

4. Anthony Oberschall, ed., *The Establishment of Empirical Sociology: Studies in Continuity, Discontinuity, and Institutionalization* (New York: Harper and Row, 1972).

5. Ibid., 2.

6. Ibid., 4.

7. Ibid., 4–5, citing Joseph Ben-David and Randall Collins, "Social Factors in the Origin of a New Science," *American Sociological Review*, 31, 4 (1966):451–465.

8. Oberschall, *Establishment of Empirical Sociology*, 5.

9. Ibid., 172.

10. Ibid., 8. Philip Abrams, *The Origins of British Sociology, 1834–1914.* (Chicago: University of Chicago Press, 1968).

11. Oberschall, *Establishment of Empirical Sociology*, 8.

12. Ibid., 187.

13. Ibid., 187.

14. Ibid.: 193.

15. Abraham Flexner, *I Remember: The Autobiography of Abraham Flexner* (New York: Simon & Schuster, 1940), 49.

16. Ibid.: 49.

17. E. Richard Brown, *Rockefeller Medicine Men: Medicine and Capitalism in America* (Berkeley: University of California Press, 1979), 132.

18. Gerald E. Markowitz and David Rosner, "Doctors in Crisis: Medical Education and Medical Reform during the Progressive Era, 1895–1915," in Susan Reverby and David Rosner, ed., *Health Care in America* (Philadelphia: Temple University Press, 1979), 185–187. See also Robert F. Arnove, *Philanthropy and Cultural Imperialism: The Foundations at Home and Abroad* (Bloomington: Indiana University Press, 1980); Lewis S. Coser, *Men of Ideas* (New York: Free Press, 1970), chapter 25, "Foundations as Gatekeepers of Contemporary Intellectual Life."

19. Oberschall, *Establishment of Empirical Sociology*, 194.

20. Ibid., 5.

21. Ibid., 12.

22. John M. Glenn, Lilian Brandt, and F. Emerson Andrews, *Russell Sage Foundation: 1907–1946*, 2 vols. (New York: Russell Sage Foundation, 1947), 6–7.

23. Oberschall, *Establishment of Empirical Sociology*, 91. Mary O. Furner, *Advocacy and Objectivity: A Crisis in the Professionalization of American Social Sciences, 1865–1905* (Lexington: University of Kentucky Press, 1975).

24. Oberschall, *Establishment of Empirical Sociology*, 87.

25. Patricia Madoo Lengermann, "The Founding of the American Sociological Review: Anatomy of a Rebellion," *American Sociological Review* 44 (1979):185–198.

26. See also Edward Shils, "Tradition, Ecology, and Institution in the History of Sociology," *Daedalus* 99, no. 4 (fall 1970): 763. Shils expands the definition of institutionalization, following closely the steps described by Ben-David.

27. Howard W. Odum, *American Sociology: The Story of Sociology in the United States through 1950* (New York: Longman Green, 1951), 276.

28. Robert Lynd and Helen Merrell Lynd, *Middletown: A Study in Contemporary American Culture* (New York: Harcourt, Brace and World, 1929).

29. William F. Ogburn, ed., *Recent Social Trends in the United States*, Report of the President's Committee on Social Trends, 2 vols. (New York: McGraw-Hill, 1933).

30. Oberschall, "Establishment of Medical Sociology," 4.

31. George Rosen, "The Evolution of Social Medicine," in Howard E. Freeman, Sol Levine, and Leo G. Reeder, eds., *Handbook of Medical Sociology*, 3rd ed. (Englewood Cliffs, N.J.: Prentice Hall, 1979), 38.

32. Elizabeth W. Etheridge, *The Butterfly Caste: A Social History of Pellagra in the South* (Westport, Conn.: Greenwood, 1972).

33. Ibid., 130.

34. Warren and Sydenstryker, *Health Insurance: Its Relation to the Public Health* (Washington, D.C.: Government Printing Office, 1916). He also repeated the recommendation while serving with CCMC: editorial, *Journal of the American Medical Association* 103 (1934): 608–609.

35. Michael M. Davis, *The Psychological Interpetations of Society* (New York: Columbia University Press, 1909).

36. Michael M. Davis, *Immigrant Health and the Community* (Montclair, N.J.: Patterson Smith, 1971; reprinted from 1921).

37. Milton Roemer, *Medical Care Administration: Content, Physicians, and Training in the United States* (San Francisco: Western Branch of APHA, UCLA School of Public Health, 1963), 53.

38. Ibid.

39. Rosemary Stevens, *American Medicine and the Public Interest* (New Haven: Yale University Press, 1971), 176.

40. Ibid.

41. Isadore S. Falk, "Proposals for National Health Insurance in the USA: Origins and Evolution, and Some Perceptions for the Future," *Milbank Memorial Quarterly* 55 (1977):164.

42. Ibid., 161.

43. Ibid.

44. See Robert Straus, *Medical Care for Seamen: The Development of Public Health Services in the United States* (New Haven: Yale University Press, 1950).

45. Ibid., 162.

46. Warren and Sydenstricker, *Health Insurance.*

47. Falk, "Proposals," 163–165.

48. Ibid., 165.

49. Stevens, *American Medicine and the Public Interest,* 134–136. Stevens shows a course that began by following closely the patterns of England and Europe: "There were . . . already, before World War I, pressures on the traditional organization of medical care. The success of scientific medicine was pushing physicians and others toward specialization, yet specialist care was largely uncoordinated. . . . Meanwhile numbers of organizations were studying the development of European social security schemes which were beginning to cover the working population for accident insurance, old-age pensions, sickness insurance, and health benefits. With the encouragement of President Theodore Roosevelt, the first federal workmen's compensation act was passed in 1908. . . . The American Association for Labor Legislation, organized in 1906, established its own Committee on Social Insurance in 1912. *Health insurance was considered the next logical step* . . . and from 1913 became the focus of the Committee's efforts.

50. Ibid., 138.

51. Ibid., 132.

52. Ibid., 169.

53. Ibid., 138–139.

54. Ibid., 170.

55. Falk, "Proposals," 166.

56. A. Hacker, "Why Our Government Doesn't Work Better," *New York Times,* November 15, 1981, section 7, 3.

57. I. S. Falk, C. R. Rorem, and M. D. Ring, *The Costs of Medical Care: A Summary of Investigations on the Economic Aspects of the Prevention and Care of Illness.* Com-

mittee on the Costs of Medical Care, publication no. 27 (Chicago: University of Chicago Press, 1933).

58. Committee on the Costs of Medical Care, *Medical Care for the American People: The Final Report of the Committee on the Costs of Medical Care* (Chicago: University of Chicago Press, 1932).

59. Ibid., 5–9.

60. Ibid., 17.

61. Stevens, *American Medicine and the Public Interest,* 184.

62. Ibid., 184.

63. This assessment does not include current forms of the health maintenance organization (HMO). The effects of the HMO movement are discussed in chapter 11 of this book.

64. Stevens, *American Medicine and the Public Interest,* 184–185.

65. Committee on the Costs of Medical Care, *Medical Care for the American People,* 152–153.

66. Stevens, *American Medicine and the Public Interest,* 186.

67. Ibid., 187.

68. *Journal of the American Medical Association* 99 (1932): 2035.

69. Stevens, *American Medicine and the Public Interest,* 187–188.

70. Isadore S. Falk, "The Committee on the Costs of Medical Care—Twenty-Five Years of Progress," *American Journal of Public Health* 48 (Aug. 1958): 979–982.

71. Margaret C. Klem, "Twenty-Five Years of Research in Medical Economics," *American Journal of Public Health* 48 (Aug. 1958): 995–1002.

72. I. S. Falk, M. C. Klem, and N. Sinai, *The Incidence of Illness and the Receipt and Costs of Medical Care among Representative Family Groups.* Committee on the Costs of Medical Care, publication no. 26 (Chicago: University of Chicago Press, 1933).

73. Falk, "Committee on the Costs," 982.

74. Throughout this section the discussion is influenced and draws from the most complete account of the Ogburn Committee that I have been able to find: Barry D. Karl, "Presidential Planning and Social Science Research: Mr. Hoover's Experts," in Donald Fleming and Bernard Bailyn, ed., *Perspectives in American History,* vol. 3 (Cambridge, Mass.: Charles Warren Center for American Studies, 1969), 347–409.

75. Karl, "Presidential Planning," 394.

76. Ibid., 365.

77. Ibid.

78. Social Science Research Council Archives, Accession 1, series 5, Rockefeller Archive Center, Sleepy Hollow, N.Y. See for index www.rockefeller.edu/archive.ctr/ssrc.html.

79. Paul F. Lazarsfeld and Jeffrey G. Reitz, *An Introduction to Applied Sociology* (New York: Elsevier, 1975), 5.

80. Karl, "Presidential Planning," 368.

81. Ibid., 373.

82. The Laura Spelman Rockefeller Memorial Archives, series 3, no. 6, Rockefeller Archive Center, Sleepy Hollow, N.Y. See entry for 1931, p. 12.

83. Karl, "Presidential Planning," 356.

84. Odum's social research institute at the University of North Carolina accounted for three chapters: T. J. Woofter, Jr., "The Status of Racial and Ethnic Groups"; Clarence Heer, Taxation and Public Finance"; and Odum, "Public Welfare Activities." Mitchell's influence can be seen in the selection of Edwin F. Gay and Leo Wolman for "Trends in Economic Organizations," as well as in Wolman, "Labor Groups in the Social Structure" (with Gustav Peck) and Robert S. Lynd, "The People as Consumers" (with Alice C. Hanson). Merriam, Ogburn, and the "Chicago School" are reflected in Leonard White, "Public Administration," Carroll Wooddy, "The Growth of Governmental Functions," Charles H. Judd, "Education," Edwin H. Sutherland and C. E. Gehlke, "Crime and Punishment," S. P. Breckinridge, "The Activities of Women Outside the Home,"

two chapters by Ogburn, "The Influence of Invention and Discovery" and "The Family and Its Functions" (with Clark Tibbitts), and Merriam's concluding chapter, "Government and Society." A solid representation of the new foundation executives also appear: Lawrence K. Frank of the General Education Board of the Rockefeller Foundation ("Childhood and Youth"), Frederick P. Keppel of the Carnegie Corporation ("The Arts in Social Life"), and Sydnor H. Walker of the Rockefeller Foundation ("Privately Supported Social Work"). See Ogburn, *Recent Social Trends.*

85. Karl, "Presidential Planning," 381–382.

86. Ibid., 390. The Ogburn Papers are cited.

87. Falk, "Proposals," 166.

88. In Ogburn, *Recent Social Trends,* 1062.

89. Karl, "Presidential Planning," cited by Lazarsfeld and Reitz, *Introduction to Applied Sociology,* 6.

90. Ibid., 5–6.

91. Ibid., 6.

92. Falk, "Proposals," 168.

Chapter 4

1. Robert E. L. Faris, *Chicago Sociology, 1920–1932* (San Francisco: Chandler, 1967), 12,128. Short 1971), xiv.

2. Fred H. Mathews, *Quest for an American Sociology: Robert E. Park and the Chicago School* (Montreal: McGill-Queens University Press, 1977), 95.

3. Interview of Milton Terris, M.D., by the author, July 7, 1982.

4. Don Martindale, "American Sociology before World War II," *Annual Review of Sociology* 2 (1976):140.

5. Robert E. Park and Ernest W. Burgess, *Introduction to the Science of Sociology* (Chicago: University of Chicago Press, 1924).

6. Ibid., 137.

7. James F. Short, *Social Fabric of the Metropolis: Contributions of the Chicago School of Urban Sociology* (Chicago: University of Chicago Press, 1971), xii.

8. Mathews, *Quest for American Sociology,* 87–88.

9. Ibid., 88.

10. Ibid., 89.

11. Bernhard Stern, "Lester F. Ward," in *Encyclopedia of the Social Sciences* (New York: Macmillan, 1933), 171. Herman Schwendinger and Julia R. Schwendinger, *The Sociologists of the Chair: A Radical Analysis of the Formative Years of North American Sociology, 1883–1922* (New York: Basic Books, 1974), 238.

12. Schwendinger and Schwendinger, *Sociologists of the Chair,* 238.

13. Mathews, *Quest for American Sociology,* 90.

14. Ibid., 97.

15. Ibid., 102.

16. Quoted in ibid., 102. See *New York Times,* April 13, p. 9. See also follow-up articles, Sept. 14, 15, 16, and 18, 1918.

17. Ibid., 4.

18. Telephone interview by the author with H. Warren Dunham, August 6, 1982.

19. Faris, *Chicago Sociology,* 64.

20. Ibid., 84.

21. Robert E. L. Faris, "The Development of the Philosophy Underlying the Durkheim School of Social Theory" (M.A. thesis, University of Chicago, 1930).

22. Faris, *Chicago Sociology,* 85.

23. H. Warren Dunham, *Sociological Theory and Mental Disorder* (Detroit: Wayne State University Press, 1959), 117.

24. Ibid., 273, n.8.

25. Ibid., 116.

26. Eleanor Leacock, "Three Social Variables and the Occurrence of Mental Disorder," in Alexander H. Leighton, John A. Clausen, and Robert N. Wilson, eds., *Explorations in Social Psychiatry* (New York: Basic Books, 1957), 311.

27. Paul V. Lemkau, Christopher Tietze, and M. Cooper, "A Survey of Statistical Studies on the Prevalence and Incidence of Mental Disorder in Sample Populations," *Public Health Reports* 58 (1943): 1909–1927. Christopher Tietze, P. Lemkau, and M. Cooper, "Schizophrenia, Manic Depressive Psychosis, and Social-economic Status," *American Journal of Sociology* 48 (1941): 167–175, "Personality Disorder and Social Mobility, *American Journal of Sociology* 48 (July 1942): 29.

28. Leacock, "Three Social Variables," 314.

29. Melvin Seeman, "An Evaluation of Current Approaches to Personality Differences in Folk and Urban Societies," *Social Forces* 25 (1946): 160–165. See also Leacock, "Three Social Variables," 320–321.

30. Edwin M. Lemert, "An Exploratory Study of Mental Disorders in a Rural Problem Area," *Rural Sociology* 13 (1949):48–64.

31. Dunham, *Sociological Theory and Mental Disorder*, 117.

32. Ibid., 117–118.

33. Ibid., 148.

34. Ibid., 133.

35. William J. Goode, *Explorations in Social Theory* (New York: Oxford University Press, 1973), 426.

36. Leacock, "Three Social Variables," 321.

37. Paul F. Lazarsfeld and Jeffrey G. Reitz, *An Introduction to Applied Sociology* (New York: Elsevier, 1975), 2; Pauline Young, *Scientific Social Surveys and Research* (Englewood Cliffs, N.J.: Prentice-Hall, 1946).

38. Harry Stack Sullivan, "Socio-Psychiatric Research: Its Implications for the Schizophrenia Problem and for Mental Hygiene," *American Journal of Psychiatry* 10 (1931):977–991, "The Modified Psychoanalytic Treatment of Schizophrenia," *American Journal of Psychiatry*, 11 (1931): 519–540.

39. Alfred H. Stanton wrote: "(White) and others helped to make the hospital a center for the attempt to reorganize psychiatric thought and practice on psychoanalytic and psychological principles. While Sullivan's duties were only those of a consultant, he had diagnostic interviews with a large number of schizophrenic patients, and his ability to reach patients who had been thought beyond contact was soon recognized. He became progressively convinced that the interviews he had as a consultant had important effects upon the patient and could not, therefore, be sharply distinguished from treatment" ("Harry Stack Sullivan: Life and Work," in David L. Sills, ed., *International Encyclopedia of the Social Sciences*, vol. 15 [New York: Macmillan, 1968], 396).

40. Ibid., 397.

41. Ibid.

42. Hadley Cantril, ed., *Tensions that Cause Wars* (Urbana: University of Illinois Press, 1950), 135–136.

43. Stanton, 397.

44. Clifford W. Beers, *A Mind That Found Itself* (New York: Longmans Green, 1908; reprint, Garden City, N.Y.: Doubleday, 1956). Beers founded the National Committee for Mental Hygiene (NCMH). For background on Beers and NCMH, see Gerald N. Grob, *Mental Health and American Society, 1875–1940* (Princeton, N.Y.: Princeton University Press), chapter 6.

45. William Seabrook, *Asylum* (New York: Harcourt, Brace, 1935).

46. J. D. Kerkhoff, *How Thin the Veil: A Newspaperman's Story of His Own Mental Crackup and Recovery* (New York: Chilton Books, 1952).

47. Mary Jane Ward, *The Snakepit* (New York: Signet Books, 1955).

48. Janet Frame, *Faces in the Water* (New York: Brazilier, 1961).

49. Howard Rowland, "Interaction Processes in a State Mental Hospital, *Psychiatry* 1 (1938): 323–337, and "Friendship Patterns in a State Mental Hospital," *Psychiatry* 2 (1939): 363–371.

50. George Devereux, "The Social Structure of a Schizophrenic Ward and Its Therapeutic Fitness," *Journal of Clinical Psychopathology and Psychotherapy* 6 (1944): 231–265.

51. Edmund H. Volkart, ed., *Social Behavior and Personality: Contributions of W. I. Thomas to Theory and Social Research* (New York: Social Science Research Council, 1951), 65; Helen Swick Perry, *The Fusion of Psychiatry and Social Science* (New York: Norton, 1964), xiii–xiv.

52. Patrick Mullahy, *Psychoanalysis and Interpersonal Psychiatry: The Contributions of Harry Stack Sullivan* (New York: Science House, 1970), 399.

53. Orville G. Brim and Stanton Wheeler, *Socialization after Childhood: Two Essays* (New York: Wiley, 1966); Daniel J. Levinson and Eugene B. Gallagher, *Patienthood in the Mental Hospital* (Boston: Houghton Mifflin, 1964).

54. Perry, *Fusion of Psychiatry and Social Science*, xv.

55. Ibid., xvii.

56. Ibid., xvii.

57. Ibid., xvii–xviii.

58. Ibid., xxiii.

59. *Proceedings: First Colloquium on Personality Investigation* (Baltimore: Lord Baltimore Press, 1929), and *Proceedings: Second Colloquium on Personality and Second Colloquium on Personality Investigation* (Baltimore: Johns Hopkins University Press, 1930), 204.

60. Perry, *Fusion of Psychiatry and Social Science*, xxix.

61. Rowland, "Interaction Processes" and "Friendship Patterns."

62. Rowland, "Interaction Processes," 323.

63. Ibid., 325.

64. Samuel W. Bloom, *The Doctor and His Patient* (New York: Russell Sage Foundation, 1963), 204–205.

Chapter 5

1. Patricia Madoo Lengermann, "The Founding of the *American Sociological Review*: The Anatomy of a Rebellion," *American Sociological Review* 44 (1979): 185–186; Henrika Kuklick, "A 'Scientific Revolution': Sociological Theory in the United States 1930–1945," *Sociological Inquiry* 43 (1973): 3–22.

2. Transcript of an interview by the author with Robert K. Merton, December 1, 1980, 19.

3. Bernhard J. Stern, *Historical Sociology: The Selected Papers of Bernhard J. Stern.* (New York: Citadel Press, 1959), xi.

4. Bernard Barber, ed. *L. J. Henderson on the Social System* (Chicago: University of Chicago Press, 1970), 40.

5. Susan Reverby and David Rosner, *Health Care in America: Essays in Social History* (Philadelphia: Temple University Press, 1979), 10.

6. Susan Reverby, personal communication, August 15, 1978, cited in Ibid., 15, n. 38.

7. Interview by the author with Milton Terris, July 12, 1982. See also Reverby and Rosner, *Health Care in America,* 10, where Stern is also called "the father of medical sociology."

8. Until recently, Henderson received little attention in medical sociology, with a few exceptions. Only Barber, *L. J. Henderson on the Social System*, described his con-

tributions full-scale. Two important works have corrected this neglect, at least in part: John Langone, *Harvard Med* (New York: Crown, 1995), 25–44; and John Pascandola, "L. J. Henderson and the Mutual Dependence of Variables: From Physical Chemistry to Pareto," in Clark A. Elliott and Margaret W. Rossiter, ed., *Science at Harvard: Historical Perspectives* (Bethlehem, Pa.: Lehigh University Press, 1992), 167–190. In the same volume, see also Lawrence T. Nichols, "The Establishment of Sociology at Harvard: A Case of Organizational Ambivalence and Scientific Vulnerability," 191–222.

9. Talcott Parsons, *The Structure of Social Action.* (New York: McGraw-Hill, 1937); Talcott Parsons, *The Social System* (Glencoe, Ill.: Free Press, 1951).

10. See Langone, *Harvard Med*, 33.

11. Bronislaw Malinowski, *Argonauts of the Western Pacific* (London, 1922), *The Sexual Life of Savages* (London, 1929), and *Sex and Repression in Savage Society* (London, 1955).

12. Lawrence J. Henderson, "The Physician and Patient as a Social System," *New England Journal of Medicine* 212 (1935):819–823, and *Pareto's General Sociology: A Physiologist's Interpretation* (Cambridge: Harvard University Press, 1937).

13. George C. Homans and Charles P. Curtis, Jr., *An Introduction to Pareto: An Introduction to His Sociology* (New York: Knopf, 1934).

14. Henry A. Murray, *Explorations in Personality: A Clinical and Experimental Study of Fifty Men of College Age* (New York: Oxford University Press, 1938). Murray dedicated this, one of his most important books, to a select list of his most important intellectual teachers: Morton Prince, Sigmund Freud, Lawrence J. Henderson, Alfred N. Whitehead, and Carl G. Jung. Next to Henderson's name he wrote: "whose expositions of scientific procedure established a methodological standard."

15. Barber, *L. J. Henderson on the Social System*, 10.

16. Alvin W. Gouldner, *The Coming Crisis of Western Sociology* (New York: Basic Books, 1970), 149–151.

17. Ibid., 149.

18. This section draws liberally from Barber, *L. J. Henderson on the Social System.*

19. Merton interview.

20. Barber, *L. J. Henderson on the Social System,* 3.

21. Arlie Bock, "Lawrence Joseph Henderson, 1878–1942," *Transactions of the Association of American Physicians* 57 (1942): 17.

22. Lawrence J. Henderson, *The Order of Nature* (Cambridge: Harvard University Press, 1917).

23. Cynthia Eagle Russett, 1966. *The Concept of Equilibrium in American Social Thought* (New Haven: Yale University Press, 1966).

24. Bock, "Henderson," 18.

25. Barber, *L. J. Henderson on the Social System,* 5.

26. Russett, *Concept of Equilibrium,* 117.

27. Barber, *L. J. Henderson on the Social System,* 5–6; Fritz J. Roethlisberger and William J. Dickson, *Management and the Worker* (Cambridge: Harvard University Press, 1939).

28. Cambridge: Harvard University Press. See also Barnard, introduction to L. J. Henderson, "*Introductory Lectures in Concrete Sociology,*" unpublished manuscript edited by Chester Barnard, Henderson Papers, School of Business, Harvard University, 1–49, especially 39.

29. The National Research Council (NRC) is an operating arm of the National Academy of Sciences (NAS). It was formed in 1916 and became an effective means for the academy to work with the professional associations of various sciences and social sciences. Henderson's survey was reported in the NRC report to the NAS, published in Washington, D.C., 1941. For history and analysis of the NRC, see Gene M. Lyons, *The Uneasy Partnership: Social Science and the Federal Government in the Twentieth Century* (New York: Russell Sage Foundation, 1969).

30. Robert Straus, "Becoming and Being a Behavioral Scientist," in Ray H. Elling and Magdalena Sokolowska, ed., *Medical Sociologists at Work* (New Brunswick, N.J.: Transaction Books, 1978), 313. Straus, writing about his career as a medical sociologist, describes his first full-time job after receiving his Ph.D. degree: "Job opportunities in 1947 were available in a metropolitan department of sociology, a medical school department of public health and in Yale's Department of Applied Physiology. For pure excitement, stimulation and opportunity, there seemed to be no choice but to remain at Yale. Howard W. Haggard, famed physiologist and medical historian, had assembled in his Laboratory of Applied Physiology one of the few truly interdisciplinary groups in the academic world. Physiology, pharmacology, biochemistry, medicine, psychiatry, psychology, anthropology, law, economics, biometrics, education and theology were all represented and a sociology group headed by Seldon Bacon, one of my most stimulating teachers."

31. Crane Brinton, ed., *The Society of Fellows* (Cambridge: Harvard University Press, 1939), 1–37. Barber describes the Society and Henderson's role in its establishment: the Society, which Henderson started thinking about as early as 1924, was finally established in 1933 with an endowment from President Lowell, to provide a prestigious place and adequate resources in the university for young men of exceptional talent and independence in any field of science and scholarship. In the small group responsible for founding the Society—Henderson, Lowell, the philosopher A. N. Whitehead, the English literature scholar John Livingston Lowes, and the lawyer and author Charles P. Curtis—Henderson took the lead; his conception of the Society was scientifically cosmopolitan, if somewhat elitist, and he was the organizer of the founding committee, the author of its founding report, and finally, the first chairman of the senior fellows of the Society, who were responsible for the selection and minor guidance of the junior fellows. . . . Henderson . . . hoped that the Society would encourage not only "isolated geniuses, but men who will do the work of the world" (Barber, *L. J. Henderson on the Social System*, 7).

32. Merton interview.

33. George C. Homans and Orville T. Bailey, "The Society of Fellows, Harvard University, 1943–1947," in Brinton, *The Society of Fellows*, 3–4.

34. Barber, *L. J. Henderson on the Social System*, 8.

35. Ibid.

36. Ibid.

37. Homans and Bailey, "Society of Fellows," 3.

38. Gouldner, *The Coming Crisis*, 149.

39. Ibid., 144–145.

40. Ibid., 92.

41. Ibid., 92.

42. Ibid., 101.

43. Anthony Oberschall, ed., *The Establishment of Empirical Sociology: Studies in Continuity, Discontinuity, and Institutionalization* (New York: Harper and Row, 1972). Joseph Ben-David and Randall Collins, "Social Factors in the Origin of a New Science," *American Sociological Review* 31 (1966): 451–465. See also Joseph Ben-David and Avraham Sloczower, "Universities and Academic Systems in Modern Societies," *Archives of European Sociology* 3: 45–84.

44. Gouldner, *The Coming Crisis*, 116.

45. Ibid., 135.

46. Ibid., 135.

47. Ibid., 136.

48. Lengermann, "Founding of the *American Sociological Review*," 186.

49. Ibid., 186; Robert E. L. Faris, *Chicago Sociology, 1920–1932* (San Francisco: Chandler, 1967), 121–122.

50. Don Martindale, "American Sociology before World War II," in Alex Inkeles, ed., *Annual Review of Sociology*, vol. 2 (Palo Alto: Annual Reviews, 1976).

51. Kuklick, "A 'Scientific Revolution.' "

52. "Founding of the *American Sociological Review*," 195–196.

53. Barber, *L. J. Henderson on the Social System*, 29.

54. Henderson, "Physician and Patient," 821.

55. Ibid.

56. Barber, *L. J. Henderson on the Social System*, 34–35.

57. *The Social System*, 428–479.

58. Ibid.

59. Lawrence J. Henderson, "The Practice of Medicine as Applied Sociology," *Transactions of the Association of American Physicians* (1936): 3.

60. Ibid., 13.

61. For more details on Stern's life and work, see Samuel W. Bloom, "The Intellectual in a Time of Crisis: The Case of Bernhard J. Stern, 1894–1956," *Journal of the History of the Behavioral Sciences* 26 (1990): 17–37. This section draws material directly from that article.

62. Bernhard J. Stern, *Should We Be Vaccinated? A Survey of the Controversy in its Historical and Scientific Aspects* (New York: Harper and Brothers, 1927), *Social Factors in Medical Progress* (New York: Columbia University Press, 1927), *Lewis Henry Morgan: Social Evolutionist* (Chicago: University of Chicago Press, 1931), *The Lummi Indians of Northwest Washington* (New York: Columbia University Press, 1934, *The Family: Past and Present* (New York: Appleton Century, 1938), *Society and Medical Progress* (Princeton: Princeton University Press, 1941), *American Medical Practice in the Perspective of a Century* (New York: Commonwealth Fund, 1945), *Medicine in Industry* (New York: Commonwealth Fund, 1946), *Medical Services by Government* (New York: Commonwealth Fund, 1946). Coauthored: with Michael M. Davis, *The Health of a Nation* (Washington, D.C.: National Education Association, 1943); with Michael M. Davis, *The Health of a Century* (New York: Commonwealth Fund, 1945); with Melville Jacobs, *General Anthropology*, 2nd ed. (New York: Barnes and Noble, 1952); with Alain Le Roy Locke, *When Peoples Meet: A Study of Race and Culture Contacts*, rev. ed. (New York: Hyde, Hayden and Eldridge, 1946).

63. See Samuel W. Bloom, "Intellectual in a Time of Crisis," for a detailed review of this part of Stern's story.

64. Throughout this section, I am indebted to Stern's widow, Charlotte Todes Stern, whom I interviewed in May 1984. Previously, little information was available about Stern's early life.

65. Stern, *Social Factors*.

66. For example, *Journal of the American Medical Association* 89 (1927): 715 and *American Journal of Medical Sciences* 174 (1927): 544.

67. Reverby and Rosner, *Health Care in America*, 8.

68. Ibid., 10, quoting from an interview, on June 24, 1978, by Reverby of Charlotte Stern, quoting Robert K. Merton.

69. Robert K. Merton, *Science, Technology, and Society in Seventeenth Century England* (Cambridge: Harvard University Press, 1938; reprint, New York: Harper and Rowe, 1970).

70. Norman Storer, ed., *Robert K. Merton: The Sociology of Science, Theoretical and Empirical Investigation* (Chicago: University of Chicago Press, 1973), 39.

71. Ibid.

72. Bernhard J. Stern, Historical Sociology: Selected Papers of Bernhard J. Stern (New York: Citadel Press, 1979), 362.

73. Merton, in Storer, *Robert K. Merton*, 39n., 316n., and 372n.

74. Terris interview.

75. References can be found in note 65.

76. *American Medical Practice, Medicine in Industry, Medical Services by Government*.

77. Charlotte Stern provided this description of Stern's experience at City College. Further evidence of the truth of this testimony is found in letters from colleagues from Columbia and the New School in the Meiklejohn Archive, section 8, file folders 121–123. See also Bloom, "Intellectual in a Time of Crisis," n.23.

78. Interview with Charlotte Stern; papers from Meiklejohn Institute Archives.

79. Meiklejohn Collection, section 11, files 002–007.

80. A separate edition was published in London by London Scientific Book Club in 1944. My interpretation is that the Committee on Research in Medical Economics was created by the Julius Rosenwald Fund, of which Davis was an officer. For more information, see the Archives of Michael M. Davis, New York Academy of Medicine, box 55, file drawer J-43.

81. T. J. McKeown, *The Role of Medicine: Dream, Mirage, or Nemesis?* (Oxford: Blackwell, 1979), and *Medicine in Modern Society* (London: Routledge and Kegan Paul, 1965).

82. *Society and Medical Progress,* 215.

83. Terris interview of July 12, 1982.

84. Straus, "Becoming and Being," 312. See also interview by the author with Straus, June 2, 1977, available at the American Sociological Association Archives, Pennsylvania State University, Pa.

85. Interview by the author with Jerome Myers, January 14, 1983.

86. Paul F. Lazarsfeld and Wagner Thielens, Jr., *The Academic Mind: Social Scientists in a Time of Crisis* (Glencoe, Ill.: Free Press, 1958). See also David Caute, *The Great Fear: The Anti-Communist Purge under Truman and Eisenhower* (New York: Simon and Schuster, 1978), and Ellen W. Schrecker, *No Ivory Tower: McCarthyism and the Universities* (New York: Oxford University Press, 1986).

87. Henry E. Sigerist, *Henry E. Sigerist: Autobiographical Writings*, selected and translated by Nora Sigerist Beeson (Montreal: McGill University Press, 1966).

88. See Bloom, "Intellectual in a Time of Crisis."

89. Reproduction of "Preliminary Report of Committee on Conference," addressed to President Kirk (Columbia University) on June 4, 1953, p. 1, in Meiklejohn Collection, F.6 021.

90. Reverby and Rosner, *Health Care in America,* 9.

91. Sigerist's successor at Zurich, Erwin Ackerknecht, is a good example. After receiving his M.D. in Germany in the late twenties, Ackerknecht studied for his Ph.D. in anthropology at the Sorbonne. A protege of Sigerist, Ackerknecht developed as his specialty the history of primitive medicine. Brought to the United States in the late thirties, Ackerknecht filled a chair in the history of medicine at the University of Wisconsin for almost two decades, writing a series of articles on primitive medicine and three books on more general medical subjects. Throughout his work, there is a highly developed sociological frame of reference. Yet beyond a small circle of historical scholars, he is relatively little known. Among medical sociology's best-known textbooks, for example, Ackerknecht, like Stern, typically receives not a single mention.

92. Albert Deutsch, *The Mentally Ill of America: A History of Their Care, and Treatment from Colonial Times* (New York: Columbia University Press, 1949); Richard H. Shryock, *The Development of Modern Medicine* (New York: Knopf, 1942).

93. George Rosen, *Madness in Society; Chapters in the Historical Sociology of Mental Illness* (Chicago: University of Chicago Press, 1968), and *From Medical Police to Social Medicine* (New York: Watson Academic, 1974) Brian Abel-Smith, *A History of the Nursing Profession* (London: Heinemann, 1960), *The Hospitals* (London: Heinemann, 1964).

94. Eliot Freidson, *Profession of Medicine* (New York: Dodd, Mead, 1970).

95. Rosemary Stevens, *Medical Practice in Modern England* (New Haven: Yale University Press, 1966), *American Medicine and the Public Interest* (New Haven: Yale

University Press, 1971). Robert Stevens and Rosemary Stevens, *A Case Study of Medicaid* (New York: Free Press, 1974).

96. Rosemary Stevens, *In Sickness and in Wealth* (New York: Basic Books, 1989).

97. George Rosen, "The Evolution of Social Medicine," in Howard Freeman, Sol Levine and Leo G. Reeder, eds., *Handbook of Medical Sociology,* 3rd. ed. (Englewood Cliffs, N.J.: Prentice Hall, 1979).

98. Bonnie Bullough and Vern I. Bullough, *Poverty, Ethnic Identity, and Health Care* (New York: Appleton-Crofts, 1972).

99. Renee Fox and Judith P. Swazey, *The Courage to Fail: A Social View of Organ Transplants and Dialysis* (Chicago: University of Chicago Press, 1974).

100. Vicente Navarro, *Class Struggle, the State, and Medicine* (New York: Prodist, 1978).

101. Howard Waitzkin, *The Second Sickness: Contradictions of Capitalist Health Care* (New York: Free Press, 1983).

102. Some examples are Elliot A. Krause, *Power and Illness* (New York: Elsevier, 1977); E. Richard Brown, *Rockefeller Medicine Men: Medicine Capitalism in America* (Berkeley, Calif. University of California Press, 1979); Barbara and John Ehrenreich, *The American Health Empire: Power, Profits, and Politics* (New York: Vintage Books, 1970).

103. Rosen, *From Medical Police to Social Medicine,* 116.

104. George A. Silver, *Family Medical Care: A Design for Health Maintenance* (Cambridge, Mass.: Ballinger, 1974), 7.

105. Thomas McKeown, "Historical Perspectives on Science and Health," presented at the Annual Meeting of the Academy of Medicine, National Academy of Sciences, Washington, D.C., March 27, 1976. See Donald L. Patrick and Jack Elinson, "Methods of Sociomedical Research," in Freeman, Levine, and Reeder, *Handbook of Medical Sociology,* 441.

106. Silver, *Family Medical Care,* 300, n.11.

107. Through Leo Srole, I discovered after this was written that Merton uses a similar metaphor to describe medicine more generally: "In historical fact medicine is at heart a polygamist becoming wedded to as many of the sciences and practical arts as prove their worth." Robert K. Merton, George G. Reader, and Patricia L. Kendall, *The Student-Physician: Introductory Studies in the Sociology of Medical Education* (Cambridge: Harvard University Press, 1957), 32; Srole, transcript of interview by the author, 1977.

Chapter 6

1. Steven J. Peitzman, "Forgotten Reformers: The American Academy of Medicine," *Bulletin of the History of Medicine* 58(1984): 516– 528. See also James L. McCartney, "Medical Sociology: A Case Study of a Special Area Receiving Much Support," in James L. McCartney, "The Support of Sociological Research: Trends and Consequences" (Ph.D. diss., University of Minnesota, 1965): 142–157.

2. Bernhard Stern was also a Visiting Professor at Yale for one year in 1944–45 and taught a course in the sociology of medicine. See Robert Straus, "Becoming and Being a Behavioral Scientist," in Ray H. Elling and Magda Sokolowska, eds., *Medical Sociologists at Work* (New Brunswick, N.J.: Transaction Books, 1978), 312.

3. Jack Elinson, "City Slums to Sociosalustics," in Elling and Sokolowska, *Medical Sociologists at Work,* 32; interview by the author of August B. Hollingshead, August 4, 1978.

4. Robin F. Badgley and Samuel W. Bloom, "Behavioral Sciences and Medical Education: The Case of Sociology," *Social Science and Medicine* 7 (1973): 927–942 (see

933); Straus, "Becoming and Being," 319; and interview by the author with Hollingshead, August 4, 1978.

5. Gene M. Lyons, *The Uneasy Partnership: Social Science and the Federal Government in the Twentieth Century* (New York: Russell Sage Foundation, 1969), 80–193.

6. Jaco published the first issue as the *Journal of Health and Human Behavior* in 1959.

7. See, for complete list, Anne G. Montegna, ed., *Guide to Federal Funding for Social Scientists* (Washington, D.C.: American Political Science Association, 1990). See Kenneth G. Lutterman, "Research Training from the Perspective of Government Funding," in N. J. Demerath, Otto Larson, and K. F. Schuessler, eds., *Social Policy and Sociology* (New York: Academic Press, 1975); Richard H. Williams, "The Strategy of Sociomedical Research," in Howard E. Freeman, Sol Levine, and Leo G. Reeder, *Handbook of Medical Sociology* (Englewood Cliffs, N.J.: Prentice-Hall, 1963), 423–448. These agencies are only the major federal sources of support for medical sociology. Project support for individual research and training are a standard part of other agencies of the National Institutes of Health and the National Science Foundation.

8. See Sharon N. Barnartt, "A Review of Medical Sociology Textbooks," *Teaching Sociology: Special Issue on Medical Sociology* 18 (1990): 372–376; Steven P. Wallace, "Institutionalizing Divergent Approaches in the Sociology of Health and Healing: A Review of Medical Sociology Readers," *Teaching Sociology: Special Issue on Medical Sociology* 18 (1990): 377–384; W. C. Cockerham, *Medical Sociology,* 7th ed. (Englewood Cliffs, N.J.: Prentice Hall, 1998); Chloe Bird, Peter Conrad, and Allen Fremont, eds., *Handbook of Medical Sociology,* 5th ed. (Englewood Cliffs, N.J.: Prentice Hall, 2000); Gary L. Albrecht, Ray Fitzpatrick, and Susan C. Scrimshaw, *The Handbook of Social Studies in Health and Medicine* (London: Sage, 2000).

9. Edward Shils, "Tradition, Ecology and Institution in the History of Sociology," *Daedalus* 99 (fall 1970): 760–825; Joseph Ben-David and Randall Collins, "Social Factors in the Origins of a New Science," *American Sociological Review* 31, 4 (1966): 451–465.

10. Robert K., Merton, George G. Reader, and Patricia L. Kendall, ed., *The Student-Physician: Introductory Studies in the Sociology of Medical Education* (Cambridge: Harvard University Press, 1957). Howard S. Becker et al., *Boys in White: Student Culture in Medical School* (Chicago: University of Chicago Press, 1961).

11. Robert Straus, "The Nature and Status of Medical Sociology," *American Sociological Review* 22 (1957): 200–204.

12. Franklin G. Ebaugh and Charles A. Rymer, *Psychiatry in Medical Education* (New York: Oxford University Press, 1942).

13. Rosemary Stevens, *American Medicine and the Public Interest* (New Haven: Yale University Press, 1971), 330–331.

14. The AAMC is the foremost professional association of medical education, matching the prestige of the American Medical Association, which represents clinical medicine.

15. Norman Cameron, "Human Ecology and Personality in the Training of Physicians," in *Psychiatry and Medical Education: Report of the 1951 Conference on Psychiatric Education* (Washington, D.C.: American Psychiatric Association, 1952), 64–66.

16. *Preventive Medicine and Medical Education: Report of the 1952 Conference on Preventive Medicine Education* (Washington, D.C.: Association of American Medical Colleges, 1953), 6–7.

17. Paul Lazarsfeld and Jeffrey G. Reitz, *An Introduction to Applied Sociology* (New York: Elsevier, 1975), 6.

18. Ibid., 6.

19. Lazarsfeld and Reitz, *Introduction to Applied Sociology,* 7.

20. Merton, Reader, and Kendall, *The Student-Physician.*

21. Nora Sigerist Beeson, *Henry E. Sigerist: Autobiographical Writings* (Montreal: McGill University Press, 1966), 192–215.

22. See chapter 3.

23. James G. Burrow, *AMA: Voice of American Medicine* (Baltimore: Johns Hopkins University Press, 1963). American Medical Association, Bureau of Medical Economics, *Group Practice* (Chicago: American Medical Association, 1933); Michael M. Davis, *Medical Care for Tomorrow* (New York: Harper, 1955).

24. I. S. Falk, "Proposals for National Health Insurance in the U.S.A.: Origins and Evolution, and Some Perceptions for the Future," *Milbank Memorial Quarterly* 55, 2 (1977): 168.

25. Ibid., 168–169.

26. Ibid., 169.

27. Ibid., 170.

28. For details, see particularly Gerald N. Grob, *Mental Health and American Society* (Princeton: Princeton University Press, 1983); also Samuel W. Bloom, *The Doctor and His Patient: A Sociological Interpretation* (New York: Russell Sage Foundation, 1963; paperback ed., New York: Free Press, 1965), 20–23.

29. Merton, Reader, and Kendall, *The Student-Physician,* 62.

30. Stouffer et al., *Studies in Social Psychology.*

31. Ibid., vol. 1, 12.

32. Edward A. Shils and Morris Janowitz, "Cohesion and Disintegration in the Wehrmacht in World War II," *Public Opinion Quarterly* 12 (1948): 280–315.

33. Eli Ginzberg et al., *The Ineffective Soldier: Breakdown and Recovery* (New York: Columbia University Press, 1959).

34. Elinson, "City Slums to Sociosalustics," 32.

35. Ibid., 32.

36. Ibid., 32–33.

37. Alexander Leighton, *My Name Is Legion* (New York: Basic Books, 1959); Dorothea C. Leighton et al., *Character of Danger: Psychiatric Symptoms in Selected Communities* (New York: Basic Books, 1963).

38. Leo Srole et al., *Mental Health in the Metropolis: The Midtown Manhattan Study* (New York: McGraw-Hill, 1962). Thomas Langner and Stanley T. Michael. *Life Stress and Mental Health* (New York: Free Press, 1963).

39. Personal interview by the author, July 23, 1977.

40. Cantril, *The Human Dimension,* 53–54; Lazarsfeld and Reitz, *Introduction to Applied Sociology,* 81.

41. Lazarsfeld and Reitz, *Introduction to Applied Sociology,* 86.

42. Ibid.

43. R. M. Dalfiume, *Desegregation in the U.S. Armed Forces* (Columbia: University of Missouri Press, 1969), 78–79.

44. Ibid., 78–79.

45. Ibid., 149.

46. Stouffer et al., *Studies in Social Psychology,* vol. 1, 100.

47. Ibid.

48. Dalfiume, *Desegregation.*

49. R. Davenport, "The Negro in the Army—A Subject of Research," *Journal of Social Issues* 3 (1947): 36.

50. Lazarsfeld and Reitz, *Introduction to Applied Sociology,* 152.

51. Ibid., 7.

52. C. Wright Mills, *The Power Elite* (New York: Oxford University Press, 1956), and *The Sociological Imagination* (New York: Oxford University Press, 1959).

53. Don Martindale, "American Sociology before World War II," in Alex Inkeles, James Coleman, and Neil Smelser, eds., *Annual Review of Sociology* 2 (1976): 140.

54. Edward Shils, *The Calling of Sociology* (Chicago: Chicago University Press, 1980), 118–119.

55. Ibid., 108–116.

56. Alvin W. Gouldner, *The Coming Crisis of Western Sociology* (New York: Basic Books, 1970), 141–142.

57. Gene M. Lyons, *The Uneasy Partnership: Social Science and the Federal Government in the Twentieth Century* (New York: Russell Sage Foundation, 1969), 48.

58. Ibid., 26.

59. Ibid., 28.

60. Ibid.; see also Robert M. Yerkes, *The New World of Science: Its Development during the War* (New York: Century, 1920), 351.

61. Lyons, *Uneasy Partnership*, 44.

62. Don K. Price, *Government and Science* (New York: New York University Press, 1954), and *The Scientific Estate* (Cambridge: Harvard University Press, 1965), 100.

63. Price, *The Scientific Estate*, 100–101.

64. Lyons, *Uneasy Partnership*, 13.

65. Shils, *The Calling of Sociology*, 120–122.

Chapter 7

1. August B. Hollingshead, *Elmtown's Youth* (New York: Wiley, 1949).

2. August B. Hollingshead and Frederich C. Redlich, *Social Class and Mental Illness* (New York: Wiley, 1958).

3. William Lloyd Warner and Leo Srole, *The Social System of American Ethnic Groups* (New Haven: Yale University Press, 1945 [vol. 3 of the Yankee City Series]).

4. Leo Srole et al., *Mental Health in the Metropolis: The Midtown Manhattan Study*, vol. 1 (New York: McGraw-Hill, 1962).

5. Interview by the author with August B. Hollingshead, August 4, 1978. Available in the files of the author; to be deposited in the Medical Sociology Archives, ASA, Pennsylvania State University, State College, Pa. See also Ray H. Elling and Magdalena Sokolowska, eds., *Medical Sociologists at Work* (New Brunswick, N.J.: Transaction Books, 1978).

6. Renee C. Fox, *Experiment Perilous* (Glencoe, Ill.: Free Press, 1959).

7. Renee C. Fox, "Training for Uncertainty," in Robert K. Merton, George G. Reader, and Patricia L. Kendall, eds., *The Student-Physician: Introductory Studies in the Sociology of Medical Education* (Cambridge: Harvard University Press, 1957), 207–241. Harold I. Lief and Renee C. Fox, "Training for Detached Concern," in Harold I. Lief, Victor F. Lief, and Nina R. Lief, eds., *The Psychological Basis of Medical Practice* (New York: Harper and Row, 1961), 12–35. Both articles are updated and reprinted in Renee Fox, *Essays in Medical Sociology* (New York: Wiley, 1979), 19–79.

8. Samuel A. Stouffer et al., *The American Soldier: Adjustment during Army Life*, vol. 1 of *Studies in Social Psychology in World War II* (Princeton: Princeton University Press, 1949).

9. Hollingshead and Redlich, *Social Class*.

10. There are three main sources for this brief description; first, John Parascandola, "L. J. Henderson and the Mutual Dependence of Variables from Physical Chemistry to Pareto," in Clark A. Elliott and Margaret W. Rossiter, ed., *Science at Harvard University: Historical Perspectives* (Bethlehem, Pa.: Lehigh University Press, 1992), 167–190; second, Robert Straus, "Becoming and Being a Behavioral Scientist," in Elling and Sokolowska, *Medical Sociologists at Work,* 313; and third, the author's interview with Eugene Brody, March, 1979.

11. Howard Odum, American Sociology: *The Story of Sociology in the United States through 1950* (New York: Greenwood, 1968), 45.

12. Leo W. Simmons, ed., *Sun Chief: The Autobiography of a Hopi Indian* (New Haven: Yale University Press, 1942).

13. Eugene B. Brody, "Maryland Psychiatry in the Context of a Personal Career," *Bulletin: University of Maryland School of Medicine* 61, 4 (1976): 4.

14. Eugene B. Brody, "Learning Social Psychiatry in the Medical School," *Yale Journal of Biology and Medicine* 51 (1977): 103. Brody offers a further explanation of Kahn's seemingly inconsistent attitude toward social science. "Eugen Kahn demonstrated in his choice of non-clinician scientist colleagues in his own department, his respect for the scholarly fields they represented. But he operated, nonetheless, an essentially closed system. He was unable to move toward a truly interdisciplinary study of social behavior and open his doors to the other inhabitants of the building at 333 Cedar Street, which had been optimistically named the Institute of Human Relations. The hints of a future social psychiatry in the Yale department were not made explicit and brought centrally into the stream of psychiatric teaching and research until Fritz Redlich became chairman" (104).

15. Ibid., 19.

16. Bernhard J. Stern, *American Medical Practice in the Perspective of a Century* (New York: Commonwealth Fund, 1945).

17. Straus, "Becoming and Being," 312.

18. Ibid.

19. Interview with Robert Straus by the author, June 2, 1977.

20. Interview with Jerome Myers, June 15, 1977.

21. Brody, "Learning Social Psychiatry," 103.

22. Ibid.

23. Leo W. Simmons and Harold G. Wolff, *Social Science in Medicine* (New York: Russell Sage Foundation, 1954).

24. The series of books were all published by the Russell Sage Foundation in New York. See works of Esther Lucile Brown listed in chapter 9, note 13. Further works included: *Lawyers, Law Schools, and the Public Service* in 1948; *Nursing for the Future*, a report prepared for the National Nursing Council, also in 1948; and *Physicians and Medical Care* in 1937—all three published in New York by the Russell Sage Foundation. After her retirement, one further work was *Nursing Reconsidered: A Study of Change* (Philadelphia: Lippincott, 1970).

25. Gene M. Lyons, *The Uneasy Partnership: Social Science and the Federal Government in the Twentieth Century* (New York: Russell Sage Foundation, 1969), 281.

26. Transcript of interview by the author with Esther Lucile Brown, November 3, 1981. Available in the author's files, to be deposited in the Medical Sociology Archives, ASA Archives, Pennsylvania State University, State College, Pa.

27. Ibid., 18.

28. Both are now emeritus professors, retired but still active.

29. Transcript of interview by the author with George Reader, June 28, 1977, 7.

30. Edmund H. Volkart, ed., *Social Behavior and Personality: Contributions of W. I. Thomas to Theory and Social Research* (New York: Social Science Research Council, 1951).

31. Transcript of interview by the author of Edmund Volkart, February 27, 1978.

32. Ibid., 4.

33. Alexander Leighton, John A. Clausen, and Robert N. Wilson, eds., *Explorations in Social Psychiatry* (New York: Basic Books, 1957).

34. Interview.

35. Edmund H. Volkart and Stanley T. Michael, "Bereavement and Mental Health," in Leighton et al., *Explorations*, 281–307.

36. Interview, 7–8.

37. Ibid., 8–9.

38. Straus, "Becoming and Being."

39. Interview.

40. Robert Straus, *Medical Care for Seamen: The Development of Public Health Services in the United States* (New Haven: Yale University Press, 1950).

41. Rosemary Stevens, *American Medicine and the Public Interest* (New Haven: Yale University Press, 1971).

42. Bernhard J. Stern, *Historical Sociology: The Collected Papers of Bernhard J. Stern* (New York: Citadel Press, 1959).

43. Straus interview.

44. Robert Straus, "Alcohol and the Homeless Man," *Quarterly Journal of Studies on Alcohol* 7 (1946): 360–404.

45. Straus, "Becoming and Being," 313–314.

46. Straus interview.

47. Straus, "Becoming and Being," 316.

48. Edward Stainbrook and Murray Wexler, "The Place of Behavioral Sciences in the Medical School," *Psychiatry* 19 (1956): 263.

49. Ibid., 266.

50. Ibid.

51. Straus interview.

52. Stainbrook and Wexler, "Place of Behavioral Sciences."

53. Interview by the author with Edward Stainbrook, November 7, 1981.

54. Interview.

55. Robert Straus, "Department of Behavioral Science," *Journal of Medical Education* 34 (1959): 666.

56. Straus, "Becoming and Being," 318–319.

57. Straus interview.

58. Ibid.

59. Ibid.

60. Hollingshead, *Elmtown's Youth.*

61. Maurice Davie, *Refugees in America* (New York: Harper and Bros., 1947).

62. Interview by the author with Frederick C. Redlich, March 1, 1983.

63. John Dollard, *Class and Caste in a Southern Town* (New Haven, Conn.: Yale University Press, 1937).

64. Interview.

65. The equivalent of American junior high school.

66. Interview.

67. Ibid.

68. All quotations from ibid.

69. Brody interview.

70. Ibid.

Chapter 8

1. Rosemary Stevens, 1971. *American Medicine and the Public Trust* (New Haven: Yale University Press, 1971), 358.

2. Ibid.

3. Ibid.

4. Ibid.; my emphasis.

5. This story is documented in E. de Brunner and J. Kolb, *Rural Sociology* (Boston: Houghton Mifflin, 1946).

6. Gene M. Lyons, *The Uneasy Partnership: Social Science and the Federal Government in the Twentieth Century* (New York: Russell Sage Foundation, 1969), 122: "When the war ended almost all the social science research programs were disbanded

and, even where they were retained or transformed, they were greatly reduced in size and in vitality. Demobilization and budget restrictions left little room for social science research, and the researchers themselves were anxious to return to the universities."

7. Raymond Bowers, "The Military Establishment," in Paul Lazarsfeld, William H. Sewell, and Harold L. Wilensky, eds., *The Uses of Sociology* (New York: Basic Books, 1967).

8. Donald G. Marquis was the committee's first chairman. Other members were Samuel A. Stouffer, Carroll Shartle, Walter S. Hunter, and William Menninger. Within the committee, Philip Hauser chaired the Manpower Panel, and Charles Dollard headed the Human Relations and Morale Division. Others included were Leland DeVinney, William H. Sewell, Hans Speier, and Irene Tauber. Raymond Bowers was the committee's deputy executive director and the executive director during the first two years, 1947–49. See Bowers, "The Military Establishment," 268.

9. "Minutes of the Conference of the National Advisory Mental Health [NAMH] Council (USPHS)," August 15–16, 1946, Washington, D.C., mimeograph, made available through the Office of the Director, Herbert Pardes, M.D., Alcohol, Drug Abuse, and Mental Health Administration, NIMH, 4–5.

10. "Minutes of the NAMH Council," 5. Mrs. Lasker was instrumental in forming the so-called Lasker Lobby, "a powerful combination of Dr. James Shannon, director of NIH in its crucial developing period, Representative John E. Fogarty of Rhode Island, Senator Lister Hill of Alabama," and Mrs. Lasker herself, "a wealthy New Yorker dedicated to expanding health programs, together with a close group of her influential physician and nonphysician friends." See Stevens, *American Medicine and the Public Trust*, 360. Also Elizabeth Brenner Drew, "The Health Syndicate, Washington's Noble Conspirators," *Atlantic Monthly*, December 1967, 75–82.

11. Julius Segal, ed., *Research in the Service of Mental Health: Report of the Research Task Force of the National Institute of Mental Health* (Washington, D.C.: Department of Health, Education & Welfare, 1975) (ADM 75–236), 7.

12. Ibid., 6.

13. Samuel W. Bloom, *The Doctor and His Patient: A Sociological Interpretation* (New York: Russell Sage Foundation, 1963), 184–196.

14. Clifford W. Beers, *A Mind That Found Itself* (New York: Longmans Green, 1908; reprint, New York: Doubleday, 1956).

15. From interview by the author with Robert H. Felix, February 8, 1983.

16. Paul Starr, *The Social Transformation of American Medicine* (New York: Basic Books, 1982), 346.

17. Mary Jane Ward, *The Snake Pit* (Garden City, N.Y.: Random House, 1946; reprint, Cutchogue, N.Y.: Buccaneer Books, 1983).

18. Albert Deutsch, *The Shame of the States* (New York: Harcourt Brace, 1949), 448–449.

19. Starr, *Social Transformation of American Medicine,* 346.

20. "Minutes of the Council."

21. A complete list of members was prepared by the Office of the Director, NIMH: "Past and Present Members, National Advisory Mental Health Council, 1946–1980." Personal correspondence, Herbert Pardes, March 31, 1983.

22. Felix interview.

23. Transcript of interview by the author with Raymond V. Bowers, February 8, 1983, 5.

24. Ibid. All these quotations from Bowers are from the interview.

25. R. H. Felix and R. V. Bowers, "Mental Hygiene and Socio-Environmental Factors," *Milbank Memorial Fund Quarterly* 26 (1948):125–147.

26. Ibid., 125.

27. Ibid., 144.

28. In his article with Bowers, ibid.

29. See Robin F. Badgley and Samuel W. Bloom, "Behavioral Sciences and Medical Education: The Case of Sociology," *Social Science and Medicine* 7 (1973):927–942; appendix 1 of this article gives extended histories and definitions of the terms "medical sociology" and "behavioral science."

30. See Otto N. Larsen, *Milestones and Millstones: Social Science at the National Science Foundation, 1945–1991* (New Brunswick, N.J.: Transaction, 1992), 30, n.3: "In the annual survey of federal funds for R & D conducted by NSF, social science is defined as follows: 'Social sciences are directed toward an understanding of the behavior of social institutions and groups and of individuals as members of a group. Social Sciences include anthropology, economics, political science, sociology, and social sciences not elsewhere classified. The latter category (n.e.c) includes linguistics; research in education; sociogeography; research in law, e.g., attempts to assess impact on the society of legal systems and practices. Psychology is a separate category and is not included. Its definitions include distinctions between biological and social aspects. . . . ' See NSF-89-304, 37, *Federal Funds for Research and Development* Washington, D.C.; NSF, 1989:3–4."

31. Dorothy Swaine Thomas was wife and collaborator to W. I. Thomas, the first graduate of the Department of Sociology at Chicago in 1896 and one of the most renowned American sociologists. Dorothy Thomas was herself equally renowned, elected President of the ASA and is cited as one of the most influential writers on population research before 1950. See Howard W. Odum, *American Sociology: The Story of Sociology in the United States through 1950* (New York: Longmans, Green, 1951), 143, 348, 351, 383, 390.

32. Felix interview, 11.

33. Ibid.

34. Samuel A. Stouffer et al., *Studies in Social Psychology in World War II: Measurement and Prediction*, vol. 4 (Princeton: Princeton University Press, 1950).

35. Felix interview, 4.

36. Sewell, for example, writes: "John Clausen has throughout his career contributed to the development of social science in the NIMH, as Chief of the Laboratory of Socioenvironmental Studies, his research and that of his colleagues [Melvin Kohn, Morris Rosenberg, Marian Yarrow, and Erving Goffman] won the respect of the social science community but also the support of the psychiatrists at NIMH." "The Changing Institutional Structure of Sociology and My Career," in Matilda White Riley, ed., *Sociological Lives*, vol. 2 (Newbury Park: Sage, 1988), 130n.

37. Joseph Eaton and Robert J. Weil, *Culture and Mental Disorders: A Comparative Study of the Hutterites and Other Populations* (Glencoe, Ill.: Free Press, 1955).

38. "Need complementarity" appears to refer to the 1952 work of Winch on process theories of mate selection. See R. F. Winch, *The Modern Family* (New York: Holt, 1952). See S. Kirson Weinberg, *Society and Personality Disorders* (New York: Prentice Hall, 1952). See also Arnold Rose, *Mental Health and Mental Disorder: A Sociological Approach* (New York: Norton, 1955). It is possible that Felix means Parsonian concepts of homeostasis here. "Complementarity" could be his term for equilibrium. But, on the other hand, he identifies "a guy from New York who did a study of complementary needs." This could be Nelson Foote (with Cottrell). All the quotations of Felix here are from the interview.

39. Edgar F. Borgatta and Marie L. Borgatta, eds., *Encyclopedia of Sociology* (New York: Macmillan, 1992), 3:1213.

40. John A. Clausen, *Sociology and the Field of Mental Health* (New York: Russell Sage Foundation, 1956). This was the second in a series published by the American Sociological Society (now known as the American Sociological Association), "seeking to explore problems raised by the professional practice of sociology." (See the foreword by Wellman J. Warner) to the preceding volume. In collaboration with Russell Sage Foundation, the Society published a series of bulletins. The first was by Lloyd F. Ohlin,

Sociology and the Field of Corrections (New York: Russell Sage Foundation, 1956), and Clausen wrote the second. He was still at NIMH, in the Laboratory of Socioenvironmental Studies.

41. Joseph W. Eaton, and Robert J. Weil, "The Mental Health of the Hutterites," in Arnold M. Rose, ed., *Mental Health and Mental Disorder* (New York: Norton, 1955), 235–236. The discussion of the study also draws from the following sources: Clausen, *Sociology and the Field of Mental Health*, 23; Bloom, *The Doctor and His Patients*, 100–101.

42. Felix and Bowers, "Mental Hygiene"; see also R. H. Felix and Morton Kramer, "Research in Epidemiology of Mental Illness," *Public Health Reports* 67 (February 1952): 152–160; and H. Warren Dunham, "Social Psychiatry," *American Sociological Review* 13 (1948): 183–197.

43. Felix interview, 8.

44. Segal, *Research in the Service of Mental Health*, 11–12.

45. Lyons, *Uneasy Partnership*, 126. This is the best source I could find about the history of the relations between social sciences and government. The story is very complex indeed.

46. Dr. M. Brewster Smith was born in 1919 and received his B.A. (1939) and M.A. (1940) at Stanford and his Ph.D. at Harvard in 1947. During the time that Felix is discussing, Smith was an assistant professor at Harvard, 1947–49, professor at Vassar, 1949–52, and on the staff of the SSRC, 1952–56. Harold Lasswell, who is regarded as one of the founders of the psychohistorical school of political science, with psychoanalytic underpinnings, was his associate. See Brewster L. Smith, Harold D. Lasswell, and R. D. Casey, eds., *Propaganda, Communication, and Public Opinion* (Princeton: Princeton University Press, 1946).

47. Both, like Clausen, pursued a substantial part of their careers at NIMH. Joseph M. Bobbitt was the chief psychologist from 1946–50; chief of the Professional Services Branch from 1950–56; assistant director, 1956–60, and associate director, 1960–64. He then went to the NICHD, where he was assistant director, 1964–66; executive director, 1966–69; and assistant director for behavioral sciences, 1969 and after. David Shakow was a professor at the University of Illinois Medical School and the University of Chicago from 1946 to 1954, serving Felix as a consultant until joining NIMH in the Intramural Research Clinical Center in 1954 as the chief laboratory psychologist, becoming in 1967 the senior research psychologist. Shakow was called by Felix "one of the great psychologists of America" (Felix interview).

48. Interview with August B. Hollingshead, August 4, 1978.

49. See chapter 5 for detailed review of the University of Chicago research.

50. Howard F. Freeman and Jeanne M. Giovannoni, "Social Psychology of Mental Health," in Gardner Lindzey and Elliot Aronson, eds., *The Handbook of Social Psychology* vol.5, 2nd ed. (Reading Mass.: Addison-Wesley, 1969), p. 629.

51. Jerome K. Myers, L. L. Bean, and M. P. Pepper, "Social Class and Mental Illness: A Ten-year Follow-up of Psychiatric Patients." *Connecticut Medicine* 28 (1964): 355–362.

52. Hollingshead interview, 1.

53. John A. Clausen, "Social Science Research and the National Mental Health Program," *American Sociological Review* 15 (June 1950): 402–408. See also Sewell, "Changing Institutional Structure," 130. Cottrell is best known as an outstanding scholar in the field of interpersonal competence, who became instrumental in building the program that developed roles for sociologists in the professions at the Russell Sage Foundation. Kingley Davis and Robin Williams were leading sociologists, both at Cornell, and Dunham was a pioneer of mental health epidemiology and professor of sociology at Wayne State.

54. Ibid., 130.

55. Ibid., 130–131.

56. See chapter 7.

57. August B. Hollingshead, and Fredrich C. Redlich, *Social Class and Mental Illness* (New York: Wiley, 1958). See also Jerome K. Myers, and Lee L. Bean, *A Decade Later: A Follow-up of Social Class and Mental Illness* (New York: Wiley, 1968).

58. Leo Srole et al., *Mental Health in the Metropolis: The Midtown Manhattan Study* (New York: McGraw-Hill, 1962).

59. It needs to be added, however, this was not the dominant pattern. An evaluation of the grants program during 1948–52 shows that the research was conducted for the most part by individual psychologists and sociologists and other social scientists: Segal, *Research in the Service of Mental Health,* 9. Less than 15 percent of all projects were conducted by biological scientists, even though grants in neurology, including grants for research on epilepsy, cerebral palsy, and multiple sclerosis, were then handled by NIMH. Such grants were later transferred to the National Institute of Neurological Diseases and Blindness after its establishment.

60. See Milbank Memorial Fund, *Epidemiology of Mental Disorder: Papers Presented at the 1949 Conference of the Milbank Memorial Fund* (New York: Milbank Memorial Fund, 1950) and *Interrelations Between the Social Environment and Psychiatric Disorders: Papers Presented at the 1952 Annual Conference of the Milbank Memorial Fund* (New York: Milbank Memorial Fund, 1953).

61. Alexander H. Leighton, John A. Clausen, and Robert N. Wilson, eds., *Explorations in Social Psychiatry* (New York: Basic Books, 1957), v.

62. William Lloyd Warner and Leo Srole, *The Social System of American Ethnic Groups* (New Haven: Yale University Press, 1945 [vol. 3 of the Yankee City Series]).

63. Freeman and Giovannoni, "Social Psychology," 680.

64. Alexander H. Leighton, *My Name Is Legion* (New York: Basic Books, 1959). Dorothea Leighton et al., *Character of Danger: Psychiatric Symptoms in Selected Communities* (New York: Basic Books, 1963).

65. Benjamin Pasaminick, "A Survey of Mental Disease in an Urban Population," part IV, "An Approach to Total Prevalence Rates," *Archives of General Psychiatry* 5 (August 1961): 151–155.

66. Freeman and Giovannoni, "Social Psychology," 680; Thomas A. Rennie and Leo Srole, "Social Class Prevalence and Distribution of Psychosomatic Conditions in an Urban Population," *Psychosomatic Medicine* 18 (1956): 449–456.

67. Interview by the author with Srole on July 23, 1977.

68. Clausen, *Sociology and the Field of Mental Health*, 11.

69. William Caudill et al., "Social Structure and Interaction Processes on a Psychiatric Ward," *American Journal of Orthopsychiatry* 32 (1952): 314–334, and *The Psychiatric Hospital as a Small Society* (Cambridge: Harvard University Press, 1958).

70. Erving Goffman, *Asylums* (Garden City, N.Y.: Doubleday, 1961).

71. Clausen, *Sociology and the Field of Mental Health,* 12.

72. Alfred H. Stanton and Morris S. Schwartz, *The Mental Hospital* (New York: Basic Books, 1954); Milton Greenblatt, D. J. Levinson, and R. H. Williams, eds., *The Patient and the Mental Hospital* (New York: Free Press, 1957).

73. Robert K. Merton, George G. Reader, and Patricia L. Kendall, *The Student-Physician: Introductory Studies in the Sociology of Medical Education* (Cambridge: Harvard University Press, 1957); Howard S. Becker et al., *Boys in White: Student Culture in Medical School* (Chicago: University of Chicago Press, 1961).

74. Clark E. Vincent, "Mental Health and the Family," *Journal of Marriage and the Family* 29 (February 1967): 22–39.

75. John A. Clausen and Marian Radke Yarrow, "Introduction: Mental Illness and the Family," *Journal of Social Issues* 11 (1955): 3–5.

76. Ibid., 3–4.

77. John A. Clausen, "Social Science Research and the National Mental Health Program," 402. I am indebted to my colleague Frederic Hafferty, who, when reading this passage, remarked that John Clausen did not hesitate to use the word "sociological" in his mission statement in spite of the trouble NIMH was encountering

at the time from Congress, which could not differentiate "sociological" from "social-ism."

78. Melvin L. Kohn and Glen H. Elder, "John Adam Clausen (1914–1996)," *Footnotes* 24 4 (1996): 7 (newsletter of the American Sociological Association).

79. John A. Clausen, "The Impact of Mental Illness on the Family," *Journal of Social Issues* 11 (1955).

80. Richard H. Williams, "The Strategy of Sociomedical Research," in Howard E. Freeman, Sol Levine, and Leo G. Reeder, eds., *Handbook of Medical Sociology* (Englewood Cliffs, N.J.: Prentice Hall, 1972), 477.

81. Clausen, *Sociology and the Field of Mental Health,* 10.

82. Vincent, "Mental Health," 20.

83. Kenneth G. Lutterman was the third executive secretary of Social Science Research Training Committee, Social Sciences Training Program, Division of Manpower and Training, NIMH. He succeeded Nathaniel Siegal, and Clark Vincent was the first appointment in the summer of 1960.

84. Kenneth Lutterman, "Research Training from the Perspective of Government Funding," in N. J. Demerath III, Otto Larsen, and Karl F. Schuessler, eds., *Social Policy and Sociology* (New York: Academic Press, 1975), 308.

85. Segal, *Research in the Service of Mental Illness,* 12.

86. Clark Vincent, "Support for Research Training in Anthropology under the National Institute of Mental Health Training Program," *American Anthropologist* 67 (1965): 754–761, 755.

87. Lutterman, "Research Training," 310.

88. Gordon W. Allport, "The Historical Background of Modern Social Psychology," in Gardner Lindzey, ed., *Handbook of Social Psychology*, vol. 1 (Cambridge, Mass.: Addison-Wesley, 1954), 4–5.

89. Ibid., 5.

90. Vincent, "Support for Research Training," 759.

91. Ibid., 756.

92. Ibid.

93. Lutterman, "Research Training," 298–299.

94. The exact place of the subcommittee was the Social Sciences Section of the Training and Manpower Resources Branch (TMRB) of NIMH.

95. Interview by the author with Frank Caffee, Director of the Office of Research Training in the NCHSR, June 23, 1975.

96. Ibid.

97. *Action for Mental Health*, Final Report of the Joint Commission on Mental Illness and Health (New York: Basic Books, 1961).

98. Lutterman, "Research Training," 309. Also Vincent, "Support for Research Training," 20–21.

99. See Segal, *Research in the Service of Mental Illness,* 18.

100. August B. Hollingshead, *Elmtown's Youth* (New York: Wiley, 1949).

101. See Edward Shils, *The Calling of Sociology* (Chicago: University of Chicago Press, 1980), 120–122, and "Tradition, Ecology, and Institution: The History of sociology," *Daedalus* 99, 4 (1970): 760–825.

102. The biographical details are based on an interview by the author with Srole on July 23, 1977.

103. A. Lawrence Lowell, president of Harvard from 1909, when he succeeded Charles W. Eliot, to 1933, when James B. Conant was appointed.

104. Lawrence T. Nichols, "The Establishment of Sociology at Harvard: A Case of Organizational Ambivalence and Scientific Vulnerability," in Clark A. Elliott and Margaret W. Rossiter, eds., *Science at Harvard University: Historical Perspectives* (Bethlehem, Pa.: Lehigh University Press, 1992), 191–222.

105. W. Lloyd Warner, A Black Civilization: Social Study of an Australian Tribe (New York: Harper Torchbook, 1964).

106. W. Lloyd Warner et al., *Social Class in America* (Chicago: Science Research

Associates, 1949); W. Lloyd Warner and Paul Lunt, *The Social Life of a Modern Community*, Yankee City Series, vol. 1 (New Haven: Yale University Press, 1941).

107. W. Lloyd Warner and Leo Srole, *Social Systems of American Ethnic Groups* (New Haven, Conn.: Yale University Press, 1945).

108. Conrad Arensberg participated in the Yankee City project but was not one of the authors. He received his Ph.D. at Harvard in 1934 and, in 1937, published his classic book, *The Irish Countryman: An Athropological Study* (London: Macmillan; reprinted in 1957 [New York: Macmillan] and in 1988 [Project Heights, Ill.: Waveland Press]).

109. Srole interview, 6.

110. Barber, *L. J. Henderson on the Social System* (Chicago: University of Chicago Press, 1970).

111. See John Parascandola, "L. J. Henderson and the Mutual Dependence of Variables from Physical Chemistry to Pareto," in Elliott and Rossiter, *Science at Harvard*, 183; reference in this quotation is to Barbara Heyl, "The Harvard 'Pareto Circle,' " *Journal of the History of the Behavioral Sciences* 4 (1968): 316–334. See also Talcott Parsons, "A Short Account of My Intellectual Development," *Alpha Kappa Delta* 29 (1959): 3–12; and George Homans and Charles Curtis, Jr., *An Introduction to Pareto, His Sociology* (New York: Knopf, 1934), preface.

112. As noted earlier, Hollingshead also worked with Warner at Chicago. They studied a small Illinois town that was to be the site of Hollingshead's first book, *Elmtown's Youth: The Impact of Social Classes on Adolescents* (New York: Wiley, 1949).

113. This is based on the testimony of Leo Srole that Margaret Mead was known to have been responsible for the rejection of the first application by Hollingshead and Redlich. Srole interview, 19.

114. Bertram S. Brown and Harry P. Cain, "The Many Meanings of 'Comprehensive.' " *American Journal of Orthopsychiatry* 34 (October 1964): 5; also Lucy C. Ozarin and Bertram S. Brown, *American Journal of Orthopsychiatry* 35 (January 1965): 1.

115. Brown and Cain, "Many Meanings of 'Comprehensive,' " 836.

116. Robert Straus, "Becoming and Being a Medical Behavioral Scientist," in Ray H. Elling and Magdalena Sokolowska, eds., *Medical Sociologists at Work* (New Brunswick, N.J.: Transaction Books, 1978), 324.

117. Ibid.

Chapter 9

1. See chapter 2 for early history of the Foundation.

2. "General director" was the original title of the chief operating officer of the foundation, or head of the staff. The Board of Trustees was led by the president. In 1954, these titles were changed. Donald Young became the president of the Foundation, still the head of the staff. Eli Whitney Debevoise, formerly the president of the board, became "chairman" of the board.

3. John M. Glenn, Lillian Brandt, and F. Emerson Andrews, *Russell Sage Foundation, 1907–1946* (New York: Russell Sage Foundation, 1947), 11. From the charter establishing the Foundation, *Laws of the State of New York Passed at the 130th Session of the Legislature,* 1:187.

4. David C. Hammack, "A Center of Intelligence for the Charity Organization Movement: The Foundation's Early Years," in David C. Hammack and Stanton Wheeler, *Social Science in the Making: Essays on the Russell Sage Foundation, 1907–1972* (New York: Russell Sage Foundation, 1994), 6.

5. Ibid., 10.

6. Eric Wanner, foreword to Hammack, "Center of Intelligence, x.

7. James A. Smith, *The Idea Brokers: Think Tanks and the Rise of the New Policy Elite* (New York: Free Press, 1991).

8. Stanton Wheeler, "The Commitment to Social Science: A Case Study of Organizational Innovation," in Hammack and Wheeler, *Social Science in the Making,* 82.

9. Ralph G. Hurlin joined the staff in January 1920 as statistician, working for (Colonel) Leonard P. Ayres and after Ayres's resignation at the end of 1920 became head of the new Department of Statistics. In 1948 he became secretary-treasurer of the Foundation, retiring in 1958, when he became consultant, until his death in 1963.

10. William F. Ogburn, *Recent Social Trends in the United States,* Report of the President's Committee on Social Trends, 2 vols. (New York: McGraw-Hill, 1933).

11. Transcription of an interview conducted by the author with Esther Lucile Brown on November 3, 1981.

12. Published by the Russell Sage Foundation (New York) and subsequently in four editions.

13. These books were all published by the Russell Sage Foundation (New York). Revised editions of *Social Work as a Profession* appeared in 1938 and 1942. *The Professional Engineer* was published in 1936; *Nursing as a Profession* in 1936, revised in 1940; *Physicians and Medical Care* in 1937; *Lawyers and the Promotion of Justice* in 1938.

14. The details of this transition in the history of the Russell Sage Foundation, especially as it affected the social sciences, is told by Stanton Wheeler, "The Commitment to Social Science: A Case Study of Organizational Innovation," in Hammack and Wheeler, *Social Science in the Making,* 81–139.

15. Milton Greenblatt, Richard H. York, and Esther Lucile Brown, *From Custodial to Therapeutic Patient Care in Mental Hospitals* (New York: Russell Sage Foundation, 1955).

16. Esther Lucile Brown, *Nursing Reconsidered: A Study of Change* (Philadelphia: Lippincott, 1970).

17. This is from Brown's personal interview (1981), but in his more recent book, David Hammack says the following: "Nothing about that commitment dictated which particular profession or professions would become dominant in the program of the Foundation, but it is evident from the record that medicine received primary attention during the early years." Hammack and Wheeler, *Social Science in the Making,* 94.

18. Ibid., 94–95. "There was also reason to believe that Dr. Young had a personal interest in medicine as a result of health problems in his family"; 95.

19. Russell Sage Foundation, *Annual Report: 1950–1951* (New York: Russell Sage Foundation, 1951), 22.

20. Ibid.

21. Benjamin Paul, *Health, Culture and Community* (New York: Russell Sage Foundation, 1955).

22. Otto von Mering and Stanley H. King, *Remotivating the Mental Patient* (New York: Russell Sage Foundation, 1957).

23. Chapter 7.

24. Leo W. Simmons and Harold G. Wolff, *Social Science in Medicine* (New York: Russell Sage Foundation, 1954).

25. Russell Sage Foundation, *Annual Report: 1950–1951,* 18–19.

26. Robert K. Merton, George G. Reader, and Patricia L. Kendall, eds., *The Student-Physician: Introductory Studies in the Sociology of Medical Education* (Cambridge: Harvard University Press, 1957).

27. *Annual Report: 1950–1951,* 24. See also Lyle Saunders, *Cultural Difference and Medical Care* (New York: Russell Sage Foundation, 1954).

28. *Annual Report,* 23.

29. These appointments were given different names from year to year. When created in 1950–51, they were called Health Service Residencies for Social Sciences; in 1951–52 "Cross-disciplinary Internships"; and in 1952–53 "Cross-disciplinary Residencies." From that point on they were called "residents."

30. Russell Sage Foundation, *Annual Report: 1952–1953* (New York: Russell Sage Foundation, 1953).

31. *Annual Report: 1952–1953,* 33.

32. Ray H. Elling, "To Strike a Balance," Ray H. Elling and Magdalena Sokolowska, eds., *Medical Sociologists at Work* (New Brunswick, N.J.: Transaction Books, 1978), 56–57.

33. Ibid., 9.

34. Ibid., 12.

35. Ibid., 13.

36. This appears to be a group jointly conducted by the Yale sociology department with the School of Medicine and the department of public health. In Russell Sage Foundation, *Annual Report: 1953–1954* (New York: Russell Sage Foundation, 1954), 14, it is reported: "Through a Committee on the Social Aspects of Medicine at Yale University, of which Professor Leo W. Simmons is chairman, plans were developed in 1953 with the school of medicine and the department of public health for a faculty seminar to discuss problems associated with interdisciplinary research, and for an experimental training program that would qualify a selected number of graduate studens in sociology for collaboration with medical personnel in the social aspects of medicine."

37. Russell Sage Foundation, *Annual Report, 1955–1956* (New York: Russell Sage Foundation, 1956), 28.

38. Apple's study was prominently featured in Irving K. Zola, "Sociocultural Factors in the Seeking of Medical Aid" (Ph.D. diss., Harvard University, 1962). This item of information is supplied by Frederic Hafferty. Simmons and Wolff, *Social Science in Medicine*; Lyle Saunders, *Cultural Difference and Medical Care* (1954); Paul, *Health, Culture, and Community*; John Clausen, *Sociology and the Field of Mental Health* (1956); Otto von Mering and Stanley H. King, *Remotivating the Medical Patient* (1957); Frances Cooke Macgregor, *Social Science in Nursing* (1960); Stanley H. King, *Perceptions of Illness and Medical Practice* (1962); Esther Lucile Brown, *Newer Dimensions of Patient Care* (1961); Eliot Freidson, *Patients' Views of Medical Care* (1961); all these were published by the Russell Sage Foundation in New York.

39. Freidson's work in this position was preparatory for his later influential books, especially: *The Profession of Medicine* (New York: Dodd, Mead, 1970).

40. Sol Levine died in 1996, shortly before this chapter's first draft was completed.

41. The other fellows were: Charles Brant, a cultural anthropologist, at Albert Einstein College of Medicine; Robert W. Hawkes, social psychologist, at the Massachusetts Mental Health Center; Eric H. Lenneberg, psychologist, at the Harvard University Medical School; Marian Pearsall, cultural anthropologist, at hospitals in Boston; Thomas F. A. Plaut, psychologist, and Steven Polgar, cultural anthropologist, at the Harvard School of Public Health; and Sam Schulman, sociologist, at the Boston University School of Nursing.

42. *Annual Report: 1950–1951,* 19. Transcript of author's interview with Robert K. Merton, February 25, 1981, 2.

43. Dana W. Atchley, M.D., born in 1892, received a B.A. from the University of Chicago in 1911 and the M.D. from Johns Hopkins in 1915. He spent most of his career at Columbia College of Physicians and Surgeons as professor of clinical medicine.

44. Merton interview, 3. Goode remained in the Columbia Sociology Department for most of his own distinguished career.

45. Wheeler, "Commitment to Social Science," 81–82. Wheeler lists the organizations as the SSRC, the social science division of the National Academy of Sciences, and the Center for Advanced Study in the Behavioral Sciences.

46. A manuscript was produced, prepared by Merton, Goode, and Mary Jean Huntington, that for years enjoyed an underground vogue in mimeographed form among insiders at the Columbia Bureau of Applied Research, but it was never submitted for publication.

47. Bureau of Applied Social Research [BASR], "*A Proposal for the Sociological Study of Medical Schools,*" Columbia University, June 1952, unpublished memorandum, copy in the files of the author. Subsequent citations will be to BASR, 1952.

48. Merton, Reader, and Kendall, *The Student-Physician*.

49. See Samuel W. Bloom, "The Sociology of Medical Education: Some Comments on the State of a Field," *Milbank Memorial Fund Quarterly* 43, 2: 143–184. The studies under the direction of the Columbia Bureau of Applied Social Research are listed on 174–176 and by the Cornell Comprehensive Care and Teaching Program on 177–178.

50. Kenneth R. Hammond and Fred Kern, Jr., *Teaching Comprehensive Medical Care* (Cambridge: Harvard University Press, 1959).

51. See George G. Reader and Mary E. W. Goss, eds., *Comprehensive Medical Care and Teaching* (Ithaca: Cornell University Press, 1967). See also Samuel W. Bloom, *Power and Dissent in the Medical School* (New York: Free Press, 1973); Robert H. Coombs, *Mastering Medicine* (New York: Free Press, 1978); Emily Mumford, *Interns: From Students to Physicians* (Cambridge: Harvard University Press, 1970); S. J. Miller, *Prescription for Leadership: Training for the Medical Elite* (Chicago: Aldine, 1970).

52. Robert Straus, "Becoming and Being a Medical Behavioral Scientist," Elling and Sokolowska, *Medical Sociologists at Work*.

53. The Foundation called these awards "residencies," but to avoid confusion with the more usual medical meaning of this word, I will call them fellowships.

54. Howard B. Kaplan is currently Distinguished Professor of Sociology and Mary Thomas Marshall Professor of Liberal Arts at Texas A & M University. He continued at Baylor College of Medicine after his two-year Russell Sage residency, becoming professor of psychiatry and community medicine, remaining there for more than twenty years until his appointment at Texas A & M. He is a past editor of the *Journal of Health and Human Behavior* and has published extensively on psychosocial stress. He holds a senior scientist award from NIDA and directs a multigeneration study of the psychosocial causes and outcomes of drug use and other deviant adaptations to life stress.

55. Donald Young grew up near Hamburg, a small town in Pennsylvania. He remained devoted to it and owned a house there to which he regularly escaped from New York. He spoke Pennsylvania Dutch to me whenever we met because I grew up in Reading, about thirty miles from his home. He never quite accepted my very primitive facility in this language, but we had some hilarious conversations in a combination of Yiddish and Pennsylvania Dutch.

56. Samuel W. Bloom, *The Doctor and His Patient: A Sociological Interpretation* (New York: Russell Sage Foundation, 1963).

57. Esther Lucile Brown was then living in a retirement community in San Francisco.

58. The Bureau of Applied Social Research. June 1952. *A Proposal for the Sociological Study of Medical Schools*. Addressed to the Commonwealth Fund. NY: Columbia University (unpublished manuscript, copy in the files of the author): pp. 3–5. I list Merton as the author, although it would probably be more accurate to include Patricia Kendall, who became the co–principal investigator, as coauthor. The face page of the manuscript lists only the BASR as the source.

59. Transcript of interview by the author of George G. Reader, June 28, 1977. Available in the files of the author.

60. BASR, 1952, 5–6.

61. George G. Reader, "The Cornell Comprehensive Care and Teaching Program," in Merton, Reader, and Kendall, *The Student-Physician*, 81–101.

62. Hammond and Kern, *Teaching Comprehensive Medical Care*.

63. David Preswick Barr was professor and chairman of internal medicine at Cornell School of Medicine, 1942–57. He received his B.A. from Cornell University in 1911 and M.D. from Cornell in 1914. He was on the faculty of Washington University in St. Louis, Missouri, from 1922 to 1944, climbing to the rank of Professor.

64. Reader interview.

65. Reader interview.

66. Ibid., 6.

67. Reader was unable to recall the name of this student.

68. The final submission of this grant application from the BASR to the Commonwealth Fund was in June 1952. However, the theoretical and methodological parts of the proposal were written earlier, for the most part prior to the contact with Cornell Medical College. The first approach to Commonwealth was also before the contact with Reader. The final proposal includes reference to consultations with Dr. George Reader and argues for a procedure that includes the evaluation of Cornell's C C & T P.

69. Goss was very soon assigned to be the Bureau's primary representative for the evaluation of C C & T P. Following her work on this project, Dr. Goss was appointed to the faculty of the Cornell Medical School. She remained there, working with Dr. Reader, until recently when she retired as a full professor.

70. See chapter 7.

71. Reader interview.

72. Dr. Renee C. Fox, currently Distinguished Unirvesity Professor at the University of Pennsylvania, joined the BASR to work on this project at the beginning of 1953. She came immediately after completing her dissertation under the direction of Talcott Parsons at the Harvard University Department of Social Relations. The dissertation was one of the earliest devoted to a topic specifically identifiable as medical sociology and was published as *Experiment Perilous* (Glencoe, Ill.: Free Press, 1959).

73. See Merton, Reader, and Kendall, *The Student-Physician,* where most of this reasoning is developed against the full background of the research up to that point. However, the original proposal is a unique document, still well worth reading. It is available in the author's files, and at the Archives of the Commonwealth Fund, Rockefeller Archive Center, Sleepy Hollow, N.Y.

74. The author similarly used the experience in this research as the launching pad of a lifetime as a medical educator. When the BASR extended its research to include the University of Pennsylvania and Western Reserve, I joined it as the chief fieldwork representative at the University of Pennsylvania, from 1953 to 1956.

75. See Robert Q. Marston and Roseann M. Jones, eds., *Medical Education in Transition: Commission on Medical Education on the Sciences of Medical Practice* (Princeton: Robert Wood Johnson Foundation, 1992).

76. Interview by the author with Lester Evans, February 18, 1980.

77. The Harkness fortune was built by Stephen, an orphan, from early success in business and investment in the Standard Oil Company from its beginnings. Anna Harkness inherited his fortune in 1888 and created the Commonwealth Fund thirty years later with a gift of ten million dollars. The Fund has been the central interest of the Harkness family since.

78. *For the Common Good: The Commonwealth Fund, 1918–1993* (New York: Commonwealth Fund, 1994), 16.

79. George L. Engel, *Psychological Development in Health and Disease* (Philadelphia: W. B. Saunders, 1962).

80. George L. Engel, "A Unified Concept of Health and Disease," in Theodore Millon, *Medical Behavioral Science* (Philadelphia: Saunders, 1975), 185.

81. Ibid., 185.

82. Ibid., 187.

83. Reader and Goss, *Comprehensive Medical Care.*

84. Hammond and Kern, *Teaching Comprehensive Medical Care.*

85. David Caplovitz, "Student-Faculty Relations in Medical School: A Study of Professional Socialization" (Ph.D. diss., Columbia University, 1961).

86. See Greer Williams, *Western Reserve's Experiment in Medical Education and Its Outcome* (New York: Oxford University Press, 1980). This is a very complete description of the Western Reserve experiment. See also T. Hale Ham, "Methods in De-

velopment and Revision of a Program of Medical Education," *Journal of Medical Education* 31 (1956): 518–521; and Milton J. Horowitz, *Education Tomorrow's Doctors* (New York: Appleton-Century-Crofts, 1964).

87. Abraham Flexner, *Medical Education in the United States and Canada: A Report to the Carnegie Foundation for the Advancement of Teaching* (New York: Carnegie Foundation, 1910).

88. Saunders, *Cultural Difference;* Hammond and Kern, *Teaching Comprehensive Medical Care.*

89. Merton, Reader, and Kendall, *The Student-Physician*; Reader and Goss, *Comprehensive Medical Care.*

90. Patricia L. Kendall, and George G. Reader, "Contributions of Sociology to Medicine," in Howard E. Freeman, Sol Levine, and Leo G. Reeder, eds., *Handbook of Medical Sociology*, 3rd ed. (Englewood Cliffs, N.J.: Prentice Hall, 1979).

91. Flexner, *Medical Education.*

92. Helen H. Gee and Rober J. Glaser, eds., "The Ecology of the Medical Student," part II, *Journal of Medical Education* 33 (October 1958): n.p.

93. Renee C. Fox, "Training for Detached Concern," in Merton, Reader, and Kendall, *The Student-Physician*; also Harold I. Lief and Renee Fox, "The Medical Student's Training for 'Detached Concern,' " in Harold I. Lief, Victor F. Lief, and Nina R. Lief, eds., *The Psychological Basis of Medical Practice* (New York: Harper and Row, 1963), 12–35.

94. Renee C. Fox, *Essays in Medical Sociology: Journeys into the Field* (New York: Wiley, 1979).

95. Howard S. Becker et al., *Boys in White: Student Cultures in Medical School* (Chicago: University of Chicago Press, 1961).

96. Mumford, *Interns;* Miller, *Prescription for Leadership.* Rue Bucher and Joan Stelling, *Becoming Professional* (Beverly Hills, Calif.: Sage, 1977).

97. Daniel H. Funkenstein, "Medical Students, Medical Schools and Society during Three Eras," in R. H. Coombs and Charles E. Vincent, eds., *Psychosocial Aspects of Medical Training* (Springfield, Ill.: Thomas, 1971), 229–284. See also Nichols A. Christakis, "The Similarity and Frequency of Proposals to Reform U.S. Medical Education," *Journal of the American Medical Association* 274 (1995): 706.

98. George G. Reader and Rosemary Soave, "Comprehensive Care Revisited," *Milbank Memorial Fund Quarterly* 54 (fall 1976): 391–414.

99. Philip V. Lee, "Medical Schools and the Changing Times: Nine Case Reports on Experimentation in Medical Education, 1950–1960," Part II, *Journal of Medical Education* 35 (December 1961):45–46.

100. Joel J. Alpert and Evan Charney, *The Education of Physicians for Primary Care* (Rockville, Md.: DHEW Publication [HRA], 1973), 74–3113.

101. Reader and Soave, *Comprehensive Care Revisited,* 400.

102. Stewart P. Mennin and Summers Kalishman, eds., "Issues and Strategies for Reform in Medical Education: Lessons from Eight Medical Schools," *Academic Medicine* supplement, 73, 9 (1998).

103. Technically, it was a single-donor foundation.

104. Clyde V. Kiser, *The Milbank Memorial Fund: Its Leaders and Its Work, 1905–1974.* (New York: Milbank Memorial Fund, 1975), 9.

105. See Kiser, *Milbank Memorial Fund.*

106. This is the same organization, founded by Clifford Beers, that is prominently mentioned in chapter 8.

107. Albert G. Milbank, 1935, as cited by Kiser, *Milbank Memorial Fund,* 9.

108. Robert F. Arnove, Introduction to Robert F. Arnove, ed., *Philanthropy and Cultural Imperialism* (Bloomington: Indiana University Press, 1982), 4.

109. Ibid.

110. Barry D. Karl and Stanley N. Katz, "Donors, Trustees, Staffs: An Historical View, 1890–1930," in *The Art of Giving: Four Views on American Philanthropy* [Pro-

ceedings of the Third Rockefeller Archive Conference, October 14, 1977] (North Tarrytown, N.Y.: The Rockefeller Archive Center, 1979), 6.

111. See chapter 3.

112. *Committee on the Costs of Medical Care, Medical Care for the American People: The Final Report of the Committee on the Costs of Medical Care* (Chicago: University of Chicago Press, 1932).

113. *Milbank Memorial Fund: Annual Report for 1933* (New York: Milbank Memorial Fund, 1933), 20–21.

114. Ibid.

115. Gerald N. Grob, *From Asylum to Community: Mental Health Policy in Modern America* (Princeton: Princeton University Press, 1991), 49.

116. Sir Arthur Newsholme and John Adams Kingsbury, *Red Medicine: Socialized Health in Soviet Russia* (Garden City, N.Y.: Doubleday, Doran, 1933).

117. Kiser, *Milbank Memorial Fund,* 57–59.

118. Daniel M. Fox, "The Fund's First Venture in Health Policy: The Crisis of 1934–35," unpublished manuscript supplied by the author.

119. I. S. Falk, *Security against Sickness* (Garden City, N.Y.: Doubleday, Doran, 1936).

120. Boudreau received his M.D. from McGill University. At the time of his appointment to the Milbank Fund, he was on the Health Secretariat of the League of Nations, conducting an assignment in Geneva, Switzerland.

121. Author of *The Mind That Found Itself* and the founder of the National Committee on Mental Hygiene. See chapter 8.

122. See Kiser, *Milbank Memorial Fund,* 76–77.

123. Grob, *From Asylum to Community,* 49.

124. Kiser, *Milbank Memorial Fund,* 77.

125. Ibid., 77–84. See also Bertram S. Brown and H. B. Cain, "The Many Meanings of 'Comprehensive,'" *American Journal of Orthopsychiatry* 34, 5 (October 1964): 834–839; and L. D. Ozarin and B. S. Brown, "New Directions in Community Mental Health Programs," *American Journal of Orthopsychiatry* 35, 1 (January 1965): 10–17.

126. The following is based on the transcript of an interview by the author with David P. Willis on June 5, 1981. All quotations from Willis are from this interview.

127. See chapter 8, note 28.

128. Willis interview, 4.

129. Brian Abel-Smith, 1960. *A History of the Nursing Profession* (London: Heinemann, 1960), and *The Hospitals, 1800–1848* (London: Heinemann, 1964). Richard M. Titmus, *The Gift Relationship: From Human Blood to Social Policy* (New York: Random House, 1972).

130. Badgley had gone from Yale to the University of Saskatchewan, where he and Robertson were colleagues.

131. Peter B. Seybold, "The Ford Foundation and the Triumph of Behavioralism in American Political Science," in Arnove, *Philanthropy and Cultural Imperialism,* 272.

132. Hammack and Wheeler, *Social Science in the Making,* 94; cited above mspage 442.

133. See chapter 8; transcript of interview by the author with August B. Hollingshead, August 4, 1978, 1.

Chapter 10

1. Joseph Ben-David, "The Scientific Role: The Conditions of Its Establishment in Europe," *Minerva* 4, 1 (autumn 1965): 15–64. Joseph Ben-David and Randall Collins,

"Social Factors in the Origins of a New Science," *American Sociological Review* 31, 4 (August 1966): 451–465.

2. Ben-David, "Scientific Role," and Edward Shils, "Tradition, Ecology, and Institution in the History of Sociology," *Daedalus* 99, 4 (fall 1970): 760–825. This quotation is from Antony Oberschall, ed., *The Establishment of Empirical Sociology: Studies in Continuity, Discontinuity, and Institutionalization* (New York: Harper and Row, 1972), 4–5.

3. See chapter 3, and Oberschall, *Establishment of Empirical Sociology*, 4–5.

4. Some examples: William Caudill, "Applied Anthropology in Medicine," in A. L. Kroeber, ed., *Anthropology Today* (Chicago: University of Chicago Press, 1953). Howard E. Freeman and Leo G. Reeder, "Medical Sociology: A Review of the Literature," *American Sociological Review* 22 (1957): 73–81. Saxon Graham, "Sociological Aspects of Health and Illness," in Robert E. L. Faris, ed., *Handbook of Modern Sociology* (Chicago: Rand McNally, 1964), 310–347. Samuel W. Bloom and Ruth Zambrana, "Trends and Developments in the Sociology of Medicine," in Julio L. Ruffini, ed., *Advances in Medical Social Science* (New York: Gordon and Breach, 1983).

5. See chapters 7 and 8.

6. Robert Straus, "The Nature and Status of Medical Sociology," *American Sociological Review* 22 (1957): 200–204.

7. This was a very modest sum of less than one thousand dollars.

8. Article 5 of the Constitution of the American Sociological Society, "Committees, Sections 14, 15, and 16." Although sections are usually thought to have been created by this change of the constitution in 1958, this was actually a reassertion of an organizational structure that first appeared in 1921. In that year, Dwight Anderson requested the formation of a Section on Rural Sociology, and it was approved by the Executive Committee of the Society. Similar status was given at the same time to a Section on Social Research. These sections, however, were only for representation on the program of the annual meetings, eventually including Social Statistics, Educational Sociology, Teaching of Sociology, Community, Sociology of Religion, Family Sociology, Sociology and Social Work, and Sociology and Psychiatry. A reorganization of the Society revised the constitution in 1942, eliminating sections except as members of the program committee. To be represented on the program committee, a section had to have twenty-five members. Sixteen years later, increasing specialization led to the creation of the modern sections. The full history is told by Lawrence J. Rhoades, *A History of the American Sociological Association: 1905–1980* (Washington, D.C.: American Sociological Association, 1981), 26, 37, 47, 58, 63, 70, 71.

9. The underlying facts here are drawn from a report written by the author that was included in an unpublished document presented by Robin Badgley to the Section on Medical Sociology in March 1968. See Robin Badgley, ed., "Medical Sociology Section of the American Sociological Association," March 1968, mimeograph, available in the files of the author and to be deposited in the Archives of Medical Sociology, American Sociological Association, Washington, D.C.

10. Kutner was trained at the Harvard Department of Social Relations and was identified closely with both sociology and anthropology in his research.

11. Badgley, *Medical Sociology Section*, 1968: 25.

12. Official membership figures are only available from 1970 forward.

13. Figures for 2001 are preliminary. At the time this table was created, the membership figures were not official.

14. Charles C. Hughes and Donald Kennedy, "Beyond the Germ Theory: Reflections on Relations between Medicine and the Behavioral Sciences" in Ruffini, *Advances*, 344.

15. Constance Holden, "Behavioral Medicine: An Emergent Field," *Science* 209 (1980): 479–481, cited by Hughes and Kennedy, "Beyond the Germ Theory," 344.

16. David Landy, "Medical Anthropology: A Critical Appraisal," in Ruffini, *Advances*, 189.

17. Nancy Adler and George Stone, "Psychology and the Health System," in Ruffini, *Advances,* 2. Over, 1,500 members were reported in 1980.

18. This occurred in 1991 and almost immediately the membership of the Medical Sociology Section began to drop. I have not been able to get data to verify the conclusion that there is cause and effect in this development; if one combines the membership of the two sections, the total represents the largest among sections of the ASA.

19. Committee on National Needs for Biomedical and Behavioral Research Personnel, *Meeting the Nation's Needs for Biomedical and Behavioral Scientists* (Washington, D.C.: National Academy Press, 1994), 52.

20. Odin W. Anderson and Milvoy Seacat, "The Behavioral Scientists and Research in the Health Field," research series no. 1 (New York: Health Information Foundation, 1957).

21. See chapter 9.

22. Oswald Hall, "Sociological Research in the Field of Medicine: Progress and Prospects," *American Sociological Review* 16 (1951): 639–644.

23. Talcott Parsons, "Some Problems Confronting Sociology as a Profession," *American Sociological Review* 24 (1959): 550–551.

24. Transcript of interview by the author with August B. Hollingshead, August 4, 1983, 1. Quotation from Hollingshead that follows is from this interview.

25. See chapter 8.

26. The discussion here is based on Odin Anderson, "The Question of Establishing Formal Criteria for the Designation of Medical Sociologist: A Report to the Officers and Members of the Section on Medical Sociology, A.S.A., for Consideration at the Annual Meeting in 1961," mimeograph, Available in the files of the author and to be deposited in the Archives of Medical Sociology, American Sociological Association, Washington, D.C.

27. Ibid., 34.

28. Ibid.

29. See the discussion in chapter 8 on the development of federal support for training in the social sciences.

30. Kenneth G. Lutterman, "Research Training from the Perspective of Government Funding," in N. J. Demerath, Otto Larsen, and K. F. Schuessler, eds., *Social Policy and Sociology* (New York: Academic Press, 1975), 370.

31. Howard E. Freeman, Edgar F. Borgatta, and Nathaniel H. Siegel, "Government Support and Graduate Training," in Demerath, Larsen, and Schnessler, *Social Policy and Sociology*, 297–306.

32. Rhoades, *History of the American Sociological Association*, 49.

33. Ibid., 49.

34. Ibid., 50.

35. This is a distinction made by Eliot Freidson, *The Profession of Medicine: A Study of the Sociology of Applied Knowledge* (New York: Dodd, Mead, 1970).

36. Rhoades, *History of the American Sociological Association*, 49.

37. These results were reported in the Minutes of the Section business meeting at the annual meeting in 1963. No more detailed report of the survey has been found.

38. See chapter 5.

39. E. Gartly Jaco ed., *Patients, Physicians, and Illness: Sourcebook in Behavioral Science and Medicine* (Glencoe, Ill.: Free Press, 1958).

40. E. Gartly Jaco, 1960. *The Social Epidemiology of Mental Disorders: A Psychiatric Survey of Texas* (New York: Russell Sage Foundation, 1960).

41. Among them were virtually all of the people mentioned so far in these pages and, in addition, Daniel J. Levinson, Talcott Parsons, Leo G. Reeder, Julius Roth, Milton Greenblatt, Milton I. Roemer, and George Rosen.

42. President of the Russell Sage Foundation, 1948–63. See chapter 9.

43. Program officer of the Commonwealth Fund, 1923–59. See chapter 9.

44. Badgley, "Medical Sociology Section," 91.

45. Ibid., 129.

46. The most recent is *Annals of Behavioral Science and Medical Education*, published since 1994 by the Association of Behavioral Science and Medical Education. Others are *Medical Anthropology*, published since 1977; the *British Journal of Medical Sociology*; and *International Journal of Health Services*, published since 1970 under the editorship of Vicente Navarro of Johns Hopkins University. The latter, it should be noted, is more a journal of public health and social medicine than specifically of medical sociology, but it is a special outlet for the social sciences of medicine. New journals continue to appear. The latest known to this author is *Health, Illness, and Medicine* (London: Sage Publications, EC2A 4PU, UK), first published in 1996.

47. E. Gartly Jaco, "Important Announcement," *American Journal of Health and Human Behavior* 7 (1966), 73.

48. Talcott Parsons, "Toward a Healthy Maturity," *Journal of Health and Human Behavior* 1 (1960): 163–172.

49. George Rosen, "Psychopathology in the Social Process," part I, "A Study of the Persecution of Witches in Europe as a Contribution to the Understanding of Mass Delusions and Psychic Epidemics," 1 (1960): 200–210; Milton I. Roemer, "On Medical Care and Human Behavior," 4 (1963): 3–4; Richard Sasuly and Milton I. Roemer, "Health Insurance Patterns: A Conceptualization from the California Scene," 7 (1966): 36–44; Leslie Falk, "Group Health Plans in Mining Communities," 4 (1963): 4–13; Robert Straus, "Planning a University Medical Center for the Student and the Patient," 4 (1963): 36–43; Renee C. Fox, "Physicians on the Drug Industry Side of the Prescription Blank," 2 (1961): 3–15; S. Leonard Syme Merton H. Hyman, and Philip E. Enterline, "Cultural Mobility and the Occurrence of Coronary Heart Disease," 6 (1965): 178–189; David Mechanic, "The Sociology of Medicine: Viewpoints and Perspectives," 7 (1966): 237–247; David Mechanic and Edmund H. Volkart, "Illness Behavior and Medical Diagnosis," 1 (1960): 86–93.

50. Everett C. Hughes, "Studying the Nurse's Work," *American Journal of Nursing* 51 (May 1951): 294–295.

51. Everett C. Hughes, *The Sociological Eye* (New Brunswick, N.J.: Transaction, 1984). See especially the discussion of Hughes as a mentor in the introduction by David Reisman and Howard S. Becker.

52. See his autobiography, *The Evolution of Health Services Research: Personal Reflections on Applied Social Science* (San Francisco: Jossey-Bass, 1991), and his articles "The Sociologist and Medicine," *Social Forces* 31 (October 1952): 38–42, and "The Roads to Social Research," *American Behavioral Scientist* 5 (March 1962): 8–11.

53. Samuel W. Bloom et al., "The Sociologist as Medical Educator: A Discussion," *American Sociological Review* 25 (1960): 95–101.

54. John A. Clausen, "The Organism and Socialization," Daniel J. Levinson "Medical Education and the Theory of Adult Socialization," and Howard S. Becker and Blanche Ger, "Comment," all in *Journal of Health and Social Behavior* 8 (1967): 243–252, 253–264, and 264–265, respectively.

55. The Leo G. Reeder Award was established in 1978 to commemorate the untimely death by airplane crash of Leo Reeder. The recipient was required to give a scholarly address; this became the Reeder Lecture.

56. The members were Samuel Bloom, Chairman, Robin F. Badgley, Lyle Saunders, and Kerr White. They prepared an ambitious set of recommendations. See Badgley, *Medical Sociology Section*," 57–58.

57. See ibid., 68.

58. Rhoades, *History of the American Sociological Association,* 70.

59. David Mechanic and Sol Levine, preface to the special supplement *Issues in Promoting Health: Committee Reports of the Medical Sociology Section, American Sociological Association* of the journal *Medical Care*, 15, 5 (1977): vi.

60. "Minutes of the First Meeting, Steering Committee for the Carnegie Grant to the Medical Sociology Section of the ASA, December 29, 1971," in unpublished doc-

ument, "ASA Medical Sociological Section: Minutes 1968–1971," currently in the files of the author, to be deposited in the ASA Archives, Pennsylvania State University, State College, Pa., 4.

61. Mary Goss, Ph.D., spent her entire academic career at Cornell University Medical College, in the departments of medicine and public health. At the time (1971–77), she was professor of sociology in public health. She is currently professor emeritus at Cornell.

62. Jack Elinson, Ph.D., emeritus professor, Division of Sociomedical Sciences, Columbia University School of Public Health. At the time (1971–77) he was professor and head of the Division of Sociomedical Sciences.

63. Research sociologist and lecturer, University of California at San Francisco.

64. Professor, Tufts University.

65. Associate professor, departments of pediatrics, behavioral sciences, and social relations, Johns Hopkins University.

66. Professor, departments of health care organization and behavioral sciences and School of Hygiene and Public Health, Johns Hopkins University.

67. "Minutes of the First Meeting," 4.

68. Mechanic and Levine, preface.

69. Ibid., vii.

70. Nancy Anderson, "A Memorandum Submitted to the Symposium on Section Day, New Orleans, Annual Meeting of the A.S.A., 1972," May 4, 1972; in the author's files, to be sent to the ASA Archives, Pennsylvania State University, State College, Pa.

71. Jan Howard and Anselm Strauss, ed., *Humanizing Health Care* (New York: Wiley, 1975); and Linda H. Aiken and David Mechanic, ed., *Applications of Social Science to Clinical Medicine and Health Policy* (New Brunswick, N.J.: Rutgers University Press, 1975).

72. ix.

73. Mary Goss et al., "Social Organization and Control in Medical Work: A Call for Research," in Mechanic and Levine, *Issues in Promoting Health,* 2.

74. See Paul M. Ellwood, Jr., "Models for Organizing Health Services and Implications of Legislative Proposals," part II, *Milbank Memorial Fund Quarterly* 50, 4 (1972):73–102. Ellwood became famous as President Richard M. Nixon's most influential health care advisor.

75. Goss et al., "Social Organization and Control," 7.

76. The following are in Aiken and Mechanic, *Applications of Social Science*: William A. Glaser, "Payment Systems and their Effects"; "Harold S. Luft, "Economic Incentives and Constraints in Clinical Practice"; Donald W. Light, "Surplus versus Cost Containment: The Changing Context for Health Providers."

77. Jan Howard et al., "Humanizing Health Care: The Implications of Technology, Centralization, and Self-Care," in Mechanic and Levine, Issues in Promoting Health, 11–26; Also Howard and Strauss, *Humanizing Health Care.*

78. Marshall H. Becker et al., "Selected Psychosocial Models and Correlates of Individual Health-Related Behaviors," in Mechanic and Levine, *Issues in Promoting Health,* 27.

79. David Mechanic and Linda H. Aiken, "Social Science, Medicine, and Health Policy," in Aiken and Mechanic, *Applications of Social Science,* 9.

80. Mechanic and Levine, *Issues in Promoting Health,* vi.

81. Letters of December 7, 1973 (to Ronald Anderson from Geoffrey Gibson), and December 19, 1973, from Malcolm Johnson, to be deposited in the Archives of Medical Sociology, Pennsylvania State University, State College, Pa., currently held by the author.

82. At the World Health Organization (WHO) Wessen joined the newly created Division of Research in Epidemiology and Communication Sciences (RECS), which in 1967 was given the mandate to create a research program. Kenneth Newell, M.D., of

New Zealand was the director. RECS was replaced in the mid-1970s by the Division of Strengthening Health Services (SHS), which was devoted mainly to primary care.

83. The committee included the following: Robin Badgley, University of Toronto; Samuel W. Bloom, Mount Sinai School of Medicine/CUNY; Margot Jefferys, Bedford College, London; Manfred Pflanz, Midizinische Hochscule, Hanover; Judith Shuval, Hebrew U-Hadassah Medical School, Israel; Henry Walton, University of Edinburgh, Scotland.

84. *Summary Report: The Advisory Group on the Sociology of Professional Training and Health Manpower* (Geneva: World Health Organization, December 1972).

85. Kosa was from the Harvard School of Medicine. See John Kosa Aaron Antonovsky, and Irving Zola, ed., *Poverty and Health: A Sociological Analysis* (Cambridge: Harvard University Press, 1969).

86. Donald Kennedy, Evan G. Pattishall, and C. Richard Fletcher, *Teaching Behavioral Sciences in Schools of Medicine*, vol. 1, *Summary Report* (Rockville, Md.: 1972) (contract no. HSM 110-69-211), 5.

87. See Donald A. Kennedy, Evan G. Pattishall, and DeWitt C. Baldwin, *Medical Education and the Behavioral Sciences* (Boulder, Colo.: Westview Press, 1985); also Joseph W. Lella, Derek G. Gill, and Thomas J. McGlynn, *Basic Curriculum Content for the Behavioral Sciences in Preclinical Medical Education* (McLean, Va.: Association for the Behavioral Sciences and Medical Education, 1985).

88. Quigg Newton, *The Commonwealth Fund Fifty-Second Annual Report* (New York: Harkness House, 1970), 1; and John Millis, *A Rational Public Policy for Medical Education and Its Financing* (New York: National Fund for Medical Education, 1971).

89. The full range of types of organization were considered, including a division or section of another department such as psychiatry or community medicine. Recognizing the difficulties, the choice was a department of its own.

90. Howard E. Freeman, Sol Levine, and Leo G. Reeder, *Handbook of Medical Sociology* (Englewood Cliffs, N.J.: Prentice-Hall, 1979). A fourth edition was published in 1989. Sharon J. Reeder wrote a foreword to the fourth edition with information included here, ix–x.

91. Howard E. Freeman, "Obituary for Leo G. Reeder, 1921–1978," *ASA Foonotes* January 1979, 10.

92. There is some discrepancy in the records about the exact dates of the first award. The ASA records 1978 as the first year, but have gaps in the list of recipients. My own reconstruction from various sources places 1977 as the beginning, and I have filled in the names for every year since.

93. See Renee C. Fox, "Reflections and Opportunities in the Sociology of Medicine," *Journal of Health and Social Behavior* 26, 1 (1985): 6–14. From that time forward, the Reeder Award article introduces each new volume.

94. Marvin Sussman, ed., *Sociology and Rehabilitation* (Washington, D.C.: American Sociological Association, 1965). A special publication of the Vocational Rehabilitation Administration. Sussman was very much the prime mover of this conference. He was, at the time, professor and chairman of the Department of Sociology at Western Reserve University in Cleveland. He was assisted by Gresham Sykes, executive officer of the ASA, and by an organizing committee composed of: Eliot Freidson, New York University, Robert Straus, University of Kentucky, Albert Wessen, Washington University of St. Louis, and myself, Downstate Medical Center, State University of New York.

95. See especially Lutterman, "Research Training," 370.

96. Ibid., 310.

97. Julius Segal, ed., *Research in the Service of Mental Health: Report of the Research Task Force of the NIMH* (Washington, D.C.: Department of Health, Education and Welfare, 1975) (publication no. ADM-75-236), 12.

98. From ibid., 152. The data were from 1972.

99. Robert Alan Day, "Toward the Development of a Critical Sociohistorically Grounded Sociology of Sociology: The Case of Medical Sociology." (Ph.D. diss., University of Missouri, Columbia, 1981; available from University Microfilms International, Ann Arbor, Michigan).

100. Talcott Parsons, *The Social System* (Glencoe, Ill.: Free Press, 1951).

Chapter 11

1. It should be noted that this was the case especially in psychiatry and public health. See Gerald N. Grob, "The Origins of American Psychiatric Epidemiology," *American Journal of Public Health* 75 (1985): 229–236.

2. Although this was the first official office for social science research at NSF, Harry Alpert was the first representative of social science in the NSF leadership. He was brought into NSF part-time in 1953 from his position in the Bureau of the Budget. His official association was with the Office of Program Analysis. Alpert, with a Ph.D. in sociology from Columbia University, had been in the federal government since the war. He analyzed public opinion and statistics for the Office of War Information, the Office of Price Administration, and the Budget Bureau. See Otto N. Larsen, *Milestones and Millstones: Social Science at the National Science Foundation, 1945–1991* (New Brunswick, N.J.: Transaction, 1992), 39.

3. Henry W. Riecken, "Social Change and Social Science," in James A. Shannon, ed., *Science and the Evolution of Public Policy* (New York: Rockefeller University Press, 1973): 135.

4. Ibid., 137. A more recent version of this sentiment is expressed by John Mirowsky in his inaugural statement as editor of *the Journal of Health and Social Behavior*, "An Informative Sociology of Health and Well-Being: Notes from the New Editor," 39 (1998): 1. Speaking about what distinguishes sociology from other disciplines in the medical school, he wrote: "For me, the single most important realization was this: The phenomena that we sociologists study are conscious beings, who can understand what we discover and will use their understandings toward their own ends."

5. See Samuel Z. Klausner and Victor M. Lidz, eds., *The Nationalization of the Social Sciences* (Philadelphia: University of Pennsylvania Press, 1986). Featuring an unpublished article by Talcott Parsons, written to argue for the inclusion of social science in NSF, this is a valuable source of information about the struggle for legitimacy of sociology immediately following World War II.

6. Riecken, "Social Change and Social Science," 137–139.

7. These figures are extracted from Larsen, *Milestones and Millstones*, 20–25. He cites the following sources: J. Merton England, *A Patron for Pure Science: The National Science Foundation's Formative Years, 1945–57* (Washington, D.C.: National Science Foundation, 1982). National Science Board, *Science and Engineering Indicators, 1989* (Washington, D.C.: U.S. Government Printing Office, 1989), 264–271. "Federal Funds for Research and Development, Detailed Historical Tables, 1955–1990," NSF Annual Series (Washington, D.C.: National Science Foundation).

8. Riecken, "Social Change and Social Science," 139.

9. Ibid., 139–141.

10. This is a fictitious name for a real institution. All the facts presented here are from the records of the university and the director of its NIMH training program.

11. See chapter 8.

12. "Report of Health Policy Committee Medical Sociology Section," August 1979, Linda Aiken, chair, with Bob Eichhorn leading the inquiry into the training area, un-

published manuscript, Archives of Medical Sociology, American Sociological Association, Washington, D.C. Presently available only through the author.

13. Ibid., 2.

14. Gene M. Lyons, *The Uneasy Partnership: Social Science and the Federal Government in the Twentieth Century* (New York: Russell Sage Foundation, 1969).

15. Ibid., 199.

16. Gene M. Lyons, "The Many Faces of Social Science," chapter 8 in Samuel Z. Klausner and Victor M. Lidz, eds., *The Nationalization of the Social Sciences* (Philadelphia: University of Pennsylvania Press, 1986), 200.

17. Kenneth Prewitt, "Federal Funding for Social Science," in Klausner and Lidz, *Nationalization of the Social Sciences*, 332.

18. Lyons, "Many Faces," 198.

19. Kenneth Prewitt and David L. Sills, "Federal Funding for the Social Sciences: Threats and Response," *Social Science Research Council Items* 35, 3 (September 1981): 39, quoted by Lyons, ibid., 200.

20. Derek Bok, *The State of the Nation: Government and the Quest for a Better Society* (Cambridge: Harvard University Press, 1997).

21. Based on an interview by the author with Russell Dynes, December 18, 1997. Currently available from the author and to be deposited in the Archives of Medical Sociology at ASA, Washington, D.C.

22. Russell Dynes received his Ph.D. from Ohio State University in 1954. He joined the Ohio State sociology faculty, started a center for the study of disasters in 1963, and later became the chairman of the Department of Sociology. After his period as executive secretary of ASA, he joined the University of Delaware (at Newark) sociology faculty, where he is currently research professor.

23. Otto N. Larsen received his Ph.D. from the University of Washington in Seattle in 1955 and was on the faculty of that university since, with time out to head the social sciences at NSF from 1980 to 1986.

24. Otto Larsen, who was the director of the Division of Social and Economic Research at NSF from 1980 to 1982 and senior associate for social and behavioral science from 1983 to 1986, has written the most complete history of NSF policy from its inception in 1950 to 1991, providing a valuable background against which to view any specialized subbranch like medical sociology. See Larsen, *Milestones and Millstones*.

25. Lyons, *Uneasy Partnership*, 98. This is one of the most authoritative studies of relations between social science and the government in this century.

26. Larsen, *Milestones and Millstones*, 6. See Vannevar Bush, *Science, the Endless Frontier: A Report to the President on a Program for Postwar Scientific Research* (Washington, D.C.: U.S. Government Printing Office, 1945; reissued by the National Science Foundation in 1980).

27. John R. Steelman, *Science and Public Policy*, 5 vols. (Washington, D.C.: U.S. Government Printing Office, 1947).

28. See Klausner and Lidz, *Nationalization of the Social Sciences*, 8–9.

29. Milton Lomask, *A Minor Miracle: An Informal History of the National Science Foundation* (Washington, D.C.: U.S. Government Printing Office, 1975), 64, cited by Larsen, *Milestones and Millstones*, 19.

30. Larsen, *Milestones and Millstones*, 19.

31. Ibid.

32. Samuel Z. Klausner, "The Bid to Nationalize American Social Science," in Klausner and Lidz, *Nationalization of the Social Sciences*, 11.

33. Lyons, *The Uneasy Partnership*, 126–127.

34. Alpert received his Ph.D. in sociology from Columbia University, and outside of his government service, the bulk of his career was on the faculty of the University of Washington at Seattle.

35. *Technical Information for Congress,* testimony of Dr. John T. Wilson, head of the NSF Program Analysis Office, before a Senate committee (Washington, D.C.: U.S. Government Printing Office, 1971), 123, cited by Larsen, *Milestones and Millstones,* 39.

36. Harry Alpert, "The National Science Foundation and Social Science Research," *American Sociological Review* 19 (1954):208–211; "Social Science, Social Psychology and the National Science Foundation," *American Psychologist* 12 (1957): 95–98.

37. Cyril S. Smith and Otto N. Larsen, "The Criterion of 'Relevance' in the Support of Research in the Social Sciences: 1965–1985." *Minerva* 27, 4 (winter 1989): 463.

38. This category includes linguistics, research in education, socioeconomic geography, and research in law, that is, attempts to assess the impact on society of legal systems and practices.

39. Larsen, *Milestones and Millstones,* 20–25. He cites NSF-89-304, 37; *Federal Funds for Research and Development* (Washington, D.C.: National Science Foundation, 1989), 3–4.

40. National Science Board, *Science and Engineering Indicators—1989* (Washington, D.C.: U.S. Government Printing Office, 1989), 89.

41. Larsen, *Milestones and Millstones,* 114.

42. Smith and Larsen, "Criterion of 'Relevance,' " 463–464.

43. Larsen, *Milestones and Millstones,* 66.

44. Julius Segal, ed., *Research in the Service of Mental Health: Report of the Research Task Force of the NIMH* (Washington, D.C.: Department of Health, Education, and Welfare, 1975) (publication no. ADM 75–236). (See chapter 9 of this book, n.11.)

45. *NIH Almanac: 1997.* (Washington, DC: National Institutes of Health, Office of the Director, 1997 (Publication no. 97–5).

46. Ibid., 76.

47. Dynes interview; here and elsewhere when Dynes is quoted, the source is this interview.

48. Hyman Witkin directed this NIMH-sponsored research training program for psychiatrists, part of what was called the Doctorate in Medical Sciences (DMS) Program. Among the social scientists on the faculty were Leo Srole, anthropologist/sociologist, Fred Pine, a social psychologist, and the author. For this and other information presented here about Pardes, the author relies on his recall from Downstate and an interview with Pardes in Washington, D.C., on February 18, 1980, available in transcript in the author's files and to be deposited in the Archives of the ASA Section on Medical Sociology at Pennsylvania State University. Quotations from Pardes are from this interview, unless otherwise indicated.

49. Kurt Massing, a political sociologist.

50. Private communication from the NIMH Office of Scientific Information, Information Resources and Inquiries Branch, April 2, 1997 (Office of Public Information, Neuroscience Center, 6001 Executive Blvd., Bethesda, Md., 20892).

51. Richard C. Simons and Herbert Pardes, eds., *Understanding Human Behavior in Health and Illness,* 1st ed. (Baltimore: Williams and Wilkins, 1977). This book was reprinted in 1978, 1979, and 1980. Simons then published second and third editions.

52. Simons and Pardes, *Understanding Human Behavior,* xi.

53. Clausen joined NIMH in 1948 and played a key role in its development. In 1951, he became the first chief of the Laboratory of Socio-environmental Studies, the intramural research arm of NIMH. For a full discussion of his role, see Chapter 8.

54. Leighton was well known as both a psychiatrist and anthropologist.

55. See chapter 8, chapter 9, and notes 60 and 63 of chapter 9.

56. Interview by the author with Herbert Klerman, February 18, 1980, 2. Quotations from Klerman hereafter are from this interview.

57. Reader and Fox were at Cornell, and this was when their study of medical student socialization for the profession was just beginning. See chapter 9.

58. Melvin L. Kohn, Ph.D. Cornell University 1952. Currently Professor, Johns Hopkins University.

59. Dickenson W. Richards, professor of medicine at Columbia University and visiting professor and director of the First (Columbia) Division of the Bellevue Hospital, New York, together with Andre Cournand and Werner Forssmann, won the Nobel Prize for Physiology or Medicine for 1956. His biography reveals that he began his research on pulmonary and circulatory physiology under the direction of Professor L. J. Henderson of Harvard.

60. Some samples: Myron R. Sharaf and Daniel Levinson, "Patterns of Ideology and role definition among Psychiatric Residents," in Milton Greenblatt, D. J. Levinson, and R. G. Williams, eds. *The Patient and the Mental Hospital* (New York: Free Press, 1957), 263–285; M. R. Sharaf and D. Levinson, "The Quest for Omnipotence in Professional Training: The Case of the Psychiatric Resident," *Psychiatry* 27 (1964): 135–149; Elvin V. Semrad et al., "A Study of the Doctor-Patient Relationship in Psychotherapy," *Psychiatry* 15 (1952): 377–386; M. Greenblatt, Daniel J. Levinson, and Gerald Klerman, *Mental Patients in Transition: Steps in Hospital-Community Rehabilitation* (Springfield, Ill.: Thomas, 1961).

61. All of the material about Sabshin is from an interview with him conducted by the author on February 19, 1980. The transcript is available in the author's files and will be deposited in the Archives of the Section on Medical Sociology at Pennsylvania State University. Quotations from Sabshin that follow are from this interview.

62. See particularly Anselm Strauss et al., *Psychiatric Ideologies and Institutions* (New York: Free Press of Glencoe, 1974).

63. Edward Berkowitz and Susan LaMountain, "Organizational Change at the National Institutes of Health: Historical Case Studies," History Associates, Germantown, Md., 1984, prepared for the Institute of Medicine, National Academy of Sciences (Washington, D.C.), mimeograph, 1.

64. Ibid., 11.

65. Ibid., 8.

66. *Congressional Record*, 79th Cong., 1945–1947, 2nd sess., 92, pt. 2:2298, cited in Berkowitz, ibid., 8.

67. Gerald N. Grob, *The Mad among Us: A History of the Care of America's Mentally Ill* (Cambridge: Harvard University Press, 1994), chapter 11, 278–311. This is the summary volume of a three-volume comprehensive history of the care and treatment of mental illness in America. See also, by the same author, *Mental Institutions in America: Social Policy to 1875* (Glencoe, Ill.: Free Press, 1973), *Mental Illness and American Society, 1875–1940* (Princeton: Princeton University Press, 1983), and *From Asylum to Community: Mental Health Policy in Modern America* (Princeton: Princeton University Press, 1991).

68. This passage is paraphrased from much more extensive and masterful argument by Grob, *The Mad among Us,* 220–221.

69. Berkowitz and LaMountain, *Organizational Change,* 13–14.

70. Grob, *The Mad among Us,* 248.

71. Congress, in 1965, passed as amendments to the Social Security Act of 1935 Title 18 (Part A) Medicare, hospital insurance for the aged, and Part B with insurance for physicians' services; and Title 19, Medicaid, grants to states for medical assistance programs for indigent persons.

72. Grob, *The Mad among Us,* 282–283.

73. Ibid., 286–287.

74. *NIH Almanac* (Bethesda, Md.: Office of Scientific Information Resources and Inquiries Branch, 1996) (NIH publication 96–5), 75.

75. Larsen, *Milestones and Millstones,* 130.

76. A summit meeting was called by the Social Science Research Council on the 12th of September 1980. See ibid., 135.

77. Mitchell C. Lynch, "Reagan's Ax," *Wall Street Journal*, March 22, 1981, 54, cited by Larsen, ibid., 152.

78. "Slicing through 'Soft' Science," *New York Times*, April 4, 1981, 22, cited in Larsen, *Milestones and Millstones,* 153.

79. On the general pattern of federal support for social science, this section is indebted particularly to Otto N. Larsen, "Sociology and Federal Research Support," in Edgar F. Borgatta and Marie L. Borgatta, eds., *Encyclopedia of Sociology* (New York: Macmillan, 1992), 2013–2022. Although I have tried to attribute specific material, inevitably, given the excellence and comprehensive nature of his article, other parts are paraphrased.

80. Ibid., 2015.

81. Ibid., 2019.

82. Ibid., 2019.

83. Ibid., 2019.

84. Ibid., 2020.

85. In 1989, NIA awarded 188 new and continuing grants allocating $26.9 million for social and behavioral research. The NIMH awared sixty-seven grants to sociologists for $8.2 million. NICHD made thirty-three awards in population research, mainly for sociologists, for a total of $4.9 million. NSF, through its program in sociology, made fifty-eight awards allocating $4.4 million to sociologists. See ibid., 2021.

86. Committee on National Needs for Biomedical and Behavioral Research Personnel, *Meeting the Nation's Needs for Biomedical and Behavioral Scientists* (Washington, D.C.: National Academy Press, 1994).

87. The discussion of Manderschied is taken from a taped telephone interview conducted on January 15, 1998, transcript available in the author's files and to be deposited in the ASA Archives of Medical Sociology, Pennsylvania State University, State College, Pa. Quotations from Manderschied that follow are from this interview.

88. Interview, 6.

89. These and subsequent comments by David Mechanic are from the transcript of an interview with the author, December 22, 1997, available in the files of the author.

90. The granting office of NIMH is the Health Services Research Branch.

91. See Barbara M. Altman coeditor, *Teaching Sociology* 18, 3, special issue on medical sociology (1990). This is an important source for this section of the discussion.

92. See table 10-1.

93. J. Stokes III, P. J. Strand, and C. Jaffe, "Distribution of Behavioral Science Faculty in United States Medical Schools," *Social Science and Medicine* 18 (1984):753–756.

94. American Sociological Association, *Footnotes*, newsletter published by the ASA, Washington, D.C., 1989. C. A. Haney, M. A. Zahn, and J. Howard, "Applied Medical Sociology: Learning from Within," *Teaching Sociology* 11 (1983): 92–104.

95. Barbara M. Altman, 1990. "Guest Co-editor's Note," *Teaching Sociology*, Special Issue on Medical Sociology 18, 3 (1990): iii.

96. Editorial, "Medical Education and the Social Sciences," *Journal of the American Medical Association* 245 (1981): 955.

97. S. Levine, "The Changing Terrains in Medical Sociology: Emergent Concern with Quality of Life," *Journal of Health and Social Behavior* 28 (1987): 1–6. This was Levine's address given on receipt of the Leo G. Reeder Award for Distinguished Scholarship in Medical Sociology. He was, in effect, extending the distinction that Straus, twenty-five years earlier, had made between the sociology *of* medicine and sociology *in* medicine, signifying the advance toward full acceptance as a basic science of medicine.

98. Selected examples are: *Future Directions for Medical Education: A Report of the Council on Medical Education* (Chicago: Americal Medical Association, 1982). C. P. Friedman and E. F. Purcell, eds., *The New Biology and Medical Education: Merg-*

ing the Biological, Information, and Cognitive Sciences, Report of a Conference Sponsored Jointly by the University of North Carolina and the Josiah Macy, Jr., Foundation (New York: Josiah Macy Foundation, 1983). "Physicians for the Twenty-first Century: Report of Project Panel on the General Professional Education of the Physician and College Preparation for Medicine," part II, *Journal of Medical Education* 59 (November 1984, the GPEP report).

99. Ibid.

100. Robert Q. W. Marston, and Roseann M. Jones, eds., *Medical Education in Transition: Commission on Medical Education and the Sciences of Medical Practice* (Princeton, N.J.: Robert Wood Johnson Foundation, 1992). D. A. Shugars, E. H. O'Neill, and J. D. Bader, eds., *Healthy America: Practitioners for 2005, An Agenda for Action for U.S. Health Professional Schools* (Durham, N.C.: Pew Health Professions Commission, Association of American Medical Schools, and Charles E. Culpepper Foundation, 1991). *Assessing Change in Medical Education: the Road to Implementation* (Washington, D.C.: Association of American Medical Colleges, 1994).

101. D. Field, "Teaching Sociology in U.K. Medical Schools," *Medical Education* 22 (1988): 294–300.

102. C. W. Aakster, "Medical Sociology Training for Medical Doctors," in Y. Nuyens and J. Vansteenkiste, eds., *Teaching Medical Sociology: Retrospection and Prospection* (Boston: Nijhoff, 1978), 141–152. J. M. Najman G. Isaacs, and M. Siskind, "Teaching Sociology to Medical Students," *Medical Education* 12 (1978): 406–412.

103. Joseph Ben-David, "The Scientific Role: The Conditions of Its Establishment in Europe," *Minerva* 4, 1 (autumn 1965).

104. Smith and Larsen, "The Criterion of 'Relevance,' " 461–482.

105. See Committee on National Needs for Biomedical and Behavioral Research Personnel, *Meeting the Nation's Needs,* 37.

106. ASA records do not allow analysis of how many individuals are members of both sections, so that no combined total can be calculated.

107. Two special journal issues have supplied background for this section: Donald W. Light, contributing ed., "New Directions in the Sociology of Medicine," *American Journal of Sociology* 97, 4 (1992); and Mary L. Fennell, ed., "Forty Years of Medical Sociology: The State of the Art and Directions for the Future," *Journal of Health and Social Behavior,* extra issue (1995). I also draw from the following earlier work: Samuel W. Bloom, "Institutional Trends in Medical Sociology," *Journal of Health and Social Behavior* 27 (1986): 265–276; and Samuel W. Bloom and Ruth E. Zambrana, "Trends and Developments in the Sociology of Medicine," in Julio L. Ruffini, ed., *Advances in Medical Social Science* (New York: Gordon and Breach, 1983), 1:93–122.

108. George Reader and Mary E. W. Goss, "The Sociology of Medicine," in Robert K. Merton, Leonard Broom, and L. S. Cottrell, Jr., eds., *Sociology Today* (New York: Basic Books, 1959), 229–248. See also Samuel W. Bloom, "Aspects of Sociology and Medicine," in Harold I. Lief, Victor F. Lief, and Nina R. Lief, eds., *The Psychological Basis of Medical Practice* (New York: Harper and Row, 1963), 70.

109. Eliot Freidson, "The Development of Design by Accident," in Ray H. Elling and Magda Sokolowska, eds., *Medical Sociologists at Work* (New Brunswick, N.J.: Transaction Books, 1978), 132.

110. Jack Elinson, "The End of Medicine and the End of Medical Sociology," *Journal of Health and Social Behavior* 26 (1985):269.

111. Renee Fox, "Reflections and Opportunities in the Sociology of Medicine," *Journal of Health and Social Behavior* 26 (1985): 1–7.

112. Howard E. Freeman, et al., eds., *Applied Sociology* (San Francisco: Jossey-Bass, 1983), xxiii.

113. Ibid.

114. Frederic W. Hafferty and Bernice A. Pescosolido, *Charting a Future Course for Medical Sociology, Final Report* (Princeton: Robert Wood Johnson Foundation, 1996), i.

115. Donald Light, 1992. "Introduction: Strengthening Ties between Specialties and the Discipline," *American Journal of Sociology* 97 (1992): 909. This is a special issue devoted to medical sociology, edited by Light.

116. Sol Levine, "Time for Creative Integration in Medical Sociology," *Journal of Health and Social Behavior*, extra issue, 36, 1–4 (1995): 1.

117. Leonard I. Pearlin, "Structure and Meaning in Medical Sociology," *Journal of Health and Social Behavior* 33 (1992): 1–9.

118. Eliot Freidson, *Profession of Medicine: A Study of the Sociology of Applied Knowledge* (New York: Dodd, Mead, 1970).

119. Kenneth Lutterman, 1975. "Research Training from the Perspective of Government Funding," in N.J. Demerath, Otto Larsen, and K. F. Schuessler, eds., *Social Policy and Sociology* (New York: Academic Press, 1975), 317.

120. Kenneth G. Lutterman, "Changing Opportunities in Applied Sociology Education," in Freeman et al., *Applied Sociology*, 436.

121. Ibid.

122. Ibid.

123. John Clausen and Leonard Pearlin are only two who come quickly to mind.

124. Robert Straus, *A Medical School Is Born* (Kuttawa, Ky.: McClanahan, 1996).

125. Daniel C. Tosteson, James Adelstein, and Susan T. Carver, eds., *New Pathways to Medical Education: Learning to Learn at Harvard Medical School* (Cambridge: Harvard University Press, 1994).

126. Erving. Goffman, "The Moral Career of the Mental Patient," *Psychiatry* 22 (1959): 123–142, and "On the Characteristics of Total Institutions," in *Symposium on Preventive and Social Psychiatry*, Walter Reed Army Institute of Research (Washington, D.C.: U.S. Government Printing Office, 1957), 43–84. This same article on total institutions was also published in Erving Goffman, ed., *Asylums* (Chicago: Aldine, 1962).

127. Thomas Scheff, *Being Mentally Ill: A Sociological Theory* (Chicago: Aldine, 1966).

128. Some examples are: William Caudill, *The Psychiatric Hospital as a Small Society* (Cambridge: Harvard University Press, 1958); Greenblatt, Levinson, and Williams, *The Patient and the Mental Hospital*. Charles Perrow, "Hospitals: Technology, Structure, and Goals," in Jame G. March, ed., *The Handbook of Organizations* (Skokie, Ill.: Rand McNally, 1965); Alfred H. Stanton and Morris S. Schwartz, *The Mental Hospital* (New York: Basic Books, 1954).

129. Both Starr and Grob make this point. See Paul Starr, *The Social Transformation of American Medicine* (New York: Basic Books, 1982), 409. Gerald N. Grob, *From Asylum to Community: Mental Health Policy in Modern America* (Princeton: Princeton University Press, 1991).

130. See chapter 7.

131. This is discussed at length in S. W. Bloom, "Institutional Trends in Medical Sociology," *American Journal of Social Behavior* 27 (1986): 265–276.

132. Norman Cameron, "Human Ecology and Personality in the Training of Physicians," in *Psychiatry and Medical Education: Report of the 1951 Conference on Psychiatric Education* (Washington, D.C.: Association of American Medical Colleges, 1952), 64–66; *Preventive Medicine and Medical Education; Report of the 1952 Conference on Preventive Medicine Education* (Washington, D.C.: Association of American Medical Colleges, 1953), 6–7.

133. Robert K. Merton, George G. Reader, and Patricia L. Kendall, eds., *The Student-Physician* (Cambridge: Harvard University Press, 1957); Howard S. Becker, Blanche Geer, Everett Hughes, and Anselm M. Strauss, *Boys in White: Student Culture in the Medical School* (Chicago: University of Chicago Press, 1961).

134. Marston and Jones, *Medical Education in Transition*. See 681, n.102.

135. Samuel W. Bloom, "The Profession of Medical Sociologist in the Future: Implications for Training Programs," in Y. Nuyens and J. Vansteenkiste, eds., *Teaching*

Medical Sociology (Leiden: Nijhoff, 1978): 38–60. Also Bloom and Zambrana, "Trends and Developments."

136. Charles L. Bosk, *Forgive and Remember: Managing Medical Failure* (Chicago: University of Chicago Press, 1979); Terry Mizrahi, *Getting Rid of Patients: Contradiction in the Socialization of Physicians* (New Brunswick, N.J.: Rutgers University Press, 1986); Frederic W. Hafferty, *Into the Valley: Death and the Socialization of Medical Students* (New Haven: Yale University Press, 1991).

137. Jeanne Harley Guillemin, and Lynda Lytle Holmsltrom, *Mixed Blessings: Intensive Care for Newborns* (New York: Oxford University Press, 1986).

138. Elliot G. Mishler, Elliot G. *The Discourse of Medicine: Dialectics of Medical Interviews* (Norwood, N.J.: Ablex, 1984); Elliot Mishler et al., "The Language of Attentive Patient Care: A Comparison of Two Medical Interviews, *Journal of General Internal Medicine* 4 (1989):325–335; Howard Waitzkin, *The Politics of Medical Encounters: How Patients and Doctors Deal with Social Problems* (New Haven: Yale University Press, 1991). David Mechanic, "Public Trust and Initiatives for New Health Care Partnerships," *Milbank Quarterly* 76 (1998):281–302.

139. Richard H. Williams, "The Strategy of Sociomedical Research," in Howard E. Freeman, Sol Levine, and Leo G. Reeder, *Handbook of Medical Sociology*, 2nd ed. (Englewood Cliffs, N.J.: Prentice Hall, 1972), 463.

140. C. Holden, "Dark Days for Social Research," *Science* 211 (1981):1397–1398.

141. B. J. Culliton, "Kennedy Hearings: Year-long Probe of Biomedical Research Begins," *Science* 193 (1976): 32–35.

142. AAHP is the trade organization for HMOs, located at 1129 20th Street NW, Suite 600, Washington, D.C. 20036.

143. Sheryl Gay Stolberg, "As Doctors Trade Shingle for Marquee, Cries of Woe," *New York Times,* August 3, 1998, A1. The figures are updates from AAHP and AMA.

144. From the Internet, National Library of Medicine medline thesaurus, MESH terms, scope note indexing annotations.

145. HMOs are defined as: organized systems for providing comprehensive prepaid health care that have five basic attributes: they (1) provide care in a defined geographic area; (2) provide or ensure delivery of an agreeed-upon set of basic and supplemental health maintenance and treatment services; (3) provide care to a voluntarily defined group of persons; (4) require their enrollees to use the services of designated providers; and (5) receive reimbursement through a predetermined, fixed, periodic prepayment made by the enrollee without regard to the degree of services provided.

Preferred provider organizations: arrangements negotiated between a third-party payer (often a self-insured company or union trust fund) and a group of health care providers (hospitals and physicians) who furnish services at lower that usual fees and, in return, receive prompt payment and an expectation of an increased volume of patients.

146. The best source for a thorough description of this development that I have found is Harry Nelson, *Nonprofit and For-Profit HMOs: Converging Practices but Different Goals?* (New York: Milbank Memorial Fund, 1997).

147. Starr, *Social Transformation of American Medicine*, 428.

148. Barbara J. Culliton, "University Hospitals for Sale," *Science* 223 (1984): 909–911.

149. Ibid., 910.

150. Ibid., 911.

151. Peter T. Kilborn, "Largest HMOs Cutting the Poor and the Elderly," *New York Times*, 6 July 1998, 1.

152. Barbara and John Ehrenreich, *The American Health Empire: Power, Profits, and Politics* (New York: Vintage Books, 1970); and Harold B. Meyers, "The Medical Industrial Complex," *Fortune* 81 (January 1970): 90. See also Starr, *Social Transformation of American Medicine*, 428–429, 493 (n.23).

153. I base this description on Rashi Fein, *Medical Care, Medical Costs: The Search for a Health Insurance Policy* (Cambridge: Harvard University Press, 1986).

154. Fein, *Medical Care.*

155. The barometers here are from the classic studies of Eliot Freidson, *Profession of Medicine* and *Professional Dominance* (New York: Atherton, 1970).

156. Henry E. Sigerist, *American Medicine*, 1st ed. (New York: Norton, 1934), and "Medical History in the U.S.," *Bulletin of the History of Medicine* 22 (1948): 47–63; and George Rosen, *From Medical Police to Social Police in Social Medicine* (New York: Watson Academic, 1974).

157. Talcott Parsons, *The Social System* (Glencoe, Ill.: Free Press, 1951), chapter 10, 428–478.

158. Nelson, *Nonprofit and For-Profit HMOs*, 9–22.

159. Lee Clarke and Carroll L. Estes, "Sociological and Economic Theories of Markets and Nonprofits: Evidence from Home Health Organizations," *American Journal of Sociology* 97 (1992): 945–969.

160. Mechanic, "Public Trust."

161. David Mechanic and M. Schlesinger, "The Impact of Managed Care on Patients' Trust in Medical Care and Their Physicians," *Journal of the American Medical Association* 275 (1996): 1693–1697.

162. Mechanic, "Public Trust," 298.

163. Clarke and Estes, "Sociological and Economic Theories," 961–964.

164. Erving Goffman, *Asylums* (Garden City, N.Y.: Doubleday, 1961); Eliot Freidson, *The Profession of Medicine* (New York: Dodd, 1970); Howard Waitzkin, *The Politics of Medical Encounters: How Patients and Doctors Deal with Medical Problems* (New Haven: Yale University Press, 1991).

165. Jenne K. Britell, "Hazards in Social Research," *New York Times*, September 7, 1980.

166. Bloom and Zambrana, "Trends and Developments in the Sociology of Medicine," 1:113.

Index